Vital Records of
DOVER
New Hampshire
1686–1850

Dover Historical Society

HERITAGE BOOKS
2011

HERITAGE BOOKS
AN IMPRINT OF HERITAGE BOOKS, INC.

Books, CDs, and more—Worldwide

For our listing of thousands of titles see our website
at
www.HeritageBooks.com

A Facsimile Reprint
Published 2011 by
HERITAGE BOOKS, INC.
Publishing Division
100 Railroad Ave. #104
Westminster, Maryland 21157

Originally published in 1894 by the Dover Historical Society under the title: *Collections of the Dover, N.H., Historical Society, Volume 1*; no subsequent editions were published.

— Publisher's Notice —
In reprints such as this, it is often not possible to remove blemishes from the original. We feel the contents of this book warrant its reissue despite these blemishes and hope you will agree and read it with pleasure.

International Standard Book Numbers
Paperbound: 978-1-55613-333-6
Clothbound: 978-0-91789-002-4

COLLECTIONS

OF THE

DOVER, N. H.,

HISTORICAL SOCIETY.

VOL. I.

DOVER:
PRINTED BY SCALES & QUIMBY.
1894.

FRED HOOPER HAYES,
ELISHA RHODES BROWN, } Publishing
CHARLES FRANCIS SAWYER, } Committee.

PREFACE.

The Publishing Committee, by vote of the Dover Historical Society, have gathered in this volume many of the widely separated records of Marriages, Births, Deaths and Baptisms in Dover, N. H., down to the year 1850.

One volume of the ancient town records has been published entire; the remainder of this volume has been extracted from the manuscript records of the N. H. Historical Society, the records of the Mass. Historical Society, the records of the local churches and of private citizens.

The thanks of the Society are due to Mr. Charles W. Tibbets who under the direction of the Publishing Committee has carefully copied the original records, and has been watchful that no errors should appear in the printed volume; and to Dr. John R. Ham who has made a complete index of the persons named in the volume, and who has also rendered valuable assistance in reading proof.

CONTENTS.

		Page.
1.	Old Book of Marriages, Births and Deaths, 1693–1838,	1
2.	Early Records of N. H. Families,	106
3.	Rev. John Pike's List of Marriages, 1686–1709,	128
4.	Rev. Jonathan Cushing's Record of Baptisms, 1717–1766,	133
5.	Rev. Dr. Jeremy Belknap's record of Baptisms, 1767–1786,	164
6.	Rev. Dr. Jeremy Belknap's Record of Marriages, 1767–1776,	170
7.	Rev. Joseph W. Clary's Record of Marriages, 1812–1829,	176
8.	Rev. Hubbard Winslow's Record of Marriages, 1829–1831,	186
9.	Nath'l Cooper's Record of Deaths, 1773–1791,	188
10.	Dea. Benjamin Peirce's Record of Deaths, 1792–1802,	197
11.	List of Members of First Church, 1718–1850,	206
12.	Baptisms by Rev. Robert Gray, 1787–1800,	241
13.	Marriages, from Methodist Church Records, 1835–1850,	243
14.	Marriages from Episcopal Church Records, 1839–1850,	253
15.	Marriages from Unitarian Church, 1829–1850,	256
16.	Marriages from Catholic Church Records, 1843–1850,	259
17.	Index of Persons,	263

ERRATA.

Page 96, Eleventh line, Chandler William is an error in the original for William Chandler.
" 97, Sixth line from bottom, Elcy A. Drew is an error in the original for Elcy O. Drew.
" 106, Thirteenth line from bottom, for moring read morning.
" 111, Eighteenth line, for Neson read Nason; and Suah is an error in the original for Shuah.
" 144, Sixth line, for Humphey read Humphrey.
" 172, Thirteenth line, insert "of Kittery &" after Shubell Mason.
" 193, Twenty-second line, Loath is an error in the original for Zoath.
" 244, Ninth line from bottom, for April 29 read April 24.
" 251, Twelfth line, for Ephriam read Ephraim.
" 254, Twelfth line, for Anasatsia read Anastasia.
" 260, Fourteenth line, for Bryne read Byrne.
" 262, Ninth line from bottom, for Thomes read Thomas.

BIRTHS AND MARRIAGES,

1693-1838.

DOVER, N. H. RECORDS.

Thomas Tebbets was marrid to His wife Judeth the 6 : Day of July in the year of our Lord 1684

John the Son of Thomas Tebbets was Boren the 29 of August by his wife Judeth Tebbets in the year of our Lord 1685

Thomas Tebbets Son of Thomas Tebbets was Boarn the 4 Day of nouember 1687

Ephrim Tebbets the Son of Thomas Tebbets was Boren the 4 of march 1690

Elezebeth The Dafter of Thomas Tebbets boren the Eight Day of September in the year of our Lord 1692

Elezebth the Dafter of Thomas Tebbets Desesed the 12 of october in the year of our Lord 1692.

Samuel the Son of Thomas Tebbets was Born the 8 Day of october 1693

Elezebeth the Second Dafter of Thomas Tebbets was boarn the 25 Day of July 1696

moses Tebbets the Son of Thomas Tebbets was Boarn the 27 Day of January 1701

Abagarl the Dafter of Thomas Tebbets was Boarn the Second Day of September in the year of our Lord 1705

Jabez garlan sonn of Jabez garlan by his wife darkis borne in douer ye 19 day of february 1693

darkis garlan daughter of Jabez garlan by his wife darkis born in douer the third day of Aprill 1698

Rebecah garlan daughter of Jabez garlan by his wife darkis born in douer ye 25th day of January 1699

Ebenezer garlan sonn of Jabez garlan by his wife darkis born in douer the 14 day of march 1703/4

Nathanaell garlan sonn of Jabez garlan by his wife darkis born in douer the 12 of aprill 1706

Lidia garlan daughter of Jabez garlan by his wife darkis born in douer the 17 day of february 1707

Paul Gerrish and Marey Leighton ware Joyned to Geather in marriage october the 2^d 1712

Nathanaell Hill son of Vallentine Hill of douer by his wife Mary was born in oyster Riuer the beginning of march 1659/60

Mrs Mary Hill alias Knight was before me on the 23^d of May 1702 and acknowledged that Nathanaell Hill was the son of her first husband Vallentine Hill/   John woodman Justs Peac

John winget and Dorithy Tebbets wear Joyned to geather in marridg in the year 1717

Pomfrett Dam son of william Dam by his wife martha was born in douer the 4th day of march Ano : dom 1681

Martha Dam daughter of william dam by his wife martha was borne the 5 day of the week being ye 29 day of march 1683

william Dam sonn of william dam by his wife martha was born in douer the first day of the weeke midnight the 14 day of Nouember 1686

Samuell Dam son of william dam by his wife martha was born in douer the 21 : day of march 6 : day of the weeke 1689

Sarah dam daughter of william dam by his wife martha was born the 21 day of Aprill 6 day of the weeke 1692

Leah dam daughter of william dam by his wife martha was born in douer the 2^d day of the weeke being the 17 day of february 1695

Jacob Allen son of Jacob Allen by his wif martha was born in douer September the 28 day the second day of the weeke midnight ano dom 1702

Edward Allen son of Jacob allen by his wife Martha born in douer the 5 day of the weeke the 17 day of may 2 aclock after noone Ano : dom 1705

Benedictus Tarr Late of old England and Leah Knight of douer widow were Joyned to geather in marriage by John woodman Esqr Justis of Peace the 17 day of July Ano : dom 1704

Elizabeth Tebbetts daughter of Joseph Tebbets by his wife Elizabeth born in douer the 10th day of march : 1697

Margery Tebbets daughter of Joseph Tebets by his wif Elizabeth borne the 18 day of January : 1700

Judeth Tebbets daughter of Joseph Tebbets by his wife Elizabeth born in douer the Third day of february : 1702

Liddia Tebbets daughter of Joseph Tebbets by his wife Elizabeth born in douer the 4th day of August 1704

Edward Euens sonn of Edward Euens by his wife darkis born in douer The 23d of october 1702

Rachell Euens daughter of Edward Euens by his wife darkis born in douer the 6 : day of Aprill 1703

Ellener Euens daughter of Edward Euens by his wife darkis born in Kittery the 3d day of march 1700

Joseph Euens sone of Edward Euens by his wife darkis borne in douer the 29 : day of october 1704

John Tuttle sone of John Tuttle Junr by his wife Judeth borne in douer the 8th day of may 1704

Ezekiell wentworth son of gersham wentworth by his wife Hannah born in douer the 4th day of february 1702

gersham wentworth sonn of gersham wentworth by his wife Hanah borne in douer the 4th day of Aprill 1705

mary Engersell daughter of Elisha Engersell by his wife mary borne in douer the 29 : day of nouember 1702

Joseph Hanson sonn of Tobias Hanson by his wife ann borne in douer the 10th day of Jnuary 1703/4

These may sertifie whome it may Concearn that Benjamin Peirce of watertowne and Elizabeth hall of douer widdow was Joyned to geather in mariage by the Reauerant Jno Buss minister of oyster Riuer in the Towneship of douer on the 7th day of September 1705

Nicholas ffollett son of Nicholas ffollett of douer marriner by his wife Hanah was borne in douer the fifth day of Nouember Ano : q : dom : 1677

Joanah Clements departed this Life being full of daies dyed in douer on the fifteenth day of January in the year 1703/4

Abraham Nute sone of Abraham Nute of douer by his wife Joanah was born in douer the ninth day of march Eleuen a Clock att night in the year 1705/6

Hanah Emerson daughter of Samll Emerson by his wife Judeth was born in douer the sixth day of Janry 1699

Micah Emerson son of Samll Emerson by his wife Judeth was born in douer the fowerth day of Janry 1701

Abigall Emerson the daughter of Samll Emerson by his wife Judeth was born in douer the 27th day of 7br 1704

Mary Pots daughter of Thos Pots by his wif Joanah born in douer the sixt day of July Ano : q dom 1690

BIRTHS AND MARRIAGES, 1693-1838.

Joyus Pots daughter of Tho Pots by his wife Joanah born in douer the 21th day of August 1693

Joseph Tebbets son of Joseph Tebbets by his wife Elizabeth was born in douer the second day of ffebruary : 1706/7

Elizabeth Tebbets the wif of Joseph Tebbets departed this Life on the Twnty fowrth day of ffebruary 1706/7 being thirty fiue years and Two months of Age wanting one day

Lidia Leighton daughter of John Leighton by his wife Sarah was born in douer the 19th day of february 1703

Ann Cromwell daughter of Phillip Cromwell Cromwell by his wife Elizabeth was born in douer the 19th day of August $\frac{1680}{1674}$*

william wentworth sonne of benjamin wentworth by his wife Sarah was born in douer the 14th day of August 1698

Sarah wentworth daughter of benjamin wentworth by his wife Sarah was born in Douer the 16 : day of Aprill 1700

Tamsin wentworth daughter of benjamin wentworth by his wife Sarah was born in douer the 4th day of Jan'y 1701

benjamin wentworth sonn of benjamin wentworth by his wife Sarah was born in douer the first day of december 1703

Ebenezer wentworth sonn of benjamin wentworth by his wife Sarah was born in douer the 9 day of September 1705

Susanah wentworth daughter of benjamin wentworth by his wife Sarah was born in douer the 9 day of december 1707

Joseph son of benjamin wentworth by his wife Sarah born the 22d day of december 1709

James Tuttle sonn of John Tuttle of douer by his wife Mary Born the seuenth day of Aprill in the year Ano : dom : 1683 and died on the fifteenth day of May 1709 being the first day of the week about 3 a Clock after Noon

will Norraway son of James norraway by his wife Elizabeth was born in Portsmoth the second day of march 1697/8

Dorrithy norraway daughter of James Norraway by his wife Elizabeth was born in douer the ninth day of July 1703

Thomas Tuttle sonne of John Tuttle of douer by his wife mary born in douer the 4th day of Aprill 1674, and dyed in the bay of Compecha the 26 day of aprill 1699

---

*In the text the original date appears to have been 1674, with the figure 7 slightly blotted. The town clerk, doubtless to make the date plain, drew a line underneath and wrote another 1674. Afterwards in another handwriting the figures 80 were written over the upper 74, making the upper date read 1680.—[ED.

Keziah Meder The daughter of Nicholas Meder by his wife Lidia was born in douer the 23ᵈ day of June in the year 1709

Bridgett Bickford daughter of John bickford by his wife Susanah born in douer the 30 : day of July 1685

Jethro Bickford son of John Bickford by his wife Susanah born in douer the 16 : day nouember 1689

John Bickford son of John Bickford by his wife Susanah born in douer the 16 : day of march 1691/2

Mary Bickford daughter of Jnᵒ bickford by his wife Susanah born in douer the 13 : day of August 1693

Joseph bickford son of John bickford by his wife Susanah born in douer the 13 day of July 1695

Anna bickford daughter of John bickford by his wife Susanah born in douer the 18 : day of September 1698

Peirce bickford son of John bickford by his wife Susanah born in douer the 9 : day of march 1701/2

Lemuell and Eliakim bickford twins sons of John bickford by his wife Susanah born in douer the 6 day of march 1703/4

doddauer bickford son of John bickford by his wife Susanah born in douer the 20 : day of August 1709

Lidia ffost daughter of william ffost by his wife Sarah born in douer the seuenth day of January 1705

ffebe Tuttle daughter of James Tuttle by his wife Rose born in douer the 26 day of September 1706

Elijah Tuttle sonn of James Tuttle by his wife Rose was born in douer the 14ᵗʰ day of may 1708

mary Tuttle daughter of John Tuttle by his wife Judeth was born in douer the 7ᵗʰ of January 1697/98

Thomas Tuttle sonn of John Tuttle by his wife Judeth was born in douer the 15ᵗʰ day of march 1699/700

Judeth Tuttle daughter of John Tuttle by his wife Judeth was born in douer the 10ᵗʰ day of may 1702

John Tuttle the sonn of John Tuttle by his wife Judeth was born in douer the Eight day of may 1704

dorithy Tuttle daughter of John Tuttle by his Judeth was born in douer the 21ᵗʰ of march 1706

nicholas Tuttle sonn of John Tuttle by his wife Judeth was born in douer the 27ᵗʰ day of July 1708

James Tuttle sonn of John Tuttle by his wife Judeth was born in douer the 9ᵗʰ day of february 1710/11

John Tuttle murdered by the Indians ye 7 : of may 1712

Sarah Horn daughter of Thomas Horne by his wif Judeth was born in douer the 14th day of January 1699

william Horn sonn of Thomas Horn by his wife Judeth was born in douer the 7th day nouember 1702

Thomas Horn sonn of Thomas Horn by his wife Judeth was born in douer the 23^d day of october 1705

Ichabod Horn sonn of Thomas Horn by his wife Judeth was born in douer the 25th of June 1710

Gershan Downes the sonne of Thomas Downes Junr borne in douer the 10 of January 1680 by his wife martha

Gersham dounes the sonne of Thomas dounes Junr marriad to Sarah Hall daughter of John Hall of douer Late of douer deceased the Twenty fowerth day of december 1707

Gersham dounes sonne of gersham downes by his wife Sarah borne in douer the 15th day of february 1708

Martha downes daughter of gersham dounes by his wife Sarah borne in douer the 14th of october 1711

Thomas downes sone of Gersham downes by his wife Sarah borne in douer the 17 day of february 1713/14

John Alle Sone of Samuell Alle born the 25 Day of January 1719/20

Expearance Heard Dafter of Samuell Heard born ye 22 : of august : 1718

Elezebeth Heard Dafter of Samuell Heard born the 25 Day of January 1719/20

Samuell Meder son of Nicholas Meder by his wife Lidia born in douer the fifteen day of January 1711

Nicholas Meader sone of Nicholas Meder by his wife Lidia born in douer the ninth day october 1712

John Meder sonn of Nicolas meder by his Lidia borne in douer the 8th day of october 1715

Daniell Meder sonn of nicholas Meder by his wife Lidia born in Douer the sixth day of Nouember 1718

Mr Daniell Titcomb And Mrs Ann Drew were Legually Joyned to geather In Marriage on the first day of Jan^{r}y 1718/19 by the Reauerand Jon^a Cushing

feb^r : 21 : 1718/9

Stephen Hawkins and Rachell Wallingsford were Legally Joyned to gether In Marriage by the Reauerand Jonathan Cushing the 14 day of Aprill 1719

Samuell Nute and Elizabeth Pinkham were Leagully Joyned to geather In Marriage by James Dauis Esqr Justis of Peace march the 18th 171$\frac{8}{9}$

Elizabeth Reckors daughter of John Reckors by his wife Hanah born the fifteenth day of June 1714

Olliue Rickor daughter of John Reckors by his wife Hanah borne the twenteth day of Nouenber 1717

Willam Welland and Hanah Heard Were Lawfully Joyned To geather in marriage on the 22^d day of march 1719/20 P^r
       Jonathan Cushing   Clark

Samuell Randell and Elezebeth macfeeld wear Lawfully Joyned to gether in marridge on the 30 Day of Nouember 1720 by James Dauis Justis of Peace

Bartholomew Stephenson was married to Mary Clark by Major Richd Waldron the tenth day of october in the year 1680

Mary Stephenson daughter of barthollomew Stephenson by his wife Mary was born the 21th day of September in the year 1681

Barthollomew Stephenson sonn of barthollomew Stephenson by his wife Mary was born the Last day of June in the year 1683

Joseph Stephenson sone of barthollomew Stephenson by his wife Mary was born the 13th day of September in the year 1686

Elizabeth Stephenson daughter of barthollomew Stephenson by his wife Mary was born the 8th day of december in the year 1688

Thomas Stephenson sone of barthollomew Stephenson by his wife Mary was born the 28th day of december in the year 1691

Sarah Stephenson daughter of barthollomew Stephenson by his wife Mary was born the 21th day of may in the year 1695

Abraham Stephenson sone of barthollomew Stephenson by his wife Mary was born the 8th day of Nouember in the year 1700

James Clements son of Job Clements of douer by his wife Abigall was born unto him In douer the Twenty sixth day of March in the year 1693/4

Sarah Hall Dafter of John Hall Junr of Douer by his wife Elezebeth was born the 25th day of July : 1696

Ichabod Haise the sonn of John haise by his wife mary was borne in douer the Eighteen day of march in the year of our Lord god 1691/2

Robard eliot Gerrish sonn of Cap^{tt} Timothy Gerrish by his wife Sarah was born in douer the Eighteen day of September 1708

John Gerrish sonn of Cap^{tt} Timothy Gerrish by his wife Sarah was born in douer the sixth day of ffebruary 1710/11

Timothy Gerrish sonn of Captⁿ Timothy Gerrish by his wife Sarah was born in douer the seuenteen day of January 1712/13

Sarah Gerrish Daughter of Capt Timothy Gerrish by his wife Sarah was borne in douer the Twenty six day of march 1714/15

Sarah Haise the daughter of Ichabod Haise by his wife Abigall was born in douer the thirtieth of Septtember in the year of our Lord 1716

John Ambler and Elizabeth Trickey was married to geather by the Reauerand Mr John Pik on the sixt day of nouember 1706

Stephen Otis and Mary young was married to geather by James Dauis Justis of Peace the 22th day of ffeb: 17$\frac{19}{20}$

John Drew & Rebecah Kook were married to geather by James Dauis Justis of Peace on the 31th day of march att Euening 1720

Mary Ambler daughter of John Ambler by his Wife Elizabeth born In Portsmoth the first day of ffebruary Ano: dom: 1709/10

John Ambler sonn of John Amblar by his Wife Elisabeth Borne In Portsmoth the Eleuenth day of february Ano: dom 1711/12

Joseph Ambler sonn of John Amblar by his Wife Elisabeth Born In douer the ninth day of Agust Ano dom 1714

Abraham Ambler the son of John Ambler by his wife Elizabeth born in douer the 2^d of September 1716

James Clark and Sarah Leighton were married To geather by Justis Dauis the 16th day of January 1717/8

Clement Drew and Mary Bunker wear married to geather by Justis Dauis the Twenty day of may 1718

Hanah Ambler daughter of John Ambler by his wif Elizabeth borne douer January 24: 1718/9

Jonthan the Son of Jonathan Crosbee by his wife Hannah was boarn August the 16th 1719

Nathaniell Heard Welland son of willam welland by his wife Hannah borne in Douer the 20 Day or nouember 1720

John Crosbee Son of Jonathan Crosbee by his wife Hannah was born October ye 3^d 1721

Sarah Crosbe Dafter of Jonathan Crosbee by his wife Hannah borne the 18 Day of January 1723/4

Patience the Dafter of Nicolas Harford by his wife Elezebeth was Born the 16 Day of September in the year 1701

Joseph Harfutt Son of Nicklas Harfutt by his wife Elesebeth was boarn the 9th Day of Aprell in the year of our Lord 1703

Charity Harford Dafter of Nicolas Harford by his wife Elezebeth was born ye 5th Day of may in the year of our Lord 1705

Stephen Harford Son of Nicolas Harford by his wife Elezebeth was borne the 12th Day of Aprell in the year of our Lord 1707

Nicolas Harford Son of Nicolas Harford was born by his wife Elezebeth Harford the first Day of September in ye year of our Lord 1709

Willam Harford was born ye 9th Day of october in the year of our Lord 1711

Elezebeth Harford was born on ye 18th Day of January in the year of our Lord 1713

Benjamen Harford was born on the 15th Day of Aprel in the year of our Lord 1716

Paul Harford was born on ye 24 Day of January in the year of our Lord 1717

Sollomon Harford was born on ye 31 : Day of march in ye year of our Lord 1720

willam Harford Departed This Life ye 10th Day of August 1716

John Harfutt son of nicklas Harfutt borne the 17th. of December 1724

Elezebeth ham Dafter of John Ham was born in the year of our Lord 1703

mary ham daughter of John ham was born in the year of our Lord 1706

Samuell ham Sone of John Ham was born in the year of our Lord 1708

nathaniell ham Sone of John Ham was born in the year of our Lord 1711

Joannah ham dafter of John ham was born in the year of our Lord 1713

doddefur ham Sone of John ham was born in the year of our Lord 1715

Patiance ham daughter of John ham was born in the year of our Lord 1718

Samuell willey Son of Samuell willey by his wife mary was borne ye 25 Day of february 1702

mary the Dafter of Samuell willey by his wife Elezebth borne ye 6 Day of September 1721

Samuell James Steuenes son of James Steuenes by his wife [———] borne the 30 Day of nouember 1723

Ann Harford Dafter of Nicklas Harford by his Wife Elezebeth was borne the Second Day of August 1722

John Smith the Son of Joseph Smith was married to his wife Susannah the 17th Day Juen 1694

John Smith Son of John Smith was boarn in may the 18—1695 by his wife Susannah

Elezebeth Smith the Dafter of John Smith was boarn by his wife Susannah in August the first 1697

Joseph Smith Son of John Smith by his wife Susannah was Born in September ye 7th Day 1701

Hannah Smith Dafter of John Smith by his wife Susannah was boarn in September the 30th Day 1703

Samuell Smith Son of John Smith by his wife Susannah was Boarn february the 6 : Day 1706

Benjamen Smith Son of John Smith by his wife Susannah was born in march the 22 Day 1709

Ebenezer Smith Son of John Smith by his wife Susannah was born in Juen the 6 Day 1712

wintrupt Smith Son of John Smith by his wife Susannah was born may the 30th Day 1714

John Giles son of John Giles by his wife mary borne the 30th Day of September in the year of our Lord 1703

Danniel Hoarn Son of Dannell by his wife mary born the 23^d Day of october 1716

Icobod Horn Son of Danniell Horn by his wife mary born the 5th Day of march 1720/1

Abegarl Church Dafter of John Church by his wife marcy born in may the 15th 1702

John Church Sone of John Church by his wife marcy born the first Day of Aprel 1704

Elezebeth Church Dafter of John Church by his wif marcy born ye 2^d Day of aprel 1706

Jonathan Church Sone of John Church by his wife marcy born the 25 Day of July 1708

mary Church Dafter of John Church by his wife marcy born the 4th Day of August 1710

Danniel young Sone of nathaniel young by his wife marcy borne the 4th Day of may 1713

marcy young Dafter of nathanniel young by his wife marcy borne ye 24 Day of may 1718

Sollomon Hanson Son of Thomas Hanson by his wife Hannah born the 29th Day of January 1719/20

Ebenezer Hanson Son of Thomas Hanson by his wife Hannah borne 16 of April 1726

Trustrim Coffen Son of Trustrim Coffen was married to Jane Heard of Kitterey the 15th Day of nouember 1719

Abegarl Coffen Dafter of Trustrim Coffen by his wife Jane was boren the 16th Day of July 1720

william welland and Hannah Heard wear Joyned in marridg march 22 : 1720

James Heard and mary Roberts Joyned together in marridg Aprel ye 7th : 1720

Benjamen Ham and Patiance Harfutt wear Joyned togeather in marridg ye 21 of Aprel 1720

Nathaniel fitts and Abigail Hayes ware Joyned togeather in marridg ye 10th : of may 1720

John Roberts and franses Emerey ware Joyned Togeather in marridg the 17th : of may : 1720

Samuell Hayes and Leah Dame wear Joyned togeather in marridg the 7th of July 1720

willam Jones and Hannah Rickers ware Joyned together in marridg the 28 of July 1720

neal mackuagh and margret Campell ware Joyned together in marridg the 31 of July 1720

Joseph farnum and Elezebeth Husse ware Joyned together in marridg ye 31 of August 1720

Ephrim Rickers and Darkcas Garland ware Joyned togeather in marridg ye first of Septembr 1720

Joseph Rickers and Elezabeth Garland was Joyned togather in marridg ye 16 : nouember 1720

John Cromuell and mary Riddley was married togather on December the 26—1720

John Buncker and Hannah Drew was Joyned together in marridg the 5 : of febrary 1720/21

Ebenezer Garland and Abigail Powel ware Joyned togather in marridg the 2^d of march : 1720/21

Willam Downes and mary Pittman ware Joyned together in marridg may the 3^d : 1721

m^r Eliezer Russel and m^{rs} margret waldron are Joyned together in marridg may y^e : 18 : 1721

These Persones aboue mentioned war Joyned together in marridg by the Reauerand m^r Jonathan Cushing as it appears under his hand
     Test Thomas Tebbets Town Clark

BIRTHS AND MARRIAGES, 1693-1838.

Samuell Tebbets and Sarah Loo was Joyned together in marridg ye 2^d Day of march 1721

Samuell Tebbets Son of Samuell by his wife Sarah was borne the forth Day of December : 1721

This Sone of Samuell Tebbets is Departed this Life a bout 3 month after his bearth

Samuell Tebbets 2^d Son of Samuell Tebbets by his wife Sarah borne the ninth Day of march in the year of our Lord 1724/5

mary Tebbets Dafter of Samuell Tebbets by his wife Sarah borne ye Eleuenth Day of february in the year of our Lord 1722/3

hur Sister Sarah borne the 29 Day of may in the year 1727

Deberah Stenpheson Dafter of bartholeme Stephenson born ye 11 of April 1709

Benjamen Heard Son of James Heard by his wife Deberrah born ye 2 of August 1715

mary Heard Dafter of James Heard borne in September 1717

Lyda Heard Dafter of James Heard by his wife Deborah born february 1720

Ephrim plumer Son of Danniel plumer borne the 12 Day of october 1720

william Hayes Sone of John Hayes born ye 6 Day of September 1698

william Hayes married to Hannah Samborn the 23^d Day of nouember 1720

mary Hayes Dafter of william Hayes by his wife hannah borne the 23^d Day of october 1721

Ephrim Tebbets and Ester Tebbets was joyned to geather in marridg by the Reuarnd m^r Jonathan Cushen the 16 : Day of nouember 1721

Catturn Tebbets Dafter of Joseph Tebbets by his Wife Catturn was born the 24th Day of August 1713

mary Tebbets Dafter of Joseph Tebbets by his wife Catturn was born the Eleuenth Day of october 1716

hannah Tebbets Dafter of Joseph Tebbets by his wife Catturn was born the 23^d Day of June 1721

Elezebeth mason Dafter of Benjamen Mason by his wife Elezebeth was boarn the fifteenth Day of may 1716

Benjamen mason Son of Benjamen mason by his wife Elezebeth was born the 27 Day of march 1718

John Tebbets Sone of John Tebbets by his wife mary was born the 27th Day of march in the year of our Lord 1711

Thomas Tebbets Son of John Tebbets by his wife mary was born the Eight Day of february in the year of Lord 1712

Ephrim Tebbets Son of Ephrim Tibbets Senr of Douer by his wife Rose was boarn the Last Day of December in the year 1694

Ann Tebbets Dafter of Ephrim Tebbets by his wife Rose was born the 8 Day of July in the year of our Lord 1697

Henrey Tebbets Son of Ephrim Tebbets by his wife Rose was born the 29th Day of July in the year of our Lord 1699

Abygarl Tebbets Dafter of Ephrim Tebbets by his wife Rose was born the 12th Day of August in the year or our Lord 1700

Joseph Tebbets Son of Ephrim Tebbets by his wife Rose was born the 4th Day of nouember in the year of our Lord 1702

Elisha Tebbets Son of Ephrim Tebbets by his wife Rose was born the 16 Day of february in the year of our Lord 1704

Aron Tebbets Son of Ephrim Tebbets by his wife Rose was born the 26 Day of february in the year of our Lord 1705

mary Tebbets Dafter of Ephrim Tebbets by his wife Rose was born the 16 Day of nouember in the year of our Lord 1707

Elijah Tebbets Son of Ephrim Tebbets by his wife Rose was born the 23 Day of march in the year of our Lord 1711

Rose Tebbets Dafter of Ephrim Tebbets by his wife Rose was born the 4th Day of february in the year of our Lord 1713

Elizebeth Tebbets Dafter of Ephrim Tebbets by his wife Rose was born the 30th Day of october in the year of our Lord 1716

Hannah Hanson Dafter of John Hanson by his wife Elezebeth born ye 11th Day of Juen 1705

Sarah Hanson Dafter of John Hanson by his wife Elezebeth born the 13th of nouember 1707

Elezebeth hanson Dafter of John Hanson by his wife Elezebeth was born ye 13th of nouember 1709

John Hanson Son of John Hanson by his wife Elezebeth was born the 17th of march 1713

Isack Hanson Sone of John Hanson by his wife Elezebeth was born the 25 of february 1714

Danniel Hanson Sone of John hanson by his wife Elezebeth was born the 26 of march 1718

Ebenezer Hanson Son of John hanson by his wife Elezebeth was born the 27 Day of february 1720

Caleb hanson Sone of John hanson by his wife Elezebeth was born the 8 Day of february 1721

Joseph Roberts Eldist Sone of Joseph Roberts of Douer by his wife Elezebeth born the 27th Day of october in the year of our Lord anoqua Dom 1692

John Roberts Son of Joseph Roberts by his wife Elezebeth born December ye 6th 1694

Elezebeth Roberts Dafter of Joseph Roberts by his wife Elezebeth born ye 13th of march 1697

Abigall Roberts Dafter of Joseph Roberts by his Elezebeth born the 16 Day of July 1701

Stephen Roberts Son of Joseph Roberts by his wife Elezebeth born the 20th Day of august 1704

Ebenezer Roberts Son of Joseph Roberts by his wife Elezebeth born ye 24th Day of february 1706

benjamen Roberts Son of Joseph Roberts by his wife Elezebeth born ye 20th of September 1709

Samuell and Lidya Twenes Son and Dafter of Joseph by his wife Elezebeth born the Eleauenth Day of Aprill in the year of our Lord 1712

mary Roberts Dafter of Joseph Roberts by his Elezebeth born ye 13th of march 1716

Jane Coffen Datter of Trustrim Coffen by his wife Jane was born the 11 Day of march 1721/2

Abegarll Giles Dafter of Mark Giles by his wife Sarah was born the 18 Day of July in the year of our Lord 1698

Ann Giles Dafter of mark Gile by his wife Sarah was born the first Day of october in the year of our Lord 1702

mark giles Son of mark giles by his wife Sarah was born ye 28 Day of June 1706

Pauel giles Son of mark gile by his wife Sarah was born ye first Day of December 1708

Sarah Gile Dafter of mark gile by his wife Sarah was born ye ninth Day of april 1711

Ester giles Dafter of mark giles by his wife Sarah was born the 21 first Day of nouember 1713

Isrial Hodgdun Sone of Isrial by his wife Ann was born the 25th Day of march in the year of our Lord 1697

Judeth Tebbets Dafter of Icobod Tebbets by his wife abagarl was born the 15th Day of may in the year of our Lord 1722   and

Abigall Tebbets Dafter of Icobod Tebbets by his wife Abigal borne the 23d of aprill in the year 1723

Timothy Tebbets Son of John Tebbets by his wife mary was born the 10 Day of January in the year 1714

hannah Dafter of John Tebbets by his wife mary was born the 25 Day of march in the year 1719

mary Dafter of Samuell Tebbets by his wife Sarah was borne the seauenth Day of february in the year of our Lord 1722/3

Ephrim Tebbets Son of Ephrim Tebbets Junr by his wife Ester was born the 21th Day of August in the year of our Lord 1722
and Departed this Life the fift Day of September 1722

Abygall the Dafter of John Tebbets by his wife mary born the tenth Day of January in the year of Lord 1720/1

Elezebeth Ham Dafter of Joseph Ham by his wife Tamson born the 22^d Day of february in the year of our Lord 1704/5

mary Ham Dafter of Joseph Ham by his wife Tamson born the 28th Day of December 1706

Tamson Ham Dafter of Joseph Ham by his wife Tamson born the 19th Day of July 1708

Abigarl ham Dafter of Joseph ham by his wife Tamson born the 15th Day of march 1710

Ann ham Dafter of Joseph ham by his wife Tamson born the : 12 : Day of December 1712

Danniel ham Sone of Joseph ham by his wife Tamson born the 24th Day of July 1714

Joseph ham Sone of Joseph ham by his wife Tamson born ye 25 of Aprill 1716

Clemant ham Sone of Joseph ham by his wife Tamson born ye 16 Day of December 1718

Jonathan ham Sone of Joseph ham by his wife Tamson born ye 8 of Juen 1720

Jane ham Dafter of Joseph ham by his wife Tamson born the 26th : of Juen 1722

william Ham the Sone of Benjamen Ham by his wife Patiance borne the 25 Day of nouember in the year 1722

william Ham the Son of Benjamin Ham by his wife Patiance borne the 25 Day of Nouember in the year of our Lord 1722

Thomas Tebbets Son of Thomas Tebbets by his wif Sarah was born the seauenth Day of January in the year of Lord 1716

Hannah Purkings Dafter of Samull Purkings by his wife mary borne the ninth Day of December 1703 franses Purkings Dafter of Samuell Purkings by his wife mary borne the Eleauenth Day of february 1705

Joseph Purkins Sun of Sam^{ll} Purkins by his wife mary born ye 25th of august 1714

Abigail Purkins Daughter of Sam^{ll} Purkins by his wife mary born ye 30 of april 1717

Sam^{ll} Purkins Sun of Sam^{ll} Purkins by his wife mary born ye 13^d of of Feb^r 1723

Jonathan Chesley Sun of Jonathan Chesley by his wife mary born ye 20^d of Nouem^r 1721

Joseph Euines Sone of Robert Euines by his wife ann borne the forth Day of June in year of our Lord 1682

Sarah Euines Dafter of Robert Euines by his wife ann born the 9: Day of nouember in the year of our Lord 1685

Benjamen Euines Sun of Robert Euines by his wife ann born the 2^d: Day of february 1687

hannah Euines Dafter of Robert Euines by his wife ann borne the 21: Day of June 1690

Patiance Euines Dafter of Robert Euines by his wife ann borne the fift Day of September 1693

Elezebeth welland Dafter of william welland by his wife hannah borne the 15th of march 1722/3

william Tebbets Son of John Tebbets by his wife mary borne the 20th Day of August in the year of our Lord 1722

moses Tebbets Son of John Tebbets by his wife mary borne the 28 of february 1723

Martha Hays Dafter of Samuell Hays by his wife Leaah borne the 16 Day of agust 1721

mary Tebbets Dafter of John Tebbets by his wife mary borne ye 3^d Day of aprill 1725

Ephrem Tebbets Son of Ephrim Tebbets by his wife Ester borne the 11th Day of nouember 1723 and

Ester Tebbets Dafter of Ephrim Tebbets by his wife Ester borne the 10 Day of march in the year of our Lord 1724/5

Wintrop watson Son of Dauid watson by his wife mary borne the Eleauenth Day of January 1723

marcy Cuck Dafter of John Cuck by his wife Lidia borne the 21 of June 1716

Hessekiah Cuck Son of John Cuck by his wife Liddia borne the first Day of January 1717 mary Cuck Dafter of John Cuck by his wife Liddia borne the first Day of april 1720

Ebenezer Cuck Son of John Cuck by his wife Liddia borne the 26 Day of april 1723

Benjamen Euenes Son of Benjamen Euene by his wife mary borne the 18 Day of June 1713

Elezebeth Euenes Dafter of Benjamen Euenes by his wife mary borne the 19 Day of January 1716

Joseph Euenes Son of Benjamen Euenes by his wife mary borne the 7th: Day of march 1719

Jonathan Euenes Son of Benjamen Euenes by his wife mary born the 17 Day of June 1722

John winget Son of John winget Desesed by his wife Ann borne the tenth Day of April 1693

John winget Son of John winget by his wife Dorethy borne the fift Day of may 1719

Samuel winget Son of John winget by his wife Dorithy borne the 19th Day of february 1721

Danniel winget Son of John winget by his wife Dorithy borne the 28 Day of January 1722

mary Chamberlin Dafter of william Chamberlin by his wife mary borne the 26 Day of october 1720

Rebeckah Chamberlin Dafter of william Chamberlin by his wife mary borne 28 Day of December 1722

nathaniel Hanson Son of nathaniel Hanson by his wife martha borne the 26 Day of April 1716

mary Hanson Dafter of nathaniel Hanson by his wife martha borne the 13th Day of August 1717

Abigal Hanson Dafter of nathaniel Hanson by his wife martha borne the 26 Day of may 1721

Pauel Hanson Son of nathaniel Hanson by his wife martha borne the 17 Day of august 1723

Ralph Twombly Son of william Twombly by his wife mary borne the 13 Day of September 1713

Isach Twombly son of william Twombly by his wife mary borne the 19 : of December 1715

william Twombly Son of william twombly by his wife mary borne the 25 of July 1717

mary twombly Dafter of william twombly by his wife mary borne the 25 Day of february 1721

Elezebeth Twombly Dafter of william twombly by his wife mary the borne first of nouember 1723

John Laton the Son of Thomas Laton by his wife Suesanah borne the 27 of June 1719

Sarah Laton Dafter of Thomas Laton by his wife Suesanah borne the tenth Day of august 1721

Dorothy Laton Dafter of Thomas Laton by his wife Susanah borne the 18 Day of october 1723

Thomas Laton Son of Thomas Laton by his wife Suesanah borne the 13th of Nouember 1725

Leidah meder Dafter of nathanill meder by his wife Elener borne ye 25 of august 1696

Danniel meder Sun of nathanill meder by his wife Elener borne ye 3^d of nouember 1698

nathanill meder Sun of nathanill meder by his wife Elener borne the 8 of march 1700

Elizebeth meder Dafter of nathanill meder by his wife Elener borne the 3^d of Aprill 1702

Elener meder Dafter of nathanill meder by his wife Elener borne the 3^d of June 1704

Samuell winget Son of John winget by his wife Ann borne the 27th of nouember 1700

Icobod Hayes Son of Icobod Hayes by his wife abbigal borne the 13 Day of December 1718

Ezekill Hayes Son of Icobod Hayes by his wife abigal borne the 21 Day of february 1720

Danniel Hays Son of Icobod Hayes by his wife abigall borne the 26 Day of August 1723

Dannill feeld Son of zacharias feeld Junr by his wife Hannah borne the 17th Day of february 1709

Zackarius feeld Son of Zackarias feeld Junr by his wife Hannah born the 9th Day of august 1712

Hannah Hussey Dafter of Richard Hussey by his wife Hannah borne the 23^d of february 1717

Mary Hussey Dafter of Richand Hussey by his wife Hannah borne the 14th Day of february 1719

Richard Hussey Son of Richard Hussey by his wife Hannah borne the 12 Day of august 1722

Mary Winget Dafter of John winget by his wife An borne the 3^d Day of october 1691

An winget Dafter of John winget by his wife An borne the Second Day of february 1694

Sarah winget Dafter of John winget by his wife An borne the 17th Day of february 1696

Moses winget Son of John winget by his wife An borne the 27 Day of December 1698

Edmond winget Son of John winget by his wife An borne the 27: Day of february 1702

Abigal winget Dafter of John winget by his wife An borne the 2: Day of march 1704

Elezebeth winget Dafter of John winget by his wife An borne the 3d Day of february 1706

mehittebel winget Dafter of John winget by his wife An borne the 14th: Day of nouember 1709

Joannah winget Dafter of Johu winget by his wife An borne the 6: Day of January 1711

Simond winget Son of John winget by his wife An borne the second Day of September 1713

John Perll Son of John Perll by his wife mary born 11 day of August 1714

Elisebeth Perll Daughter of John Perll by his wife mary born 28 day of December 1718

Abraham Pearll Son of John Pearl born ye: 5 of aprill 1726

Joseph Pearll Son of John Pearll by his wife mary borne the 30th Day of march 1721

Benjamen Pearl Son of John Pearl by his wife mary borne the 28 Day of nouember 1723

Pomfrett Whithous Son of Pomfret whithous by his wife Rebeckah borne the 14 Day of october 1703

william whithous Son of Pomfret whithous by his wife Rebeckah born the 8 Day of January 1705

Elezebeth whithous Dafter of Pomfret whithous by his wife Rebeckah born ye Last of february 1707

Judeth and Edward whithous twenes Dafter Son of Pomfret whithous by his Rebeckah borne the 10: Day of nouember 1710

Thomas whithous Son of Pomfret whithous by his wife Rebeckah born the 8 Day of Aprill 1713

Rosemes whithous Dafter of Pomfret whithous by his wife Rebeckah born the 31 Day of march 1715

Samuell whithous Son of Pomfret whithous by his wife Rebeckah borne the 15 Day of Aprill 1716

John whithous Son of Pomfret whithous by his wife Rebeckah borne the 8 Day of January 1718

Moses whithous Son of Pomfret whithous by his wife Rebeckah borne the 13 of June 1720

Hannah Drew Dafter of John Drew borne the 26 of february : 1709

John Drew Son of John Drew borne the 18 Day of october 1712

Abigall Drew Dafter of John Drew borne 21 of June 1714

Rebeckah Drew Dafter of John Drew borne the 24 of April 1716

franses Drew Son of John Drew by his wife Rebeckah borne the 9 Day of August in the year of our Lord 1720

frances Drew Departed This Life the 16th Day of february 1726/7

Zebulon Drew Son of John Drew by his wife Rebeckah borne the 9 Day of nouember 1721

Limuell Drew Son of John Drew by his wife Rebeckah borne the 26 Day of may 1722

Benjamen Demerritt Son of Eli Demerritt Senr by his wife Hopstill borne the 29 Day of nouember 1708

Job Demerritt Son of Eli Demerritt by his wife Hopstill borne the 29 Day [——] in ye year of our Lord 1705

Samuel Demerrit Son of Ely Demerritt by his wife Tabathy borne the 8 Day of may in the year 1723

John Twombly Son of John Twombly Junr by his wife Sarah borne the 28 Day of october 1712

Sarah Twombly Dafter of John Twombly by his wife Sarah borne the 21 Day of february 1714

Danniel Twombly Son of John Twombly by his wife Sarah borne the 18 Day of January 1716

martha Twombly Dafter of John Twombly by his wife Sarah borne the 25 Day of february 1719

John Heard Son of Trustrim Heard Desesed by his wife Jane borne the 20th Day of July 1718

Jane Heard Dafter of Trustrim Heard Desesed by his wife Jane borne the 12 of nouember 1719

Ruben Heard Son of Trustrim Heard Desesed by his wife Jane borne the 9th Day of march 1721/2

Tristrim Heard Son of Tristrim Heard Desesed by his wife Jane borne the 5 Day of December 1723

John winthworth Son of Benjamen wintworth by his wife Elezebeth borne the 30 Day of march 1719

Elezebeth winthworth Dafter of Benjamen winthworth by his wife Elezebeth borne the 15th Day of february 1721

Abigall winthworth Dafter of Benjamen winthworth by his wife Elezebeth borne the 12 Day of february 1723

Hannah Hayes Dafter of william Hayes by his wife Hannah borne the 27th Day of october 1723

Benjamen Hays Son of John Hayes by his wife mary borne the 6 Day of September in the year 1700

Trustrim Coffen Son of Trustrim Coffen by his wife Jane the 22 Day of January in the year 1723

and Desesed the tenth Day of february 1723

mary Ham Dafter of Benjamen Ham by his wife Patiance borne the 8 Day of october 1723

John Heard Son of Samuell Heard by his wife Elezebeth borne the 4 Day of october 1721

Samuell Heard Son of Samuell Heard by his wife Elezebeth borne the 13 Day of nouember 1723

Ruben Garland Son of Jabus Garland by his wife Abigall borne the 20th of february 1723

Samuell Alle Son of Samuell Alle by his wife Elezebeth borne the 19 Day of Aprill 1723

Samuell Clements Son of Job Clements by his wife Hannah borne the 4th Day of may 1717

Job Clements Son of Job Clements by his wife Hannah borne the 19th : Day of nouember 1722

febe heard Dafter of James Heard by his wife Daberah borne the 13 Day of December 1722

mary Rawlings Dafter of Jeremiah Rawlings by his wife Elezebeth borne the 23 Day of January 1714

Lidia Rawlings Dafter of Jeremiah Rawlings by his wife Elezebeth borne the 18 Day of march 1717

Debarah Rawlings Dafter of Jeremiah Rawlings by his wife Elezebeth borne the 26 of January 1719

Icobod Rawlings Son of Jeremiah Rawlings by his wife Elezebeth borne the 18th Day of July 1722

Bridgett Tebbets Dafter of nathaniel Tebbets Desesed by his wife Elezebeth borne the 28 Day of September 1700

Hannah nock Dafter of Thomas nock by his wife abigall borne the 9 Day of August 1714

nathaniell and mary twenes Son and Dafter of Thomas nock by his wife Abigall borne the 26 Day of January 1717

James nock Son of Thomas nock by his wife abigall born the first Day of August 1720

marcy nock Dafter of Thomas nock by his wife abigall borne the 4 Day of Aprill 1723

marcy Hobs Dafter of James hobs by his wife Rebeckah borne the 7 Day of December 1719

febe Hobs Dafter of James Hobs by his wife Rebeckah borne the 19 Day of September 1722

Hannah Twombly Dafter of of Benjamen Twombly by his wife Hannah borne the 16th of may 1722

James Hobs Son of morris Hobs by his wife Joannah borne the 20th Day of march 1700

Sarah Hobs Dafter of morris Hobs by his wife Joannah borne the Last Day of october 1703

Abigall Hobs Dafter of morris Hobs by his wife Joannah borne the 20 Day of December 1707

Joannah Hobs Dafter of morris Hobs by his wife Joannah borne the 26 day of may 1711

morris Hobs Son of morris Hobs by his wife Joannah born the 6: Day of august 1717

Daborah Hobs Dafter of morris Hobs by his wife Joannah borne the 6 Day of July 1720

John Rickers Son of Joseph Rickers by his wife Elezebeth borne the 28 Day of August 1721

Sarah Ricker Dafter of Joseph Ricker by his wife Elezebeth borne the 3^{d} Day of february 1723/4

Abigall Ricker Dafter of maturin Ricker by his wife Hannah borne the 14 Day of August 1713

mary Rickers Dafter of maturin Rickers by his wife Hannah borne the 14 Day of June in the year 1715

George Ricker Son of maturin Ricker by his wife Hannah borne the 23^{d} Day of february 1717

maturin Rickers Son of maturin Rickers by his wife Hannah borne the 23^{d} Day of July 1719

Richard Ricker Son of maturin Ricker by his wife Hannah borne 8th : Day of August 1721

BIRTHS AND MARRIAGES, 1693-1838.   23

Bridget Ricker Dafter of maturin Ricker by his wife Hannah borne the 3ᵈ : Day of may 1723

Darkis Ricker Dafter of Meaturin by his wife Hanna born the 24ᵈ of Septemʳ 1727

Samˡˡ Ricker the Son of meturen Ricker by his Wife Hanna born the 20ᵈ of May 1730

Zebelon Corson Son of Samuell Corson by his wife mary born the 17 Day of June in the year 1712

Hatiuell Corson Son of Samuell Corson by his wife mary born the 9 Day of December 1714

Joannah Corson Dafter of Samuell Corson by his wife mary borne the 15 Day of June in the year 1717

Samuell Corson Son of Samuell Corson by his wife mary born the 2ᵈ Day of nouember 1719

mary Corson Dafter of Samuell Corson by his wife mary borne the 9 Day of September 1722

Hannah wallinford Dafter of Thomas wallingford by his wife margritt borne the 5 : Day of may 1720

Judeth wallingford Dafter of Thomas wallingford by his wife Margrit borne the 25 Day of march 1722

James the Son of mary Silley borne the 22ᵈ Day of august 1715

william Perey Son of mathue Perey by his wife mary borne yᵉ 15 of april 1722

Robert Euenes Son of Joseph Euenes by his wife marcy born the Eleauenth Day of January 1704

John Euenes Son of Joseph Euenes by his wife marcy borne the 3ᵈ Day of february 1705

Joseph Euenes Son of Joseph Euenes by his wife marcy borne the 28 Day of march 1708

william Euenes Son of Joseph Euenes by his wife marcy borne the 9 : Day of february 1711

Dannil Euenes Son of Joseph Euenes by his wife marcy borne the 28 Day of June 1715

marcy Euenes Dafter of Joseph Euene by his wife marcy borne the 6 : Day of December 1717

mary Euenes Dafter of Joseph Euene by his wife marcy borne the 6 : Day of march 1720

Jonathan young Son of Jonathan young by his wife Abigall borne the 5 Day of June 1710

Thomas young Son of Jonathan young by his wife Abigall borne the 15 : Day of July 1712

Elezer young Son of Jonathan young by his wife Abigall born the 10th Day of nouember 1714

Isack young Son of Jonathan young by his wife Abgall borne 15 : Day of march 1716

James young Son of Jonathan young by his wife Abigall borne the 10 : Day of September 1718

nathaniel young Son of Jonathan young by his wife Abigal borne the first of february 1720

Abigal young Dafter of Jonathan young by his wife Abigall borne the 15 Day of September 1723

Nathaniel Cuck Son of Peter Cuck by his wife Abigal borne the 23 of January 1716/7

Joseph Cuck Son of Peter Cuck by his wife Abigal borne the 23 Day march 1719

Peter Cuck Son of Peter Cuck by his wife Abigal borne the 4th : of october 1722

Elezebeth Stiles Dafter of william Stiles by his wife Deborah borne the 6 Day of march 1702

Abigal Stiles Dafter of william Stiles by his wife Deborah borne the first of July 1703

Deborah Stiles Dafter of william Stiles by his wife Deborah borne the 10 : of march 1706

mary Stiles Dafter of william Stiles by his wife Deborah borne the first Day of march 1708

william Stiles Son of william Stiles by his wife Deborah borne the first Day of march 1709

Samuell Stiles son of william Stiles by his wife Deborah borne the 10th : Day of august 1710

Pauel Roberts Son of Nathaniel Roberts by his wife Elezebeth borne the 18 of february 1706/7

Mirriam Roberts Dafter of nathaniel Roberts by hi wife Elezebeth borne the 4th Day of January 1708/9

Thomas Roberts Son of nathaniel Roberts by his wife Elezebeth borne the 23 Day of July 1710

Nathaniel Roberts Son of Nathaniel Roberts by his wife Elezebeth borne the 27 of aprill 1713

Aron Roberts Son of nathaniel Roberts by his wife Elezebeth borne the 16 Day of April 1716

Moses Roberts Son of nathaniel Roberts by his wife Elezebeth borne the 22^d Day of June 1718

Elezebeth Roberts Dafter of Nathaniel Roberts by his wife Elezebeth borne the 3^d Day of february 1722/3

Abigall Hall Dafter of Joseph Hall by his wife Ester borne the 3^d of July in the year 1708

John Purkings Son of Nathaniell Purkings by his wife Hannah borne the 2^d Day of october 1705

Hannah Pinckham Dafter of Amos Pinckham by his wife Elezebeth borne the 10 Day of January 1713/4

Joannah Pinckham Dafter of Amos Pinckham by his wife Elezebeth borne the 11 Day of August 1718

Benjamen Tebbets Son of Henrey Tebbets by his wife Joyce borne the Last of october 1700

Edward Tebbets Son of Henrey Tebbets by his wife Joyce borne the 2^d Day of february 1702

Pauel Tebbets son of Henrey Tebbets by his wife Joyce borne the 26 Day of June 1705

Susannah Tebbets Dafter of Henrey Tebbets by his wife Joyce borne the Last of october 1707

Olliue Stephens Dafter of Thomas Stephenes by his wife martha borne the 14 of march 1717/8

Elezebeth Stephenes Dafter of Thomas Stephenes by his wife martha borne the 26 of may 1719

Elijah Stephenes Son of Thomas Stephenes by his wife martha borne the 29 of August 1721

Joannah Roberts Dafter of John Roberts by his wife Deborah borne the 20th of october 1705

Sarah Roberts Dafter of John Roberts by his wife Deborah borne the 18th of february 1708/9

mary Roberts Dafter of John Roberts by his wife Deborah borne 20th of July 1711

Phebe Roberts Dafter of John Roberts by his wife Deborah borne the 20th of September 1716

Ebenezer Roberts Son of John Roberts by his wife franses borne the 5th Day of february 1721/2

Abigal Cenney Dafter of Joseph Cenney by his wife Leah borne the 27 of September in the year 1709

Ellenar Jones Dafter of william Jones by his wife Hannnh borne the 3^d Day of april 1723

Thomas Starbord Son of Thomas Starbord by his wife margret borne the 23 of march 1713/4

Nathaniel Starbourd Son of Thomas Starbord by his wife margret borne the 27th Day of Aprel 1716

Jethro Starbord Son of Thomas Starbord by his wife margret borne the 29 of June 1718

Hannah Starbord Dafter of Thomas Starbord by his wife margret the 31 Day of January 1719/20

John Starbord Son of Thomas Starbord by his wife margret borne the 16th of nouember 1721

Samuel Starbord Son of Thomas Starbord by his wife margret borne the 16th of nouember 1723

margrett Sarbird Dafter of Thomas Starbird by his wife margrett borne ye Last Day of may 1725

Otis Cenney Son of Richard Cenney by his wife Rebeckah borne the 23 Day of January 1718

Richard Cenney Son of Richard Cenney by his wife Rebeckah borne the 11 Day of march 1720/21

Judeth Cenney Dafter of Richard Cenney by his wife Rebeckah borne the 2d Day of march 1722/23

Elezebeth Winthworth Dafter of Benjamin Wenthworth by his wife Sarah borne the 8 Day of June 1712

Dorithy Wenthworth Dafter of Benjamen wenthworth by his wife Sarah borne the 26 of July 1714

Marthe Wenthworth Dafter of Benjamen wenthworth by his wife Sarah borne the 25 Day of July 1716

Abre wenthworth Dafter of Benjamen Wenthworth by his wife Sarah borne the 14 Day of february 1718

Markes Wenthworth Son of Benjamen wenthworth by his wife Sarah borne the 30th Day of may 1720

Hannah Plumer Dafter of Danniel Plumer by his wife Sarah borne the 25 Day of April 1722

Joshua Nock Son of Zacharias Nock by his Wife Sarah borne the 13th of october 1715

Joseph nock Son of Zackarias Nock by his wife Sarah borne the 12 Day of nouember 1717

Zacharias Nock Son of Zackarias Nock by his Wife Sarah borne the first of August 1720

Benjamen Nock Son of Zackarias Nock by his wife Sarah borne the 12 : of July 1722 mary Nock Dafter of Zackarias Nock by his Wife Sarah borne the 26 Day of march 1724

Hannah Hobs Dafter of Henrey Hobs by his wife mary borne the 2^d Day of march 1704

Benjamen Peirce Son of Benjamen Peirce by his wife Elezebeth borne th Eleauenth of December 1706

Joseph Peirce Son of Benjamen Peirce by his wife Elezebeth borne the 22^d of october 1709

Benjamen Peirce Senr and Hannah Ash was Joyned Togeather in marridg the 30th Day of may 1714

John Peirce Son of Benjamen Peirce by his wife Hannah was borne the 19th Day of may 1715

Elezebeth Peirce Dafter of Benjamen Peirce by his wife Hannah was borne the 17th Day of may 1717

Hannah Peirce Dafter of Benjamen Peirce by his wife Hannah was borne the 10th of January 1718

Ebenezer Peirce Son of Benjamen Peirce by his wife Hannah was borne the 2^d of february 1720/21

Israel Peirce Son of Benjamen Peirce by his wife Hannah borne the 16th of february 1723/4

Hannah Rawlings Dafter of Icobod Rawlings by his wife Elezebeth borne the 16 : of July 1706

martha Pearce by His wife Hannah borne the 18 of october 1725

Thomas Pearce Son of Benja Pearce by his wife Hannah born 15 of may 1727

James Chesley Son of James Chesley by his wife Tamson borne the 18 Day of may 1706

John Hayes Son of John Hayes by his wife Tamson borne the 19 Day of october 1711

Pauel Hayes Son of John Hayes by his wife Tamson borne the 16th Day of September 1713

Thomas Hayes Son of John Hayes by his wife Tamson borne the 29 of September 1715

Elehue Hayes Son of John Hayes by his wife Tamson borne the 16 of December 1717

Hezekiah Hayes Son of John Haye by his wife Tamson borne the 2^d Day of february 1719/20

Thire Sister Elezebeth borne the 5 Day of Apriel 1721

and Their Sister Abra borne the 17th Day of february 1723/4

Anne Hanson Dafter of Benjamen Hanson by his wife Elezebeth borne the 23 Day of July in ye year 1703

William Hanson Son of Benjamen Hanson by his wife Elezebeth borne the 11 : Day of September 1705

Elezebeth Hanson Dafter of Benjamen Hanson by his wife Elezebeth borne the 12 of September 1707

Benjamen Hanson Son of Benjamen Hanson by his wife Elezebeth borne the 26 Day of october 1709

Ester Hanson Dafter of Benjamen Hanson by his wife Elezebeth borne the 26 Day of April 1711

Joseph Hanson Son of Benjamen Hanson by his wife Elezebeth borne the 15 Day of october 1714

marey Hanson Dafter of Benjamen Hanson by his wife Elezebeth borne the 14 Day of June 1717

George Hanson Son of Benjamen Hanson by his wife Elezebeth borne the 13th of october 1719

John Drew Son of John Drew by his wife Elezebeth borne ye 17 of october 1707

Elezebeth Drew Dafter of John Drew by his wife Elezebeth borne the 2^d of nouember 1709

franses Drew Son of John Drew by his wife Elezebeth borne the 24 Day of January 1711/2

James Pinckham Son of James Pinckham by his wife Elezebeth borne ye 21 Day of of July 1714

Urselah Pinckham Dafter of James Pinckham by his wife Elezebeth borne ye 4th of october 1716

mary Pinckham Dafter of James Pinckham by his wife Elezebeth born the 14 of September 1719

Loes Pinckham Dafter of James Pinckham by his wife Elezebeth borne the 2^d Day of march 1721/2

Hannah Pinkham Dafter of James Pinkham by his wife Elezebeth borne ye 16th of September 1725

martha Stephenes Dafter of Thomas Stephenes by his wife martha borne the 18 Day of June 1724

Joseph Heard Son of Tristrum Heard by his wife Abigall born the fifteenth Day of february 1692

John Heard Son of Tristrim Heard by his wife Abigall borne the first Day of January 1700

Abigall Heard Dafter of Tristrim Heard by his wife Abigall borne the 15 Day of Aprill 1702

Samuell Heard Son of Tristrm Heard by his wife Abigall borne the Last Day of february 1703/4

Elezebeth Heard Dafter of Tristrim Heard by his wife Abigall borne the Eight Day of february 1706/7

mary Heard Dafter of Tristrim Heard by his wife Abigarll borne the 10 Day of June 1709

Kezia Heard Dafter of Tristrim Heard by his wife Abigall borne the first Day of December 1712

Nathaniell Heard Son of Tristrim Heard by his wife Abigall borne the 23^d of January 1696/7 and Desesed or Departed this Life ye 10 Day of october 1723

Tristrim Heard Son of Tristrim Heard by heard by his wife Abegall borne the 26 of march 1695 and the Sd Heard was killid by the Indianes ye 31st Day of August 1723

An Hayes Dafter of Peter Hayes by his wife Sarah borne the 3^d Day of June in the year of our Lord 1718

Ruben Hayes Son of Peter Hayes by his wife Sarah borne the Eight Day of may 1720

Joseph Hayes Son of Peter Hayes by his wife Sarah borne the 15th Day of march 1722

Benjamen Hayes Son of Peter Hayes by his wife Sarah borne the first Day of march 1723/4

Ebenezer Dauis Son of moses Dauis by his wife Rueanah borne ye 10th of June 1702

Benjamen Wamouth Son of Benjamen by his wife mary borne the first Day of february in ye year 1693/4

Hannah Roberds Dafter of Loue Roberds by his wife Elezebeth Roberds borne the 10 of may 1713

Loue Roberds Son of Loue Roberds by his wife Elezebeth borne the 21 of april 1721

James Stephens Son of James Stephen borne the the first of february in the year 1724/5

Abigal Hanson Dafter of Thomas Hanson by his wife Hannah borne ye 23^d of December 1721

mary Downes Dafter of Thomas Downes by his wife Sarah borne the 22^d of february 1710/11

Sarah Downes Dafter of Thomas Downes by his wife Sarah borne the 25th of nouember 1712

Elezebeth Downes Dafter of Thomas Downe by his wife Sarah borne the 25 of July 1714

Anne Downes Dafter of Thomas Downe by his wife Sarah borne the 3d of february 1716

marcy Downe Dafter of Thomas Downe by his wife Sarah borne the 25 of July 1719

Patiance Downe Dafter of Thomas Downes by his wife Sarah borne the 13 of April 1721

Abigal Downes Dafter of Thomas Downes by his wife Sarah borne the 10 of July 1724

Ruben Rickers Son of maturin Rickers by his wife hannah borne the 29 January 1724

mary Horne Dafter of Dannill Horne by his wife mary borne the 13 of April 1724

Joseph Allen Son of Jacob Allen by his wife martha borne ye 30th Day of July 1715

Samuell Hayes Son of John Hays by his wife mary borne the 16th Day of march 1694/5

Samuell Nock Son of Silluenas Nock by his wife Sarah borne the 20th Day of September in the year 1707

Ebenezer nock Son of Siluenas nock by his wife Sarah borne the 16th of may 1710

Henrey nock Son of Siluenes nock by his wife Sarah borne the 23d of August 1714

Ester nock Dafter of Siluenes nock by his wife Sarah borne the 21th of nouember 1717

Drisco nock Son of Siluenes nock by his wife Sarah borne the 21 of march 1719

Sarah nock Dafter of Siluenes nock by his wife Sarah borne the 11th of July 1721

marcy nock Dafter of Siluenes nock by his wife Sarah borne the 11th of october 1723

Samuell Roberds Son of Hateuill Roberds by his wife Lydia borne ye 12 of December 1686

Abigal Roberds Dafter of Hateuill Roberds by his wife Lydia borne the 29 of July 1689

Joshua Roberds Son of Hateuill Roberds borne the 11th of october 1698

mary Roberds Dafter of Hateuil Roberds by his wife Lydia borne the 20th of July 1701

Lydia Guding Dafter of Danniel Guding by his wife Abigal borne the 29th of march 1710

Abigal guding Dafter of Danniel Guding by his wife abigal borne the 22ᵈ of September 1713

Danniel Guding Son of Danniel by his wife abigal borne the 15ᵗʰ of August 1715

Ame Guding Dafter of Danniel guding by his wife abigal borne the 15ᵗʰ of nouember 1718

mary Guding Dafter of Daniell guding borne the 15ᵗʰ of January 1720

Sarah Guding Dafter of Daniell Guding by is wife abigal borne the 3ᵈ of August 1723

James guding Son of Daniel guding borne the 22 of June 1724

Samuel Downes Son of william Downes by his wife mary borne the 18ᵗʰ of December in the year of our Lord 1721

william Downes Son of william Downes born the 18 Day of January 1723

Nathanil Perkins of Sligo and Abigal wear married yᵉ 15ᵗʰ of march 1715

Pennaeh Dafter of nathanil Purkins by his wife abigal borne the 15 of June 1716

Lemuel Purkings the Sun of nathaniell Purking by his wife Abigal borne the 6 of December 1718

Abigial Purkings Dafter of nathanil Purkings borne the 16 of february 1720/21

Ann Purkings Dafter of nathaniell Purkings borne the 6 of September 1723

Jethro Starbird the Son of Thomas and Abigail Starbird was borne the 28 Day of august in the year 1689

Thomas Starbird the Son of Thomas Starbird by Abigal his wife borne the 19 of october 1691

Agnes Starbird the Dafter of Thomas Starbird by Abigal his wife borne the 4 of october 1693

Abigal Starbird Dafter of Thomas Starbird by his wife abigal borne the 29 of September 1695

Elezebeth Starbird Dafter of Thomas Starbird by his wife abigal borne the 15 of february 1699

John Starbird Son of Thomas Starbird by his wife abigarl borne the 16 of march in the year 1701

Samuell Starbird the Son of Thomas Stirbird by his wife abigal borne the 22ᵈ Day of April in the year 1704

Samuell Roberds Son of Samuell Roberds by his wife Sarah borne the 16 of July in the year 1717

Benjamen Roberds Son of Samuell Roberds by his wife Sarah borne the first Day of September 1719

Lydia Roberds Dafter of Samuell Roberds by his wife Sarah borne the 16 of may in the year 1721

Samuell Roberds Son of Samuell Roberds by his wife Sarah borne the 7th of may 1723

Zackariah Pitman and Marcy Conner was Joyned togeather in marridg by the Reuerand m^r Jeremiah wise ye 13th Day of December 1723

Samuell Crumwell and Betty Penkham was Joyned togeather in marridg the 4 Day of December 1727 by

James Dauis Justis of Pece

Elenor Horne Dafter of william Horne by his wife margret borne the 17th July 1726

James Nute Son of James Nute Desesed by his wife Elezebeth borne the 27 of July in the year of our Lord 1687

Elezebeth nute Dafter of James nute by his wife Prudance borne ye 28 of Decembr 1706

James nute son of James nute by his wife Prudance borne the 12 of march in the year 1712/13

Paul Nute Son of James nute by his wife Prudance borne the 19 of August 1714

Ann Nute Dafter of James nute by his wife Prudance borne the 21 of march 1721

Cattern Aystin Dafter of Nathnill aystin by his wife Cattern borne the 12 Day of January in the year of our Lord 1715

febe aystin Dafter of nathanill aystin by his wife Cattern borne ye 14 of march 1718

Sarah Aystin Dafer of nathanill aystin borne the 14 of nouember 1719

Ann Astin Dafer of nathanel aystin borne the 17 day of July 1721

Nathnill Aysten Son of nathanell aysten borne the 25 of June 1723

mary Tebbets Dafter of Samuell Tebbets by his wif Judeth borne the 18 Day of nouember 1718

Judeth Tebbets Dafter of Samuell Tebbets by his wife Judeth borne the 10 Day of December 1720

Samuell Tebbets Son of Samuell Tebbets by his wife Judeth borne the Last Day of January 1722/3

Samuell Tebbets Departed This Life ye 24th of December 1724 and
Icobod Tebbets Son of ye Desesed Samuel Tebbets by his wife Judeth borne ye 2^d Day of march 1724/5

Meheteble Hayse Dafter of Peter Hayes by his wife Sarah was borne the Eleauenth Day of December in the yeare 1725

Benjamen Horne Son of Danniel Horne by his wif mary borne the 14 Day of January 1726

Judeth Horne Dafter of Thomas Horne Senr by his wife Ester borne the 16th of august in the year 1721

margrett Horn by his wife Ester borne the 16th of aprill 1722

Samuell Horne by his wife Ester borne the 16 of february 1724

Abigal Horne by his wife Ester borne the 7th Day of December 1725

Dreusila Horn Dafter of Thomas Horne by his wife Ester borne ye 18th of June 1727

Loue Clark Dafter of Abraham Clark by his wife Annah borne ye 30th of may 1721

Annah Clark Dafter of Abraham Clark by his wife Annah borne ye 2^d Day of July 1723

Richard Hussey Son of Richard Hussey by his wife Jane borne the 26 of october in the year 1691

Job Hussey Son of Richard Hussey by his wife Jane borne the 25 of December 1693

Roberd Hussey Son of Richard Hussey by his wif Jane borne the 28th of nouember 1695

mary Hussey Dafter of Richard Hussey by his wife Jane borne the first of June 1697

Joseph Hussey Son of Richard Hussey by his wife Jane borne the 23^d of June 1699

Elezebeth Hussey Dafter of Richard Hussey by his wife Jane borne ye 28 of october 1701

Elener Hussey Dafter of Richard Hussey by his wife Jane borne ye 23^d of aprill 1705

Abigarl Hussey Dafter of Richard Hussey by his wife Jane borne ye 25 of aprill 1707

Jane Hussey Dafter of Richard Hussey by his wife Jane borne the 27th of June 1708

william Hussey Son of Richard Hussey by his wife Jane borne ye 24 of march 1711

margrett Hussey Dafter of Richard Hussey by his wife Jane borne ye 28 of february 1712

Benjamen Hussey Son of Richard Hussey by his wife Jane borne the first of april 1718

John Ambler and Elezebeth Edgerly wear Joyned Togeather in marridg the 20th Day of July in the year 1725

Elezebeth Ambler Dafter of John Ambler by his wife Elezebeth borne the 14th Day of June 1724

Peter mason Son of Benjamen mason by his wife Elezebeth borne the 22d Day of September 1725

John Tebbets Son of John Tebbets by his wife Sary borne the 14th Day of nouember 1711

Jeremiah Tebbets Son of John Tebbets by his wife Sarah borne the 4 Day of may 1713

nathaniell Tebbets Son of John Tebbet by his wife Sarah borne the 28 Day of february 1720

Sarah Tebbets Dafter of John Tebbets by his wife Tamson borne the 18 Day of august 1725

margrett wallingford Dafter of nicolas wallingford by his wife Rachel borne the 4th Day of aprill 1714

John Hakings Son of Stephen Hakings by his wife Rachell borne the 19th Day of march 1720

Elezebeth whithous Dafter of Thomas whithous by his wife Rachell borne the first of nouember 1725

Martha Bickford Dafter of John Bickford by his wife Elezebeth borne the 23d Day of July 1692

Thomas Bickford Son of John Bickford by his wife Elezebeth borne the 18th Day of may 1694

John Bickford Son of John Bickford by his wife Elezebeth borne the 10 Day of march 1698

Henrey Bickford Son of John Bickford by his wife Elezebeth borne the first Day of Jnnuary 1702/3

Joseph Bickford Son of John Bickford by his wife Elezebeth borne the 8 Day of march 1705/6

Benjamen Stanton Son of Benjamen Stanton by his wife Elener borne the 12 of february 1724/5

Elener Stanton Dafter of Benjamen Stanton by his wife Elener borne the 9 : of July 1727

Kezia Tebbets Dafter of moses Tebbets by his wife mary was Borne the 22d of September 1725

Abigal Hobs Dafter of James Hobs by his wife Rebeckah borne the 30 Day of march in the year of our Lord 1725

Dorithy Crumwell Dafter of Samuell Crumwell by his Rachil borne the 13 Day of may in the year 1713

Eliphalet Crumwell Son of Samuell Crumwell by his wife Rachil borne the 12 of nouember 1716

Stephen Euenes Son of Benjamen Euenes by his wife marey borne the 13 Day of nouember 1724

Samuell Cearll Son of Samuell Cearll by his wife Patiance borne ye 9th of february 1709/10

Sarah Cearll Dafter of Samuell Cearll by his wife Patiance borne the 27th Day of february 1711

Nathaniell Cearll Son of Samuell Cearll by his wife Patiance borne the first of nouember 1713

Ann Cearll Dafter of Samuell Cearll by his wife Patiance borne the 26 : of october 1715

Patiance Cearll Dafter of Samuell Cearll by his wife Patiance borne the 26 of february 1717/18

Timothy Cearll Son of Samuell Cearll by his wife Patiance borne the 6 Day of June 1721

Robert Cearll Son of Samuell Cearll by his wife Patiance borne the 7 Day of August 1723

Benjamen Cearll Son of Samuell Cearll by his wife Patiance borne the 15th Day of august 1725

marey wentworth Dafter of Benjamen wentworth by his wife Elezebeth borne the 29th Day of July in the year 1725

Joshua winget Son of John winget by his wife Dorithy borne the 28th Day of July in the year of our Lord 1725

Rebeckah Aystin Dafter of Nathaniell aystin by his wife Cattern borne the 23^d Day of march 1724/5

mary Clark Dafter of Abraham Clark by his wife Anne borne the 21 first Day of December 1725

Silas Buncker Son of John Buncker by his wife Hannah borne the 5 Day of Juen in ye year 1723

Elezebeth Buncker Dafter of John Buncker by his wife Hannah borne the 28 Day of Aprill 1726

Thomas aystin Son of Joseph aystin by his wife Sarah borne the 7th Day of may in the year 1723

Debrah and Alexander Son and Dafter being Twens of John Roberds by his wife frances borne ye 15th of January 1725/6

marey Steuens Dafter of Thomas Steuens by his wife martha borne the first Day of may in the year 1726 marey young Dafter of Jonathan young by his wife Abigall borne the 30th Day of December 1725

John Twombly Son of william Twombly by his wife mary borne the 19th of September 1725

moses Hayes Son of Icobod Hayes by his wife Abigall borne the 30th Day of January 1725/6

mary Brock Dafter of Benj Brock by his wife marey ye 6th Day of January 1719/20

mary Cenney Dafter of John Cenney by his wife Sarah borne the 19 Day of august 1713

Sarah Cenney Dafter of John Cenney by his wife Sarah borne the 22^d of December 1716

william Jones Son of william Jones by his wife Hannah borne y^e : 7 : Day of July 1725

Sarah Hix Dafter of Joseph Hix by his wife Sarah borne the 22^d Day of may in the yeare 1721

John Hix Son of Joseph Hix by his wife Sarah borne the 20th Day of october in ye yeare 1723

marey Hix Dafter of Joseph Hix by his wife Sarah borne the first Day of January 1725

Rubin and Araham kuck twenes Sons of Peter kuck by his wife Abigall borne the 12th Day of Juen 1725

Susanah Stephens Dafter of James Stephens by his wife Debrow borne ye 10 of Aygst 1726

Sarah walland Dafter of william welland by his wife Hannah borne the 19th Day of December 1726

These may Certifi any Person that william Giddes and Ann Pinckham is Joyned togeather in marridg the Second Day of march 1726/7 by James Dauis Justis of Peace

Joseph Hall Son of Thomas Hall of oyster Riuer by his wife mary borne the 13th Day of Aprill in the year 1707

John hall Son of John Hall of oyster Riuer by his wife Sarah borne the 17th of December 1726

william Dam Son of will Dam by his wife Sarah borne the 20 Day of february 1710

Sarah Dam Dafter of william by his wife Sarah borne the 26 Day of August in ye year 1714

John Dam Son of will Dam by his wife Sarah borne the 12 Day of Juen in ye year 1723

The above written John Dam Desesed ye 11 of august 1724

Abigall Dam Dafter of william Dam by his wife Sarah borne the 18 of July in ye year 1725

Samuel Lamaes Son of nathanil Lames by his wife Abigal borne the 6 Day of July in the year 1721

Elezebeth Lumas Dafter of Nathaniell Lumas by his wyfe Abigall borne 26 Day of march 1723

James Lumas Son of nathanil Lumas by his wife Abigal borne the 10th Day of September 1725

Samuell Pinckham Son of otis Pinckham by his wife Abigal borne the 26 Day of September 1722

Ann Pinckham Dafter of otis Pinckham by his wife Abigal borne the 30th Day of april 1724

Rose Pinckham Dafter of otis Pinckham by his wife abigal borne the 18 Day of march 1725/6

Ebenezer wallingford Son of Thomas wallingford by his wife margret borne the 21 Day of July 1724

Abigal wallingford Dafter of Thomas wallingford by his wife margret born the Last of Septembr 1726

Abigal Purkings Dafter of Joshua Purkings by his wife Dorothy borne the 11 Day of January 1723/4

Ephrim Purkings Son of Joshua Purkings by his wife Dorothy borne the 10 Day of July 1726

Doddeuer Garland Son of Ebenezer Garland by his wife abigal borne the 6 Day of Decembr 1722

abigal Garland Dafter of Ebbenezer garland by his wife abigal borne the 13th of nouember 1724

Hannah Garland Dafter of Ebenezer Garland by his wife abigal borne the 18 of february 1726/7

James Heard Son of James Heard by his wife Debrah borne the 6: of may 1725

Sarah wentworth Dafter of Benjamen wentworth by his wife Debrah borne the 19 of nouember 1727

Elezebeth Starbord Dafter of Samuell Starbord by his wife Rebeckah borne the 4th Day of July 1725

Samuell Starbord Son of Samuell Starbird by his wife Rebeckah borne the 29th Day of may 1727

Sam^{ll} Twombly Son of John Twombly by his wife Rachal born the 10th march 1699

Ann Twombly Dafter of Sam^{ll} Twombly by his wife Judey born the 15th aug^t 1724

Sam^ll Twombly Son of Sam^ll Twombly by his wife Judey born march 18th 1726

Jonathan Twombly the Son of Sam^ll Twombly by his wife Judey Born octo^r 21th 1727

Judeth Tebbets the Wife of Thomas Tebbets Desesed the 22 Day of October in the year of our Lord 1728

John Gline and marey Basford ware Joyned in Marrage Novem^r 27th 1728

Judeth Tebbets Dafter of Icobod Tebbets by his wife Abigal borne the 15 Day of may in the yeare 1722

Abigal Tebbets Dafter of Icobod Tebbets by his wife Abigal borne the 23^d Day of aprial in the yeare 1723

Icobod Tebbets Son of Icobod by his wife abigal borne the 25 Day of July in the yeare 1726 and Departed this Life the 25 Day of September 1726

Nathaniel Tebbets Son of Icobod Tebbets by his wife Abigal borne the 30th Day of august 1727

francis Drew and Ann winget Joyned togather in marridg the third Day of June in the yeare of our Lord 1713

the Sd francis Drew Departed this Life the ye 10 of may 1717

Joseph Drew Son of francis Drew by his wife Ann borne the Eight Day of aprill in the yeare of our Lord 1717

Ann Titcomb Dafter of Dannil Titcomb by his wife Ann borne the fifteenth Day of october in the yeare 1719

william Titcomb Son of Dannil Titcomb by his wife ann borne the 20 of December 1721

Sarah & marey Titcomb Dafters of Dannil Titcomb by his wife Ann borne the 27th Day of January in the year 1724

John Titcomb Son of Danniel Titcomb by his wife Ann borne the 20th Day of march 1726/7

Paul Gerrish Son of Paul Gerrish by his Wife Marey born the 2 day of august 1713

Elizabeth Gerrish the Dafter of Paul Gerrish by his wife Marey born the 13th day of November 1714

Marey Gerrish the Dafter of Paul Gerrish by his wife Marey born the 15 day august 1719

Sam^ll Gerrish the Son of Paul Gerrish by his wife Marey borne July 30 1722

Jonathan Gerrish the Son of Paul Gerrish by his wife Marey born the 24 day of May 1726

Aron Hayes the Son of Icobod Hayes by his wife Abagal Born March 3th 1727/8

John Glines and Mary Bassford was Joyned in Marriage Novmr 27th 1728

James Davis the Sone of James Davis by his Wife Elizabeth Born July the tenth 1689

James Davis of Dover & Ruth Ayer of Havrhill Was Joyned in Marraige Novembr the fifth 1728

Mary Hayes the Dafter of Samll by his Wife Leah born Augts 12 1728

Marey Carrtar the Dafter of John Carrter by his Wife ffransse born may the 11d 1726

Abigel Carrter the Dafter of John Carrter by his Wife ffransse born Fevbery 14d 1728

Ann Chesley the Dafter of Samll Chesley by his wife Ann born october the 29th 1723

Suanah Chesley the Dafter of Samll Chesley by his wife Ann born october the 21 1725

Matha Chesley the Dafter of Samll Chesley by his wife Ann born october the 7 1728

Willm Hill & Patience Drew was Joyned in Marrage auguest 21th 1729

Ruth Davis the Dafter of James Davis by his wife Ruth born November the 5th : 1729

Ruth Davis the wife of James Davis Desesed the 28 Day of April 1730

Sarah Hobs the Dafter of James Hobs by his wife Rebacah born the 20 Day of Jully 1727

James Hobes the Sun of James Hobes by his wife Rebacah born the 11th Day of Januarey 1729

Leidea Gerrish the Dafter of Paul Gerrish by his wife Marey Born the 24th April 1730 and deceasd August yu 12—1732

Benja Gerrish the Son of Paul Gerrish by his wife Mary born August ye 7th 1732

Elizt Hanson the Dafter Nathanil Hanson by his Wife Martha Born the 30th Day April 1725

Silos Hanson the Son of Nathal Hanson by his Wife Martha Born the 5th Day April 1727

Paul Hanson the Son of Nathal Hanson by his Wife Martha Born the 26 Day May 1729

Joseph Hall the Son of Ralph Hall by his Wife Mary Born the 26 Day of March 1706

Joseph Hall and Peniel Bean were Joyned in Marriage Decembr ye 19th 1731

P   Jon^a Cushing   Cler

Abgial Heays the Dafter of Ichobod Heays by his wife Abgial born the 28th August 1730

Matha Moses the Dafter of Timothy Moses was Born the 5th : May 1732

Willam Fost the son of John Fost by Mary his Wife was born March the 11th : 1673

Mary Fost the Dafter of Willam Fost by his wife Mary was Born June the 24th 1728

Chadbourn Fost the Son of Willam Fost by his wife Mary was Born March the 26th 1731

Paul Horn the Son of Danil Horn by his Wife Mary Born 24^d May 1730

Temprnce Nock the Dafter of Zachariah Nock by his wife Sarah Born April the 1^d 1726

Ollive Nock the Dafter of Zachariah Nock by his wife Sarah Born the Febury 23^d 1728/9

Thomas Nock the Son of Zachariah Nock by his wife Sarah Born January 23^d 1730/1

Jonathan Nock the Son of Zachariah Nock by his wife Sarah Born the June 2^d 1733

Martha Moses the Daughter of Tim^o Moses by his wife Mary Born ye 5 of May 1700.

Tim^o Moses ye Son of Tim^o Moses by his wife Mary Born ye 2^d of Sep^t 1707.

Abigail Horn the Daughter of Daniel Horn by his wife Mary Born March ye 28th 1734.

Elezabeth Titcomb the Dafter of Danil Titcomb by his wife Ann Born 21 April 1728

Daniel Titcomb the Son of Daniel Titcomb by his Wife Ann born April ye 31 1731

David Titcomb the Son of Daniel Titcomb by his wife Ann born July 25 1733

Robert Heays the Son of John Hayes by his wife Tamsen Born 21^d March 1725/6

Wentworth Hayes the Son of John Hayes by his Wife Tamsen Born 27ᵈ Janueray 1727/8

Samˡˡ Hayes the Son of John Hayes by his Wife Tamsen Born 12ᵈ March 1729/30

Jonathan Hayes the Son of John Hayes by his Wife Tamsen Born 17ᵈ April 1732

Hannah Hayes the Posthumous Daughter of Ichabod Hayes by Abigail his Widdow Born Janʳʸ yᵉ 5, 1734/5

Anna Gerrish yᵉ Daughter of Timᵒ Gerrish by his wife Sarah Born 4 July 1717

William Gerrish yᵉ son of Timᵒ Gerrish by his wife Sarah Born 24 August 1719

Abagail Gerrish yᵉ Daughter of Timᵒ Gerrish by his wife Sarah Born 6 June 1721

Andrew Gerrish yᵉ son of Timᵒ Gerrish by his wife Sarah Born 4 August 1724

Elizᵃ Gerrish yᵉ Daughter of Timᵒ Gerrish by his wife Sarah Born 28 May 1727

Benjᵃ Gerrish yᵉ Son of Timᵒ Gerrish by his wife Sarah Born 6 June 1728

Jane Gerrish yᵉ Daughter of Timᵒ Gerrish by his wife Sarah Born 22 May 1729

Joseph Gerrish yᵉ Son of Timᵒ Gerrish by his wife Sarah Born 13 Septʳ 1732

William Horn yᵉ Son of Wᵐ Horn By his wife Margret Born the 30 Decʳ 1728

James Horn yᵉ Son of Wᵐ Horn by his wife Margret Born 18 Janʳʸ 1730/31

John Buncker yᵉ son of John Buncker by his wife Dorcas Born yᵉ 16 July 1696

Sarah Buncker yᵉ Daughter of John Bunker by his wife Dorcas Born 20 Octobʳ 1699

Daniel Buncker yᵉ Son of John Buncker by his wife Dorcas Born 22 Octobʳ 1702

Zachariah Buncker and Elizᵃ Buncker yᵉ Son & Daughter of John Buncker by his wife Dorcas Born 25ᵗʰ Februᵃ 1707

This may Certifie that Stephen Otis and Catherine Astin were Joyned in mariage July 29ᵗʰ 1736   Jonᵃ Cushing . Clerk
  Dover July 30ᵗʰ 1736

This is to Certifie that Betty & Anna Harford were Baptised June 12th 1737   P   Jon^a Cushing   Clerk

Dover June 28, 1737

John Gerrish the Son of John Gerrish by his wife margery Born Sepr 5, 1735

George Gerrish the Son of John Gerrish by his wife Margery Born April 9, 1737

Mary Wood Daughter of John Wood by his Wife Elizabeth Born Novr 12, 1737

Susannah Wood Daughter of John Wood by his wife Elizabeth Born Sep^t 21, 1739

Benjamin Gerrish Son of Paul Gerrish Jun. by his wife Mary Born July 3^d 1739

Samuel Ricker the Son of Meturan Ricker by his wife Hannah Born May 20th 1730

Beiley Ricker Daughter of Meturan Ricker by his wife Hannah Born March 15th 1734

Marcy Ricker Daughter of Meturan Ricker by his wife Hannah Born March 31, 1736

Sarah Gerrish Daughter of John Gerrish by his wife Margery Born Aprill 11th 1740

Elizabeth Wood Daughter of John Wood by his wife Elizabeth Born Feb^{ry} 22, 1740/1

Lidia Wood Daughter of John Wood by his Wife Elizabeth Born Novr 17, 1742

Col^o Paul Gerrish Esq: Departed This Life June the 6th 1743 and was honourably buried June 10th following being attended to his grave by Near about a Thousand People

Ephraim Roberts Son of Ens: Joseph Roberts by his wife Eliz^a Born March y^e: 23 1727

Joseph Roberts Son of the above named Joseph & Eliz^a Born February 7th 1729

Betty Roberts Daughter of the aboue Named Joseph & Eliz^a Born april 21 : 1731

Mary Roberts Daughter of the aboue Named Joseph & Eliz^a Roberts Born October 8th 1733

Abigail Roberts Daughter of the above Named Joseph & Eliz^a Born February 18th 1736

Liddia Roberts Daughter of the aboue Named Joseph & Eliz^a Born Octob^r 22 : 1738

Esther Horn Daughter of Thomas Horn by his wife Esther Born april 26th 1729

Paul Horn Son of Thomas Horn By his wife Esther Born Septemr 5th 1737

Benjamin Church Son of John Church by his wife Mary Born April 5 : 1740

Ebenezer Church Son of Jonathan Church by his wife abigail Born January ye 9 1742/3

John Daniel Son of Joseph Daniel by his wife Jane born May 25 : 1709

Sarah Tebbets Daughter of Jeremiah Tebbets By his wife Martha Born Novemr 1744

Margery Gerrish Daughter of John Gerrish by his wife Margery was born March the 30 : 1742

Samuel Hanson Son of Thomas Hanson by his wife Margaret Born July 19 : 1717

Samuel Hanson of Dover & Sarah French of Stratham Were Joyned in marriage Octobr 20 : 1743

Zacheus Hanson son of Solomon Hanson by his wife Ann Born in Dover Septemr 17 : 1742

John Cook Born in Dover May the 5th 1692

Liddia Cook the wife of John Cook Born in Dover Novemr 29th 1694

John Cook Son of John Cook by his wife Liddia was Born in Dover Novr 6 : 1725

Richard Cook Son of John Cook by his wife Liddia was Born in Dover Decemr 21 : 1727

Phebe Cook Daughter of John Cook by his wife Liddia was Born in Dover March 17 : 1729/30

Daniel Cook son of John Cook by his wife Liddia Was Born in Dover Septemr 11, 1732

Ebenezer Cook Son of John Cook Died on his Passage home from Cape breton the 17th Day of august 1745 in the 23d year of his age

John Wood Son of John Wood By his wife Elizabeth was Born In Dover april 11th 1745

Joseph Hanson Son of Tobias Hanson by his Wife Ann Born January 10th 1704

Joseph Hanson and Rebekah Shepard was Joyned in Marriage by the Revd Mr Hugh Adams The 23d Day of Novemr 1727

Rebekah Hanson Wife of Joseph Hanson Departed This Life april 18th 1736 in ye 29th year of her age

Joseph Hanson and Sarah Scammon Was Joyned in Marriage By the Revd Mr Saml Willard on the 25th Day of August 1737

Sarah Hanson Wife of Joseph Hanson Departed Th is life the 2^d Day of Septem^r 1738 being in y^e[——] year of her age

Joseph Hanson and Susanna Burnum Were Joyned in Marriage By the Revd Mr Jonathan Cushing ye 6th Day of June 1739. The Said Susanna being Daughter of Robert Burnam by his wife Elizabeth Born March ye 1st 1715/16

Ephraim Hanson Son of Joseph Hanson by his Wife Rebekah Born June 15th 1728

Humphry Hanson Son of Joseph Hanson by his Wife Sarah Born August 27th 1738

Rebekah Hanson Daughter of Joseph Hanson by his Wife Susanna Born Decr 28th 1739

John Burnam Hanson Son of Joseph Hanson by his wife Susanna Born Novem^r 29 : 1741

Susanna Hanson the wife of Joseph Hanson Esq. Departed this Life March 4th 1758 N S aged 41 years

Thomas Canney Son of Samuel Canney by his wife Susanna was born in Dover October 26, 1730

Samuel Canney Son of Samuel Canney by his wife Susanna was Born in Dover Novr 27, 1736

Susanna Canney Daughter of Samuel Canney by his wife Susanna was Born in Dover May 22^d 1739

Sarah Canney Daughter of Samuel Canney by his Wife Susanna Was Born in Dover Feby 14 : 1741/2

John Canney Son of Samuel Canney by his wife Susanna was born in Dover August 24 : 1744

Elihu Hayes Son of John Hayes by his Wife Tamson Born Decem^r 16, 1717

William Hayes Son of Elihu Hayes by his wife Martha was Born in Dover July 22^d 1739

John Hayes Son of Elihu Hayes by his wife Martha was Born in Dover Feby 26 : 1741/2

Elihu Hayes Son of Elihu Hayes by his wife Martha Born May 14th 1743

Tamson Hayes Daughter of Elihu Hayes by his wife Martha was Born in Dover Jan^{ry} 31 : 1745/6

Tamson Hayes Second Daughter of Elihu Hayes by his wife Martha Born in Dover September ye 4th 1746

Elihu Hayes Son of Elihu Hayes Died august 8th 1744

William Hayes Son of Elihu Hayes Died august 28 : 1744

Tamson Hayes Daughter of Elihu Hayes Died Octob^r 31 : 1745

William Shannon Son of Cutt Shannon By his Wife Mary born in Dover Jany the Sixth 1747/8

John Pinkham Son of Richard Pinkham By his wife Elizabeth was Born in Dover August ye 19 : 1696

John Alley Son of Samuel Alley by his wife Elizabeth was Born in Dover Jany 25 Anno Dom 1720/1

Thomas Alley Son of Samuel Alley by his wife Elizabeth was Born in Dover april 21st A. D. 1727

Sarah Alley Daughter of John Alley by his wife Martha was Born Dover July 26 : 1742

Phebe Alley Daughter of John Alley by his Wife Martha was Born in Dover Decem^r 16 : 1743

John Alley son of John Alley by his wife Martha was Born in Dover Jany 19 : 1747/8

Liddia Harfard Daughter of Paul Harfard by his wife Liddia Born in Dover Jany 15th 1701

Paul Harfard Son of Paul Harfard by his wife Liddia Born in Dover January 2^d 1744

Israel Hodgdon and Hannah Hanson were Joyned in marriage august 9th 1725

Sarah Hodgdon Daughter of Israel Hodgdon by his wife Hannah was born Novem^r 12th 1725

Timothy Hodgdon Son of Israel Hodgdon by his wife Hannah was born May the 22^d 1726

Caleb Hodgdon Son of Israel Hodgdon by his wife Hannah was born January 27th 1732/3

Hannah Hodgdon the wife of Israel Hodgdon Departed this life January 1st 1737/8

Israel Hodgdon of Dover & Mary Johnson of Hampton were Joyned in Marriage Sep^t 21st 1738

Edmond Hodgdon Son of Israel Hodgdon by his wife Mary was born Agust 20th 1739

Israel Hodgdon Son of Israel Hodgdon by his wife Mary was born Jnly 26th 1741

Peter Hodgdon Son of Israel Hodgdon by his wife Mary was born October 7th 1742

John Hodgdon Son of Israel Hodgdon by his wife Mary was born April 22d 1745

Abigail Hodgdon Daughter of Israel Hodgdon by his wife Mary was born april yr 8th 1749

Ezekiel Hayes Son of Thomas Hayes by his wife Hannah Born in Dover October 14th 1742

Susea Hayes Daughter of Thomas Hayes by his wife Hannah Born in Dover October 11th 1745

Abigail Hayes Daughter of Thomas Hayes by his wife Hannah Born in Dover March 5th 1748/9

Eliphalet Ricker Son of John Ricker jun by his wife Elener Born at Summersworth Decr 13th 1745

Elisha Ricker Son of John Ricker jun by his wife Elener Born at Summersworth Decemr 16th 1747

Joseph Ricker Son of John Ricker jun by his wife Elener Born at Summersworth Septemr 5th 1750

James Davis the Son of James Davis by his Wife Elizabeth Born July the tenth 1689

James Davis of Dover and Ruth Ayers of Haverhill was Joyned in Marriage Novemr the fifth 1728

Ruth Davis the Daughter of James Davis by his wife Ruth Born Novemr 5th 1729

Ruth Davis the wife of James Davis Deceased the 28th Day of april 1730

James Davis of Dover and Elizabeth Pain of York Were Joyned together in Marriage April the 14th 1743

James Davis Son of James Davis by his wife Elizabeth Born in Dover Feby 14th 1744/5

Mary Davis Daughter of James Davis by his wife Elizabeth Born in Dover March 28th 1746

Daniel Davis Son of James Davis by his wife Elizabeth Born in Dover June 7th 1748

Daniel Davis Son of James Davis Departed this life May 27th 1749

Jacob Hossom Son of Jacob Hossom by his wife Bridget Born in Dover Sept 22d 1735

Thomas Davis Son of James Davis by his wife Elizabeth Born in Dover Sept 7th 1750

John Davis Son of James Davis By his wife Elizabeth Born in Dover July 6th 1754

John Leghton Son of Thomas Leghton by his wife Susanna Born June ye 27th 1719

Sarah Leighton Daugh^r of Thomas Leighton by his wife Susanna Born August ye 10th 1721

Dority Leighton Daugh^r of Thomas Leighton by his wife Susanna Born Octob^r ye 18th 1723

Thomas Leighton Son of Thomas Leighton by his wife Susanna Born Novem^r 13th 1725

George Leighton Son of Thomas Leighton by his Wife Susanna Born Novem^r ye 18th 1727

Samuel Leighton Son of Thomas Leighton by his wife Susanna Born Decr 20th 1729

Gideon Leighton Son of Thomas Leighton by his wife Susanna Born Feby 14th 1731

Joseph Leighton Son of Thomas Leighton by his wife Susanna Born april ye 23^d 1733

Elizabeth Leighton Daugh^r of Thos Leighton By his wife Susanna Born March ye 11th 1737

Theodore Leighton Son of Thos Leighton By his wife Susanna Born March 22^d 1739

Susanna Leighton Daugh^r of Thos Leighton By his wife Susanna Born Decr 6th 1742

Moses Hodgdon Son of Israel Hodgdon by his wife mary Born in Dover November 10th 1750

Ebenezer Church, Son of Jonathan Church by his wife Abig^l Born in Barrington Jan^{ry} 9th 1742/3

John Church, Son of Jonathan Church By his wife Abig^l born in Barrington Octob^r 30th 1745

James Church Son of Jonathan Church by his wife Abig^l Born in Barrington Jan^{ry} 20th 1747/8

Ann Church Daughter of Jonathan Church by his wife Abig^l born in Barrington Octob^r 6th 1749

Nathaniel Church Son of Jon^a Church by his wife Abig^l Born in Barrington Sep^t 28th 1751

Isaac Hanson ju^r Departed this Life January ye 12th 1758

Isaac Hanson Departed this life January the 15th 1758 on Sabbath Day about 4 oclock afternoon of an an apperplect fit

Joseph Hanson Esqr Departed this Life September the 5th 1758 Sun about two hours high at night after 4 Days Sickness with the Numb Palsie

Tobias Hanson Departed this Life the 27th day of august 1765—In the 65th year of his age

The Revd Mr Jonathan Cushing Departed this Life on Saturday ye 25th Day of March 1779—& was Decntly Interr^d on Thursday Following being the 30th day of s^d march.

John Alley Son of Samuel Alley by his wife Elizabeth Born in Dover January ye 5th 1720

Samuel Alley Son of Samuel Alley by his wife Elizabeth Born in Dover April ye 19th 1723

Ephriam Alley Son of Samuel Alley by his wife Elizabeth Born in Dover april ye 3^d 1725

Thomas Alley Son of Samuel Alley by his wife Elizabeth Born in Dover april 21st 1727

Daniel Alley Son of Samuel Alley by his wife Elizabeth Born in Dover april ye 10th 1739

John Whitehouse and Abigail Wentworth were Joyned together in marriage by Joseph Hanson Esqr April ye 30th 1756

William Horn and Jane Davis were Joyned together in marriage by Joseph Hanson Esqr the 14th day of July 1756

Jonathan Bickford of Dover and Sarah Wilmet of Somersworth were Joyned together in Marriage by the Revd Mr James Pike the 26th Day of May 1757

John Hammack and Rachel Whitehouse were Joyned in marriage by Joseph Hanson Esqr Septem^r 22^d 1757

Elizabeth Horn Daughter of Nathaniel Horn by his wife Sarah was born in Dover February ye 15th 1738/9

Sarah Horn the Daughter of nathaniel Horn by his wife Sarah was born in Dover August 13th 1742

Hannah Horn Daughter of Nathaniel Horn by his wife Sarah Born in Dover Septem^r 24th 1745

John & Benjamin Kielle (twins) & Sons of James Kielle by his wife Deborah Born in Dover april ye 23^d 1731

James Kielle Son of James Kielle by his wife Deborah Born in Dover Decr ye 1st 1733

William Kielle Son of James Kielle by his wife Deborah Born in Dover april 23^d 1736

Samuel Kielle Son of James Kielle By his wife Deborah Born in Dover Novr ye 8th 1738

Moses Kielle Son of James Kielle by his wife Deborah Born in Dover Feby 13th 1740/1

Aron Kielle Son of James Kielle by his wife Deborah Born in Dover Octob^r 11th 1743

Ebenezer Kielle son of James Kielle by his wife Deborah Born in Dover March 14th 1746

Joseph Mesarve Son of Daniel Mesarve jun^r by his wife abigail Born in Dover Octr 4th 1729

Deborah Mesarve Daghter of Danl Mesarve jun by his wife abigail Born in Dover May 14th 1732

Daniel Mesarve Son of Danl Mesarve jun By his wife abigail Born in Dover March 18th 1734

Jonathan Mesarve Son of Danl Mesarve jun by his wife abigail Born in Dover March 4th 1738

Clement Mesarve Son of Danl Mesarve jun By his wife Abigail Born in Dover Jany 23^d 1741

Abigail Mesarve Daughter of Danl Mesarve jun by his wife abigail Born in Dover Augst 27th 1745

Molly Gerrish Daughter of Jonathan Gerrish By his wife Eunice Born in Kittery March 1st 1751

Nanny Gerrish Daughter of Jon^a Gerrish By his wife Eunice Born in Dover Sep^t 31st 1753

Eunice Gerrish Daughter of Jon^a Gerrish by his wife Eunice Born in Dover Octob^r 3^d 1755

James Tobey Gerrish Son of Jon^a Gerrish by his wife Eunice Born in Dover Sep^t 10th 1758

William Hanson Son of William Hanson by his wife Bathsheba was born in Dover Decr 19th 1732

Anna Hanson Daughter of Wm Hanson by his wife Bathsheba born in Dover feb^y 27, 1735

Mary Hanson Daughter of Wm Hanson by his wife Bathsheba Born in Dover June 19th 1737

Bridget Hanson Daughter of Wm Hanson By his wife Bathsheba Born in Dover Octr 13th 1739

Joseph Hanson Son of Wm Hanson by his wife Bathsheba Born in Dover June ye 13th 1742

Israel Hanson Son of Wm Hanson by his wife Bathsheba Born in Dover March 12th 1744

Jacob Hanson Son of Wm Hanson by his wife Bathsheba Born in Dover march 14th 1747

Bathsheba Hanson Daugh^r of Wm Hanson by his wife Bathsheba Born in Dover Septem^r 14th 1749

Joanna Hanson Daugh^r of Wm Hanson by his wife Bathsheba Born in Dover Feby 11th 1752

Ephraim Hanson Son of Wm Hanson by his wife Bathsheba Born in Dover feb^y 6th 1754

Elizabeth Hanson Daugh^r of Wm Hanson by his wife Bathsheba Born in Dover May 18th 1757

Benjamin Watson Son of Isaac Watson by his wife Lylle Born in Dover April ye 3^d 1734

Sarah Gerrish Daughter of Andrew Gerrish by his wife Hannah Born in Providence July ye 12th Anno Dom: 1748

Elizabeth Gerrish Daughter of Andrew Gerrish by his wife Hannah Born in Providence May ye 9th 1750

Hannah Gerrish Daughter of Andrew Gerrish by his wife Hannah Born in Dover April ye 25th 1752

Joseph Gerrish Son of Andrew Gerrish by his wife Hannah Born in Dover July ye 6th 1754

Timothy Gerrish Son of Andrew Gerrish by his wife Hannah Born in Dover April ye 7th 1756

Hannah Sawyer Daughter of Moses Sawyer By his wife Huldah Born in Dover Decr 6th 1748 O. S.

Samuel Sawyer Son of Moses Sawyer by his wife Huldah Born in Dover July ye 19th 1751 O. S.

Mary Sawyer Daughter of Moses Sawyer By his wife Huldah Born in Dover June ye 1st 1753 : N. S.

George Sawyer Son of Moses Sawyer by his wife Huldah Born in Dover Augst 1st 1758 : N. Stile

Jonathan Gage and Rebeckah Hanson were Joyned together in Marriage by the Revd Mr Jon^a Cushing the 29th Day of March 1759

Ephraim Hanson & Margaret Lord were Joyned together in Marriage by the Revd Mr Moses pastor of the upper Parrish Church in Berwick on March ye 24th 1756

Joseph Hanson Son of Ephraim Hanson by his wife margaret Born Octob^r 1st 1756

Abraham Hanson Son of Ephraim Hanson by his wife margaret Born in Dover July 15th 1759

Margaret Hanson wife of Ephraim Hanson Departed this Life the 24th Day of August 1769 In the 32d year of her age

Ephraim Hanson Son of Joseph Hanson Esqr Departed this Life the 24 Day of March 1772 In the 43d year of his age

Mary Hawkins Daughter of Stephen Hawkins By his wife Sarah Born in Dover Decemr 14th 1739

Stephen Hawkins Son of Stephen Hawkins By his wife Sarah Born in Dover Decr 14th 1741

Rachel Hawkins Daughter of Stephen Hawkins By his wife Sarah Born in Dover augst 26th 1744

John Hawkins Son of Stephen Hawkins By his wife Sarah Born in Dover March 5th 1745/6

Abigail Hawkins Daughter of Stephen Hawkins By his wife Sarah Born in Dover Feby 27th 1747/8

Elizabeth Hawkins Daughter of Stephen Hawkins By his wife Sarah Born in Dover July 4th 1750

Hannah Hawkins Daughter of Stephen Hawkins By his wife Sarah Born in Dover June 3d 1752

Benjamin Hawkins Son of Stephen Hawkins By his wife Sarah Born in Dover July 26th 1755

William Hawkins Son of Stephen Hawkins By his wife Sarah Born in Dover June 19th 1757

Thomas Hawkins Son of Stephen Hawkins by his wife Sarah Born in Dover June 25th 1759

George Hawkins Son of Stephen Hawkins By his wife Sarah Born in Dover May 20th 1761

Ann Hawkins Daughter of Stephen Hawkins By his wife Sarah Born In Barrington May 29th 1765

Samuel Hall Son of Benjamin Hall By his wife Frances Born in Dover May ye 19th 1744.

Recorded ye 22d Day of Janry 1761 :
                                      By Ephm Hanson   Town Cler.

Nicholas Canada & Abigail Merrow ye Daughter of Jonathan Merrow & Elizabeth merrow his wife, were Joyned together in Marriage by the Revd Mr Jonathan Cushing the 12th Day of march 1754

Sarah Canada Daughter of Nicholas Canada & his wife Abigail was Born in Dover the 27th Day of may 1755

John Canada Son of Nicholas Canada & his wife Abigail was Born in Dover the 18th Day of February 1757

George Canada Son of Nicholas Canada & his wife Abigail was Born in Dover the 8th Day of January 1759

Abigail Canada the wife of Nicholas Canada Departed this Life the 12th Day of July 1761 in the 34th year of her age

John Hussey Layn son of Edmund Layn By his wife Jane was Born In Dover the 22d Day of December 1739

Moses Brown of Portsmouth In New Hampshire and Mary Young of Dover was Joyned together In Marriage By the Revd Mr Jeremy Belknap of Dover the 4th Day of June 1770

Recorded ye 22d Day of October 1770

By Ephm Hanson   Town Cler.

Abigail Hayes Daughter of Ichabod Hayes By his wife Eliza was Born in Dover may ye 9th 1742

Ichabod Hayes Son of Ichabod Hayes By his wife Elizabeth was Born in Dover Jany ye 17th 1744

Ezekiel Hayes Son of Ichabod Hayes by his wife Eliza was Born in Dover February 19th 1746

Daniel Hayes Son of Ichabod Hayes by his wife Eliza was Born in Dover June 24th 1748

Moses Hayes Son of Ichabod Hayes by his wife Eliza was Born in Dover June 14th 1750

Aaron Hayes Son of Ichabod Hayes by his wife Eliza was Born in Dover Sept 19th 1752

Tamson Hayes Daughter of Ichabod Hayes By his wife Eliza was Born in Dover march 21st 1755

Abrey Hayes Daughter of Ichabod Hayes by his wife Eliza was Born in Dover Augst 2d 1757

James Chesley Hayes Son of Ichabod Hayes By his wife Eliza was Born in Dover Jany 29th 1760

Betty Hayes Daughter of Ichabod Hayes By his wife Eliza was Born in Dover march 10th 1762

Tamson Hayes Daughter of Ichabod Hayes Departed this Life Jany 10th 1758

John Hayes Son of Ichabod Hayes By his wife Elizabeth was Born In Dover Sept 15th 1764

Nicholas Otis Son of Joshua Otis By his wife Jane was Born in Dover march ye 29th 1746

Micaiah Otis Son of Joshua Otis By his wife Jane was Born in Dover may ye 21st 1747

Elijah Otis Son of Joshua Otis By his wife Jane was Born in Dover December ye 25th 1749

Sarah Otis Daughter of Joshua Otis by his wife Jane was Born in Dover may 18th 1751

 Bro^t to Record May 28th 1763

Patience Hanson Daughter of Thomas Hanson Jun. by his wife Hannah was Born In Dover May 28th 1752

Sarah Hanson Daughter of Thomas Hanson Ju^r by his wife Hannah was Born In Dover aug^t 26 1754

Elizabeth Hanson Daugh^r of Thos Hanson Junr by his wife Hannah was Born In Dover may 23^d 1756

Lois Hanson Daughter of Thos Hanson Junr by his wife Hannah was Born In Dover april 11th 1758

Merriam Hanson Daughter of Thomas Hanson Ju^r By his wife Hannah was Born In Dover Feby 21st 1760

Thomas Hanson ye 3^d, Son of Thos Hanson Junr By his wife Hannah was Born In Dover July 30 : 1763

William Laighton Son of John Laighton By his wife Abigail Born in Dover august ye 20th 1729

Hatevil Laighton Son of John Laighton By his wife Abigail Born In Dover may ye 13th 1731

Tobias Laighton Son of John Laighton By his wife Abigail Born In Dover may ye 9th 1736

Paul Laighton Son of John Laighton By his wife Abigail Born In Dover april ye 3^d 1738

Abigail Laighton Daughter of John Laighton By his wife Abigail Born In Dover may ye 2^d 1740

Jonathan Laighton Son of John Laighton By his wife Abigail Born In Dover Jany 20th 1742

Olive Laighton Daughter of John Laighton By his wife Abigail Born In Dover October 29th 1743

Mary Laighton Daughter of John Laighton By his wife Abigail Born In Dover Feby 19th 1746

Deborah Laighton Daughter of John Laighton By his wife Abigail Born In Dover Octob^r 23^d 1747

James Laighton Son of John Laighton By his wife Abigail Born In Dover October ye 12th 1749

 Bro^t to Record July 26, 1764

M:rs Mary Gerrish Consort to Colo Paul Gerrish Decd Departed this Life, the Sixteenth Day of April 1765 & was Honourably Buried ye 19th Day of Sd April

James Libbey Son of Benjamin Libby By his wife Elizabeth Born In Dover ye 27th Day of July 1739

Benjamin Kielle Son of John Kielle By his wife Abigail Born In Dover Augd 23d 1763

Hannah Kielle Daughter of John Kielle By his wife Abigail Born In Dover March 22d 1765

Sarah Hanson Daughter of Timothy Hanson By his wife Kezia Born In Dover March 23d 1733

Sarah Sawyer Daughter of Jacob Sawyer By his wife Susanah Born In Dover Novr 8th 1744

Stephen Sawyer Son of Jacob Sawyer By his wife Sarah Born In Dover June ye 8th 1752

Patience Sawyer Daughter of Jacob Sawyer by his wife Sarah Born In Dover Sept 26th 1753

Susanah Sawyer Daughter of Jacob Sawyer By his wife Sarah Born In Dover Decr 17th 1758

Micajah Sawyer Son of Jacob Sawyer By his wife Sarah Born In Dover May ye 19th 1760

Kezia Sawyer Daughter of Jacob Sawyer By his wife Sarah Born In Dover Jany 12th 1762

Lydia Sawyer Daughter of Jacob Sawyer By his wife Sarah Born In Dover Novr 30th 1763

Timothy Sawyer Son of Jacob Sawyer By his wife Sarah was Born In Dover ye 5th Day of October 1766

The Revd Mr Jeremy Belknap of Dover & Mrs Ruth Eliot of Boston were Joyned together In Marriage By the Revd Mr Andrew Eliot of Boston the 15th Day of June 1767

Sarah Belknap Daughter of the Revd Mr Jeremy Belknap By his wife Ruth was Born In Dover the 7th Day of april 1768

Zaccheus Sawyer Son of Moses Sawyer By his wife Huldah Born In Dover May 24th 1760

Isaac Watson Son of Joseph Watson By his wife Elizabeth was Born In Dover ye 23d Day of october 1760

James Watson Son of Joseph Watson By his wife Elizabeth was Born In Dover ye 8th Day of March 1763

Sarah Watson Daughter of Joseph Watson By his wife Elizabeth was Born In Dover ye 2d Day of Jany 1766

Elizabeth Giles Daughter of Mark Giles By his wife Lydia was Born In Dover May ye 2^d 1737

Mark Giles Son of Mark Giles By his wife Lydia was Born In Dover June ye 22^d 1739

Lydia Giles Daughter of Mark Giles By his wife Lydia was Born In Dover Decr 15th 1741

Paul Giles Son of Mark Giles By his wife Lydia was Born in Dover July 22^d 1743

Joseph Giles son of Mark Giles by his wife Lydia was Born In Dover May 22^d 1746

Avery Copp, Daughter of Benjamin Copp By his wife Elizabeth was Born In Dover March 20th 1762

Joseph Belknap, Son of the Revd Mr Jeremiah Belknap By his wife Ruth, Was Born In Dover Decr 2^d 1769

Jacob Sawyer Son of Jacob Sawyer By his wife Sarah, was Born In Dover ye 1st Day of octob^r 1769

Samuel Belknap, Son of the Revd Mr Jeremy Belknap By his wife Ruth was Born In Dover, Decr 31st 1771

Elizabeth Daughter of Jeremy & Ruth Belknap was born April 3^d 1774

John, Son of Jeremy & Ruth Belknap was born Decr 30, 1776.

Andrew Eliot, Son of Jeremy & Ruth Belknap was born June 4, 1779.

Humphry Hanson Departed this Life November the 13th 1766

Dominicus Hanson Son of Humphry Hanson By his wife Joanna was Born In Dover Decr 19th 1760

Sarah Hanson Daughter of Humphry Hanson By his wife Joanna was Born In Dover Decr 22^d 1762

Joseph Hanson Son of Humphry Hanson By his wife Joanna was Born In Dover Decr 18th 1764

Elizabeth Hanson Posthumous Daughter of Humphry Hanson By his wife Joanna was Born In Dover ye 12th Day of May 1767

The Births of Jonathan Gages Children By His Wife Rebeckah are as follows (Viz)

Susanna born In Dover Octr 30th 1759

Hannah Born In Dover June 25th 1763

Elizabeth Born In Dover June 4 1768

Peggey Born In D^o Jany 5 1771

Joseph Hanson Born in D^o March 4 1779

Mr Jonathan Gage Departed this Life on Tuesday about ten : o : Clock in the forenoon after being sick about three days & in the 66th year of his age and was Decently Inter'd on Thirsday the 16th Octr 1800

Hatevil Hall Son of Hatevil Hall By his wife Marcy was Born In Dover February 15th 1708/9

Hatevil Hall of Dover & Sarah Furbush of Kittery was Joyned together In Marriage By the Reverand Mr Jonathan Cushing of sd Dover, april 11th 1733

Dorothy Hall Daughter of Hatevil Hall By his wife Sarah was Born In Dover August 28th 1733

Daniel Hall Son of Hatevil Hall By his wife Sarah was Born In Dover March 24, 1735/6

Hatevil Hall Son of Hatevil Hall by his wife Sarah was Born In Dover March 24th 1736/7

Marcy Hall Daughter of Hatevil Hail By his wife Sarah was Born In Dover October ye 6th 1738

Abigail Hall Daughter of Hatevil Hall by his wife Sarah was Born In Dover February 12th 1739/40

Ebenezer Hall Son of Hatevil Hall by his wife Sarah was Born In Dover July 20th 1741

William Hall Son of Hatevil Hall By his wife Sarah was Born In Dover December ye 6th 1742

John Hall Son of Hatevil Hall By his wife Sarah was Born In Dover, June ye 19th 1744

Jedediah Hall, son of Hatevil Hall By his wife Sarah was Born In Dover, June ye 21st 1748

Andrew Hall Son of Hatevil Hall By his wife Sarah was Born In Dover September ye 15th 1750

Nicholas Hall Son of Hatevil Hall By his wife Sarah was Born In Dover, March ye 8th 1753

July 4 1776 This May Certify whom may Concern That Benjaman Evans & Lydia Widden Was Married By Me   Samuel Hutchins

Bro't To Record June 29th 1779 Examined
                    By Thos Wk Waldron   Town Clerk

The Births of the Children of Saml. Emerson of Dover by his Wife Dorothy &c here followeth Viz.

Sarah Emerson born ye 25th Augt 1749 & Died Feby 10th 1753

Hannah Emerson Born ye 28th of June 1753

Mary Emerson Born ye 14th of January 1756

Micah Emerson Born y⁰ 1ˢᵗ May 1758
Abigail Emerson Born y⁰ 3ᵈ October 1760
Deborah Emerson Born y⁰ 18ᵗʰ November 1762
Samuel Emerson Born y⁰ 17ᵗʰ December 1765
William Emerson Born y⁰ 13ᵗʰ September 1768
Joseph Emerson Born y⁰ 4ᵗʰ October 1772
The Births of the Children of Paul Welland of Dover by his Wife Elizabeth here followeth Viz.

Lydia Welland Born y⁰ 28ᵗʰ of February 1765
Paul Welland Born y⁰ 9ᵗʰ of August 1768
Nathaniel Welland Born y⁰ 28ᵗʰ of April 1775

  Recorded Decʳ 22ᵈ 1779 P Thoˢ Wᵏ Waldron Town Clerk

Loas Sawyer Daughter of Moses Sawyer by his Wife Rebeckah Born in Dover July 24ᵗʰ 1769

Moses Sawyer Son of Sᵈ Moses by his wife Rebeckah born in Dover october 5ᵗʰ 1771

Sarah Sawyer Daughter of Sᵈ Moses by his wife Rebeckah Born in Said Dover may 17 1774

  Recorded march 24ᵗʰ 1786 by John Bᵐ Hanson Town Clerk

The Births of the Children of Joshua Wingate by his Wife Abigail &c here follows Viz.

Edmund Wingate born Sepᵗ 22ᵈ 1757
Stephen Wingate born Novʳ 14ᵗʰ 1759
Elizᵃ Wingate born May 5ᵗʰ 1762
Joshua Wingate born April 26ᵗʰ 1765
Mary Wingate born March 18 1769

John Titcomb son of Jnᵒ Titcomb by his Wife Sarah born in Dover Febʸ 25ᵗʰ 1760   april 1ˢᵗ 1780

Mʳ George Watson Departed this Life on thirsday the 9ᵗʰ Day of October A Dom: 1800. In the [——] year of his age.

At a legal Town Meeting held at Dover on the Twenty Ninth Day of March 1784

Voted	The Honᵇˡᵉ Meshach Weare President	Nᵒ	155
Voted	General Sullivan	Dᵒ	11
Voted	Wiseman Clagett	Dᵒ	2
Voted	For Senators Colᵒ Ebʳ Smith	Dᵒ	51
	Jnᵒ Wentworth Esqʳ	Dᵒ	137
	Colo Jnᵒ Waldron	Dᵒ	86
	Capt Jnᵒ Gage	Dᵒ	1
	Capt James Calef	Dᵒ	1

At a Legal Town Meeting held at Dover in the twenty Eighth day of March 1785

Voted the following men Candidates for a President

    George Atkinson Esqr 124
    General Sullavin Esqr 36
    John Langdon Esqr 7

    Senators

    John Wentworth Esqr 124
    Otis Baker Esqr 71
    Coll John Waldron   53

This Return made by
    Benjamin Peirce who was Clerk Protempore

The Hon. Thomas W^k Waldron Esqr Town Clerk Departed this Life april 3^d 1785 in Sixty fourth year of his age

    these Minutes Sent by the Revd Mr Belknap

The Births of Peter Hodgdon his Wives & Children & his Marriages as follows

Peter Hodgdon Born in Dover Octr 18, 1742

Mary Boody born in Madbury June 23, 1749

Peter Hodgdon Was Married to Mary Boody Decr 11 1766

John Hodgdon Son of Peter Hodgdon by his wife Mary Born in Notingham Novr 4, 1768

Mary Wife of the above Peter Departed this Life in the 22^d year of her age Octr 30 1770

Patience Chase born in Kensington June 26 1750

Peter Hodgdon Was Married to Patience Chase July 9, 1772

Stephen Hodgdon Son of Peter Hodgdon by his wife Patience Born in Kensington March 16, 1774

Jonathan Hodgdon Son of the above by D^o born in Kensington Feby 13. 1776

Mary Hodgdon Daughter of D^o Born at Wolfeborough August 20, 1778

Peter Hodgdon Son of D^o Born in Dover Sep^t 12, 1781

Sarah Hodgdon Daughter of D^o born in Dover Decr 25, 1783

Chase Hodgdon Son of D^o Born in Dover May 19 1786

Abigail Hodgdon Daughter of D^o } Born in Madbury 27th March 1791   1791

Patience Hodgdon Daughter of D^o } Born in Madbury 14 June 1793   1793

Brought to Record the two Last March 27th 1805,
and Recorded by	Dominicus Hanson	Town Clerk

John B^m Hanson was Born In Dover Novr 29th 1741
Elizabeth Rogers Born in Durham May 20th 1744
John B^m Hanson was Married to Elizabeth Rogers September ye 20th 1764
The Births & Deaths of their Children are as follows Recorded February 11th 1786
Susanna Born in Durham June 15th 1765
Susanna Died Sep^t 23^d 1765
Hannah Born In Durham July 11th 1766
Susey Born In Durham May 25th 1768
Two Sons Called Daniel & Robert Born In Durham Ap^ll 30th 1770
Robert Died May 4th 1771
Salley Born in Dover Decr 18th 1772
Two Children Robert & Bettey Born In Dover March 14th 1776
Robert Died June 6th 1777
John Burnham Born In Dover June 13 1778
Two Sons Ephraim & Humphry Born In Dover Sep^t 16 1780
Joseph Born in Dover March 12 1783
Peter Cushing Born in Dover February 22 1757
Hannah Hanson Born in Durham July 11th 1766
Peter Cushing was Married to Hannah Hanson the 11th of april 1784
The Births of their Children
John Born October 25th 1784
Betty Born November 26th 1786

Nathanael Cooper and Abigail Hayes were Married May 23^d 1765 by the Revd Mr Jonathan Cushing

Martha the Daughter of Nath^el Cooper and Abigail Born 25th September 1772.

Walter the Son of Nath^el Cooper and Abigail Born Septr 2^d 1774.

Elizabeth the Daughter of Nath^el Cooper & Abigail Born January 24th 1777.

Deborah Shackford Daughter of Nath^el Cooper & Abigail Born 24th October 1778   Died April 3^d 1787

William Shackford Son of Nath^el Cooper & Abigail Born January 5th 1782

1790 Jany 31 Recorded by	Nath^el Cooper Town Clerk

Ezekiel Varney born Decr 20th 1736, and Married to Susannah Hanson Septr 10th 1761, who was born June 15th 1738

Dorothy, Daughter of Ezekiel Varney and Susannah Varney born Sept' 2ᵈ 1766.

Ezekiel, Son of Ezekiel & Susannah Varney born March 6ᵗʰ 1769.

Ezekiel Varney died April 13ᵗʰ 1769.

  Recorded April 26ᵗʰ 1791 by   N. Cooper Town Clerk

Stephen Sawyer and Mary Varney both of Dover Married at Dover 4ᵗʰ day of 3ᵈ Month 1778

      Their offspring
   Names of Children and dates of their Births

Elizabeth 12ᵗʰ day 6ᵗʰ Month 1778
Nahum 6ᵗʰ day 11ᵗʰ Month 1779
Justin 16ᵗʰ day 6ᵗʰ Month 1781
Hosea 25ᵗʰ day 5ᵗʰ Month 1783
Walter 1ˢᵗ day 11ᵗʰ Month 1784
Benaiah 6ᵗʰ day 7ᵗʰ Month 1787
Ruth 10ᵗʰ day 9ᵗʰ Month 1789
Levi 11ᵗʰ day 8ᵗʰ Month 1791
Edward 2ᵈ day 7ᵗʰ Month 1793

  Dover the 25ᵗʰ of 3ᵈ Month 1794.

           Pʳ Stephen Sawyer
  Recorded by   Nathel Cooper Town Clerk

Lydia daughter of Stephen & Mary Sawyer born the 20ᵗʰ of the 8ᵗʰ Month 1796

The names of David Jewetts children and the dates of their births.

David H. Jewett born Novʳ 5ᵗʰ 1792

Clarissa Jewett born March 2ᵈ 1795

  Brought to record May 19 in 1795 &
  Recorded by   Walter Cooper Town Clerk

John Riley & Mary Hanson were Married Octʳ 13, 1777.

Mary Riley born March 5ᵗʰ 1779

John Riley born Janʸ 24ᵗʰ 1781

Catherine Riley born March 15, 1783

Anna Riley born Octʳ 28ᵗʰ 1785

Sarah Riley born Febʸ 22ᵈ 1787

Susannah Riley born March 25ᵗʰ 1791

Eliza Riley born Febʸ 19, 1793

  brought to Record May 19ᵗʰ 1795 half past 6 OClock in the afternoon

  Recorded by,   Walter Cooper Town Clerk

William Mann and Susannah Hanson were Married Octʳ 2ᵈ 1791

Susanna Mann daughter of William & Susanna Mann born June 25th 1792 at 12 O.Clock
    brought to Record May 20th 1795
        Recorded by   Walter Cooper   Town Clerk

Maria Sise daughter of Edward & Nancy Sise born Feby 18, 1790 on Thursday at 4 O.Clock P. M.

Shadrach Hodgdon Sise son of Edward & Nancy Sise born Friday Novr 11th 1791 at 3 O'Clock Afternoon

John Sise son of Edward & Nancy Sise born Sept^t 1st [17]93
    departed this life 23^d of s^d Month Aged 23 days

John Hodgdon Sise son of Edward & Nancy Sise born Novr 13th 1794 which was a day of Publick Thanksgiving throughout ye State:
    Brought to record May 20th 1795
        Recorded by   Walter Cooper   Town Clk

David Boardman & Abigail Waldron were Married Decr 5th 1790

Anna Boardman daughter of David & Abigail Boardman born Feby 9th 1792

Harriot Boardman daughter of David and Abigail Boardman born 2^d Feby 1794
    Brought to Record May 20th 1795
                        Walter Cooper   Town Clerk

Israel Estes son of Samuel & Mary Estes born July 1st 1785

Samuel Estes son of Samuel & Mary Estes born March 13th 1788, died Feby 6th 1791

Robert Estes son of Samuel & Mary Estes born May 6th 1790, died Feby 10th 1791

Elizabeth Estes daughter of Samuel & Mary Estes born March 15th 1792

Olive Estes daughter of Samuel & Mary Estes born May 30th 1794
    recorded May 21st 1795 by   Walter Cooper   Town Clk.

Elizabeth Smith daughter of Joseph & Judith Smith born May 20th 1794
    brought to record May 25th 1795

Rebeccah Elizabeth Wheeler daughter of John and Rebeccah Wheeler born March 21st 1794
    brought to record May 27th 1795

Maria Kimball daughter of Ezra and Mary Kimball born March 3^d 1794.
    1795 Augt 14th

Abigail Gray Kimbal Daughter of D^o born Augt 15th 1800

Liberty E. Kenney daughter of Daniel & Jane Kenney born October 12th 1794

[1795 Aug¹] 14th
Susanna Daughter of Zaccheus & Sarah Hanson born 3d day 3d month 1768

Sarah Hanson daughter of Zaccheus & Sarah Hanson born 3d day 3d Month 1771, died 26th 1 Month 1777

Ezra, son of Zaccheus & Sarah Hanson born 22 day 5 month 1773

Amos, son of Zaccheus & Sarah Hanson born 1st day 6 Month 1776

Stephen, son of Zaccheus & Sarah Hanson born 26th day 3 Month 1779

Abijah, son of Zaccheus & Sarah Hanson born 16th day 8 month 1783
  Recorded March 4, 1796

Samuel Ladd son of Eliphalet & Elizabeth Ladd born February 12th 1793.

Eliza Ladd daughter of Eliphalet & Elizabeth Ladd born January 4th 1795

Wm Ladd Son of do Born august 26th 1797

James C. Twombley son of William & Mehitable Twombley born November 11, 1787

William Twombley son of William & Mehitable born September 18, 1793

Christina Twombley daughter of William & Mehitable Twombley born September 20, 1795

Henry Orlando Mellen son of Henry & Martha Mellen born June 22d 1797

George Gains Mann son of Wm & Susanna Mann born Saturday the 5th of December 1795

Statira Mann Daughter of Wm & Susanna Mann born October 16, 1797.

William Jarvis Smith son of Joseph & Judeth Smith born 25th March 1796.

David Copp Jr and Polly Watson Were married in Portsmouth by the Revd Mr Saml Haven March 4th 1795

John Manning Copp Son of David and Polly Copp Born April 12th 1795

Polly Copp Daughter of David & Polly Copp Born Septr 11th 1796

Adeline Copp Daughter of David & Polly Copp Born April 24th 1798

  Recorded Jany 6th 1800

Philemon Chandler Born Dec'r 28th 1766

Betsey Torr Born Dec'r 20th 1779

and were married by the Rev'd Robert Gray in Dover on the 19th Jan'y 1797

Eliza Chandler Daughter of Philemon & Betsey Chandler Born Sept'r 10th 1797

Mary Ann Chandler Daughter of Philemon & Betsey Chandler Born March 15th 1799

  Recorded Jan'y 6th 1800 by   Dom's Hanson T. Clk.

John Prentyce Mellen son of Henry & Martha Mellen Born March 21st 1799

Martha Wentworth Daughter of Henry & Martha Mellen Born Dec'r y'e 9th 1800

  Rec'd for Record June 18th 1801 &

  Recorded by   Dom's Hanson Town Clerk

Lydia Gray Chandler Daughter of Philemon & Betsey Chandler Born in Dover June 20th 1801

William Lovejoy Chandler Son of Philemon & Betsey Chandler Born in Dover May 29th 1805

    Dom's Hanson : T. Clerk

Oliver Crosby of Dover & Harriot Chase of Portsmouth Were Joined in Marriage at Portsmouth by the Rev'd Joseph Buckminster Sept'r y'e 11th 1800

Harriot Daughter of Oliver & Harriot Crosby Was born in Dover June y'e 12th 1801

Oliver Son of Oliver & Harriot Crosby was Born in Dover November y'e 30th 1802

  Recorded April 15th 1803

    by Domi's Hanson T. Clerk

W'm Chase Crosby Son of d'o born in Dover Dec'r 2'd 1806.

Cornilia Crosby Born in Dover March 27th 1810

  Recorded by   Dominicus Hanson T. Clk.

Henriettee Daughter of Oliver and Harriot Crosby borne Nov'r 29th 1814 in Dover

    Dom's Hanson

Jacob M. Currier, Son of Jacob Currier &———Morril born in Hamstead 16th March 1771

Sally Chase wife of J. M. Currier born in Hampton falls Sep't y'e 24th 1773.

John Currier Son of Jacob M & Sally Currier born in Dover July ye 11th 1798.

Thomas Currier Son of J. M. & Sally Currier born in Dover May ye 28th 1801.

  Rec^d for Record July 20th 1803, &
  Recorded by   Dominicus Hanson   Town Clerk

Sarah K. Sweazey Daughter of Nathl & Sarah Sweazey Born Decr 12th 1786

Henry S. Sweazey Son of Nathl & Sarah Sweazey Born In Dover June 16th 1788

Joanna Sweazey Daughter of Nathl & Sarah Sweazey Born in Dover Octr 10th 1790

Nathl Sweazey Son of Nathl & Sarah Sweazey Born in Dover January 28th 1791

Ambrose Sweazey Son of Nathl & Sarah Sweazey Born in Dover August 27th 1792.

Asa Sweazey Son of Nathl & Sarah Sweazey Born in Dover Feby 9th 1794.

Sophia Sweazey Daughter of Nathl & Sarah Sweazey Born in Dover Feby 5th 1796.

Charles Sweazey Son of Nathl & Sarah Sweazey Born in Dover June 19th 1798.

  Recorded March 8th 1804 by   Dom^c Hanson   T. Clk.

Hannah Hanson Daughter of Thomas Hanson By his Wife Polly Was born in Dover November ye 1st 1793

Polly Hanson Daughter of Thomas & Polly was Born in Dover August ye 17th 1795.

Nabby Hanson Daughter of Thomas Hanson by his Wife Polly was born in Dover May 20th 1797

Elizabeth Hanson Daughter of Thomas Hanson By his Wife Polly was born in Dover March the 17th 1799.

  Bro^t to Record Sep^t 10th 1804 &
  Recorded by   Dominicus Hanson   T. Clerk

Jane Margaret Andrews Daughter of George & Ann Sinclair Andrews Born in Dover Feby 2nd 1800.

Edmund Charles Andrews Son of D^o Born in Dover Septr 5th 1802.

Elizabeth Neil Andrews Daughter of D^o Born in Dover May 8th 1804.

William Neil Andrews Son of George & Ann Andrews born in Dover May 16th 1806.

 Recorded by   Doms Hanson

William Brown Born in Salisbury March 28th 1752.

Abigail Brown Wife of Wm Brown Born in Haverhill July 4th 1760. Married April 1778.

Births of their Children.

Amos Brown Son of Wm & Abigail Brown born in Dover the 6th July 1779.

Lydia Brown Daughter of d° born ye 26th Apl 1781.

John Brown Son of D° born in Dover 30th June 1783.

Alice Brown Daughter of D° born 13th July 1785.

William Brown Son of D° born 10th Jany 1788.

Jeremiah Brown Son of D° born 28th Feby 1791.

Moses Brown Son of D° born 17th Sept. 1793.

Anna Brown Daughter of D° born 19th May 1796

David Sands Brown Son of d° born 27th July 1800

Abigail Brown Daughter of D° born 5th Apl 1803

 Recorded by   Dominicus Hanson, T. Clerk

Stephen Hanson Son of Stephen Hanson Born in Dover the 18th of the 11th month 1774

Lydia Brown Daughter of Wm & Abigail Brown Born in Dover 26th 4th Month 1781

Married 25th of the 5th month 1797

Children's Births.

Ivory Hanson Son of Stephen & Lydia Born In Dover 16th of the 7th month 1798

Parmela Hanson Daughter of D° Born in Dover 23d of the 3d Month 1801

Mary Ann Hanson Daughter of D° Born in Dover 2d of the 2nd Month 1803.

Record from the Friends Monthly Meeting

 1806 Augt 22.—Recorded by   Doms Hanson, T. Clk.

Lydia Rotch Hanson Daughter of D° Born in Dover 30th 3d month 1808

William Rotch son of D° Born in Dover 4th month 26th 1810

 Recorded by   Dom Hanson T Clk.

Ivory Hanson Son of Stephen & Lydia Hanson Drowned in Cochecho River Opposite the Landing the 25th of the 6th Month 1809.

Albert Franklin Hanson Son of Stephen & Lydia Hanson Born in Dover 10th Mo 11th 1813

*Mary Ann Died 11 M" 24 day 1816

Recorded by   D. Hanson   T. Clerk.

Mary Hanson Consort of Stephen Hanson Departed This life June 1st 1812.

Stephen Hanson Consort of Mary Hanson Departed this Life November 14th 1812.

Richard F. Chesley and Nancy Twombly was Joined in Marriage By the Revd Joseph Haven of Rochester 29th January 1806.

Elizabeth Chesley Daughter of Richd & Nancy Chesley Born in Dover Novr 21st 1806

Recorded by   Doms Hanson, T. Clk.

Daniel Meserve Durrell Esqr and Elizabeth Wentworth Were Married at Somersworth By the Revd Parson Thurston June 1st 1800.

Births of D. M. Durell's Children by his Wife Elizabeth, Viz.

Mary Jane, born February 24th 1801.

Sarah Adeline Durell Born April 19th 1802.

Elizabeth Salter Durell Born Octr 25th 1803.

Nicholas Saint John Durell Born Sept 7th 1805.

Charles James Fox Durell Born April 28th 1807.

Recorded By Dominicus Hanson T. Clerk, Sept 26th 1807

Births of the Children of Willm K. Atkinson by His Wife Abigail Atkinson.

Charlotte King Atkinson Daughter of Wm & abigail Atkinson Born in Dover Feby 26th 1790.

Susanna Sparhawk Atkinson Daughter of Do Born in Dover January 30th 1792.

Theodore Atkinson Son of Do Born in Dover Feby 5th 1794.

Frances Atkinson Daughter of Do Born in Dover June 21st 1797.

John Pickering Atkinson Son of Do Born in Dover December 15th 1800.

William King Atkinson Son of Do Born in Dover March 22nd 1807.

Brought to Record 26th Sept [——] &

Recorded by   Dominicus Hanson, Town Clerk.

Ezekiel Hayes Born in Dover Feby 19th 1746.

Hannah Money Born February 4th 1752.

---

*This death record is interlined, without doubt by some other town clerk, as Dominicus Hanson had ceased to be town clerk at this time.—[Ed.

BIRTHS AND MARRIAGES, 1693-1838.

Ezekiel Hayes and Hannah Mooney Were Jioned in Marriage June 15th 1769.

Their Children.

Betsey Hayes Daughter of Ezekiel & Hannah Hayes Born in Dover Jany 10th 1775.

Samuel W. Hayes Son of Ezek^l & Hannah Hayes Born in Dover April 23^d 1777

Mary Hayes Daughter of D^o Born in Dover Sep^t 6, 1779.

Ezekiel Hayes Junr Son of D^o Born in Dover March 25th 1783.

Joseph M Hayes Son of Ditt^o Born in Dover July 22nd 1786

Herculese M Hayes Son of D^o Born in Dover May 4th 1790

Mary Hayes Daughter of D^o Died Decr 1st 1800

Betsey Hayes Died Augt 1801

Hannah Hayes Died Jany 24th 1804

Brought to Record Jany 12th and Recorded by
 Dominicus Hanson   T Clerk

Thomas Varney Son of Thomas Varney of Rochester Born in Rochester in the year 1779 June 29th

Hannah Long Born In Newbury Port 1786 Jany 31st

Thomas Varney and Hannah Long, were Joined in Marriage in Dover by the Revd Mr Gray 1805, March 7th

Their Children.

Samuel Varney Son of Thomas & Hannah Varney Born in Dover July 1st 1806.

Sarah Ann Varney Daughter of Thom^s & Hannah Varney Born in Dover January 17th 1808.

Brought to Record April 2nd 1808 and Recorded,
 By Dominicus Hanson   Town Clerk.

John Calef Son of Co^l James Calef & Sally Calef, Born in Dover November 5th 1782.

Mary Calef Danghter of James & Sally Calef, Born in Dover June 14th 1789.

Zachariah Z Calef Son of James & Sally Born in Dover, October 17th 1791.

Brought to Record the 24th of May 1808, &

Recorded by   Dominicus Hanson,   T. Clerk.

Horace Parmale was Born August 20th 1780.

Polly Parmale was Born February the 29th 1780

Horace & Polly Parmale Were Joined in Marriage Octr 27th 1803

Horace Gerrish Parmale Son of Horace & Polly Parmale Was Born Octr 12th 1806.

  Recorded by   Dominicus Hanson T Clerk.

Horace G. Parmale Son of Horace & Polly Died in Dover Novr 2^d 1807.

Jesse Shearman Parmale Son of D^o D^o Born in Dover July 23rd 1809.

Horace age 1 y^r 20 days

John Hanson Born in Dover Jany 27th 1745

Marcy Hanson Wife of John, Born in Dover Decr 7th 1759

  their Children as Follows to Witt.

John Hanson Son of John Hanson Born in Dover March ye 18th 1787.

Samuel Hanson Son of D^o Born in Dover May 24th 1789

Phebe Hanson Daughter of D^o Born in Dover Jany 21st 1793.

 Brought to Record 1809 Jany 11th 1 O. Clock afternoon & paid

  Recorded by   Dominicus Hanson Town Clerk

           Births.

Capt William Blake Junr Son of Wm Blake Born in Barrington May ye 11th 1777.

Elizabeth Blake Wife of Wm Blake Born in Dover May ye 5th 1762.

Elizabeth Blake Daughter of W^m & Elizabeth Born in Dover October 3^d 1800.

Nabby Blake Born in Dover & Daughter of D^o Sept 8th 1803

Lydia Ham Blake Daughter of D^o born in Dover August 4th 1806.

Mary Gage Daughter of Joseph Gage & Polly his wife Born in Dover March 9th 1799.

 Received of Capt Blake to Record Octr 31st 1809 and

  Recorded By   Dominicus Hanson Town Clerk.

  Births & Deaths of Doct^r Kittredge & Family.

Doctor Jacob Kittredge was Born in Andover the 15th of March 1761—and Died July 15th 1807 Aged 46 years.

   The Births and Deaths of his Children.

First Child, Son of Jacob and Abigail his Wife, John, & Born in Dover Feby 5th and Died Feby 22^d 1792.

John Son of Jacob & abigail Born in Dover April 25th 1793.

Jacob Son of D^o & D^o Born in Dover oct^r 1st 1794.

Thomas Wallingford Son of D^o Born in Dover August 1st 1796

Hannah Daughter of D^o Born in Dover June 21st 1798

George Washington son of Ditt^o Born in Dover February 15th 1800.

William Wight Son of Jacob & Abigail Born in Dover October 6th 1801

    Rec'd For Record 27th May 1810
    Recorded By   Dominicus Hanson, T Clk.

Births of Mellen's Children Brought from page 96. [pages 62-3.]

Eliza Hovey Mellen Daughter of Henry & Martha Mellen Born in Dover June 17th 1802.

George Washington Frost Son of D" D" Born in Dover April 28th 1804.

William Pepperill Mellen Son of D" D" Born in Dover July 18th 1806.

    Brought to Record Jan'y 9th 1811, at 2 O.Clock and Recorded By
        Dominicus Hanson, T Clerk.

Births of the Children of Ephraim Bickford & Wife

Aaron Bickford son of Ephraim & Sarah Bickford Born in Dover June the 29th 1773.

Deborah Bickford Daughter of Ditt" & D" Born in Dover December 9th 1774

Joseph Bickford son of D" D" Born in Dover Sept 14th 1776
Mary Bickford Daughter of D" & D" Born in Dover March 11th 1779
Hannah Bickford Daughter Born in Dover February 14th 1781
Sarah Bickford Daughter of D" D" Born in Dover July 14th 1783.
Ephraim Bickford Son of D" D" Born in Dover November 8th 1785
Susanna Bickford Daughter of D" D" Born in Dover Sept 8th 1788.
Thomas Bickford Son of D" & D° Born in Dover August 8th 1791.

    Brought to Record January 20th 1811 and Recorded by
        Dominicus Hanson T Clerk.

Births of the Children of Benjamin Kielle & Wife

Abigail Kielle Daughter of Benja Kielle Born in Dover November 13th 1790

William Kielle Son of Ditt" & D" Born in Dover May 25th 1794
John Kielle Son of D" & D" Born in Dover December y" 10th 1796
James Kielle Son of D" & D" Born in Dover Sept 11th 1801
Ivory Kielle Son of Benjamin & Keziah his wife Born in Dover May 1st 1804

    Recorded By   Dominicus Hanson, T. Clerk.

Births of the Children of Nicholas Peaslee by his Wife Hannah.

*Nicholas Peaslee Son of Nicholas & Hannah Born in Dover July 15th 1770

*Hannah Peaslee Daughter of Do Born in Dover July 5th 1786

Joseph Tibbits Peaslee Son of Do Born in Dover September 15th 1808

Benjamin Titcomb Peaslee Son of Do Born in Dover August 4th, 1810

John Noble Peaslee son of Do Do Born in Dover September 4th 1812

Recorded and Examined By

Dominicus Hanson T. Clk.

Children of Joseph & Mary Smith Born in Dover N. H.

Mary Emerson Smith, Born January 11th 1812.

Caroline Smith, born Novr 30th 1813.

Joseph Benknap Smith, born March 30th 1815

Thomas Elliot Smith, born January 13th 1817.

Recorded by request of Joseph Smith Esq. July 24th 1817

A. Peirce, Town Clerk.

Children of Jeremy & Hannah Young

Ezra Young, Born September 30th 1803

Wm Augustus Young, born Novr 28th 1805

Mary R. Young, born Feby 12th 1808

Timothy R. Young, born Nov. 19th 1810

Lydia D. Young, born July 26th 1815

Recorded by request of Jeremy Young January 3d 1818

A. Peirce, Town Clerk

Frances Ellen Young Born March 29th 1821

Jany 1830   J. Richardson Ck

Mary Ellen Hanson Daughter of Stephen & Lydia Hanson was born in Dover 12 Mo 23d 1818.

Recorded by request of said Stephen 26th April 1819

A. Peirce, Town Clerk.

---

*Here is an error in the record. The family record in the Peaslee Bible reads: "Nicholas Peaslee married to Hannah Titcomb, Oct. 8th, 1807.
Nicholas Peaslee, born July 15th, 1770.
Hannah (Titcomb) Peaslee, born July 5th, 1786.
Joseph Tibbetts Peaslee, born Sept. 15th, 1808.
Benjamin Titcomb Peaslee, born Aug. 4th, 1810.
John Noble Peaslee, born Sept. 4th, 1812.
Elizabeth Austin Peaslee, born Aug. 15, 1814.
Mary Noble Peaslee, born January 26th, 1817.
Hannah Peaslee, deceased Feb. 8, 1817.
Nicholas Peaslee married Anna Hall, Dec. 28, 1820, aged 21 years, April 4th, 1820.
Nicholas Peaslee deceased Sept. 16, 1826, aged 56 years.
Ann Peaslee deceased October the [——] 1880, aged 31 years."

From another family record in the same Bible it appears that Nicholas Peaslee was son of Amos and Elizabeth (Tibbetts) (Austin) Peaslee, of Dover, N. H. —[ED.

Children of Andrew & Abigail Smith Peirce, Born in Dover.
Rebecca Elizabeth Wheeler Peirce born Decr 31, 1809
Abigail Smith Peirce born July 9th 1811
Mary Ann Peirce born April 7th 1813 & Died Augt 25th 1814
Clarissa Wheeler Peirce born Novr 7, 1814
Lydia Peirce born 5th Jany 1817.
Joseph Andrew Peirce born Decr 18th 1818
    A true Record
    March 1819   A. Peirce, Town Clerk

Children of Artemas Rogers & his wife Abigail, born in Dover.
William Harris Rogers born Jany 19th 1817
Abigail Ann Rogers born Jany 3^d 1819.
    Recorded by request of said Artemas Jany 23^d 1821
                             J. Richardson Town Clerk

Barnabas H. Palmer was Married to Betsy Haggens March 26th 1815 by Revd Hilliard at Berwick.

        Children of Barnabas H. and Betsy Palmer
Susan Haggens Palmer born Jany 15th 1816
Mary Elizabeth Palmer born July 29th 1817
Susan Hamilton Palmer born Jany 6th 1819
Edmund Haggins Palmer born July 22^d 1821
    Recorded by request of said Palmer 1822 Jany 30th
            Att.   J. Richardson Town Clerk

Children of Nathaniel and Elizabeth Young, born in Dover.
John K. Young, born March 22^d 1802
Thomas J. Young, born Augt 2^d 1804
Fordyce R. Young, born July 10th 1806
Effalina Emmela Young, born Feby 26th 1809
Elizabeth Jane Young, born May 7th 1812
Roxary Augusta Young, born April 19th 1819
    Recorded by request of N. Young, March 15th 1823
            Att.   J. Richardson Town Clk.

Mary Ann Paul, daughter of Ambros & Abigail Paul, Born March 30th 1823.
    May 1823. Recorded by request of s^d Paul
                           J. Richardson Town Clerk

James Richardson born in Woburn Mass. July 7th 1779.
Tammy Tibbets born in Dover N. H. November 4th 1783.

BIRTHS AND MARRIAGES, 1693-1838.

James Richardson and Tammy Tibbets were married in Dover by the Rev'd C. Shearman Dec. 21^t 1808.

Their Children.

Charlotte King Atkinson, born Octr 12th 1809.
Augustus, born Feby 14th 1811.
John Tibbets, born Dec. 7th 1813.
James, born Octr 17th 1816.
Lydia Ann, born March 20th 1821.

Recorded July 26th 1823 by   J Richardson   Town Clerk

Thomas Lenoard Smith son of Lenoard & Sarah Smith, born April 29th 1820.

Recorded by request.   J. Richardson   Town Clk.

Alexander Crawford son of Alexander & Lucy Crawford born April 8th 1825

Recorded by request May 26th 1825

J. Richardson   Town Clk.

Children of Joseph & Mary Smith born in Dover N. H.
Sophia Smith born August 7th 1819
Susanah Smith born July 14th 1821
Nathaniel Emerson Smith born April 14th 1823
Catherine Smith born Sep^t 16th 1824

Recorded by request of Joseph Smith esq. Dec. 19th 1825

J. Richardson   Town Clerk

Children of Joseph & Ann Whittier born in Dover N. H.
Samuel Hall Locke Whittier born Nov. 20th 1818
Joseph Albert Whittier born July 6th 1820
Adaline Mendum Whittier born April 14th 1822
Lydia Ann Whittier born April 7th 1824

Rec^d by request of Joseph Whittier Jany 2^d 1826.

J. Richardson   Town Clk.

Child of James N. & Hannah Hadley born in Dover.
David F. Hadley born Oct. 7th 1824.

Recorded by request of J. Hadley Jany 27th 1826.

J. Richardson   Town Clerk

Francis Peter Scanlan Son of Phillip Scanlan & his wife Ann, Born in Dover Jany 31^t 1826.

Recorded by the request of P. Scanlan, May 1827.

Att.   J. Richardson   Town Clerk

Nathaniel Whittier Ela, born Feby 5th 1766.
Esther Emerson, born April 22^d 1766.

BIRTHS AND MARRIAGES, 1693-1838.   73

Nath¹ W. Ela & Esther Emerson were Married Nov. 7th 1790
                    Their Children.

Nathaniel   Ela born Nov. 8th 1791.
George   "   born July 11th 1793.
Susanna   "   born June 19th 1795.
Caroline   "   born March 13th 1797, died Sept 16th 1798.
Caroline 2ᵈ "   born Jany 10th 1799, died Nov. 23ᵈ 1801.
John Furnald "   born Jany 20th 1801.
Esther   "   born Feby 2ᵈ 1803.
Charles   "   born Dec. 26th 1804, died Nov. 16th 1807.
Benjamin   "   born April 23ᵈ 1807.
Ruth   "   born Jany 4th 1809.
Charles 2ᵈ   "   born Feby 28th 1811.

Esther Ela wife of Nath¹ W. Ela, Died Feby 28th 1826.
    Recorded by request of N. W. Ela April 6th 1826.
                          J. Richardson   Town Clk.

Andrew Quincy Hadley son of James N. & Hannah Hadley born Octʳ 1ᵗ 1826.
    Recorded by request of Mrs. Hadley July 30th 1827.
                          J. Richardson   Town Clerk.

John Smith born Nov. 14th 1784
Sarah Locke "   July 27th 1783
        Children of John Smith by his wife Sarah.

John   Smith Jun born Sept. 21ᵗ 1810
George   "   born Jany 16th 1813
Sarah Ann   "   born April 3ᵈ 1815
Hamden Sidney   "   born July 30th 1818
Susan Hodgdon   "   born March 17th 1820
Susan Watkins   "   born Feby 20th 1823
Mary Jane   "   born Jany 3ᵈ 1826

    Recorded by request of J. Smith April 21ᵗ 1826.
                          J. Richardson, Town Clk.

Benjamin Wiggin born in Stratham January 27th 1792.
Mary wife of said Benjamin born in Stratham January 18th 1797
        Children of said Benjamin & *Mary.

Mary H.   Wiggin born in Dover March 13th 1817.
Nancy D.   "   born "   "   July 29th 1819.
Benjamin Horace   "   born "   "   April 19th 1822.
Zelia   "   born "   "   Augt 17th 1824.
Norris Dow   "   "   "   "   Augt 9th 1827.

    Recorded by the request of Benjᵃ Wiggin Sept 26th 1826.
                          J. Richardson   Town Clerk

*Name is indistinct and bears marks of attempted erasure.

Martha Jane Wiggin born February 1st 1830
Ellen Frances Wiggin born January 16th 1833
  Recorded by Request of Benjamin Wiggin Sept. 16, 1836
        Charles Young Town Clerk

George Piper was born in Stratham January 23d 1797.
Sally Fisher Smith was born in Dover February 13th 1801.
George Piper & Sally Fisher Smith were Married by Revd Joseph W. Clary in Dover July 11th 1822.

     Their Children.

Sarah Bell Piper born in Dover May 9th 1823
Ellen Clark " " " " April 13th 1825
Mary Smith " " " " Oct° 30th 1827
  Recorded March 31t 1829, by request of G. Piper
        J. Richardson, Town Ck.

 Ages of the Children of Jesse & Abigail Varney, born in Dover.

Mary Ann Boardman Varney born May 24th 1810
Theodore Varney   " Oct° 20th 1813
Jesse Varney Jun.   " May 16th 1816
Samuel Bragg Varney   " Dec. 28th 1818
Charles Green Varney   " January 16th 1822
  Recorded April 8th 1829 by the request of Jesse Varney.
        J. Richardson, Town Ck.

Isaac Dollive Street, son of John F. & Ellen Street, born in Dover January 13th 1829.
  Recorded by request. J. Richardson, Town Ck.

Mary Scanlan, daughter of Philip and Ann Scanlan, born in Dover October 18th 1827.
  Recod by request of P. Scanlan May 13th 1829.
        J. Richardson, Town Ck.

Margaret Stuart born June 21t 1827
Ann Stuart born February 11th 1829 daughters of William & Ann Stuart.
  Recorded by request of W. Stuart May 13th 1829
        J. Richardson, Town Ck.

Willard Stevens son of Jacob & Olive Stevens, born June 5th 1827.
Olive Stevens, daughter of Jacob & Olive Stevens born Dec. 15th 1828.
  Recorded June 18th 1829 per request of J. Stevens
        J. Richardson, Town Ck.

Children of Mathew and Mary Bridge born in Dover N. H.
Samuel Ingersoll Bridge born July 17th 1827
Mathew Harrington Bridge born Dec. 13th 1828.
   Recorded Sept 23d 1829 per request.
                           J. Richardson, Town Ck.
Teresa Scanlan, daughter of Phillip & Ann Scanlan, Born in Dover Augt 27th 1829
   Recd by request, Nov. 23d 1829. J. Richardson, Town Ck.
Children of Joseph Hanson 3d and his Wife Abigail, Born in Dover (viz.)
   Clarissa Jane Hanson, born Augt 24th 1828
   Joseph Hanson   " Feby 24th 1830.
   Recorded Feby 1830 by request of J. Hanson
   Att.   J. Richardson, Town Ck.
James Alpha Stevens son of Alpha Stevens by his wife Sarah born in Dover January 5th 1831
   Recorded Dec. 31t 1831, by request of Mr Stevens
   Att.   J. Richardson, Town Ck.
George Graham Griffin and Olive Minnort Griffin children of William H. Griffin by his wife Olive, born in Dover.
George Graham, born Octr 15th, 1813
Olive Minnort, born Nov. 13th 1815.
   Recd Dec. 31t 1831 by request of Wm H. Griffin.
   Att.   J. Richardson, Town Ck.
Asa Alford Tufts (son of Asa & Martha Tufts) was born in Dover Nov. 13th 1798.
Hannah Phillips Gilman (daughter of John P. & Elizabeth Gilman) was born in Dover, March 22d 1800.
Asa A. Tufts & Hannah P. Gilman were Married by Revd Joseph W. Clary Nov. 13th 1820.
      Names of their children born in Dover.
Charles Augustus, born Nov. 6th 1821.
John Wheeler, born May 12th 1825.
Ellen Foster, born Feby 19th 1828.
Caroline, Gilman born Jany 19th 1832.
   Recorded Jany 28th 1832 by request of Asa A. Tufts—By
                           J. Richardson, Town Clerk
Catherine Elizabeth, daughter of Robert McKenley and Sarah his wife, born in Dover May 4th 1831.
   Recorded by the request of Mrs Smith
   Att.   J. Richardson, Town Clk.

Aroet Lucius Little son of Jonathan H. Hale & Olive Hale, Born in Dover May 18th 1828

 Rec'd by the request of Mr Hale.

 Att.   J. Richardson, Town Clk.

Mary Woodman, daughter of John and Elizabeth B. Chadwick, Born in Dover August 1st 1831.

 Recorded by request of Mr Chadwick.

 Att.   J. Richardson Town Clk.

Births of Samuel Abbot's children by his wife Jane, born in Dover N. H.

Mary Ann, born Agust 22d 1814

John Sullivan, born January 20th 1816.

 Rec'd Sept 3d 1834, by the request of Mr Abbot

 Att.   J. Richardson, Town Clerk

Births of John Smiley's children by his wife Rhodia M. born in Dover.

Ellen Marria Smiley born August 16th 1828.

Susan Gilgrist " " September 17th 1829.

Ephraim Haley " " October 17th 1830.

John Sam " " July 3d 1832.

Josiah Haley " " December 6th 1833 and Departed this Life Augt 29th 1834.

 Recorded by the request of Mr Smiley Jany 8th 1835

 Att.   J. Richardson Town Clerk

Nathaniel Gookin, Son of John & Elizabeth B. Chadwick born in Dover, Feby 5th 1834.

 Recorded by request of Mr Chadwick, April 8th 1835.

 Att.   J. Richardson Town Clk.

William Francis McDavitt, Son of William and Eminty McDavitt, Born Feby 13th 1834.

Ann McDavitt Born August 29th 1835.

 Recorded by request of Mr W. McDavitt Sept. 16th 1835.

          J. Richardson, Town Clerk

James B. Varney Born July 17th 1784.

Sarah B. Riley " Feby 22d 1787.

 Married May 14th 1812.

     Their Children.

Abigail Ann Varney Born March 29th 1813.

Mary Riley "   " Octo 30th 1815.

James Varney   " July 14th 1817.

John Riley Varney " March 26th 1819.

Sarah B. "   " May 4th 1821.

Moses Lafayett Varney [born] August 4th 1823.
Mercy Matilda   "   "   Augt 1^t 1826.
Charlotte Augusta Varney   "   Dec. 5th 1828.
    Recorded by the request of J. B. Varney, Feby 8th 1836.
                               J. Richardson, Town Clk.

John Boardman Morse son of Thomas G. and Eliza Jane Morse Born in Dover April 9th 1835.
    Recorded by request of Mr. Thomas G. Morse, May 9th 1836.
    Att.   Charles Young   Town Clerk

{ Seal } Circuit Court of the United States.
New Hampshire, SS.   May Term 1832.
    I hereby certify that Thomas Hough has by order of Court been admitted to take and has taken the oath of allegiance as a naturalized citizen of the United States. In testimony whereof I have hereto set my hand and affixed the seal of the said Court this eighth day of May A. D. 1832.
                              Charles W. Cutter,   Clerk.
    Received and Recorded November 12, 1836.
    Ex^d by   Ch^s Young   Town Clk.

George Washington Whitehouse born Saturday August 3, 1822
Charles Carroll Whitehouse born Friday May 20, 1825
Laura Ann Whitehouse born Thursday November 15, 1827
Walter Scott Whitehouse born Thursday August 11, 1836.
Children of George L. and Liberty N. Whitehouse now resident in
    Dover N. H.—November 1836.
    Received Nov. 30, 1836.
    Attest   Charles Young   Town Clerk

John Brown was born June 30, 1783
Mary Thornton Brown was born July 3rd 1788
    Married Septr 1806.
                    Their Children
William Henry Brown was born Jany. 6, 1810.
George Thornton Brown was born April 6th 1812.
Nathaniel Howland Brown was born May 24th 1815.
Edward Brown was born May 26, 1817.
Walter Brown was born Decr 16, 1820.
John R. Brown was born May 31, 1823.
David S. Brown was born May 16, 1827.
Mary Anna Brown was born Novr 15, 1831.
    Received from Edward Brown July 25, 1837.
    Recorded and Examined by   Charles Young   Town Clerk.

John Wesley Place son of Harrel and Eliza Place born in Dover January 3d 1838.

Recorded by request of Mr. Harrel Place February 24, 1838 by
Charles Young Town Clerk

At A meetting of the Select men in Douer the 20th of may 1723 ordered that 2 Schoolmasters be Procured for the Towne of Douer for the year Ensuing and that ther Sallery Exceed not £30 Payment a Peece and to attend the Directtions of the Select men for the Seruis of the Towne in Equill Propotion

Test   Thomas Tebbets   Towne Clark

At the Same time mr Sullefund Exseps to Sarue the Towne as abouesd as Scoole master three months Sertin and begines his Seruis ye 21th Day of may 1723 and also the Sd Sullefund Promesed the Select men if he Left them Soonner he woold giue them a month notis to Prouide them Selues with a nother and the Select men was also to giue him a month notis if they Dislikd him

Test   Thomas [Tebbets] Toune Clark

Dover September Six One Thousand Seven Hundred Seventy Six here followeth The Record of Marriages as Delivered the Town Clerk by Minesters & Justices in Consequence of a Law made by the general Court this Present year requiring them So to Do

Thomas Clements & Alice Powers both of Dover were Married Sepr 4th 1776 by Jer. Belknap

Examined Sepr 6 1776   Thos Wk Waldron Town Clerk

Samuel Furber of Rochester & Mary Emerson of Dover were Married Sepr 12th 1776 by Jer. Belknap

Examined Sepr 14th 1776   Thos Wx Waldron Town Clerk

Gershom Lord & Esther Hanson were Married Sepr 30th 1776 by J. Belknap

Examined Octr 1st 1776   Thos Wk Waldron Town Clerk

Aaron Davis of Madbury & Susanna Otis were Married Novr 7th 1776 by Jer. Belknap

Exd   Thos Wk Waldron Town Clerk

Josiah Folsom of Rochester & Hannah Cushing were married Novr 18th 1776 by Jeremiah Belknap

Exd   Thos Wk Waldron T Clk.

Simeon Brock of Berwick & Judeth Bunker were Married Decr 2d 1776 by Jer. Belknap   Exd By Thos Wk Waldron T Clk.

Thos Clark of Portsmo & Esther Tibbets were Married Decr 5 1776 By Jer. Belknap   Exd By Thos Wk Waldron T Clk.

Capt Thos Peirce of Portsm^o & Kezia Wentworth were Married Decr 11th 1776 By Jer. Belknap

Ex^d By Thos W^k Waldron T Clk.

A List of Marriages by Jeremy Belknap Minester of Dover, duly returned to the late Town Clerk & now first recorded, December 1, 1785.

Anno Dom
1777

Jany 13, Joseph Ricker of Somersworth & Esther Bunker.
Feb 11, Caleb Horn & Molly Randel both of Somersworth.
20, Samuel Waldron & Hannah Gage.
April 1, Benjamin Ham of Rochester & Mary Waldron.
8, James Chesley & Lydia Horn.
26, James Young & Susanna Loyns.
June 12, James Hanson & Mary Evans.
July 9, Moses Medar jun^r of Durham & Jane Otis of Barrington.
12, Morris Hurn & Hannah Jose both of Portsmouth.
Augt 28, Andrew Bickford of Durham & Rebecca Canney.
Sepr 28, Samuel Bodge of Lee & Rebecca Gear of Barrington.
Oct^o 6, Jeremiah Garland of Chichester & Lydia Cook.
13, John Riley & Mary Hanson.
Decr 4, John Walker of Rochester & Hannah Emerson.
31, Jonathan Whitehouse & Mehetabel Seavey.

A D 1778

Jany 3, Samuel Tuttle & Molly Roberts.
15, Philip Chesley jun^r of Durham & Abigail Hayes of Madbury.
15, Samuel Howard & Sarah Hanson.
Feb 12, Thomas Cushing & Anna Tuttle.
24, Josiah George of Leavit's town & Elisabeth Brown.
March 8, Michael Reade & Deborah Horn.
23, Elijah Clements of Somersworth & Mary Waldron.
24, Benjamin Field of Falmouth & Hannah Hanson.
April 9, James Bishop & Elisabeth Dwyer both of Portsmouth.
23, William Brown & Abigail Peaslee.
May 7, Reuben Twomly of Madbury & Anna Twomly.
14, Jacob Chadwick of Somersworth & Sarah Cromwell.
Augt 6, William McNeal of Rochester & Mary Hartford.
Novr 3, Hatevil Leighton & Abigail Nock.
29, Thomas Leathers jun^r & Elisabeth Medar both of Durham.

A D 1778.
Dec* 8, Jeremiah Foss & Abra Hayes both of Barrington.
8, John Kimbal & Lydia Chesley.
10, John Hanson & Abigail Scagel.
21, Silas Hoag of Newtown & Mary Morrill.
22, John Philpot & Kezia Wentworth both of Somersworth.
28, John Nason & Rebecca Perkins.
30, Ezra Green & Susanna Hayes.

A D 1779.
Jany 28, John Aken of Barrington & Hannah Brock of Madbury.
Feb 8, Samuel Tasker of Barrington & Sarah Tuttle.
11, Samuel Small of New Durham & Sarah Hanson.
March 4, Stephen Roberts & Mary Canney.
April 1, Ezra Young & Susanna Demerritt of Madbury.
16, William Waldron & Susanna Ham.
May 6, James Hayes of Barrington & Elizabeth Ham.
11, Jonathan Morrison of Rochester & Sarah Hartford.
July 14, William Larry & Mary Larry, both of Durham.
Augst 14, Thomas Footman & Susanna Gage.
Sepr 9, Samuel Wigglesworth & Mary Waldron.
9, Samuel Cook & Anna Daniels.
Oct 10, Robert Varney & Molly Gage.
25, Peirce Powers & Mary Wingate.
Novr 18, Ephraim Perkins & Mary Walker of Rochester.
18, Richard Philpot of Somersworth & Molly Clements.
22, John Davis & Deborah Tasker both of Madbury.
25, Elijah Varney & Sarah Roberts.
28, Eliphalet Mace of Pitch Hill & Abigail Underwood of Stratham.
Decr 2, Samuel Jefferds of Wells & Lois Storrs.

A D 1780.
Feby 1, Thomas Dame & Anna Medar both of Durham.
18, George Foss of Barrington & Lois Drew.
24, Seth Jacobs of Madbury & Phebe Tuttle.
May 25, Ebenezer Demerrit of Madbury & Elizabeth Young.
27, Sylvanus Tripe & Love Henderson.
June 20, James Bracket of Greenland & Lucy Gerrish.
July 6, Joseph Leavit of Wolfborough & Elizabeth Hodgdon.
20, Nathaniel Garland & Susanna Young both of Barrington.

BIRTHS AND MARRIAGES, 1693-1838.

Aug^t	3, Ebenezer Hall & Susanna Tibbetts both of Barrington.
Sep^r	21, Benjamin Church & Eunice Smith.
Oct	5, Ephraim Twomly & Abigail Wingate.
Nov	26, Robert Hanson & Patience Waldron, both of Barrington.
Dec^r	4, John Murray of Northwood & Rose Canney.
	17, Ephraim Leighton of the Gore & Olive Perkins.
	19, Joseph Runnells & Abigail Pinkham.
	19, Benjamin Foss of Rochester & Judeth Whitehouse.
	21, Thomas Wright Hale & Lydia Drew both of Barrington.

A D 1781

Jan^y	22, John Garland & Mary Ham.
	31, Samuel Heard Horn & Hannah Vicker.
Feb^y	6, William Tuttle & Anna Pinkham.
	16, Jonathan Hanson & Alice Roberts.
March	15, Adam Perkins & Abigail Tibbetts.
May	2, John Titcomb & Sarah Ham.
July	24, Jonathan Davis & Hannah Gerrish.
Sep^r	16, Francis Winklay jun^r of Barrington & Sarah Libbey.
	16, Disco Wentworth & Anna Libbey.
	24, John Bartlet & Esther Clark.
Oct	25, Fabian Holden & Elisabeth Foss.
	31, George Ricker & Abigail Snell.

A D 1782.

Jan^y	17, Ichabod Cook & Joanna Hartford.
	17, George Roberts & Elisabeth Horn.
April	4, Abraham Hanson & Susanna Odiorne.
July	10, Jonathan Horn & Elisabeth Peaslee.
Aug^t	1, David Twomly & Sarah Garland.
	29, William Shannon & Eleanor Gerrish.
Sep^r	10, James Remick & Mary Kinsman.
	16, Paul Gerrish & Mary Dorset.
Oct	10, Jonathan Trickey & Lydia Pinkham.
October	20, Daniel Whitehouse & Elisabeth Canney.
Nov^r	18, Benjamin Bennett of the Gore & Elisabeth Bell.
Dec^r	16, Stephen Lee of Durham & Hannah Waldron.

A. D. 1783

March	18, Nathaniel Hayes & Elisabeth Bickford.
	24, John Bennett jun^r of New Durham & Lydia Gage.
June	29, Richard Canney & Deborah Emerson.

July	2, James Young of Rochester & Mary Kimball.
Sept^r	25, Ebenezer Cook & Hannah Brown.
Dec^r	14, Joseph Richardson & Sarah Hanson.
	25, Nathaniel Evans & Parnel Coffin.

A D 1784.

Jan^y	18, John Hayes & Mary Hanson.
Feb	19, Hanson Hodgdon & Mary Caldwell.
March	1, John Wingate of Rochester & Susanna Canney.
	6, Mark Ricker of Cogshall & Susa Bunker.
	7, Zoath Henderson & Elizabeth Henderson.
	14, David Twomly & Mary Horn.
	16, John Bragdon & Charity Howard.
April	11, Peter Cushing & Hannah Hanson.
June	10, Micah Emerson & Betty Meserve.
	24, Edmund Thompson of Durham & Abigail Emerson.
Sep^r	9, Thomas Burrows & Anna Garland.
	23, Israel Ham of Rochester & Mehetable Hayes of Madbury.
	30, Samuel Estes & Mary Kielle.
Nov^r	10, Nathaniel Cook & Bathsheba Horsam.
	11, William Ricker & Nancy Tripe.
	25, Joseph Drew & Sarah Conner.
	30, Daniel Twomly & Priscilla Nute.
Dec^r	5, James Smith of Durham & Eleaner Waldron.
	21, Daniel Randel & Rachel Hussey both of Somersworth.
	23, Thomas Young of New Durham & Thomasin Hayes.

A D 1785.

Jan^y	13, Joseph Stimson & Mary Crocket.
Feb	6, Amos Peaslee & Lydia Ham.
	17, Isaac Brown of Rochester & Lois Gage.
March	24, Ephraim Ham jun^r & Hannah Kielle.

Dover December 1, 1785. I do certify that the List of Marriages contained in this & the four preceeding Pages is a true Record of the Persons joined together in Marriage since the beginning of the year 1777, by me

         Jeremy Belknap, Minister of Dover.

The foregoing Returns were formerly made to the former Clerk but not Recorded Therefore it has been Entered as above by the Reverend Mr. Belknap & Examined by John B^m Hanson Town Clerk

 A Return of Marriages given in by the Reverand Jeremy Belknap are as follows.

1785
September 13, Stephen Nason & Mary Brown, Dover.
Novr 7 1785 Benjamin Roberts, Rochester, & Sarah Stevens, Dover.
Novr 13, Amos Cogswell & Lydia Wallingsford, Dover.
Decr 11, Richard Waldron J^r & Sarah Titcomb, Dover.
    Recorded By   John B^m Hanson   Town Clerk
Jany 8th 1786 Daniel Cushing & Thomasin Hayes, Dover.
   19   " Solomon Lowd & Sarah Heard, Dover.
1788
Dec   7th John P. Gilman and Elizabeth Hanson (Daughter of Humphrey & Joanna Hanson) Married.—

1790 May 4th Sarah Gilman their Daughter, Born.

1794 June 20th Eliza Gilman Daughter of John Phillips and Eliza Gilman, Born.

Mary Ann Gilman Daughter of John Phillips and Eliza Gilman, Born in Dover August 22nd 1797.

Joanna Gilman Daughter of John & Eliza Gilman, Born in Dover March 22nd 1800. .

This is to Certify to the Clerk of the Town of Dover, That the following Named Persons were Married in the Meetings of the Society of Friends in Dover and Kittery and at the dates against their names.

Ebenezer Jenkins of New Durham and Hope Varney of Dover, Married at Dover 25th of 4th M^o 1792.

James Varney of Dover and Sarah Allen of Kittery, Married at Kittery 3^d of 1st M^o 1793.

Cyrus Beede of Sandwich and Judith Varney of Dover, Married at Dover 27th of 3^d M^o 1793.

Moses Hanson and Sarah Varney both of Dover, Married at Dover 6th of 11th M^o 1793.

Samuel Varney of Berwick and Mary Hussey of Somersworth, Married at Dover 25th of 12th M^o 1793.

                            Dover the 8th of 3^d M^o 1794.

Agreeable to an Act of the General Court of this State, the above is Certifyed by me the Subscriber, as Clerk of the Meeting of Friends in Dover.
                                  Stephen Sawyer

Marriage was Administered by and between Jacob Wentworth and Martha Heard the Eighth day of Septr 1794.
                          by Levi Dearborn   Jus. Peace
                          Nathe^l Cooper   Town Clerk

BIRTHS AND MARRIAGES, 1693-1838.

Nicholas Meader & Susanna York of this Town were married by the Revd Robert Gray August 1st 1798.

A List of Marriages Brought by the Revd Mr Caleb H. Shearman since his Admission in this Parish in Dover May the 6th 1807.

1807

May [—] Mr Jon^a Robinson of Dover & Miss Nancy Brown of Deerfield.

July 20th Capt William Twombley & Miss Lydia Horn Both of Dover.

July 27th Mr George Foss and Miss Alice Holland Both of Dover.

Augt 18th Mr James Twombley and Miss Hannah Reynolds Both of Dover.

Octr 1st Mr Jedediah Wentworth and Miss Betsey Hanson.

Octr 8th Mr Nicholas Peaslee & Miss Hannah Titcomb Both of Dover.

Octr 28th Mr James Ladd & Miss Sellars of Portsmouth.

Novr 4th Mr Edward Jerrill, Boscawan, and Miss Abigail Kimball, Dover.

12 Mr Nehemiah Cram to Mrs Hannah Ham both of Dover.

26 Mr Reuben Webster to Miss Betsey Eliot both of Dover.
Mr James Durant to Miss Esther Tuttle both of Dover.
Mr Robert Spurling of Madbury to Miss Tamy Drew of Dover.

Decr 13 Mr John Varney to Miss Mary Varney both of Dover.

14 Mr Jeremiah Banks to Mrs Eliza Chase of Dover.

17 Mr Saml Blake to Miss Sally T. Swazey both of Dover.

1808

Jany 11 Mr George Pendexter to Miss Nabby Titcomb of Dover.

Ap^l 10 Mr John Tebbetts to Miss Polly Bodge Both Dover.

21 Mr Ezekiel Hayes to Mrs Lucy Hodgdon both of Dover.

Sepr 11 Mr James Brown of Somersworth to Miss Abigail Hanson of Dover.

Novr 1st Mr Job Hodgdon to Miss Hannah Bolo, Dover.

13 Mr William Coffin of Saco to Miss Susanna Tebbetts of Dover.

Decr 12th Mr Jesse Varney to Miss Abigail Bragg of Dover.

20 Mr Jeremiah Jordan to Miss Martha Flood of Portsmouth.

21 Mr James Richardson to Miss Tammy Tebbets both of Dover.

1809
Jany 3^d Mr James Kielle to Miss Hannah Cushing, Dover.
Feby 12 Mr William Clements to Miss Nancy Tripe, Dover.
       26 Mr Nathl Hilton of Wells, Massachusetts, to Miss Joanna Chase of Dover.
March 13 Mr William Kimball to Miss Tammy Tebbetts both of this Town.
       30 Mr Moses Eliot to Miss Martha Tuttle.
May   14 Mr Benjamin Horn to Miss Hannah Watson both of Dover.
Septr 10 Mr William Blake to Miss Abigail Libbey of Dover.
Oct^r   8 Mr Robert Perkins to Miss Relief Earl of Dover.
           Mr Joshua Nute to Miss Hannah Chick.
Novr 16 Mr James Twombly to Miss Lucy Mann both of Dover.
Decr 14 Mr Daniel Watson to Mrs Polly Walbridge both of Dover.

The foregoing minutes were handed to me before the March meeting 1810 by Mr Shearman.

    Exam^d By   Dominicus Hanson

1810
March 5th Mr John Smith to Miss Sally Lock both of this Town.
       22^d Mr Plato Waldron, Dover, to Miss Betsey Cole, Somersworth.
       24   Mr Benj^a Carter of Dover to Miss Mehitable Lapish of Durham.
July   3^d Doct^r Jon^a Greeley of Dover to Miss Susan Richardson of Durham.
        9   Mr John Jenkins of Milton to Miss Nancy Patten of Dover.
       16   Mr Jon^a Young to Miss Nabby Coffin both of this Town.
1810
Aug^t   2^d Mr John G. Tebbetts to Miss Elizabeth Smith both of this Town.
       21   Mr John Libbey Junr of Durham to Miss Hannah Wells of Dover.
Sepr 27   Mr William Taylor to Miss Sally Phillips Gilman both of Dover.
Nov.   22   Mr Seth S. Walker of Dover to Miss Sarah Smith of Durham.
       25   Mr Daniel Ham to Miss Sarah Varney both of Dover.
Dec^r   2^d Mr Robert Rogers to Miss Rebecca Patten both of this Town.

   12 Capt Benjamin Brown of Moultonboro to Mrs Polly Libbey of this town.

   15 Mr Otis Tuttle to Mrs Hannah Footman Both of Dover.

1811
Jany 27 Mr William Titcomb of Dover to Miss Eunice Whitehouse of Somersworth.

   30 Mr Joseph W. March of Portsmouth to Miss Susan S. Atkinson of Dover.

These minutes were handed to me by Mr Shearman March 9th 1811 to be Recorded.

              Dominicus Hanson.
  Examined By   Dominicus Hanson, Town Clerk.

1812 Decr 31st Philemon Chandler & Abigail Nute both of Dover Were Joined in Marriage at Portsmouth by the Revd Mr Parker.

Joseph Socrates Chandler son of Philemon & Abigail Born in Dover October 7th 1813.

  Recorded & Exam^d by   Dom^s Hanson, T. Clerk.

MARRIAGES.

1816-1838.

DOVER, N. H. RECORDS.

This may certify that Mr. Titus Ham and Miss Nancy Peirce were both married by me, as the law directs, this 30th day of Nov., 1816.

HARVEY MOREY,
Pr. of the Gospel in Rochester.

Copy of the original.
Attest.   A. PEIRCE, Town Clerk.

Strafford, SS. On this 28th day of January, A. D. 1820, then Edmund Downs and Hannah Watson personally appeared and was joined in marriage by me.

SAM'L KIMBALL, Jus. of the Peace.

Recorded from the original Feb'y 22d, 1820.

Ex'd by   A. PEIRCE, Town Clerk.

Strafford, SS. On this 27th day of June, 1822, Mr. Isaiah Varney and Miss Rhoda Ann B. Varney were lawfully joined in marriage.
Before me,

SAMUEL KIMBALL, Justice of the peace.

Rec'd from the original.

J. RICHARDSON, Town Clerk.

Strafford, SS. On this 28th day of November, 1822, Mr. Oliver Peavey and Mrs. Mary Hurd, both of Dover, were join'd in marriage according to the laws of the State of New Hampshire, by me.

SAMUEL KIMBALL, Justice Peace.

Recorded from original.

J. RICHARDSON, Town Clerk.

STATE OF NEW HAMPSHIRE.

Strafford County: On the 3d day of October, A. D., 1824, Mr.

MARRIAGES, 1816-1838.

Benjamin L. Colby and Miss Dorothy Colby were united in holy matrimony, agreeable to the laws of said state.

          A. PEIRCE, Jus. of the Peace.
 Recorded from the original.
 Att.   J. RICHARDSON, Town Clerk.

STATE OF NEW HAMPSHIRE.

Strafford County: On the 14th day of October, A. D. 1824, Mr. Augustus Stackpole of Somersworth and Miss Mary Courson of Dover were united in holy matrimony, agree'ble to the laws of said state.

          A. PEIRCE, Justice of the Peace.
 Recorded from original.
 Att.   J. RICHARDSON, Town Cl'k.

This certifies that the marriage between Mr. Samuel Howard of Dover, State of New Hampshire, and Miss Mary Ann H. Hanson of Thomaston, State of Maine, was celebrated by the Subscriber in Thomaston, this third day of March in the year of our Lord, one thousand eight hundred and twenty-five.

 Witness my hand,
          JOHN H. INGRAHAM.
 A true copy from the original.
 Att.   J. RICHARDSON, Town Clerk.

I, Jotham*Horten, Minister of the Gospel in the town of Dover, N. H., do certify that the following persons have been lawfully joined in holy matrimony by me, in the period included within the following dates, viz: from the first of July, 1824, to the first of June, 1825.

 1st Mr. Joseph L. Neal to Miss Susan Young, both of Dover.
 2d Mr. Andrew Tetherly to Miss Mary Nute, both of Dover.
 3d Mr. Samuel Kimball Jr. to Miss Hannah H. Tasker, both of Dover.
 4th Mr. Alexander Crawford to Miss Lucy Nichols, both of Dover
 5th Mr. Richard P. Smith of Waterborongh, to Miss Ann Plumer of Dover.
 6th Doct. Robert Woodbury of Barrington, to Miss Content Neal of Dover.
 7th Mr. Peter Cushing 2d to Miss Sarah Austin, both of Dover.
 8th Mr. Nathaniel R. Hill to Miss Esther Ela, both of Dover.

 DOVER, May 27th, 1825.
 A true copy of the original.
 Att.   J. RICHARDSON, Town Clerk.

*An error in the record, should read Horton.—[ED.

DOVER, Octo. 28th, 1825: This certifies that Mr. William W. Stackpole and Miss Judith T. Tuttle, both of Dover, N. H., were lawfully joined in marriage on the 27th inst. by me.

HERSHEL FOSTER, Minister of the Gospel.

Ex'd by   J. RICHARDSON, Town Cl'k.

DOVER, Octo. 2d, 1827: Married Mr. Francis Nute to Miss Ruth Whipple, both of Dover.   JOHN FLANDERS.

Copy the original. Att.   J. RICHARDSON, Town C'k.

1825, July 4th: Married Mr. Ebenezer Lane to Miss Sarah Emery both of Hampton.   JOHN N. MAFFITT.

1825, July 10th: Married Mr. Robert C. Miller to Mrs. Rebecca Pollard, both of Dover.   J. N. MAFFITT.

1825, July 17th: Married Mr. Lewis Richardson to Miss Lucy Cox, both of Dover.   J. N. MAFFITT.

1825, July 31st: Married Mr. John N. Knap of Dover, to Miss Rachael Bennett of Loudon.   JACOB SANBORN.

1825, Sept. 11th: Married Mr. Levi W. Houson to Miss Mary Blake, both of Dover.   JOHN N. MAFFITT.

1825, Nov. 27th: Married Mr. Ivory Fry to Miss Statira A. Ellison, both of Dover.   JOHN N. MAFFITT.

1825, Dec. 4th: Married Mr. William Abott of Shapleigh to Miss Hannah S. Canney of Somersworth.   JOHN N. MAFFITT.

1826, April 2d: Married Mr. Robert Spurling of Madbury to Mrs. Eunice Twombly of Dover.   J. N. MAFFITT.

1826, Sept. 23d: Married Mr. Thaxter Russell to Miss Mary Ann Joy, both of Dover.

Sept. 24th: Mr. John Tuttle of Durham to Miss Sarah Young of Somersworth.

Nov. 26th: Mr. Asa White to Miss Jane Kenniston, both of Dover.

Nov. 26th: Mr. Benjamin Boardman to Miss Clarissa Straw.

Jan'y 30th, 1827: Mr. Dudley Carr to Miss Sarah Ann Hanson, both of Dover.

Jan'y 26th: Mr. Ezekiel Heard to Miss P. Henderson, both of Dover.

Feb'y 27th: Mr. Theodore Littlefield to Miss E. Saltmarsh, both of Dover.

March 20th: Mr. James Hopkins to Miss Harriet Watson, both of Dover.

March 17th: Mr. John Sales to Miss Sarah Ann Grant, both of Dover.

March [—] 1827: Mr. John G. Cate to Miss Deborah R. Prime, both of Dover.

April 12th : Samuel H. Henderson of Dover to Miss Delia Paul of Somersworth.

April 14th : Mr. Nathan Whittier to Miss Mary A. Ricker, both of Dover.

May 25th : Mr. Moses Quimby to Miss Mary A. Richardson.

The foregoing, recorded from original minutes left by the Rev'd John N. Maffitt.

Att.   J. RICHARDSON, Town C'k.

I certify that the following persons have been joined in Marriage as the Law directs, viz :

Mr. Thomas Wright & Miss Abigail Farnham, both of Dover, Aug't 30th, 1827.

Mr. John Stephens of Sanford and Miss Mary Jane Mitchel of Dover, Sept. 6th, 1827.

Mr. Henry Harriden & Miss Mary Ann Hayes, both of Dover, Oct. 12th, 1827.

Mr. Nathaniel Growdy of Ossipee and Miss Lydia Tasker of Somersworth, Oct. 18th, 1827.

Mr. Jacob Bodge of Biddiford & Miss Elizabeth Brackett of Somersworth, Nov. 1st, 1827.

Mr. Joseph Hanson 3d & Miss Abigail Paul, both of Dover, Nov. 8th, 1827.

Mr. Samuel S. Huchinson & Miss Susan Warren, both of New Market, Dec. 4th, 1827.

Mr. Elisha Murdock & Miss Mary Nute, both of Dover, Dec. 6th, 1827.

Mr. John Guppy of Rochester and Miss Ann Dame of Dover, Dec. 9th, 1827.

Mr. Meshach Weare & Miss Hannah Wadleigh, both of Dover, Dec. 23d, 1827.

Mr. John B. Sargent & Miss Mercy Hussey, both of Dover, Dec. 30th, 1827.

Mr. James Plumer & Miss Mary Ann Roberts, both of Dover, Jan'y 10th, 1828.

Mr. James Clark of Berwick & Miss Mary Burnham of Dover, Jan'y 31st, 1828.

Mr. Osgood Putnam & Rhoda A. Hall, both of Dover, March 23d, 1828.

Mr. George P. Hooper of Berwick & Miss Abigail Guppy of Dover, April 6th, 1828.

Mr. John Smiley & Miss Rhoda M. Haley, both of Dover, Apr. 20th, 1828.

  By   BENJAMIN R. HOYT, Minister of the Gospel.

  True copy of the original.

  Att.   J. RICHARDSON, Town Clerk.

The following persons have been duly joined in Marriage, viz:

Mr. Wm. G. Webster & Miss Hannah J. Foss, both of Dover, May 15th, 1828.

Mr. Henry Y. Graham of Worwick, R. I., & Miss Lydia H. Hussey of Somersworth, May 28th, 1828.

Mr. David Gotham & Miss Maria Bishop, both of Dover, July 18th, 1828.

  By   BENJA. R. HOYT, Minister of the Gospel.

  Ex'd by   J. RICHARDSON, Town C'k.

Mr. Jeremiah Locke & Miss Elizabeth Wentworth, both of Dover, Feb'y 14th, 1828.

Mr. Charles Paul & Miss Lois Foss, both of Dover, April 10th, 1828.

  By   JOHN ADAMS, Minister of the Gospel.

  Ex'd by   J. RICHARDSON, Town Clerk.

Mr. James Rollins of Somersworth & Miss Abigail Wingate of Dover, Sept. 7th, 1828.

Mr. Ivory Paul & Miss Judith S. Wentworth, both of Somersworth, Sept. 21st, 1828.

Mr. James R. Lewis & Miss Angeline Warren, both of Somersworth, Sept. 28th, 1828.

Mr. David S. Hanson of Somersworth & Miss Betsy Drew of Dover Octo. 20th, 1828.

Capt. Timothy Ricker & Miss Betsy Clark, both of Dover, Octo. 25th, 1828.

Mr. Simeon Hartford & Miss Rebeckah Peirce, both of Dover, Octo. 25th, 1828.

Mr. Orlo Guilford & Miss Clarissa Gilman, both of Dover, Nov. 9th, 1828.

Mr. Phillip Harty Jr. & Miss Eliza Hanson, both of Dover, Nov. 13th, 1828.

Mr. George Wentworth & Miss Judith Brown, both of Somersworth, Nov. 16th, 1828.

Mr. Daniel Newall & Miss Betsy Tibbets, both of Dover, Nov. 24th, 1828.

Were all joined in marriage as the law directs by

                BENJA. R. HOYT, Minister of the Gospel.

    True copy.   Att.   J. RICHARDSON, Town Clerk.

Mr. Robert Holden & Miss Mary Hook, both of Dover, Nov. 30th, 1828.

Mr. Thomas Parol & Miss Susan French, both of Somersworth, Dec. 31st, 1828.

Mr. Palfrey Downing & Miss Eliza Hanson, both of Dover, Jan'y 4th, 1829.

Mr. Henry Dore & Miss Betsy S. Young, both of Dover, Jan'y 4th, 1829.

Mr. Nicholas Chase & Miss Hannah Pinkham, both of Dover, Jan'y 15th, 1829.

Were all joined in marriage as the law directs by

                BENJA. R. HOYT, Minister of the Gospel

    True copy.   Att.   J. RICHARDSON, Town Clerk.

The following persons were join'd in marriage, viz:

Mr. Wm. B. Hayes and Miss Diana Hall, both of Dover, Jan'y 25th, 1829.

Mr. Elkanah Barrows & Miss Mary Drew, both of Dover, Feb'y 5th, 1829.

In this town March 1st, 1829, Mr. Samuel A. M. Moulton & Miss Mary Young, both of Somersworth.

Mr. Joseph Prime & Miss Mahala Vickery, both of Dover, March 11th, 1829.

Mr. Lewis Wentworth & Miss Hannah Watson, both of Dover, April 1st, 1829.

Mr. James Kenney & Miss Lavina Whidden, both of Dover, April 2d, 1829.

    By me   BENJAMIN R. Hoyt,

        Minister of the Gospel in the Methodist E. Church.

    True copy of the original.

       Att.   J. RICHARDSON, Town C'k.

The following persons have been joined in Marriage by me, viz:

Mr. Uriah S. Smith & Miss Emmela Prime, both of Dover, April 13th, 1829.

In this town, Mr. Calvin Chaplin of Danverse, Mass., & Miss Hannah H. Snell of Dover, April 19th, 1829.

In Somersworth, Mr. Jacob Wentworth & Miss Mercy Wentworth, both of Somersworth, April 22d, 1829.

MARRIAGES, 1816-1838.

In this town, Mr. Ezra Rumney & Miss Charlotte Lougee, both of Dover, April 30th, 1829.

In this town, Mr. Aaron K. Frederick and Miss Lydia G. Smith, both of Dover, May 14th, 1829. BENJAMIN R. HOYT, Preacher of the Gospel in the Methodist Epis'opal Church in Dover.

True copy. Att. J. RICHARDSON, Town C'k.

The following is a list of the Marriages I have solem'ized in this town, with the dates to the present time:

Aug't 9th, 1829: Mr. Calvin Thomson to Miss Hannah Martin, both of Somersworth.

" 13th, " Mr. Joseph Reynolds to Miss Deborah Stiles, both of Dover.

" 16th, " Mr. Jonathan Spurlin to Miss Lydia Goodridge, both of Dover.

" 23d, " Mr. Wright H. Wigglesworth to Miss Keziah Emery, both of Somersworth.

Sept. 20th, " Mr. William T. Howard to Miss Mary Glidden, both of Dover.

Octo. 17th, " Mr. James Miller to Miss Sarah Ann Perkins, both of Somersworth.

Dec. 24th, " Mr. Robert McKinly to Miss Sarah K. Smith, both of Dover.

Jan'y 5th, 1830: Mr. Nathaniel Berry to Miss Sarah Severance, both of Dover.

" 10th, " Mr. Joseph Plummer to Miss Mary Clemment, both of Dover.

" 13th, " Mr. James Ross to Miss Sarah Jones, both of Dover.

" 20th, " Mr. James Sanborn to Miss Mary Ann Babb, both of Dover.

Feb'y 21st, " Mr. Horace Clark to Miss Clementine Waldron, both of Dover.

BARTHOLOMEW OTHEMAN,
Minister of the Methodist E. Church in Dover, N. H.
Dover, March 23d, 1830.

True copy. Att. J. RICHARDSON, Town Clerk.

The following marriages were consummated by me:

1829, Oct. 25th: Mr. Oliver H. Emery was married to Miss Hannah Porter, both of Dover.

MARRIAGES, 1816-1838.

1830, Mar'h 18th: Mr. Bracket Hayes of Rochester to Miss Rebecca Grant of Chester.

" " 28th: Mr. Smith M. Shaw to Miss Susannah Cady, both of Dover.

ELIJAH FOSTER.

Mar'h 30th, 1830. True copy. Att.

J. RICHARDSON, Town C'k.

Mr. John Adams, minister, certified on the back of my certificate, that he joined in marriage Simeon W. Taylor & Susan D. Ford, both of Dover, Nov. 26th, 1830.

Att. J. RICHARDSON, Town Clerk.

PERSONS MARRIED BY ELIJAH FOSTER IN DOVER DURING YEAR 1830.

Bracket Hayes & Rebecca Grant, March 18th, 1830.
Smith M. Shaw & Susan Cady, " 28th, "
Walter Durgin & Hannah Woodman, May 19th, "
William Henderson Jr. & Maria Dimon, both of Rochester, July 4th, "
Charles C. P. Moody & Frances Evans, both of Dover, Aug't 24th, "
Russel F. Elliot & Mary Jane Whitehouse, both of Somersworth, Sept. 19th, "

True copy from minutes left by Hosea Evans.

Att. J. RICHARDSON, Town Clerk.

STATE OF NEW HAMPSHIRE, STRAFFORD COUNTY, SS.

To the Town Clerk of Dover.

Sir: This certifies that the bonds of matrimony have been duly Solem'ized by me according to the following schedule:

At Dover August 12th, 1830, Mr. Joseph H. Scruton of Madbury to Miss Lucinda Bolo of Somersworth.

At Dover Aug't 18th, 1830, Mr. Daniel Goodwin to Miss Mary F. Keniston, both of Dover.

At Somersworth Aug't 29th, 1830, Mr. Richard Ayers of Dover to Miss Mary F. Spencer of Somersworth.

At Dover Sept. 16th, 1830, Mr. John James to Miss Sally Edgerly, both of Lee.

At Dover, Sept. 16th, 1830, Mr. Samuel H. Hanson to Miss Maria Dealing, both of Dover.

At Dover Nov. 21st, 1830, Mr. Joseph Butler of Me. to Miss Lydia Hatheway of Dover.

At Dover January 27th, 1831, Mr. Eli Cook to Miss Sarah Horn, both of Somersworth.

At Dover Feb'y 17th, 1831, Mr. Daniel Purrington to Miss Sarah Varney, both of Dover.

At Dover Feb'y 27th, 1831, Thomas E. Sawyer Esq., to Miss Elizabeth Watson, both of Dover.

Dover, Mar'h 29th, 1831. Att. JOHN G. DOW,
Minister of the Gospel.

True copy. Att. J. RICHARDSON, Town Clerk.

Mr. James Richardson: I wish you to make record that marriage was solem'iz'd between Mr. George Wendell & Miss Prudence Jenness, both of Dover, on the 19th Feb'y, 1832, by

SAMUEL RABBIN.

A true copy of original. Att. J. RICHARDSON, Town C'k.

STATE OF NEW HAMPSHIRE.

Strafford County: In the month of May, 1831, Mr. John Otis and Miss Martha Gage were united in holy matrimony agreeable to the laws of said state, by me.

EZEKIEL HURD, Jus. of the Peace.

True copy. Att. J. RICHARDSON, Town Clerk.

This certifies that the following persons have been duly joined in marriage by me as follows, viz:

April 11th, 1831: Mr. James Page of Rochester to Miss Mary Furber of Lee.

" 21st, " Mr. Moses C. Young to Miss Mary Nutter, both of Dover.

May 29th, " Mr. Israel Ricker Miss Mary Ann Stearns, both of Dover.

June 19th, " Mr. Oliver L. Reynolds to Miss Sarah H. Watson, both of Dover.

July 3d, " Mr. William Ricker to Miss Mary H. Downing, both of Dover.

" 11th, " Mr. Daniel W. Kimball to Miss Sabrina Carver, both of Dover.

" 17th, " Mr. Samuel Currier to Mrs. Mary S. Jenkins, both of Dover.

" 31st, " Mr. Eli Grant to Miss Mary Ann Snell, both of Dover.

Aug't 2d,	"	Mr. William B. Wiggin of Milton to Miss Philena Graves of Dover.
" 11th,	"	Mr. General S. Baker to Miss Susan S. Piper, both of Dover.
" 18th,	"	Mr. John B. Nealley to Miss Maria J. Drown, both of Dover.
Sept. 18th,	"	Mr. John E. Armstead of Lloyd, Cannada, to Miss Emila Edson of Dover.
Octo. 9th,	"	Mr. Joseph Doe to Miss Mary E. N. Drew, both of Dover.
" 27th,	"	Mr. Chandler William to Mrs. Mary Murdock, both of Dover.
" 29th,	"	Mr. John P. Rogers to Miss Mary Prime, both of Somersworth.
Nov. 7th,	"	Mr. Benja. Magoon of Kingston to Miss Catherine Barstow of Dover.
" 15th,	"	Mr. Enoch Berry to Miss Eliza Hurd, both of Dover.
Dec. 15th,	"	Mr. James Allen to Miss Sophia Baker, both of Rochester.
" 19th,	"	Mr. Moses Hussey of Somersworth to Miss Clarissa M. Ham, Dover.
Jan'y 1st, 1832 :		Mr. George W. Williams to Miss Mary Wingate, both of Dover.
" 2d,	"	Mr. Joseph D. McNeal to Miss Sarah Beal, both of Dover.
" 5th,	"	Mr. William P. Baker of Kennebunk to Miss Rebecca Roberts, Dover.
" 8th,	"	Mr. Thompson L. Newall to Miss Sophia Tibbets, both of Dover.
" 19th,	"	Mr. Samuel Lawrence of Tamworth to Miss Lydia G. Roberts, Dover.
Feb'y 1st,	"	Mr. Nicholas Lougee to Miss Hannah S. Bickford, both of Lowell.
" 5th,	"	Mr. Jacob S. Clark to Miss Rebecca Peirce, both of Dover.
" 8th,	"	Mr. Robert Guptill to Miss Ruth Roberts, both of Somersworth.
" 23d,	"	Mr. Moses Guptill to Miss Betsy Garvin, both of Somersworth.

MARRIAGES, 1816-1838.   97

Mar'h 1st,   "   Mr. Stephen Hanson Jun. of Dover to Miss Eunice Wentworth, Somersworth.
" 18th,   "   Mr. Ebenezer Faxon to Miss Olive Thompson, both of Dover.

Dover, March 31st, 1832.
                    JOHN G. Dow, Minister of the Gospel.
True copy of the original.
Att.   J. RICHARDSON, Town Clerk.

DOVER, July 23d, 1832 : A list of marriages solem'ized by John G. Dow.

1832, April 5th: At Dover, Mr. John Dunn to Miss Mary Tuttle, both of Dover.
" " 15th: "   Mr. Robert Perkins Jr. to Miss Mary Webster, both of Dover.
" " 15th: "   Mr. Nathan F. Seavey of Berwick, Me., to Miss Mary Ann Gile of Dover.
" " 22d: "   Mr. James Littlefield to Miss Sarah C. Bean, both of Dover.
" " 29th: "   Mr. Luther Sampson to Miss Mary Leighton, both of Dover.
" June 2d : At Durham, Mr. John Yeaton to Miss Elizabeth French, both of Durham.
" "   3d : At Dover, Mr. John Kenniston to Miss Sarah Hodgdon, both of Dover.
" "   4th: "   Mr. Geo. P. Robinson of Berwick, Me., to Miss Drusella Adams of Dover.
" "   24th: "   Mr. Amos Brown to Miss Elizabeth Emery, both of Dover.
" July 15th: "   Mr. William H. Stevens of Dover to Miss Irena Osborne of Alna, Me.

                    JOHN G. Dow, Preacher of the Gospel.
Rec'd August 3d, 1832.
True copy. Att.   J. RICHARDSON, Town Clerk.

To the Town Clerk of Dover: This is to certify that Joseph Rounds & Miss Elsy A. Drew were duly joined together in marriage on the 24th ultimo, their intention of marriage having been previously published according to law.
      By me   DAVID ROOT, Minister of the Gospel.
Dover, April 1st, 1833.
True copy. Att.   J. RICHARDSON, Town Cl'k.

Marriages solemnized by myself, Nathan'l Thurston:

Mr. Samuel Beede of Boston, formerly of Sandwich, N. H., to Miss Mary E. Spa'lding of Dover, N. H., formerly of Smithfield, R. I., May 25th, 1832.

Mr. James Kelly to Miss Elizabeth Jepson, both of Somersworth, May 27th, A. D. 1832.

Mr. Mark L. Ferber to Miss Eliza Ricker, both of Dover, July 5th, 1832.

Mr. Gershom Horn to Miss Eleanor Horn, both of Dover, Aug't 2d, 1832.

Mr. Daniel Stillings to Miss Cynthia Webster, Dover, Sept. 2d, 1832.

Mr. Wentworth Dore to Miss Sarah Meader, both of Somersworth, Sept. 9th, 1832.

Mr. *Moses Hall Hall and Miss Henrietta Horn, both of Dover, N. H., Oct. 17th, 1832.

Mr. Stephen S. Cook and Miss Rosamond Russell, both of Shapleigh, Me., Nov. 8th, 1832.

Mr. Woodbury M. Simpson and Miss Eliza H. Sumner, both of Somersworth, Nov. 15th, 1832.

Marriages solemnized by myself, 1833, Nathaniel Thurston:

Mr. Phillip McCrellis to Miss Lydia Runnels, both of Dover, Jan'y 27th, 1833.

Mr. Eliphalet Cloutman Esq'r to Miss Sarah Berry, both of Rochester, N. H., Feb'y 25th, 1833.

Mr. Samuel Ham 3d to Miss Sarah Morrill, both of Dover, N. H., Mar'h 3d, 1833.

Mr. Nathaniel Whitan to Miss Betsy Richardson both of Rochester, N. H., Mar'h 10th, 1833.

True copy from Nathaniel Thurston's minute book.

Dover, April 5th, 1833.
Att. J. Richardson, Town Cl'k.

List of persons united in marriage by the Rev'd R. H. Deming:

1832, Sept. 6th: Thomas Goodwin Jun. of Lebanon to Betsey Glidden of Dover.

" " 6th: Augustus Stackpole, Saco, Me., to Joanna Roberts, Dover.

" " 9th: Zebulon Y. Wentworth of Weston to Mary Drew of Dover.

" " 19th: Stephen Otis Jun. to Abigail Ham, both of Dover.

" Octo. 21st: James Sampson to Mary Sands, both of Dover.

*The publishment says simply Moses Hall.—[Ed.

"   Nov'r 24th: Hammon Hutchinson to Almira Paul, both of Dover.
"   "   24th: Josiah Hall to Rachel Peirce, both of Dover.
"   "   26th: At Dover, Thomas Fall to Louisa M. Durgin, both of Somersworth.
"   Dec. 24th: Benjamin Owen Jun. of Ashford, Con't., to Harriet Bowen of Dover.
1833 Jan'y 1st: Mr. William Potter of Somersworth to Miss Olive Reynolds of Dover.
"   "   2d: Jacob J. Demeritt to Martha H. Fernald.
"   "   27th: Henry Knox to Abigail Leighton, both of Dover.
"   Feb'y 3d: Mr. Elijah Jenkins of New Durham to Abigail B. Drew of Dover.
"   March 10th: Mr. Thomas T. Ham to Sarah Nason, both of Dover.
"   "   21st: John Webster to Sophia L. Wendell, both of Dover.
"   "   31st: Mr. Nathaniel Mason to Martha W. Piper.
"   May 1st: Ebenr. F. Odell of Randolph, Mass., to Mary Conner of Dover.
"   July 4th: Ezekiel Adams to Jane Adams, both of Gilmanton.
"   "   "   Tho's Gray of Barnstead to Olive F. Davis of Dover.
"   "   14th: Nathaniel Hobbs to Luranah Young, both of Dover.
"   "   14th: Mr. D. W. Foss of Bangor, Me., to Harriet M. Clifford of Dover.

True copy, Aug't 6th, 1833. Att.

J. RICHARDSON, Town Clerk.

To J. Richardson, Town Clerk, Dover:

Sir: You will please record the following marriages solemnized by me, Gibbon Williams, pastor of the regular Baptist Society, Dover, N. H.   DOVER, March 6th, 1834.

1833.
  Octo. 4th: Mr. John D. Smith to Miss Mary Ann Kay, both of Dover.
  "   17th: Mr. John Warburton of Dover to Miss Louisa Hodgdon of Newington.

" 20th: Mr. Henry Barnes to Miss Mary Ann Whittle, both of Dover.
" 28th: Mr. George W Leavett of Lynn, Mass., to Miss Louisa Hodgdon of Dover.
Dec. 29th: Capt. Wm. B. Lyman of Milton to Miss Lydia Jones of Dover.
March 7th, 1834. A true copy. Att.

J. RICHARDSON, Town Clerk.

1833, March 22d, I married George Deere to Lydia F. Fall.

EZEKIEL HURD, Justice of the Peace.

1833, August 4th, I married Henry Quimby to Tamson Ricker.

EZEKIEL HURD, Justice of the Peace.

Rec'd Mar'h 29th, 1834.
A true copy. Att. J. RICHARDSON, Town Clerk.

Strafford, SS This first day of March, A. D. 1835, personally appear'd before me at Somersworth in said county, Nathaniel D Wetmore of said Somersworth and Lydia McIntosh of Dover in said county and were joined in marriage.

CHARLES W WOODMAN, Justice of the peace.

Rec'd Mar'h 6th, 1835.
A true copy. Att. J RICHARDSON, Town Cl'k.

DOVER, N. H., June 8th, 1835: I hereby certify that I have solemnized the following marriages:

1 Between Gardner Ruggles & Eliza Gilman, June 23d, 1834.
2 Between William S McCollister & Abigail K. Estes, Octo., 1834.
3 Between John Abbot & Mercy Hartwell, July 24th, 1834.
4 Between John McDaniel & Elizabeth R. Foss, Nov., 1834.
5 Between Benja. Lord & Harriet Sargent, Nov., 1834.
6 Between John S Chadwick & Sarah Clark, Nov., 1834.
7 Between Benjamin Pray & Dorcas Pray, Octo., 1834.
8 Between Abraham Clark & Judith Davis, April 9th, 1835.
9 Between John L. Currier & Ann Currier, March, 1835.
10 Between Samuel Robinson & Elizabeth A Hussey, May, 1835.
11 Between William Keillee & Hannah Rollins, May, 1835.
12 Between Levi Shaw & Charlotte L. Wyatt, Nov, 1833.
13 Between Samuel Twombly & Nancy Worcester, June, 1833.
14 Between Joseph Stickney & Mary J. Middleton, Nov., 1833.
15 Between Horatio G. Tasker & Patience Hall, Sept, 1833.
16 Between Sidney Paul & Louisa Ann Chesley, Nov., 1833.
17 Between Joseph Footman & Ann Foy, Dec, 1833.

MARRIAGES, 1816-1838.

18 Between Joseph Rounds & Elcy O. Drew, March, 1833.
19 Between Benja. F. Curtis & Mary Tredwick, Sept., 1833.

DAVID ROOT, Minister of the Gospel.

True copy, July 1835. Att.

J. RICHARDSON, Town Cl'k.

DOVER, Sept. 11th, 1835.

To the Town Clerk:

Dr. Sir: This certifies that on Wed. Sept. 9th, 1835, I married Mr. John Gillpatrick and Miss Abigail Young, both of Dover.

Respectfully Yours,

DANIEL P. CILLY, Minister of the Gospel.

True copy. Att. J. RICHARDSON, Town Cl'k.

To the Town Clerk of Dover N. Hampshire.

Sir: The following is a list of marriages which I have solemnized in the Town of Dover, State of N. Hampshire, viz:

Sept. 18, 1834: Mr. Albon Glines to Miss Sarah P. Goodwin, both of Dover, N. H.

Oct. 18, 1834: Mr. Wm. S. Adams to Miss Sophia H. Mathews, both of Dover, N. H.

Oct. 30, 1834: Mr. Ebenezer Gilman to Caroline T. Whitehouse, both of Dover, N. H.

Nov. 13, 1834: Mr. William Hanson to Miss Sarah Colomy, both of Dover, N. H.

Nov. 16, 1834: Mr. John Kimball to Miss Elizabeth Dore, both of Dover, N. H.

April 15, 1835: Mr. James V. Clark of Strafford to Miss Elizabeth Nute of Dover, N. H.

April 23, 1835: Mr. Jeremiah Moulton of York, Me., to Miss Abigail Stackpole of Dover, N. H.

May 7, 1835: Mr. John Canney of Lagrange, Me., to Miss Elizabeth Willey of Dover, N. H.

May 7, 1835: Mr. Stoten Austin to Miss Sarah Varney, both of Dover, N. H.

June 14, 1835: Mr. William Melcher to Miss Susan Brown, both of Dover, N. H.

July 5, 1835: Mr. James Shumway to Miss Charlotte Pickering, both of Dover, N. H.

August 2, 1835: Mr. Andrew Lynn to Miss Eliza P. *Emory, both of Dover, N. H.

*The publishment says Emery.—[Ed.

August 9, 1835: Mr. Samuel Gerry of Portsmouth, N. H. to Miss Lucretia S. Foss of Somersworth, N. H.

August 8, 1835: Mr. John N. Champion to Miss Eunice R. White, both of Dover, N. H.

August 23, 1835: Mr. John Hubbard to Miss Deborah Morgan, both of Dover, N. H.

Sept. 21, 1835: Mr. Dearborn Wedgewood to Miss Ursula Dealand, both of Dover, N. H.

Oct. 18, 1835: Mr. Stephen Jenness to Miss Maria Paul, both of Dover, N. H.

Oct. 26, 1835: Mr. John S. Hall to Miss Hannah N. Brock, both of Exeter, N. H.

Nov. 8, 1835: Mr. Cyrus Munroe of Concord, N. H. to Miss Sylvina H. Foss of Dover, N. H.

Nov. 26, 1835: Mr. Richard Berry to Miss Maria Ayers, both of Dover, N. H.

Nov. 30, 1835: Mr. Joseph Leighton of Farmington, N. H. to Mrs. Mary Hayes of Dover, N. H.

Dec. 13, 1835: Mr. Joseph Walker to Miss Elizabeth Hildrup, both of Dover, N. H.

Dec. 13, 1835: Mr. George F. Guppy to Miss Abigail F. York, both of Dover, N. H.

Jan'y 12, 1836: Mr. William Trickey of Brookfield, N. H. to Mrs. Martha Norris of Dover, N. H.

" " " Mr. James B. Guppy to Miss Sophia Brock, both of Dover, N. H.

Feb. 29, 1836: Mr. Charles E. Burleigh to Miss Mary Bean, both of Dover, N. H.

Yours with Resp't,

JARED PERKINS, Minister of the Gospel.

DOVER, March 1, 1836.

True copy. Attest. CHARLES YOUNG, Town Clerk.

I certify that James Cole and Jane Spooner both of Dover were on the 22d inst. married by me.

EZEKIEL HURD, Justice Peace.

May 30, 1836.

Received May 30th, 1836.

Exam'd by CHARLES YOUNG, Town Clerk.

This certifies that the following persons have been united in marriage by me in the order and at the times severally specified:

1836.
March 20: Mr. Andrew Tuttle and Miss Susan Demeritt, both of Dover.
" 31: Mr. John Hough and Mrs. Lurania Hobbs, both of Dover.
July 3d: Mr. Charles White and Miss Susan Rogers, both of Dover.
ditto Mr. Enoch T. Willey and Miss Sarah Hodgdon, both of Dover.
July 4: Mr. Joseph Whitehouse and Miss Catherine Harvey, both of Dover.
ditto Mr. Hiram Burley and Miss Susan Whitehouse, both of Dover.
Aug. 17: Mr. George Porter of Concord and Miss Clara Ayers of Haverhill, Mass.
Sept. 4: Mr. Jeremiah Cole and Miss Mary Ann Whidden, both of Dover.
Sept. 7: Mr. William F. Estes and Miss Sarah A. Torr, both of Dover.
Oct. 23: Mr. Joseph Chamberlin of Dover and Miss Mary Ann Wendell of Portsmouth.
Nov. 13: Mr. Amos Wright and Miss Ann Dunn, both of Dover.
Dec. 11: Mr. Ezra Young of South Berwick, Me., and Miss Catherine N. Tredick of Dover.

1837.
Jan. 10: Mr. Nicholas P. Horn and Miss Betsy Chase, both of Dover.
" 19: Mr. Thomas L. Nudd of Wolfborough and Miss Fanny Lord of Dover.
" 26: Mr. Joseph Ham 3d and Miss Mary M. Randall, both of Dover.

Yours Respectfully,

BENJ. BRIERLY.

Mr. Charles Young.
Received March 13, 1837.
Ex'd by   CHARLES YOUNG, Town Clerk.

List of marriages solemnized in 1836 by the pastor of the Unitarian Society in Dover, N.H:

Oct. 2: William B. Smith and Mary A. Hardy.
Oct. 19: William N. Melcher and Harriet N. Meder.

Nov. 29 : Hiram Gleason and Abigail Twombly.
Dec. 11 : Edwin Whitehouse and Harriet A. Torr.
    Att.   EDGAR BUCKINGHAM, Pastor.
    March 25, 1837.
    Received March 29, 1837.
    Ex'd by   CHARLES YOUNG, Town Clerk.

March 31, 1837 : The following persons have been duly united in marriage by me in this town during the last year, viz :

March 24, 1836 : Sam'l Ham of Barrington to Miss Sally Tebbets of Dover.

June 9, 1836 : Mr. William Pickering of Rochester, N. H., to Miss Laura Percival of D.

July 3, " Mr. Jesse Mansfield of Salisbury, N. H. to Miss Hannah Lufkin of D.

" 5th, " Mr. Oran Dudley of Springfield, Mass , to Miss Elizabeth A. Waldron of D.

" 20th, " Mr. Geo. W. T. Rogers to Miss Betsy Nason, both of Somersworth, N. H.

Oct. 2d, 1836 : Mr. Jonathan J. Davis Jr. to Miss Betsy W. Gray, both of Dover, N. H.

" 16th, " Mr. Henry G. Abbott of Boston, Mass. to Miss Phebe Bickford of Dover.

" 19th, " Mr. Samuel S. Clark to Miss Irena Tebbets, both of Dover.

Nov. 13th, " Mr. Dexter Jackson to Miss Lucinda Fuller, both of Dover.

Oct. 30, 1836 : Mr. Harrel F. Place to Miss Eliza Blaisdell, both of Dover.

Dec. 25, " Mr. Charles Jones to Miss Mary Hartford, both of Dover.

Jan. 12, 1837 : Mr. Josiah A. Corson to Miss Hannah C. Nutter, both of Dover.

RECORD OF MARRIAGES CONTINUED.

Jan'y 25, 1837 : Mr. Elisha Howard to Miss Ann Maria Lncas, both of Dover.

Feb. 27. „ Mr. William Deland of Wolfborough, N. H. to Miss Sarah Deland of D.

    14 in all. Dover, March, 1837.   JARED PERKINS.
    Received May 16, 1837.
    Ex'd by   CHARLES YOUNG, Town Clerk.

List of marriages solemnized by Edgar Buckingham, pastor of the Unitarian Society in Dover, N. H.

To Mr. Young, Town Clerk:

1837.
April 2, Aaron Bridge and Ann Clark.
Sept. 13, Charles D. Jackson and Elizabeth C. Wheeler.
1838.
Jan. 23, John Tredick and Mary W. Copp.

EDGAR BUCKINGHAM, March 14, 1838.

Received March 14, 1838.
Examined by   CHARLES YOUNG, Town Clerk.

EARLY RECORDS

OF

NEW HAMPSHIRE FAMILIES.

[Published by permission from manuscript in library of the New Hampshire Historical Society.]

These following Were Entered pr booke from another being truely kept by Theodore Attkinson ye 26th Novb^r 1700

Elizabeth Daughter of Theodore Attkinson and Mary his Wife was born att Boston 28 of Nouem 1692 about 3 of Clock afternoon being 2^d day of week

Mary ye Daughter born att New Castle 6th June 1695 abo^t 9 att night being Thursday—5th day

Theodore there Son born att New Castle ye 20th of Decemb^r 1697 about 6 In the moring being Monday or 2^d

Theodore Atkinson Theodore & Mary N : Castle July 10

Memo : look for A after Z

B.

Robert Burnam Son : of Rob : Burnam dyed 25 ffebru : 1663.

Robt Burnam 2^d Son : of Robt Burnam bo : 21 of August 1664

Wm Beard Son : of Tho : Beard by Mary his wife bor : 12 : May 1664 & dyed the 27th day of ye same m^o following

Hannah Beard dau : of Thomas Beard by Mary his wife bo : 24 Octob^r 1666

Hannah Bickford dau : of Jno Bickford by Temperance his wife born ye 5 Nouem : 1665

Benjamin Son : of Jno Bickford by Temperance his wife bor : ye 20 : octob : 1672

Phillip Benmore Married to Rebecca Nock: Wid: 28th of Sep' 1669
Rebecca Benmore wid. dyed the 30: of march: 1680
Michael Brawne Son of George Brawn by Mary his wife borne y" 1: June 1679
Annabell Barsham dau: of Jo" Barsham by Mehetabel his wife bo: 31 May 1670
Mary dau of Jn" Barsham by Metabel his wife bo: 26: ffebru: 1671
Dorothy dau: of Jn" Barsham by Mehetabel his wife bo: 23 ffebru 1673
Sarah dau: of Jn" Barsham by Mehetabel his wife bor: 11 Augt 167—
William Son of Jn" Barsham by Mehetabel his wife bor 25 April 1678
Samuel Son of Jacob Browne by Sarah his wife bor: ye 4th nouem^r 1686
John Browne aged 98 years died the 28 ffeb: 1686
Thomas Son of Tho: Brown by Abial his wife bo: 14: Decem^r 1686
Dorothy dau: of John Blake by ffrancis his wife bor. 8th April 1686
Nicholas Badcock mar: to Ann Cole the 11th [—] 1686: pr Jus: Barefoote.
Wm Bussell mar: to Ruth Stileman ye 5th of Septem^r 1687
4th Oct 1689 Elisha Bryer Maryed Abigail Drew Portsm^o
30 Nov: 1693 Margerit there Daug: born
11 Dec. 1695 Abigail there Daug: born
18 Sep^t 1697 Sam^{ll} there Son born
2 Feb: 1700 Sarah there Daugh: born
21 Aug: 1702 Mary there Daughter born

NEW CASTLE

The Children of William Berry & Judah
15 Oct: 1686 Eliz^a there Daug: born
13 Feb: 1688 Nath: there Son born
18 Jan^{ry} 1690 Stephen there Son born
18 Nov: 1693 William there Son born
8 March 1695 Jeremiah there Son born
15 Jan^{ry} 1697 Frederick there Son born
15 March 1699 Abigail there Daug: born
26 Jan^{ry} 1701 Jane there Daug: born

3 July 1685 Shadrach the Son of Shadrach Bell and Rachel his wife was born

19 March 1687 Eliz[a] there Daughter was born
29 Jan[ry] 1689 Meshak there Son was born
5 Aug: 1695 Benjamin there Son was born
12 March 1699 Thomas there Son was born

C.

John Cutt Maried to Hannah Star y[e] 30th of July 1662 pr m[r] Danforth

Jn[o] Cutt Son of Jn[o] Cutt borne y[e] 30 : June 1663, by hannah : his wife

Elizabeth Cutt daugh[r] of Jn[o] Cutt by Hannah his wife bo : 30 : of Nouem 1664 & departed this Life y[e] 28 Sep[tr] 1665

Hannah Cutt dau[r] of Jn[o] Cutt by Hannah his wife bo : y[e] 29 July 1666

Mary Cutt dau : of John Cutt by Hannah his wife bo : 17 : of Nouemb 1669

Sam Cutt Son of Jn[o] Cutt by Hannah his wife bo : the : [———]

Jn[o] Cutt Sen[r] Prsid[t] of y[e] Pro. of N. Hampsh : dyed y[e] 27 of March 1681

Abigall Coffin daugh[r] of Peter Coffin by Abigall his wife bo : 20 octob[r] 1657

Peter Coffin Son of Pet[r] Coffin by Abigall his wife bo : 20 Augu[t] 1660

Jethro Coffin Son of Peter Coffin by Abigall his wife bo : 16 Sep[t] 1663

theire son Trustrum bo : 18 Janua : 1665

Edward Son of Peter Coffin by Abigall his Wife bor : y[e] 20th ffebru : 1669

Judeth dau : of Peter Coffin by Abigall his wife bor : ye 4th ffeb : 1672

Elizabeth dau : of Peter Coffin by Abigall his wife bo : y[e] 27 January 1680

James Coffin Maried to Mary Seauerne y[e] 1[t] Nou. 1663 pr Cap[t] Pike theire daught[r] Mary bo : 18 : Aprill 1665 :

Thomas chesley & Elizabeth Thomas were marryed the 22[d] of August 1663 by m[r] Ed : Hilton

Thomas chesley Son of Tho : chesly by Elizabeth his wife bo: 4th June 64

Robert chapman Son of Rob[t] Chapman by Elizabeth his wife bo : the 18th decem : 64 : & dyed y[e] 6th of Janua : following

Robert Clemons Maried to Joanna Carr y[e] 2[d] of Aprill 1667

Jonathan Church Son: of Jn" church by Abigall his wife borne y" 12 Apr: 1666

John Church Son of Jn" church by Abigall his wife borne ye 12: Aprill 1668

Ebenezer Son of Jn" church by Abigall his wife bo: 25: ffebb: 1669

Abigall: daugh. of Jn" church by Abigall his wife bo: 12 August 1672

Joseph Canny Son: of Tho: Canny Senr mar: to Mary Clements ye 25th Decemb: 1670

Joseph: the Son: of Joseph Canny by Mary his wife bo: 14th octob. 1674

Jane Canny dau: of Joseph Canny by Mary his wife bo ye 16: Decem: 1671

Mary dau: of Joseph Canny by Mary his wife bo: ye 25: ffeb: 1678

Job Clements Senr mar: to Joane Laighton ye 16th of July 1673 pr. Maj^r Waldren

Henry Crowne married to Alice Rogers y^e 1: of May 1676

John Son: of Hen: Crowne by Alice his wife bo: y^e 10th Nouem: 1679

Elizabeth dau: of Hen: Crowne by Alice his wife bo: y^e 27th May 1684

Agnes dau: of Hen: Crowne by Alice his wife bo: y^e 19th July 1686

Rebecka, dau: of Hen Crown by Alice his wife bo. y^e 23: Jan'y $\frac{89}{90}$

William, Son, of Hen: Crowne by Alice his wife bo. 1 Jan'y 9$\frac{1}{2}$

Jonathan Clarke mar: to Mary Magoone y^e 6th Septr 1686 pr. Jus: Wadleigh

John Vrin mar: to Rebecca Cate y^e 12: Nouem^r 1686: pr Jus: Craffort

Jn" Cluff maried to Mathew [Martha?] Silly the 15th Janua: 1686: pr. Jus: Green

Joseph: Son of Jos: Cash dyed 22: Janua 1686

Moses Cox aged aboute 93 years died y^e 28: May 1687

Mehetabel dau: of Israel Clifford by Ann his wife bo: 9th July 1686

John Son of John Clifford Junr by Sarah his wife bo: 6th ffebr^y 1686

Mary dau: of Joseph Cass by Mary his wife bo: 26: ffebr: 1686

Jonathan So: of Sam^{ll} Colcord by Mary his wife born y^e 4th March 168$\frac{3}{4}$

Elizabeth dau: of Sam^{ll} Colcord by Mary his wife bor: y^e 26: decem^r 1686

John Cook mar: to Mary Downes Nouem^r 26: 1686: pr m^r Pike
John Cromwell mar: to Elizabeth Thomas y^e 13th Janua: 169$\frac{1}{2}$
The Children of Sam^{ll} Cutt and Elioner his wife
2 Decem: 1694 John there Son was born
23 Feb: 1697 Sam^{ll} there Son was born

HAMPTON.

7 Dec: 1706 Sam^{ll} the Son of Sam^{ll} Chapman Junr & Phebee born
8 Feb: 1704/5 Eliz^a the Daug: of Benj^a Cram Junr & Sarah born
6 Aug: 1706 Hibzibah the Daug: of the S^d Cram &c: born
22 Aug: 1706 Jonathan the Son of John & Mary Cram born

D.

Hannah Dauis daugh^r of Jno Dauis bo 24 decem: 1653
Jane Dauis dau: of John Dauis bo 29 Decem: 1655
Moses Dauis Son of John Dauis bo 30 Decem: 1657
Joseph Dauis Son of Jno Dauis bo 26: Janua 1659
James Dauis Son of Jno Dauis bo 23 May 1662
Jane Dauis dau. Jno Dauis dyed ye 23: Sep^{tr} 1656
Jane Dauiss 2^d daugh: Jno Dauiss bo: 15 May 1664
Elizabeth Dam: dau. of Jno Dam Senr bo 1 may 1649
Mary Dam dau: Jno Dam Senr by Elizabeth his wife bo. 4th Sep^t 1651
William Dam Son of Jno Dam Senr by Elizath his wife bo: 14 octob: 1653
Susanna Dam dau of Jno Dam Senr by Elizabth his wife bo 14 dec: 1661
Judeth Dam: dau: of Jno Dam by Elizabeth his wife bo: 15: Nou: 1666
Abigall Dam: daugh^r of Jno Dam Junr bo: ye 5th Aprill 1663.
John Dam Junr maryed Elizabeth furber his 2^d wife 9: Nou. 64 by Capt Walden
there Son: Jno bo: 11: Janu: 65
John Dam: Son: of Jno Dam Junr by Elizabeth his wife bo: 23: ffebru: 1667
Alice ye daugh: of Jno Dam Ju^r by Elizab: his wife bo ye 14th decem: 1670
Elizabeth Downes daugh of Tho: Downes by Katherne his wife borne the 17 Nouem 1663

Patrick Denmark Son: of Patrick Denmarke by Hannah his wife bor: ye 8th of Aprill: 1664

theire Son: James bo: 13 march: 65:

Jno Doe Son of Nicholas Doe by Martha his wife bo: ye 25 August 1669

Samson Doe Son of Nicho. Doe by Martha his wife bo: ye 1^t of Aprill 1670

Elizabeth Doe dau: of Nicho: Doe by Martha his wife bo: ye 7th ffebr: 1673

Sarah dau: of Abraham Drake Junr by Sarah his wife bor: 7th Nouem^r 1686

Jonathan Son of Thomas Dearborn by Hannah his wife bor. 18: Nouem^r 1686

Mary dau: of Simon Dow by Sarah his wife bor: ye 19: Nouem^r 1686

Joseph the Son of Samuel Dow by Abigail his wife bor: 13: decem^r 1686

John Duglas mar to Suah Neson Wid: 16: Sep^t 1687:

24 June	1703	Joseph Dennet Maryed Eliz^a Meed both of Portsm^o
13 Jan^{ry}	1705	Eliz^a there Daug: born
1 Oct:	1707	Hanah there Daug: born
29 Dec:	1709	Lydia there Daug: born
8 Nov:	1703	Timothy Davis Maryed Eliz^a Badger Portsm^o
12 July	1704	John there Son born
12 Oct:	1705	Mary there Daugh: born
13 Apr:	1707	Joanah there Daugh: born

PORTSM^o

The Children of John Dennet and Ame his wife

15 Dec:	1675	John there Son born
9 Apr:	1679	Ame there Daugh: born
19 July	1681	Joseph there Son born
2 Aug:	1683	Epha: there Son born
1 March	1688/9	Sam^{ll} Douse Maryed Sarah Berry New Castle
2 March	——	Joanah there Daug: born
4 Oct	1690	Sam^{ll} there Son born
8 Feb:	1692/3	John there Son born
16 Feb:	1694/5	Anna there Daug: born
3 Jan^y	1696/7	Sollomon there Son born
6 Nov:	1699	Susanah there Daug: born
12 Dec:	1701	Ozem there [———] born

E

Thomas Edgerly Maried to Rebecka Hallwell 28 : Sep^t 65 pr. Capt Walden

Robert Euens Son of Robert Euens by Elizabeth his wife born ye 30th Sep^t 1665

Edward ye Son Roberts Euens by Elizabeth his wife bo ye 28 June 1667

Jonathan the Son of Robt Euens by Elizab : his wife bo : 10 : Aprill 1669

Elizabeth Euens : dau : of Robert Euens by Elizabeth his wife bo : 25 : January 1671

Nathaniel Eastwick Son of Phesant Eastwick by Sarah his wife bo : ye 7th Aprill 1682

Thomas Euens mar : to Hannah Browne ye 30 : Septr 1686 pr. Jus : Greene

Thomas Edgerly married to Jane Whedon ye 3^d Decemb^r 1691

F.

Susanna ffurber dau : of W^m ffurber by Elizabeth his Wife borne the 5th of May 1664

Mehetabel dau : of Benjamin ffifield by Mary his Wife bo : 9th April 1687

John ffootman mar : to Sarah Cromwell ye 18 Decem^r 1691

12 Sep^t 1700 Nich : ffollet Maryed Mary Hull both of Portsm^o

8 Dec : 1704 Sam^{ll} there Son born & Dyed 4 May 1709

25 Aug : 1707 Nich : there Son born & Dyed 11 Dec : 1707

G.

John Greene Marryed to Mary Jenkins ye 12 : 9 m^o 1666

Elihu Gullison Married to Martha Trickie ye 10th of Nouem : 1674

Thomas Graffort mar : to Bridget Daniel widow ye 11 Decem^r 1684 pr. Jus ffrost

Peter Son of Peter Garland by Elizabeth his wife bor : 4th octob^r 1686

30 Oct : 1701 Caleb Griffeth Maryed Eliz^a the Daug : of Ed : Ayers

8 Aug : 1702 Caleb there Son born

Ed^w there Son born 1 Feb : 1703 & Dyed the 24 March 1703/4

1 Feb : 1704 Joshua there Son born

23 Sep^t 1707 Gershom there Son born

H.

Benjamin Heard Son of Jn⁰ Heard by Elizabeth his wife bo 20 ffeb: 1643

Mary Daugh^r Jn⁰ Herd by Elizabeth his wife bo 26 Jan: 1649

Abigall dau: of Jn⁰ Heard by Elizabeth his wife bo. 2 Augt 1651

Elizabeth: dau: Jn⁰ Heard by Elizabeth his wife bo. 15 Sep^{lr} 1653

Hannah: dau. Jn⁰ Heard by Elizabeth his wife bo 25 Nou. 1655

John: Son of Jn⁰ Heard by Elizabeth his wife bo 24: ffeb: 1658

Joseph: Son of John Heard by Elizabeth his wife bo 4th Janu 1660

Samuell Heard Son: Jn⁰ Heard by Elizab his wife bo: 4 aug^t 1663

Nathaniell Son of Jn⁰ Heard by Elizabeth his wife bo: 20th Septmb^r 1668

Trustrum Son of Jn⁰ Heard by Elizabeth his wife bo: ye 4th March 1666

John Horne Son of Wm Horne by Elizabeth his wife bo: 25 octo. 63

William: So: of Wm Horne by Elizabeth his wife bo: 11: of May 1674

Thomas: So: of Wm Horne by Elizabeth his wife bo: y^e 28th Nouem: 1676:

Margarit dau: of Wm Horne by Elizabeth his wife bo: 10th of May 1679

Grace Hall dau of Jn⁰ Hall by Elizab: his wife bo 16: March $\frac{63}{64}$

Sarah Hall dau: of Ralph Hall by Mary his wife dyed y^e 16 July 63

Benjamin Hill Son of Jn⁰ Hill by Elizabeth his wife bo: 8th Apr^{ll} 65

Enock Hutchins Married to Mary Steeuenson y^e 5th of Aprill 1667

John Hunking Son of John Hunking by Agnis his Wife borne y^e 2^d of March 1651 & dyed in England, In July 1666

Herculis Hunking So of Jn⁰ Hunking by Agnis his Wife bo: ye 11th July 1656

Jn⁰ Hunking So of Jn⁰ Hunking by Agnis his Wife bo: ye 6th Aprill 1660

Peter Hunking So of Jn⁰ Hunking by Agnis his Wife bo: 20: March: 1662

Agnis daugh^r of Jn⁰ Hunking by Agnis his Wife bo: ye 2^d June 1665

Willia Hunking 2^d, So of Jn⁰ Hunking by Agnis his Wife bo: ye 6th Janua: 1667

Marke Hunking son of Jn⁰ Hunking by Agnis his Wife bo: 17 May 1670

John Ham: Married to Mary Heard 6th of May 1668

Mary Daugh: of Jn" Ham by Mary his wife born y" 2ᵈ october 1668
Elizabeth dau: of Jn" Ham, by Mary his wife bo: 29ᵗʰ January 1674
Joseph: So: of John Ham by Mary his wife bo: yᵉ 3ᵈ June 1678
John Hall Junʳ Married to Abigall Roberts 8ᵗʰ of Nouem: 1671 pr Capt Waldren

Jn" Hall So: of Jn" Hall pr Abigall his wife bor: 27ᵗʰ June 1673
Thomas Son of Jnᵒ Hall pr Abigal his wife bo: 19ᵗʰ June 1675
Abigall dau: of Jn" Hall by Abigall his wife bo: 24 ffebru: 1679

Sam: Haynes Married to Mary ffifield yᵉ 9: Jannuary 1672 before mʳ Sam Dolton of Hampton comissoʳ entred againe on a leafe

Soloman Hambleton Son of Dauid Hambleton by his wife bo: yᵉ 10ᵗʰ Auguᵗ 1666

Jonathan: Son: of Dauid Hambleton bo: 20: of Decemb: 1672

Jn" Haise & Mary his wife were marᵈ yᵉ 28 June 1686 pr Jus: Coffin

Jn" Horne & Mary his wife were mar: yᵉ 30 June 1686: pr Jus: Coffin

Sarah Huggins dau: of James Huggins by Sarah his wife bo: 12ᵗʰ Decem: 1672

Sarah dau: of James Huggins by Sarah his wife bo: 12ᵗʰ decemb 1674

James Son of James Huggins by Sarah his wife bo: 16: July 1675
John Hodey mar: to Mary Reddan yᵉ 21: June 1675
Mary dau: of Jn" Hoddey by Mary his wife bo: 1ᵗ march 167⅞
Jn" Son of Jn" Hodey by Mary his wife bo 27: August 1679
Arthur So: of Jn" Hody by Mary his wife bo: 25: August 1681
Samˡ So: of Jn" Hodey by Mary his wife bo: 4ᵗʰ octobʳ 1683

Samˡˡ Haynes Junʳ mar: to Mary ffifield yᵉ 9ᵗʰ January 1672
Sarah dau: of Sam: Haynes by Mary his wife bo: yᵉ 6ᵗʰ octob: 1673
Elianor dau: of Sam: Haynes by Mary his wife bo: yᵉ 23: auguᵗ 1675
Mathias Son: of Sam Haynes by Mary his wife bo: yᵉ 7ᵗʰ march 167⅚
Wᵐ Son of Sam Haynes by Mary his wife bo: yᵉ 7ᵗʰ of January 1678
Vide: Mary & Sam pr contra:

Mathias Haynes Mar: to Jane Bracket yᵉ 28ᵗʰ of Decem: 1671
Samˡˡ Son of Mathias Haynes by Jane his wife bo: yᵉ 25ᵗʰ Decem: 1674
Joshua Son of Mathias Haynes by Jane his wife bo: yᵉ 5ᵗʰ of Aprill 1678

Mary Hanson dau: of Isaac Hanson by Mary his wife bo: y" 18: May 1679

Apphia dau: of Timothy Hilliard by Apphia his wife bor. 29 August 1686

Mary dau: of Morris Hobbs Junr by Sarah his wife bor: 5th march 168 6/7

20 Nov: 1705 Tho: the Son of Joseph & Jane Hart born

Reuben Hull maried to Hannah ffarniside the [———]

yr dau{r} Elizabeth bor: 9 Septb{r} 1673

Joseph: Son of Reuben Hull by Hannah his wife borne y" 31 march 1676

Dodauah Son of Reuben Hull by Hannah his wife bor: 31 decem{r} 1681

Reuben Son of Reuben Hull by Hannah his Wife bor y" 2d August 1684

Sarah dau: of Reuben Hull by Hannah his Wife bor: 25: Sept 1886

Mary dau: of Reuben Hull by Hannah his Wife bor: first Sep{tr} 1688

Mary Haynes: dau: of Samll Haynes by Mary his wife bor: 27 Jan: 1685

Samuel Haynes Son: of Sam: Haynes by Mary his wife bor: 5 July 1687

2d May	1699	Samuel Hart Maryed Mary Euans
18 Jan{ry}	1701	Mary there Daughter born
20 Sept	1701	Samll there Son born
7 Apr:	1703	Sarah there Daug: born: Dyed 6 Sept 1703
16 Aug:	1704	Robert there Son born
8 July	1706	John there Son born
30 Aug:	1708	Tho: there son born
28 Oct:	1680	Samll Hill Maryed Eliza Williams
30 Nov:	1681	John there Son born
7 Nov:	1683	Eliza there Daugh: born
6 Apr:	1685	Mary there Daugh: born
29 Sept	1687	Hanah there Daug: born
29 Sept	1689	Abigail there Daug: born
13 Dec:	1696	Samll there Son born
28 July	1701	Sarah there Daug: born
2 July	1703	Benja: there Son born
28 July	1706	Joseph there Son born

J

Steeuen Jones Maried to Elizabeth ffield 28 Jan 1663 by Capt Waldren

Richard Joce So: of xtopher Joce by Jane his wife bo: ye 10: Nouem 1660

Thomas Son: of christop^r Joce by Jane his wife bo ye 27: June 1662

Joanna dau: of xtop^r Joce by Jane his wife bo: ye 13: march 1664
Margaritt dau: of xtop^r Joce by Jane his wife bo 10: octob^r 1666
John So: of xtop^r Joce by Jane his wife bo: 27 of May 1668
Jane dau of christop^r Joce by Jane his wife bo: 18: July 1670
Samuel So: of christop^r Joce by Jane his wife bo: 6 May 1672
Mary dau: of Christoph^r: Joce by Jane his wife bo: ye 8^t July 1674
John Johnson Mar: to Elianor Bracket ye 26: Decemb^r 1661
John Son: of Jno Johnson by Elianor his wife bo: 2 Nouem: 1662
Rosamon dau: of Jno Johnson by Elianor his wife bo: 10 June 1665
Hannah: dau: of Jno Johnson by Elianor his wife bo: ye 7th ffeb^r 1670

James Son: of Jno Johnson by Elianor his wife bo: 13th Nouem 1673

Ebenezer: Son of Jno Johnson by Elianor his wife bo: 27th Nouem^r 1676

16 Oct	1683	Richd Joce Maried Hanah Martyn of Portsm^o
17 Nov:	1685	Joanah there Daughter borne
20 July	1689	Jane there Daughter borne
20 Jan^y	1694	Mary there Daughter borne
17 Oct:	1696	Rich^d there Son borne
28 Dec	1700	Martyn there Son borne
20 Apr:	1704	Sarah there Daughter borne
14 May	1694	Nath: Jackson Maryed Margeritt Ellins Portsm^o
6 Apr:	1705	Joshua there Son born
26 Oct:	1702	Nath: there Son born
11 Dec:	1707	John Son of John and Margeret Jackson born

HAMPTON.

| 11 Dec: | 1706 | Anne the Daug: of Hez: & Anne Jenings born Ham^{ton} |

K.

Sarah Kettle dau: of Jno Kettle by Sarah his wife bo: y^e 8: of march 166$\frac{2}{3}$

John Kettle So: of Jno Kettle by Sarah his wife bo: y^e 6th August 1666

Richard Kenney mar: to Deborah Stokes Augt 15: 1687

17 March 1698/9 W^m the Son of Daniel & Mary King born

4 Feb: 1695 Sam^{ll} Keais Maried the Wido^w Mary Hoddy

11 Apr: 1697 They had there Son Sam^{ll} borne

27 Aug: 1699 There Son William borne

L.

Elizabeth Ludecas Wife of Dauid Ludecas dyed 16 Nouem 1663
Allen Lyde Maried to Sarah ffirnald ye 3^d of Decemb^r 1661
Allen Son of Allen Lyde by Sarah his wife bor: ye 29th July 1666.
Thomas Layton of Dou^r Senr dyed ye 22^d January 1671
Mary daugh^r of Jno Light by Dorothy his wife bo: 20th March 1677
Robert Son of Jno Light by Dorothie his wife bo: 15 sep^t 1680
John Son of Jno Light by Dorothy his wife bo: 8^t ffebru: 1682
Dorothy dau: of Jno Light by Dorothy his wife bo: 28^t April 1685
Henry Lamprell mar: to Elizabeth Mitchel ye 24: July 1686 pr. Jus: Green

Thomas Son of Aretas Louit by Ruth his wife bor 15 Janua: 1686
Abraham Lee: mar: to Hester Elkins widow: 21: June 1686
Tobias Langdon mar: to Mary Hubbart 17th Nouem^r 1686
Elizabeth dau: of Tobias Langdon by Mary his wife was bor: y^e 17th of Nouem^r 1687

11 Oct:	1689	Tobias there Son born
7 March	169$\frac{2}{3}$	Martha there Daug: born
14 Apr:	1694	Rich^d there Son born
28 ffeb:	169$\frac{5}{6}$	Joseph there Son born
15 Sep^t	1698	Marks there Son born
6 Sep^t	1700	Samuel there Son born
30 Oct:	1702	William there Son born
28 May	1707	John there Son born
16 Jan^y	1701	John Low Maryed Joanah Partridge Portsm^o
1 Feb:	170$\frac{1}{2}$	Sarah there Daugh: born
3 Apr:	1704	Mary there Daug: born
10 Sep^t	1706	John there Son born
6 Feb:	1708/9	Joanah ther Daug: born

9 June   1698   James Leby Maryed Mary Hanson Portsm"
23 Nov: 1700   James there Son born
14 Feb: 1702/3 Mary there Daughter born
10 June   1705   Sarah there Daug: born
15 Nov: 1691   Allen the Son of Allen and Eleoner Loyde born
28 Sep¹   1695   ffrancis there Daug: born

M.

Elizabeth Meader dau: of Jn" Meader by Abigal his wife bo: 26: march 1665

Sarah, Daughʳ of Jn" Meader by Abigall his wife borne 11 January 1668

Nathaniel Son: of Jn" Meader by Abigall his wife bor 14: June 1671

Mary yᵉ dau: of Rich: Martyn by Sarah his wife bo: yᵉ 7ᵗʰ June 1655

Sarah dau of Ric: Martyn by Sarah his wife bo 3ᵈ July 1657

Richard Son: of Ric: Martyn by Sarah his wife bo 10ᵗʰ Janua 1659

Elizabeth dau: of Ric: Martyn by Sarah his wife bo 31 July 1662

Hannah: dau of Ric: Martyn by Sarah his wife bo: 2ᵈ Janua 1664

Michaell Son: of Ric: Martyn by Sarah his wife bo: 3ᵈ ffebru: 1666

John Son of Rich Martyn by Sarah his wife bo: yᵉ 9ᵗʰ June 1668

Elias Martyn So: of Ric: Martyn by Sarah his wife bo: yᵉ 18: Aprill: 1670

Josiah Son of Josiah Moulton by Lucy his wife bor: 21 Nouemʳ 1686

James yᵉ Son of Benjamin Moulton by Hannah his wife bor: 13: decemʳ 1686

Margery Marion aged aboute 78 years died yᵉ 2ᵈ May 1687

Thomas Marshall mar: to Abizag Palmer febʳ 4: 1686 pr Just Barefoote

ffrancis Mathewes mar: to Ruth Bennet 23ᵈ ffebru 169½

Samuel Moodey married Esther Green of Boston April 4ᵗʰ 1695

Joshua Son of Samuel Moodey by Esther his Wife was born at New Castle in New Hampshire Feb: 11ᵗʰ 9⅝ Died may 27, 1696

Joshua 2ᵈ Son of Samˡˡ Moodey by Esther his Wife born at New Castle Ocbr. 31, 1697 on Sabbath day at Night

Samuel Son of Samˡˡ Moodey by Esther his Wife was born at New Castle Ocbʳ 29, 1699 on Sabbath day night between 11 & 12 a Clock.

Mary Daughter of Sam^ll & Esther his wife was born at New Castle Nov^br 16, 1701 on a Sabbath day Night about 11 a Clock

25 Feb:	170½	Geo: Marshal Maryed Eliz^a Hill Portsm^o
19 March	170⅔	Lydia there Daug: born
21 Aug:	1705	Geo: there Son born
23 Oct:	1695	James Mardin Maryed Abigail Webster New Castle
25 Sep^t	1697	James there Son born
28 Aug:	1699	Stephen there Son born
20 July	1701	Rachel there Daug: born
30 Apr:	1703	John there Son born

HAMPTON.

6 Dec:	1706	John the Son of John & Mary Moulton born
16 Dec:	1706	Mary Daugh: of Daniel & Mary Moulton born

N.

Elizabeth Nock daugh^r of Tho: Nock by Rebecka his Wife bo 21 Nou 1663

Thomas Nock himselfe dyed ye 29 octob^r 1666

Henry Nock Son of Tho: Nock by Rebecka his Wife born eight ffebru, 1666

Elizabeth: daughter of Tho: Nock dyed ye 12: may 1669

John Nutter Son of Anthony Nutter by Sarah his wife bo 27 Dec 1663

John Nason mar: to Hannah Heard ye 6th of Nouem^r 1674 pr Capt Waldren

Samuel Neale Son of Walter Neale by Mary his wife bo: ye 14th June 1661

Mary daugh of Walter Neale by Mary his wife bo: ye 31: mar: 1668 she herselfe dyed ye first friday in Aprill following: 1668

Siluanus Nock was married to Elizabeth Emry the 20: of Aprill 1677

Elizabeth: dau: of Siluanus Nock by Elizabeth his wife bo ye 12: ffeb: 1677

Sarah Dau: of Siluanus Nock by Elizabeth his wife bo ye 4 of May 1680

Benjamin Nason mar: to Martha Kenny 30: June 1687

Henry Nock mar. to Sarah Adams ye 10th January 169½

O.

Solomon Oates Son of Rich: Oates by Rose his wife bo: 15 octo. 63 & dyed aboute the first of march following

Experience Oates daught[r] of Ric: Oates by Rose his wife bo: 7 Nouem 1666

Steuen Oates the Son of Ric: Oates Sen[r] was married to Mary Pittman dau[r] of W[m] Pittman y[e] 16: of Aprill: 1674: pr. Cap[t] Waldren:

P.

John Partridg Maried to Mary ffurnald the 11: of Decemb. 1660

Hannah: daugh[r] of Jn[o] Partridg by Mary his wife bo: y[e] 14th of octob: 1661

Jn[o] y[e] Son of John Partridg by Mary his wife bo: y[e] 3[d] of January 1663

Mary y[e] daugh[r] of Jn[o] Partridg by Mary his wife bor: y[e] 26: ffebrua 1665

Sarah y[e] dau: of Jn[o] Partridg by Mary his Wife, bo y[e] 3[d] of Sept[r] 1668

Rachel the dau: of Jn[o] Partridg by Mary his wife borne y[e] 4th of march 16$\frac{70}{71}$

Elizabeth dau: of John Partridge by Mary his wife bo: y[e] 4th July 1673

Abigall dau: of Jn[o] Partridge by Mary his wife bo: y[e] 2: ffeb: 1675

Patience dau: of Jn[o] Partridge by Mary his wife bo: 4th July 1678

Brian Pendleton So. of James Pendleton by Hannah his Wife born the 27: of Septemb[r] 1659

Joseph Pendleton So of James Pendleton by Hannah his Wife bo Decem 1661

Edmund Pendleton So of Ja: Pendleton by Hannah his Wife bo: 24: June 1665

Ann Pendleton dau: of Ja: Pendleton by Hannah his Wife bo 12: Nou: 1667

Caleb Pendleton So: of James Pendleton by Hanah his Wife bo: 8th aug[t] 1669

John Pickering Jun[r] Married to Mary Stannyan y[e] 10th of Janu 1665

Theire Son John borne y[e] 1[t] of December 1666

Theire daughter Mary borne y[e] 18th July 1668

Thomas Son of John Pickering by Mary his wife bo: y[e] 6th Aprill: 1670 & died y[e] 3 July 1671

Sarah there dau : bo : the 15 feb : 1671 & dyed y^e [————]
Sarah theire 2^d dau : bo : ye 3 : Janua 1673
John Pickering the Eld^r dyed the 18th of Janua 1668
Lt Wm Pomfret died ye 7th of August 1680
Ruth dau : of Joseph Palmer by Deborah his wife bo : ye 31 : August 1686
Elizabeth dau : of Thomas Philbrook Junr by Mehetabel his wife bo : 17th octo^r 1686
Mary dau : of James Perkins by Leah his wife bor 2^d Decem^r 1686
Joseph Son : of ffrancis Page by Merabah his wife bor : 25th Nouem^r 1686
Joseph, a child of Josep Philbrook dyed the 21 ffeb : 1686 being aboute 8 weeks old who was born the 14th decemb^r before —1686
Christopher Son of Samuel Palmer by Ann his wife bo : 12th ffebru 1686
Abigale dau : of Jonathan Perkins by Sarah his wife bor : 30th April 1687
John Son of John Plaisted by Mary his wife bor : 2^d January 1682
Joshua Son of Jno Plaisted by Mary his wife bor : 20th Septem^r 1685
Mary dau : of Jno Plaisted by Mary his wife bor : 29 : March : 1687
Samuel Penhallow maried to Mary Cutt ye first day of July 1687
Thomas Packer mar : to Elizabeth Hall Wid : 7 Augu^t 1687
John Pickerin Junr mar : to Elizabeth Munden 17 July 1688
Walter Philbrook Son : of Wm Philbrook by Mary his Wife bo : 10th Nouem^r 1690
Mary dau : of Wm Philbrook by Mary his Wife bo : ye 20th May 1692

4 May	1699	Tho : Phips Maryed Eleoner Cutt both Portsm^o
11 Aug :	1701	Eleoner there Daughter born
7 Nov :	1703	Mary there Daughter born
22 Nov :	1676	Tho : Phipps by Solomon & Mary born at Charles Town
8 March	1704/5	Noah Parker by Noah & Eliz^a his wife born
11 Jan^{ry}	1692/3	William Partridge Maryed Abigail Reading
2 Feb :	1695/6	Nehemiah there Son borne
8 Dec :	1694	Sarah there Daug : born
22 Jan^{ry}	1697/8	William there Son born and Dyed the 19 Feb 1677/8
9 Apr :	1699	Mary there Daug : born
24 Dec	1700	William there Son born And Dyed 4 March 1701/2

25 Feb:	1702	William there Son born
10 Feb:	1703/4	Abigail there Daug: born
29 Aug:	1704	Abigail the Wife of William Patridge Dyed
28 Nov:	1710	William Partridge Maryed the Widd^{w} Hanah Griffin
26 Feb:	1702/3	William Parker Maryed Surviah Stanley
9 Dec:	1703	William there Son born
5 Jan^{ry}	1704/5	Katherine there Daug: borne
22 Dec:	1706	John there Son borne

Tho: Peirse by Mehetible his Wife had Children

4 Jan^{ry}	1702/3	Viz: Mary there Daughter born
14 July	1704	Sarah there Daug: born
9 June	1706	Hanah there Daug: born
5 Jan^{ry}	1692	Icabod Plaisteed Maryed Mary Joce
10 June	1696	Samuel there Son borne
21 July	1700	Icabod there Son borne
6 Oct	1702	Mary there Daughter borne
29 Aug:	1708	Oliue there Daughter borne
22 May	1711	Robt Pike & Eliz^{a} Atkinson Ware Married

Robt there Son borne at New Castle y^{e} 17th of Jan^{ry} 17$\frac{12}{13}$ About 5 a Clock After Noon It being Saterday

John their Son Born [———]

Theodore Their 3^{d} Son born Jan^{ry} 9th 1718/19

Eliz^{a} Pike Dyed Feb^{ry} 5th 1719/20

June 28 1722 Theodore their Son Dyed

HAMPTON.

| 8 Dec: | 1706 | Eliz^{a} Daug of Joseph & Tryphane Philbrook born |

R.

HAMPTON.

| 30 Dec: | 1706 | Satchel Runlet Maryed Mercy Leavet |
| 13 Jan^{ry} | 1706/7 | Icabod Robey Maryed Mary Cass |

S.

Margerit Steeuenson W: of Tho: Steeuenson dyed ye 26: Nou 1663

Thomas Steeuenson dyed ye 7th decemb 1663

Elias Stileman Maried to Ruth Mannyard ye 10th of Aprill 1667

John Shepway Son: of John Shepway by Ann: his wife borne ye 26: July 1662

John Smith Son of Joseph Smith by Elizabeth his wife bo : 9th January 1669

Mary Steeuens dau : of Nath[ll] Steeuens by Mary his Wife bo : 4th octob. 1672

William So : of Rich : Scamon by Prudence his wife bo : y[e] 29 : ffebrua : 1664

Jane : dau : of Rich : Scamon by Prudence his wife bo : y[e] 21 : July 1667

Prudence, dau : of Ric : Scamon by Prudence his wife bo : 29 : August 1669

Elizabeth : dau : of Ric : Scamon by Prudence his wife bo : 22 : Aprill : 1671

Mary dau : of Rich : Scamon by Prudence his wife bo : 31 : May 1673

Moses Son of Aron Sleper by Elizabeth his wife bor : 22 : January 1684

Thomas Son of Aron Sleeper by Elizabeth his wife bor : 3[d] Nouem 1686

Mary dau : of Rich[d] Stileman by Mary his wife bo : y[e] 6th January 1657

Elizabeth dau : of Rich : Stileman by Mary his wife bo y[e] 8[t] May 1663

Sarah : dau : of Rich : Stileman by Mary his wife bo : the 30th June 1665

Richard Son : of Rich : Stileman by Mary his wife bo : y[e] 20 : March 1667/68

himself dyed the 11 : of October 1678 :

Jn[o] Seauey mar : to Hannah Walker widow 29 July 1686 pr Jus Barefoot

Mary Sanburne wife of W[m] Sanburn Jun[r] dyed the 11th octob[r] 1686

Their daughter not having a name dyed y[e] 3 Nou : 1686

Moses Swet mar : to Mary Hussey 12th May 1687 pr. Just : Green

Lidia dau : of John Samborn Jun[r] by Judeth his wife bor : 24th ffeb : 1686

Abigaile dau : of John Smith, Coop. by Huldah his wife bo : 19 : May 1687

Richard Shortridge mar : to Alice Creeber may the 16 : 1687 : pr Jus : Barefoote

Thomas Starbeard mar : Abigal Damm 4th January 1687

15 March 1707/8 Tho : Sevy of New Castle Dyed

HAMPTON.

22 Jan^ry 1706/7 Sam^ll Smith Maryed Eliz^a Pees
11th May 1702 Joseph Simpson & Hanah Lewis were Married
26 June 1712 Hanah Simpson Dyed
17 March 1713/14 Joseph Simpson & Merriam Easmon were Married
16 Jan^ry 1714/15 Joseph their Son born
14 Octob^r 1716 Abigail their Daughter born
14 ffeb^y 1722/3 John their Son Born

T.

Jeremiah: the Son of Jeremiah Tibbet by Mary his wife bo: ye 5 June 1656

Mary theire daught^r borne ye 15 Aprill: 1658:

Thomas Tibbet Son of Jer: Tibbet by Mary his wife bo: 24 feb: 1659

Hannah Tibbet daught^r of Jer: Tibbet by Mary his wife bo: 25 feb: 1661

Joseph Tibbett Son: of Jer: Tibbet by Mary his wife bo: ye 7th August 1663

William Thomson Married to Mary Loueren ye 4th Sepr 1682 pr Elias Stileman

Joshua Towel married to Sarah Reed the 2^d Decem^r 1686 by Justis Green

John Son: of John Tuck by Bethia his wife bo: 19 April 1687
Mary dau: of John Taylor by Debora his wife bor 3^d May 1687
John Twamly mar: to Mary Kenny April 18: 1687
Samuel Tibbets mar: to Dorothy Tuttle Sep^t 1^t 1686
Stephen Tobey mar: to Hannna Nelson 29: Nouem^r 1688:
Elias Tarelton Son of Richard Tarleton by Ruth his Wife borne the 13 of August 1693 being L^ds day

V.

Humphrey Varney Maried to Sarah Storer ye 2^d of March: 64
Theire Son: Peter bo: 29 March: 1666

Jno: Verney Son of Vmph: Varney by Sarah his wife died 14 aug^t 1666

Joseph Varney So: of Hump: Varney by Sarah his wife borne y^e 8 octob^r 1667

Abigall the daughter of Hump^r Varny by Sarah his wife borne 10th July 1669

Wm Vaughan Married to Margarett Cutt y^e 8th of December 1668:

Ellinor dau: of Wm Vaughan by Margarett his wife bo: y^e 5th march 16$\frac{69}{70}$

Mary dau: of Wm Vaughan by Margarett his wife bo: y^e 6 march 16$\frac{71}{2}$

Cutt y^e So: of Wm Vaughan by Margaret his wife bo: y^e 9: march 1673/4

George y^e Son of Wm Vaughan by Margeret his wife bo: 13 Aprill 1676

Bridget dau: of Wm Vaughan by Margeret his wife bo: 2: July 1678

Margerit dau: of Wm Vaughan by Margerit his wife bo: 30th of December 1680

Abigall dau: Wm Vaughan by Margaret his wife bor: y^e 5: of May 1683

Elizabeth dau: of Wm Vaughan by Margaret his wife bo: 26: of April 1686

Mrs Margaret Vaughan died y^e 22 day of January 169$\frac{0}{1}$ ben mar: 22 years 6 weeks

John Vrin mar: to Rebecca Cate the 12th Nouem: 1686 pr Jus: Crafort

9 Jan^ry	1701	Geo: Vaughan Maryed Eliz^a Eliot
8 Feb:[170]1		Sarah there Daug: born
12 Sep^t	1703	William there Son born
21 Aug:	1705	Margeret there Daug: born Dyed 9 Sep^t 1706
22 July	1706	Geo: there Son born
3 Oct	1707	Eliz^a there Daug: born

W.

William Williams Son off Wm Williams by Margarit his wife bo: 22 Decem *16

John Williams Son of Wm Williams by Margarit his wife bo: 30 march 64

Elizabeth Williams daught^r of Wm Williams by Margaret his wife bo 25: octob: 1665

Edward Waymouth Maried to Hester Hodsdon 25 Dec: 63 by Capt Walden

Eliazer Waldren Son of Capt Ric: Waldren by Ann his Wife bo: the first day of may 1665

*Last two figures of the year torn off.—[Ed.

Elizabeth Waldren dau: of Capt Ric: Waldren by Ann: his Wife bo 18: octo^r 1666

Marah Waldren dau: of cap^t Ric: Waldren by Ann his wife bo 17 July 1668

Samuel Wentworth Son: of Samuel Wentworth by Mary his wife borne ye 9th Aprill 1666

Daniel Son of Sam^ll Wentworth by Mary his wife bo: 21 octob^r 1669

John So: of Sam: Wentworth by Mary his wife borne ye 16: January 1671

Mary daught^r of Sam Wintworth by Mary his wife bo: ye 5: ffebr: 1673

Ebenezer: So: of Saml Wintworth by Mary his wife bo: ye 9: Aprill 1677

Dorothy dau: of Sam Wintworth by Mary his wife bo: ye 27th June 1680

Bening So: of Sam: Wintworth by Mary his wife bo: ye 28th June 1682

Ann Wingett daugh^r of Jno Winget by Mary his wife bo: ye 18th ffebru: 1667

John: Sonn of Jno Wingett by Mary his wife bo: 13: July 1670

Allexand^r Waldren died ye 7th of June 1676

Richard Son of Rich: Waterhouse by Sarah his Wife bo: ye 19th Aprill 1674

Samuel Son: of Rich: Waterhouse by Sarah his wife bo: ye 9th May 1676

Jno Weekes Son: of Leonard Weekes by Mary his wife bo: ye 14th June 1668.

Sam: Son: of Leonard Weekes by Mary his wife bo: ye 14th decemb: 1670

Joseph: So: Leonard Weekes by Mary his wife bo ye 11 may: 1671

Joshua: So: of Leonard Weekes by Mary his wife bo: 30: June 1674

Mary dau: of Leonard Weekes by Mary his wife bo: y^e 19 July 1676

Margaret dau: of Leonard Weekes by Mary his wife bo: y^e 4th June 1679

George Wollis mar: to Ann Shortridge Nouem^r 18: 1686 pr. Jus: Barefoote

John Wallinsford mar: to Mary Tuttle 6: Decem^r: 1687

Edward Wakeham mar to Sarah Meader 16: March 169$\frac{1}{2}$

10 July 1701 Richd Wiberd Maryed the Wido^w Eliz^a Redford Portsm^o

7 July	1702	Rich^d there Son borne
20 Oct	1705	John there Son born
Oct:	1707	Tho: there Son born
27 Aug:	1709	Eliz^a there Daug: born
6 Feb:	1692/3	Richd Waldron and Elloner Vaughn Maryed Portsm^o
21 Feb:	1693/4	Rich^d there Son born
16 Nov:	1695	Margeret there Daug: born
*Aug:	1697	William there son born
*9 Aug:	1698	Anna there Daug: born
*8 July	1704	Abigail there Daug: born
7 Apr:	1706	Eleoner there Daug: born

*The day of the month has been wholly or partly torn off; in 1853, according to John Wentworth, these dates read respectively: 4 Aug., 29 Aug., and 28 July.—[ED.

MARRIAGES

BY

REV. JOHN PIKE.

1686-1709.

[Published by permission, from his diary now in library of the Massachusetts Historical Society.]

Mr Abraham Lee married to Ester Elkin widdow Jun. 21, 1686.
Tho: Packer married to Elizab: Hall widdow Aug. 7, 1687.
Sam^{ll} Tibbets married to Dorothy Tuttle Sep: 2, 1686.
Robert Alkins married to Patience Evens widdow Nov: 9, 1686.
John Cook married to Mary Downs Nov: 25, 1686
John Twomley married to Mary Kenney, Ap: 18, 1687.
Ben: Nason married to Martha Kenney Jun. 30, 1687.
Richd Kenney married to Deborah Stokes Aug. 15, 1687.
Clemment Rummeril married to Rebecca Pommery widow, Sep: 6, 1687.
John Wallingsford married to Mary Tuttle Dec: 6, 1687.
John Dugles married to Suah Nason widow Sep: 16, 1687.
Tho: Starboord married to Abigal Damm Jan. 4, 1687[-8].
John Pickerin married to Eliz: Munden July 17, 1688
Stephen Tobey married to Hanna Nelson Nov: 29, 1688.
Job Clements married to Abigail Heard Feb. 28, 1688[-9].
John Hudsen married to Mary Beard, July 25, 1689.
Fran: Graves married to Amy Puddington widdow, Aug: 27, 1689.
Edw: Howard married to Martha Row Aug. 22, 1689.
Tho: Rouse married to Rebecca Rummeril widow Sep: 2, 1689.
Tho: Puddinton married to Rachell Williams, Sep: 20, 1689.
Jeremiah Homes married to Sarah Walker, Sep: 22, 1689.
Elisha Plasted married to Eliz: Harvey Octo: 11, 1689.

MARRIAGES BY REV. JOHN PIKE, 1686-1709.

William Rackley married to Dorathy Lord widow Octo: 18, 1689.
Willm Berry married to Sabina Lock, Decem^r 19, 1689.
George Walker married to Mary Jackson Decem^r 25, 1689.
Tho: Potts married to Johanna Roberts Mar: 24, $\frac{89}{90}$
John Heard married to Phebe Littlefield April 27, 1690.
Wiiliam Grant married to Jane Warren Aug 4, 1690.
Mr Henry Green married to Mary Page widow, Mar: 10, $\frac{90}{91}$
Nath^ll Berry married to Eliz: Philbrick July 2, 1691.
Jonathan Sanburn married to Eliz. Sherburn Feb: 4, 1691[-2].
Willm Hunkins married to Sarah Partridge May 12, 1692.
Nath^ll Sanburn married to Rebecca Presket Dec. 3, 1691.
John Lovit married to Sarah Hobbs, Dec. 30, 1691.
Peter Wear married to Eliza: Wilson Jan. 6, 1691[-2].
John Twomley married to Rachel Allin, Octo: 3, 1692.
Joseph Randal married to Eliz: Garmine Octo: 20, 1692.
John Bickford married to Eliz: Tibbets Dec. 1, 1692.
Rob: Mac-kenney married to Rebec: Sparkes wid. Dec. 1, 1692.
John Cooper married to Sara Lord Dec. 13, 1692.
James Houston married to Mary Door Dec. 23, 1692.
John Lebbey married to Elianor Kirk Dec. 29, 1692.
John Kase married to Joanna Johnson, Ap. 27, 1692.
Robert Goss married to Jane Berry Jan. 5, 1692[-3].
Augustine Bullard married to Hanna Dyer widow Octo: 12, 1693.
Sam^ll Jackson married to Mary Melcher Octo. 12, 1693.
Sam^ll Piper married to Abigail Church, April 23, 1694.
John Cox married to Hanna Hill wid: May 22, 1694.
Michael Whidden married to Eliz: Messervey Jun. 6, 1694.
Henry Sewer married to Mary Huntress Jun. 21, 1694.
William Furbur married to Eliz: Nute wid: Aug. 13, 1694.
William Richards married to Mary Dow, Aug. 23, 1694.
Edward Sargeant married to Joanna Homan, Pemmaquid, Jun. 3, 1695.
John Hayte married to Sara Childe wid: Nov. 10, 1695.
Mr John Wade married to Elizabeth Gerrish, Sep. 3, 1696.
Anthony Lowden married to Sarah Osburn Sep: 16, 1696.
Richard Sanders married to Mary Moss Jun. 17, 1697.
Mark Hunkins married to Mary Harvey Jun. 29, 1697.
Thomas Silley married to Ann Stanian July 2, 1697.
Joseph Richards married to Abigal Rawlins Aug. 12, 1697.
Andrew Wiggin married to Abigal Follett Sep. 2, 1697.

MARRIAGES BY REV. JOHN PIKE, 1686-1709.

Tho : Avery married to Abigal Coomes widow Octo. 8, 1697.
Philipp Lambeth married to Susanna Leer Octo. 14, 1697.
Daniel Jacob married to Abig: Field Octo. 24, 1697.
Moses Boudey married to Ruth Wittum Nov. 29, 1697.
Richard Pommery married to Deliverance Berry Feb. 14, $169\frac{7}{8}$.
John Hamm married to Elizabeth Knight Mar. 14, $169\frac{7}{8}$.
Edward Cloutman married to Sara Tuttle April 22, 1698.
Tobias Hanson married to Ann Lord Aug. 28, 1698.
John Waldron married to Mary Horn wid : Aug. 29, 98.
Thos : Downs married to Abig : Hall wid : Octo : 24 1698.
Benjamin Tubbs married to Eliza : Kim wid : Jan. 12, 1698[-9].
William Monsey married to Rosamond Jacklin Jan. 10, 1698[-9].
Sam^{ll} Kenney married to Sarah Rankin wid : Mar. 15, $16\frac{98}{99}$.
Tho : Horn married to Judith Riccar Apr : 14, 1699.
Joseph Kenny married to Leah Allin Dec. 1, 1699.
John Church married to Mercy Hanson Dec : 1, 1699.
Henry Tibbets married to Joyce Otice wid : Feb. 25, $\frac{1699}{1700}$.
George Brawn married to Sarah Sanders widow. Ap. 1, 1700.
Mark Giles sen: married to Frances Perkins wid : Sep. 2, 1700.
John Cole married to Elizabeth Allin Sep. 23, 1700.
Tho : Pinkham married to Mary Allin Dec. 2, 1700.
Rowland Jenkins married to Tabitha Joy Feb. 10, 1700 [-1].
James Tompson married to Eliz : Fry Mar. 3, $170\frac{0}{1}$.
John Morrel married to Hannah Dixon Mar. 18, $170\frac{0}{1}$.
Joseph Beard married to Eliz : Waldron Mar. 24, $170\frac{0}{1}$.
Ralph Hall married to Mary Chesley May 26, 1701.
George Huntrys married to Sara Morrill Aug. 4, 1701
Jacob Allin married to Martha Damm Feb. 5, $170\frac{1}{2}$.
William Hayt married to Eliz : Nelson wid : Mar. 10, $170\frac{1}{2}$
Jonathan Nason married to Adah Morrel Ap. 27, 1702.
Samuel Shorey married to Mary Roads Ap. 28, 1702.
Samuel Willey married to Mary Canny Jun. 8, 1702.
Richard Chick married to Martha Lord July 11, 1702.
Nathaniel Furnel marrid to Ann Allen Sep. 10, 1702.
Clement Messervy married to Eliz : Jones Sep. 24, 1702.
Benjamin Richards married to Elizabeth Hodgesden alias Galloway Nov. 19, 1702.
John Fabian married to Mary Pickirin Dec. 25, 1702.
John Giles married to Mary Tibbets Dec. 29, 1702.
William Foss married to Sarah Heard widow Ap. 26, 1703.

MARRIAGES BY REV. JOHN PIKE, 1686-1709.

Henry Nutter married to mary Shackford July 26, 1703.
John Wentworth married to Martha Millar Dec. 24, 1703.
Joseph Evens married to Mercy Horn Ap. 6, 1704.
Howard Henderson married to Sarah Roberts Jun. 8, 1704.
Abraham Nute married to Johanna Stanton widow Sep. 2, 1704.
Jacob Roades married to Elianor Brawn Sep. 7, 1704.
John Roberts married to Deborah Church Octo. 16, 1704.
Icabod Rawlings married to Mary Perkins Dec. 25, 1704.
James Chesley married to Thamsin Wentworth Dec. 29, 1704.
Samuel Willey married to Elizabeth Rendal Feb. 19, 170$\frac{4}{5}$.
John Pugsley married to Elizabeth Small Mar. 7, 170$\frac{4}{5}$
Richard Randal married to Elizabeth Blanchant wid. Ap 10, 1705.
John Drew married to Elizabeth Hopley May 24, 1705.
Adrian Fry married to Mercy Chapman Jun. 8, 1705.
John Hall married to Hester Chesley Aug. 9, 1705.
Sylvanus Nock married to Hester Beard wid : Nov. 12, 1705.
Timothy Carle married to Eliz : Hall Dec. 18, 1705.
David Thomas marrried to Elizabeth Brawn Jan. 28, 1705[-6].
Nathaniel Roberts married to Eliz : Mason Apr. 11, 1706.
Henry Jaquis married to Rebecca Pickering Jun. 28, 1706.
Mr John Jambrin of Jersey (belonging to England) was Legally married to Elizabeth Knight alias Sheavalleir, of the town of Dover in New England, upon the 12 of September, 1706, as attest John Pike.
William Eyres married to Mary Hopley Octo. 24, 1706.
John Ford married to Hanna Tydie, Nov. 4, 1706.
John Amblar married to Elizab : Trickey Nov. 6, 1706.
Sylvanus Nock married to Sarah Drisco Dec. 13, 1706.
Solomon Pinkham married to Mary Field Dec. 13, 1706.
John Field married to Sarah Drew Jan. 16, 1706[-7].
Joseph Jones married to Mary Spencer Feb. 7, 170$\frac{6}{7}$.
Hatevil Hall married to Mercy Cromwell March 14, 170$\frac{6}{7}$.
Joseph Wilson married to Elizabeth Chapman Aug. 27, 1707.
Joseph Hall married to Easter Beard Nov. 3, 1707.
Joshua Shuckford married to Elizabeth Barnes Dec. 4, 1707.
Joshua Crocket married to Mary Bickford Dec. 8, 1707.
Gershom Downs married to Sarah Hall Dec. 24, 1707.
Pomfret Dam married Easter Twomley Jan. 14, 1707[-8].
William Dam married to Sarah Kimmin July 29, 1708.
Thomas Tibbets married to Sarah Tibbets Aug. 12, 1708.
Elias Parcher married to Grace Allard Aug. 12, 1708.

William Marrifield married to Margarit Frost Octo: 18, 1708.
John Horn married to Eliz: Heard Dec: 29, 1708.
Jonathan Young married to Abigal Hanson May 12, 1709.
Edward Andrews married to Sarah Churchill Aug. 11, 1709.
Zechariah Field married to Hannah Evens Jan. 12, 1709[-10].
Samuel Smith married to Hannah Burnam Feb. 16, 1709/10.

BAPTISMS

BY

REV. JONATHAN CUSHING

1717-1766.

RECORDS OF FIRST CHURCH, DOVER, N. H.

1717
October 6 Anna, Daugh^r of Capt Timothy Gerrish.
Novr 20 John & Elizabeth, Childⁿ of Benj^a Pierce.
1718
March 30 Thomas & Elihu, Childⁿ of John Hayes.
Aug 17 Gershom Downs.
Septr 28 James Heard & Deborah his Wife; Benjamin, Deborah & Mary their Childⁿ.
Mary, Wife of Daniel Horn; Daniel their son.
Mary, Wife of Saml Jones; John, Abigail & Mary, their Childⁿ.
Widow Mary Ash; Judith her Daugh^r.
Esther Jones.
Abigail Powers.
Octob^r 12 Abigail Hayes.
Peter Cushing, born 9th Inst.
1719
May 31 Samuel & Bridget, Childⁿ of Joseph Bierd.
July 5 Martha Wentworth & her Childⁿ, Richard, Thomas, Ezekiel & Damaris.
19 John, Son of John Wingate.
Aug 2 Joseph, Son of Ann Drew, now Titcomb.

Sept[r]	13	William, Son of Tim[o] Gerrish.
		Mary, Daugh[r] of Paul Gerrish.
Sept[r]	—	Ichabod Hayes & his Child[n].
Nov[r]	29	Gershom, Martha, Thomas, Rebekah, John, Child[n] of Gershom Downs.

1720

March	6	Sarah Hall.
	27	Jonathan Cushing, born 24th Inst.
		Hezekiah, Son of John Hayes.
May	22	Mary, Daugh[r] of James Pinkham.
July	3	Hannah, Wife of Nat[ll] Perkins.
		Eliz[a], Wife of John Bickford, & their Son John.
		Mary, Wife of Jacob Allen, & their Child[n].
		Sam[l], Son of Job Clements.
		The Child[n] of Tristram Heard.
	31	Humphry Foss.
		Sam[l] Heard & Eliz[a] his Wife; Experience & Elizabeth their Child[n].
Aug	14	Lydia, Daugh[r] of James Heard.
Octob	2	Gershom Wentworth.
		Fidellah Harby, negro.
	30	Ann Evans, Widow.
		Ann, Daugh[r] of Daniel Titcomb.

1721

Feb	12	Mary, Daugh[r] of William Chamberlain.
April	16	Ezekiel, Son of Ichabod Hayes.
		Samuel, Son of John Wingate.
June	11	Abigail, Daugh[r] of Cap[t] Tim[o] Gerrish.
		Ichabod, Son of Daniel Horn.
July	2	Samuel, Son of Paul Gerrish.
	30	Abigail, Daugh[r] of Tristram Coffin.
Sept[r]	3	Peter Hayes; Ann & Reuben his Child[n].
Octob	15	Eliz[a], D[r] of Richard Goodwin.

1722

Jan	7	Deborah Cushing, born 5th inst.
Mar	18	Jane, D[r] of Tristram Coffin.
	25	Hannah, Wife of William Jones.
April	22	Reuben, Son of Tristram Heard.
May	6	Maturin Ricker & Hannah his Wife.
		Elizabeth Twombly.

May	13	Joseph Ricker & Eliz^a his Wife, & John their Child.
June	3	John, Son of Saml Heard.
July	1	Hannah, Nathl, Mary, James, Child^n of Thomas Nock.
		Joseph, Son of Peter Hayes.
	8	William, Son of Daniel Titcomb.
		Lois, Daugh^r of James Pinkham.
Sept^r	2	Elizabeth, D^r of John Hayes.
Octob	14	Tamsen, Wife of Joseph Ham, & their Daugh^r Jane.
Nov	25	Capt Benj^a Wentworth.
Dec^r	16	John & Elizabeth, Child^n of Benj^a Wentworth.

1723.

Feb	10	Rebekah, D^r of William Chamberlain.
Mar	17	Daniel, Son of John Wingate.
	18	Job, Son of Job Clements.
April	19	Eleanor, D^r of William Jones.
May	26	Nathaniel, Son of Timothy Gerrish.
July	14	Susanna, D^r of Paul Gerrish.
Aug	4	Mercy, D^r of Thomas Nock.
	25	Thomas Starboard.
Octob	13	——— Son of Ichabod Hayes.
Dec^r	8	Tristram, Son of Tristram Heard jun^r.
	15	Phebe, D^r of James Heard.
	29	William Cushing, born 26th Inst.

1724.

Jan	12	Edward Pevey.
Feb	2	Tristram, Son of Tristram Coffin.
		Abigail, D^r of Capt Benj^a Wentworth.
		Sarah, D^r of Doct^r Jonathan Crosbee.
Mar	8	Joseph Daniels.
	15	Hannah, D^r of Benj^a Twombly.
April	19	Abra, D^r of John Hayes.
		Sarah & Mary, twin Daugh^{rs} of Daniel Titcomb.
		Richard, Son of Richard Goodwin.
May	3	John, Hannah & Elizabeth, Child^n of Richard Plummer.
June	21	Richard, Son of Gershom Downs.
	26	Saml Canny sen^r.
July	5	Benj^a, Son of Peter Hayes.
	16	John Twombly sen^r.
	19	Mary, D^r of Daniel Horn.

Aug	2 Sarah, D^r of Joseph Ricker.
	9 Sarah, Wife of Daniel Plummer.
	Tamsen Wentworth.
Sept^r	13 Ephraim & Hannah, Child^n of Danl Plummer.
Octob	25 Hannah, D^r of James Pinkham.
1725.	
Feb	21 Tamsen, D^r of Benj^a Twombly.
Mar	25 Judith, wife of Capt Thomas Tibbetts.
April	4 Margery & Lydia Foss.
May	9 Thomas Tibbetts & Sarah his Wife, & Thomas their Son.
	Widow Judith Tibbetts & her Child^n, vizt: Mary, Samuel, Judith & Ichabod.
	Samuel Willey.
	Simon, Son of Nathaniel Randel.
	16 Sarah Horn.
June	20 Abigail, D^r of Joshua Perkins.
July	31 Benj^a Foss.
Aug	22 William Foss.
	William Wentworth.
Sept^r	26 Joshua, Son of John Wingate.
	James, Son of James Heard.
	William, Son of William Jones.
Octob	11 Philip Eaton.
1726.	
April	24 Moses, Son of Ichabod Hayes.
May	8 Robert, Son of John Hayes.
	29 Jonathan, Son of Paul Gerrish.
June	12 John, Son of Daniel Titcomb.
	Mehetabel, D^r of Peter Hayes.
July	3 Joseph Heard & Rebecca his Wife.
	John Waldron, jun^r & his Son John.
	7 Reuben, Son of Maturin Ricker.
	17 The other Child^n of Maturin Ricker.
	Samuel & Judith, Child^n of Sam^ll Heard.
	Ephraim, Son of Joshua Perkins.
	24 Daniel, Son of Daniel Plummer.
	Noah, Son of Joseph Ricker.
	31 Samuel Cromwell & Rachel his Wife, & their Child^n.
	William Downs & his Child^n, Samuel, William & Phebe.
	James Hobbs & Child^n.

Aug	7	Bidfield, Son of Richard Plummer.
		Hannah, Daugh^r of Richard Goodwin.
Sept^r	25	Rachel, D^r of Benj^a Twombly.
Octob	23	Love, D^r of Thomas Nock.
1727.		
Jan	15	Elizabeth Cushing, born 5 inst.
April	2	Dorcas, D^r of Maturin Ricker.
June	4	Sarah, D^r of James Pinkham.
Sept^r	3	Benjamin, Son of Daniel Horn.
	17	Lydia Canney.
Octob	22	Jonathan, Son of John Wingate.
1728.		
Jan	7	Benjamin Hayes & his Son Benjamin.
Feb	18	Deborah Canney.
		Elizabeth Hanson.
	25	Daniel, Son of Joseph Libbey.
March	19	Temperance, D^r of Zachary Nock.
April	7	Jeremiah Rallings, & Elizabeth his Wife, & their Child^n, Mary, Lydia, Deborah, Sarah, Ichabod & Elizabeth.
		Samuel Randel & Eliz^a his Wife, & their Child^n, Mary, Samuel & Eliphalet.
		Samuel Corsen & Mary his Wife, & their Child^n, Joanna, Mary, Samuel, Ichabod & Hannah.
		Joseph Pevey & Child Esther.
		Sarah, Wife of Zachary Nock, & their Child^n, Joshua, Joseph, Zachary & Benjamin.
		John Tibbetts & Mary his Wife, & their Child^n, Timothy, William, Moses, Joshua, Hannah, Abigail & Mary.
		The Child^n of Saml Jones, Samuel, Ebenez^r, Eliz^a, Dorcas, Mary & Esther.
		Hannah, D^r of William Jones.
		Ebenezer, Son of John Roberts.
		The Child^n of Philip Yeaton, Phebe, William, Philip.
		Abigail Pitman.
		Judith Power.
		Richard Clay.
April	21	Aaron, Son of Ichabod Hayes.
May	12	William Whitehouse & his Dr Elizabeth.
		Wentworth, Son of John Hayes.

BAPTISMS BY REV. JONATHAN CUSHING, 1717-1766.

May	12	Hannah, D^r of William Wentworth.
June	3	Benjamin, Son of Daniel Plummer.
	9	Elizabeth, D^r of Daniel Titcomb.
		Joseph, Son of Joseph Ricker.
		Abigail, D^r of Benjamin Hayes.
June	16	Abigail, Wife of John Ham, & their Child^n, Elizabeth & Abigail.
	23	John Horn & Elizabeth his Wife, & their Child^n, Isaac, Elizabeth & Mary.
		Abra, Daugh^r of Benjamin Twombly.
		Joseph Hall.
Aug	18	Sarah, D^r of Gershom Downs.
Sept^r	1	William, Son of John McDuffee.
	8	Joseph, Son of Joseph Heard.
Octob	27	John, Son of Peter Hayes.
	31	Nathaniel Perkins.
Dec^r	8	Mary, D^r of Daniel Greeno.
	26	Abigail, Wife of Ichabod Tibbetts, & their Child^n, Judith, Abigail & Nathaniel.
1729.		
Feb	18	Margaret, Wife of Thomas Wallingford.
	23	Thomas, Son of Doct^r Thomas Miller.
		Thomas, Son of William Downs.
		Elizabeth, D^r of Sam^{ll} Randel.
		Sarah, D^r of James Hobbs.
		Sarah, D^r of Benjamin Weymouth.
March	2	Jane, D^r of John Scovy.
	16	Tamsen, Wife of John Hayes.
May	25	Benj^a, Son of Gershom Wentworth.
		Ebenezer, Son of William Chamberlain.
June	15	Elizabeth Church.
	29	Hannah, D^r of Micah Emerson.
July	27	Daniel, Son of Joshua Perkins.
Aug	18	William, Son of Robert Knight.
	24	Abigail, D^r of John Carter.
	26	Hannah, D^r of Maturin Ricker, (in private).
	31	Joseph Richards.
		Joseph Connor & Sarah his Wife.
Sep^t	12	Hannah Cushing, (in private) born 11th Inst. & Died 12th.

Sept	14	Abigail, Wife of Moses Wingate, & their Child{n}, Edmund & Abigail.
Octob	26	Abigail, Dr of John Carter.
Novr	9	Ruth, Dr of James Davis.
	23	Moses & Elizabeth, twin Child{n} of John Wingate.
Decr	7	Mary Lord.
1730.		
Jan	4	Ephraim, Son of Joseph Hanson.
	18	Philip Stagpole & Child{n}, Sarah, William, Lydia, & Elisha.
April	12	Thomas, Son of Doctr Thomas Miller.
	26	Lydia, Dr of Major Paul Gerrish.
May	3	Jonathan, Son of James Pinkham.
		Abigail, Dr of Jonathan Copps.
	31	Samuel, Son of Maturin Ricker.
June	7	George, Son of Benja Hayes.
		Joseph, Son of Robert Knight.
	14	Hannah, Dr of James Heard.
	21	John, Son of Tristram Coffin.
July	26	Mary, Wife of William Foss & her Child{n}, viz : Lydia & Timothy Hanson (by her 1st Husband, Benja Hanson) & Mary, (by Wm Foss.)
		Bethiah Hall.
Aug	2	John Hanson, Son of Mary Foss, Wife of Wm Foss.
		Deborah, Dr of Moses Wingate.
	9	Mary, Dr of John Ham, junr.
	23d	Rebecca, Dr of Joseph Heard.
Septr	13	Abigail Messerve, Wife of Danl Messerve, junr, and their Child Joseph.
	20	Tamsen Ham.
		Samll, Son of John Hayes.
Octob	4	John, Son of Wm Whitehouse.
	11	Eliza, Wife of Ezra Kimbal & their Child Mary.
		Paul, Son of Daniel Horn.
		Abigail, Dr of Ichabod Hayes.
	25	Jonathan, Son of Nathan{l} Randel.
1731.		
March	21	Dorothy, Dr of Wm Chamberlain.
	23	Matthew, Son of John MacScovy.
April	18	Ebenezer, Son of Daniel Plummer.
	25	Mary, Dr of Wm Wentworth.

BAPTISMS BY REV. JONATHAN CUSHING, 1717-1766.

May	2	Hobart & Mary, Child[n] of Hobart Stevens.
June	20	Daniel, Son of Daniel Titcomb.
		Sarah, D[r] of Joseph Bickford.
	24	At Rochester, at y[e] Dedication of y[e] new meet[g] House, baptiz'd by M[r] Adams:
		Jonathan, Son of Jonathan Copps.
		James, Son of John MacDuffee.
		John, Son of John Blackden.
	27	Ann, D[r] of John Bickford, baptiz'd by M[r] Cush[g] at Roch[r].
July	4	Daniel & Elizabeth, Child[n] of Doct[r] Jonathan Crosbee.
Aug	22	Eunice, D[r] of W[m] Twombly.
	29	Richard, Son of Ezra Kimbal.
Oct	31	Welthean, D[r] of John Huckins.
Nov[r]	28	Chatborn, Son of W[m] Foss.

1732.

April	30	Mary Church.
May	14	Eliz[a], D[r] of Benjamin Hayes.
June	25	Jonathan, Son of Deac[n] John Hayes.
July	2	Neiobe, D[r] of Ezekiel Wentworth.
Aug	20	Benjamin, Son of Col. Paul Gerrish.
Oct	22	Abigail, D[r] of Mica Emerson.
Nov[r]	22	Sarah, D[r] of Sam[ll] Heard, in private.
	26	Susanna, D[r] of Tristram Coffin.

1833.

March	18	Ebenezer, Son of Moses Wingate.
April	25	Lydia & Joanna, twin Child[n] of Peter Hayes, in private.
May	13	Lucy, D[r] of W[m] Whitehouse.
July	22	John, Son of John Ham.
		Mary, D[r] of John Blackden of Rochester.
	29	Mary, Wife of Timothy Emerson & their Daugh[r] Hannah.
		Ann, D[r] of Joseph Hall.
Aug	26	Daniel, Son of W[m] Foss.
Sept[r]	2	Eliz[a] & Hannah Bampton.
	23	Dorothy, D[r] of John Wingate.
	30	John Church & Child[n], John & Daniel.
Oct[o]	28	Hannah, D[r] of Benj[a] Hayes, by M[r] Cushing of Haverhill.
Nov[r]	11	John, Son of W[m] Twombly, jun[r].

Decr	16	Mary, wife of Wm Twombly.
1734.		
Feb	10	John Horn & Child{n}, Mary & Sarah.
	24	Mary Ditte.
May	13	David, Son of Daniel Titcomb.
June	16	Thomas, Son of Samll Davis.
July	28	Samll, Son of Timothy Emerson.
		Deborah, Dr of John Demerritt.
Aug	4	Abigail, Dr of Ezra Kimbal.
Septr	22	Abigail, Dr of Daniel Horn.
Octo	6	William, Son of William Cate.
	13	Thomas Horn & Child{n}, Judith, Margaret, Samuel, Abigail, Drusilla, Esther, Nathan & Elizabeth.
Nov	8	Joseph Chesley, in private.
Decr	15	Eliza & Martha Varney.
1735.		
March	2	Hannah, Dr of Widow Abigail Hayes.
June	22	Abigail, Dr of John Huckings.
July	13	Hannah, Dr of Capt Tristram Coffin.
		Dodavah, Son of Benja Hayes.
		Job, Son of Job Demerritt.
		Susanna, Dr of Edward Tibbetts.
Aug	10	Lydia, Dr of Peter Hayes.
	17	Mary, Wife of Nehemiah Kimbal & Children.
		Moses, Son of Ezek{l} Wentworth.
Septr	7	John, Son of John Gerrish.
	21	John, Son of Zech{r} Edgerly.
		Wm, Son of Wm Whitehouse.
	27	Noah, Son of John Wingate, in private.
	28	Moses & Jonathan, Child{n} of John Gage.
	30	Stephen, Son of Saml Heard, in private.
Oct	24	William, Paul & Ebenezer, Child{n} of John Heard, all of whom died within 2 Days after.
Novr	9	Ephraim Ham & Anna, his Wife, & their Child{n}, Joshua, Ephraim, Moses & Aaron.
	23	Abigail, Dr of Daniel Titcomb.
Decr	28	Daniel, Son of Saml Heard, in private.
1736.		
Jan	13	Mary, Dr of Benja Foss ⎫ at Rochester on a fast Saml Son of Wm Chamberlain, ⎭ Day.

Jan	30	Anna & Isaac, the Child[n] of Isaac Libbey, in private.
Feb	22	Deborah & Daniel, Child[n] of Daniel Harvie, jun[r].
Mar	21	John Roberts & Child[n], Sam[l] & Eliz[a], & his Wife's Child, Joseph.
		Eliz[a], Wife of Solomon Emerson & their Child, Micah.
		Benj[a], Son of Robert Tomson.
		Benj[a] & Hannah, Child[n] of John Bussell.
		Samuel, John, Ebenezer & Rebekah, Child[n] of John Tasker.
		Joseph & Benjamin, Child[n] of Archibald Smith.
		James & Robert, Child[n] of James Jackson.
		Sam[ll], Son of Sam[ll] Chesley.
		Abig[l], D[r] of Tim[o] Emerson.
March	28	Eliz[a], Wife of John Young, & their Child[n], Thomas, Ann, Mary & John.
		Eleanor, Wife of Thomas Ash & their Child[n], Mary, Thomas, Judith & Benjamin.
		James & Dorothy, Child[n] of Joshua Perkins
May	9	Hannah Hall.
	23	Mary, D[r] of Joseph Hall.
	29	Eliz[a] & Sam[ll], Child[n] of Sam[ll] Drown, in private.
July	18	Eliz[a], D[r] of James Hanson.
	25	Eliz[a] & William, the Child[n] of Samuel Wille, jun[r].
Aug	8	Eliz[a], Wife of Sam[ll] Wille, jun[r], & Mary their Daugh[r].
		Ebenezer, Son of John Ham.
Sept[r]	5	Charles, Son of John Blackden.
	12	Lydia, Daugh[r] of Nehemiah Kimbal.
		Mary, D[r] of Joseph Bickford.
Octob	3	Ann, D[r] of Moses Wingate.
	10	Shadrach Hodgdon & Mary, his Wife, & their Child[n], Ann & Israel.
	17	Dudley Watson & his Son, Dudley.
		Nathaniel Horn & his Son, Nathaniel.
	31	John, Son of John Heard.
		Eliz[a], D[r] of Ezra Kimbal.
Dec[r]	9	Mary Hanson—upon her Death bed.
1737.		
Jan	21	Joseph & Paul, Child[n] of Gershom Downs, in private.
	27	Pumfret Dam, aged 14 y[rs], in private.
	29	John, Son of John Marden, in private.

Feb	6	Aaron, Son of John Wingate.
April	17	George, Son of John Gerrish.
	25	Spencer Wentworth, in private.
	30	William, Son of John Gage, in private.
May	15	Paul, Son of John Demeritt.
June	12	Betty & Anna Harford.
		Henry, Son of Edward Tibbetts.
	26	Anna, D^r of Ephraim Ham.
Aug	21	Mary & Sarah, Child^n of John Marden.
Sept^r	12	Benj^a, Son of Capt Thomas Millet, in private.
	25	John, Son of John Huckins.
Octo	2	Ichabod, Son of Peter Hayes.
	12	John, Son of Capt Thomas Millet, in private.
	23	Patience, Wife of Benj^a Ham & their Child^n, Mary & John.
		Martha, D^r of Saml Heard.
		Joseph, Son of Shadrach Hodgdon.
Oct	23	Mary, D^r of John Wood.
Nov^r	27	Joshua, Son of Joshua Perkins.
Dec^r	4	Love, Wife of Capt Thos Millet, & their Child^n, Abigail, Thomas, Hannah, Elizabeth & Lydia.

1738.

March	9	Sarah Watson, on a sick bed.
April	2	Mary, D^r of Wm Whitehouse.
	30	Enoch, Son of Daniel Titcomb.
		Eliz^a, D^r of Nathaniel Horn.
May	7	James, Son of Ichabod Tibbetts.
		Sarah, D^r of Joseph Bickford.
	14	Lydia, D^r of Wm Foss.
	21	Elizabeth, D^r of Samuel Hodge.
June	25	Jacob, Son of Wm Chamberlain.
July	2^d	Israel, Son of John Ham.
		Eli, Son of Job Demerritt.
	9	Benjamin, Son of Paul Gerrish.
	23	Widow Eliz^a Jones & her Daugh^r, Ann.
Aug	6	Daniel, Son of Nehemiah Kimbal.
		John, Son of John Church.
		John Davis, Son of Daniel Rogers.
	13	Mary, D^r of George Horn.

Aug	20	Sarah, D^r of John Wingate.
		Moses, Son of Moses Wingate.
	27	Paul, Son of Thomas Horn.
		Lydia, Wife of Arthur Danielson & their Child^n, Sarah & Mary.
Sept^r	3	Humphey, Son of Joseph Hanson, in private.
	17	Deborah, D^r of Capt Tristram Coffin.
Octob	15	William, Son of John Heard.
Nov^r	5	Joseph, Son of Joseph Hall.
Dec^r	12	Paul Roberts, upon a sick bed.
	25	John Foye, upon a sick bed.
1739.		
Jan	4	Daniel, Son of Zechariah Edgerly.
Feb	14	Sarah, D^r of John Roberts, in private, being sick.
	18	Lucy, D^r of Dudley Watson.
Mar	11	Abigail & Joseph, Child^n of Jonathan Thomson, at Durham.
	13	John, Son of John Sanburn, in private.
	18	Sarah, D^r of Timothy Emerson.
		Joseph, Son of Solomon Emerson.
		Isaac & James, Sons of James Leighton.
	25	Patience, D^r of Benjamin Ham.
		Elizabeth, D^r of John Mardin.
Ap^l	5	Susanna, D^r of Capt Thomas Millet, in private.
	15	Ichabod, Son of Eph^m Ham.
		Sarah, D^r of Sam^{ll} Whitehouse.
May	3	Sam^{ll} Ham, on a sick bed.
	27	Patience, Wife of Wm Hill, jun^r.
June	10	Sarah, D^r of William Cate.
	24	Levi, Son of Arthur Danielson.
July	1	Sarah Dittey.
Aug	19	Ezra, Son of Ezra Kimbal.
	26	Samuel, Stephen & Lydia, Child^n of Widow Lydia Ham.
Sept^r	20	Baptiz'd at ye Meeting H^o in ye S. W. part of ye Town, now Madbury.
		Rebekah & Sarah, Child^n of Thomas Bickford.
		Jonathan, Son of Danl Harvie.
		Abraham, Son of John Bussell.
		Solomon, Son of Sol^o Emerson.

Sept^r	20	Baptiz'd at ye Meeting H^o in ye S. W. part of ye Town, now Madbury.

            Judith, D^r of Saml Jackson.
            Thomas, Son of Joseph Johnson.
            Joanna, D^r of David Daniel.
            Abigail, Benj^a & Lydia, Child^n of Wm Hill, jun^r.

	23	Mary Tibbetts.
	30	Susanna, D^r of John Wood.
Octob^r	1	Mary Twombly, on her Death bed.
	7	Samuel, Son of Richard Jones.

1740.

Jan	27	Samuel, Son of Sam^ll Hodge.
Mar	21	Daniel & Shadrach, Child^n of Danl Ham, in private.
Ap^l	13	Sarah, D^r of John Gerrish.
May	4	John, Son of John Woodman, at Durham.

            Sarah, D^r of Stephen Jones,   "   "
            Nathaniel, Son of Eliph^t Daniel, "   "
            Hannah, D^r of Thomas Chesley, "   "

June	8	George Horn & his Daugh^r Elizabeth.
	15	Mary, D^r of Shadrach Hodgdon.

            Sarah, D^r of Wm Whitehouse.

	22	Benjamin, Son of John Church.
	30	Samuel, Son of Isaac Clark of Durham, in private.
July	29	Love Clark, in private, being sick.
	31	Eliz^a, Daugh^r of Joseph Hicks.

            Betty & Lois, Child^n of Francis Drew.
            Clement, Son of Daniel Messerve.
            Nathaniel, Son of Henry Bussell.
            David, Son of Joseph Johnson.

Aug	10,	Robert, Son of Wm Hill.
	24	Ephraim Wentworth & Child^n, viz : Mary, Grant, Willm, Ephraim & Martha.

            Anna, D^r of Joshua Perkins.
            Mary, D^r of John Roberts.

Sept^r	21	Paul, Son of John Ham.

            Eliz^n, D^r of Wm Twombly.

	28	Benj^a, Son of Moses Wingate.

            Spencer, Son of Eph^m Wentworth.

Nov^r	23	Hannah Jackson.

1741.

Mar 1 Eliz^a, D^r of John Wood, bpz^d by Mr Pike.
  12 Mary Young & Hannah & Susanna, D^{rs} of John Young, & Rebekah, D^r of Ichabod Tibbetts, in John Young's house.
  21 Susanna & Benj^t, Child^n of George Chesley, at Durham in private.

May 24 Francis & Elijah, Child^n of Joseph Drew.
   Rachel, D^r of George Horn.
  31 Mercy, D^r of Cheney Smith.
   Moses, Son of Ezekiel Wentworth.

June 7 Mary, D^r of Vincent Tarr.
  14 John, Son of William Cate.
   David, Son of Dudley Watson.
  17, Joseph, Son of John Demerritt.
   Rebekah, D^r of John Huckins.

July 19 Richard, Son of Richard Jones.

Aug 9 Abigail, D^r of Job Demerritt.
   Aaron, Son of James Leighton.

Septr 10 Sarah, D^r of John Bussell.
   John, Son of John Rowe.
   Samuel, Son of Solomon Emerson.
   Meribah, D^r of Joseph Jackson.
  27 Josiah, Son of John Heard.
   Elijah, Son of Peter Hayes.
   Jacob, Mary & Sarah, Child^n of Jacob Horsum.
   Sarah, D^r of Nath^ll Horn.

Octob 5 Ebenezer, Son of Wm Jackson, jun^r, in private.
  10 Mary, Frances & Hannah, Child^n of Stephen Willey, priv^t.
  25 Thomas Young.

Novr 1 John, Son of Doct^r Moses Carr.
  22 Mary Pinkham, Stephen Pinkham & Child Abigail.
   Patience Pinkham & Hepzibah Pinkham.
  26 Jonathan, Son of Sam^ll Davis.

Decr 13 John Starbird & Sarah his Wife.
   Daniel Ham & his Son Joseph.
   Ambrose Bampton & Deborah Kielle.
  16 Nathaniel Young, upon a sick bed.
  27 John Drew & Patience his wife.

Dec[r] 27 Jonathan Hanson & Anna Willey.
  30 Baptized at the Meeting House in y[e] westerly part of y[e] Town, now Madbury :
  Sarah, D[r] of Eli Demerritt.
  Benjamin Hall & his Wife Frances, & their Child[n], Benjamin, Isaac, Joseph, John & Abigail.
  Christian, Wife of Joseph Rines, & their Child[n], Betty & John.
  Anna, D[r] of Nathan[l] Davis.
  Robert Willey & his D[r] Anna.
  Joseph, Son of Thomas Bickford.

1742.
Jan   1 Baptized at Durham :
  Eliz[a] and Frances, the Child[n] of Jon[n] Brew.
  Eliz[a] & Hannah, Child[n] of Eliph[t] Hill.
  Lucretia, D[r] of Abig[l] Hill.
  Hannah, D[r] of Robert Huckings, sick.
   2 Ebenez[r], Sam[l], Will[m] & Ichabod, Tabitha & Mary, Child[n] of Will[m] Bussell.
  Joseph, Paul & Elizabeth, Child[n] of Widow Eleanor Perkins, in y[e] house of W[m] Bussell.
   3[d] Lord's day, Martha, Wife of Elihu Hayes; William & John, their Child[n].
  Mary & Anna Bampton.
  Jonathan Watson.
  William Twombly & his Son Moses.
  Elizabeth Twombly.
  Clement & Jonath[n] Ham.
  Josiah, Son of Jonathan Hanson.
   8 At Durham :
  John Crockett, on a sick bed.
  Deborah, D[r] of Ichabod Follett.
  Anna, D[r] of John Laskey.
  Joseph, Son of Joseph Jackson.
  10 John Tebbetts, Moses Whitehouse, Ebenezer Demerritt, Ezekiel Willey, Richard Glover, Abigail Bampton.
  17 Sarah Pinkham.
  Anna, Wife of Abraham Clark & their Child[n], Anna & Mary.
  24 Zechariah Bunker & his Wife, Deborah Bunker.

Jan 24 Sarah Drew.
     Margery Tibbetts.
     30 Elizabeth, Frances, Solomon, Ralph, Lois & Joseph, the Child^n of Ralph Hall, in his own house.
     31 Jon^a Young & Abigail his Wife, and their Child^n, Isaac, James, Abigail, Mary, Elizabeth & Mercy, all adult excepting Mercy. Also Joshua Perkins, Sobriety Young, Mary Brock, William Ham & Venus, Col^t Gerrish's negro.

Feb 4 Shadrach, Son of Shadrach Hodgdon, in private.
     14 Ichabod Tibbetts, Jerusha Hill & Lydia Twombly.
     28 Daniel Jacobs & Wife Mary, & their Child^n, Danl & Abig^l.
     Mary Evans & Child^n, Benj^a, Joseph & Stephen Evans & Elizabeth Mooney.
     John Mills & John Twombly.

March 7 Jane Layn & her Child^n, Saml, Styles, Edmund & John Hussey Layn.
       8 Nathan^l Garland, on a sick bed, Nath^ll his Son.
       9 Dodivah Ham, on a sick bed.
       14 Eph^m Tibbetts & Child^n, viz: Eph^m & Judith, adult, & Sam^ll.
       James Thomson. Mary Tuttle.
       Ann, Daugh^r of John Wingate.
       31 Eliz^a Hall.
       Mehetabel Daniel, Wife of Joseph Daniel, jun^r & their Child^n, viz; Sam^ll, Joseph, Pelatiah, Abig^l & Obadiah.
       Anna, D^r of Wm Demerritt.
       John, Son of Thomas Rines.

April 4 Henry Bickford & Eliz^a his Wife.
       Jeremiah Tibbetts.
       William Hayes.
       Sarah Pinkham.
       Dorothy Tibbetts.
       Margery, D^r of John Gerrish.
       11 Sam^ll Starbird & Rebecca his Wife.
       Hannah Hayes & her Dr Patience.
       Mercy Watson.
       David Polley, Mr Hanson's Servant.

April	18	Israel Hodgdon.
		William Twombly & his Daugh^r Eleanor.

April   18 Israel Hodgdon.
William Twombly & his Daugh^r Eleanor.
Eliz^a Pinkham.
Mercy Evans
Mary, Wife of John Horn, jun^r & their Childⁿ, John & Eleanor.
           25 Allis, Wife of Eliezer Young & their Childⁿ, Solomon & Lucy.
Abigail, Wife of Meshech Drew & their Daugh^r Patience.
Elizabeth Bunker.
Benj^a Son of Wm Twombly, jun^r.

May   9 Primus, Negro Servt to Col^o Gerrish.
           23 Ebenezer, Son of Moses Wingate.

June   11 Mary, D^r of Wm Brown of Nottingham.
           16 Joanna, D^r of Isaac Watson.
           20 Abigail, D^r of Ichabod Hayes.
           27 Nehemiah, Son of Nehemiah Kimbal.

July   4 Ann, D^r of Ichabod Tibbetts.
           11 Mary. D^r of John Horn.
John, Son of John Mills.
Philip, Negro Servt of Thomas Hanson.
           25 Joseph, Son of Wm Hanson.
Eliz^a, Wife of Joseph Roberts, in their house, she being sick.
Phebe, Negro Servt of Vincent Tarr.

Aug^t   22 Abigail Starbird, Widow.
Daniel, Son of Joseph Hall, jun^r.

Sept^r   5 Benedictus, Son of Vincent Tarr.
           26 Stephen, Son of Stephen Pinkham.
Deborah, D^r of John Messerve.

Oct^o   7 Betty, Mary, Abigail & Lydia, Childⁿ of Joseph Roberts, on their Mother's acco^t who was sick.

PERSONS WHO OWNED THE COVENANT.

1741.
Dec^r   30 Nathaniel Davis & Hannah his Wife.
Joseph Rines.

1742.
Jan   1 Eliphalet Hill & Abigail Hill.

Jan	2d	William Bussell & Wife.
		Eleanor Perkins, Widow.
	3	Elihu Hayes.
	10	Eliza Hobart & Judith Heard.
	17	Daniel, Hezekiah, Benja & Mehetabel Hayes.
	24	Eliza Mills.
Feb	28	Reuben Hayes.
April	4	Hannah Pinkham.
	18	Abra Hayes.
May	16	Robert & John Hayes 3tius.
Sepr	26	John Messerve & Wife.

1742.
Octr 14 BAPTIZED.—David, Son of David Daniel.
17 John, Abigail, Hannah & Sarah, Childn of John Starbird.
24 Eliphalet, Son of Tristram Coffin.
Jonathan, Son of John Layton.
Novr 21 Mary & Joseph, Childn of Joseph Dam.
28 Lydia, Dr of John Wood.
Ann, Dr of Samuel Hodge.
Decr 19 Turner, Son of Wm Whitehouse.

1743.
Jan 12 John & Elizabeth, Childn of —— Matthews.
Feb 21 Aaron, Son of Ezekl Wentworth, in private.
May 8 Sobriety, Dr of Wm Hill.
22 John, Son of John Roberts.
Joseph, Son of Joseph Bickford.
June 4 Timothy, Son of Timo Moses, in private.
12 Benja, Son of Danl Titcomb.
Eliza, Dr of Isaac Watson.
16 John Ham, on a sick bed.
19 Elihu, Son of Elihu Hayes.
Sarah, Dr of Geo. Horn.
26 Thomas, Son of Danl Ham.
July 3 Elihu Son of Ephm Wentworth.
Joshua, Son of Wm Twombly.
10 Eliza, Dr of Jacob Horsum.
19 Mary, Dr of Samll Chesley, in private.

July	24	Tamsen, Wife of John Tibbetts & their Child[n], viz[t]: Daniel, Mary, Nathan[l] & Sarah.
Aug[t]	10	Thomas, Son of Dudley Watson, in private.
	21	Hannah Tibbetts.
	25	At y[e] West Part of y[e] Town:
		Paul, Son of Paul Gerrish.
		Jane, D[r] of Henry Buzzell.
		John, Son of Sol[o] Emerson.
		James, Son of John Row.
		Benaiah, Son of Francis Drew.
		Eleazer, Son of Sam[ll] Davis.
		Sam[ll], Son of Benj[a] Hall.
		Robert, Son of Azariah Boody.
		Eliz[a], D[r] of Stephen Willey.
	28	Molly, D[r] of W[m] Gerrish.
Sept	18	Eunice, D[r] of Cheney Smith.
	23	Andrew, Son of Andrew Marshall, in private.
Oct[o]	2	Abigail, D[r] of Dan[l] Horn.
	30	Mary, D[r] of John Mills.
Nov[r]	6	Daniel Young.
	28	Moses & Aaron, Twin Child[n] of John Wingate.
1744.		
Jan	8	John, James, W[m], Sam[ll], Moses & Aaron, Child[n] of James Kielle.
Feb	16	Solomon, Son of David Daniel, in private.
March	11	Ichabod, Son of Ichabod Hayes.
Ap[l]	15	Tim[o], Son of John Gerrish.
		Anna, D[r] of Eph[m] Ham.
	17	Martha M[c]ElRoy, upon a sick bed.
	22	Israel, Son of W[m] Hanson.
		W[m], Son of Mary Tuttle.
	29	Mary, D[r] of George Hern.
May	12	Sam[ll], Son of James Pinkham, in private.
	13	Ebenezer, Son of W[m] Twombly.
		Eph[m], Son of Joseph Bickford.
	20	John, Son of John Messerve.
		Hannah, D[r] of Arthur Danielson.
		Judith, D[r] of George Horn.
	27	James, Son of James Davis.
July	8	Patience, D[r] of John Horn.

Sept^r	9	James, Son of Jonathan Young.
		Sarah, D^r of Clement Ham.
	16	Jane, D^r of Jonathan Ham.
	30	Olive, D^r of John Leighton.
Oct^o	7	Abigail, D^r of Joseph Hall.
Nov^r	6	Patience, D^r of Daniel Jacobs, in private, she being sick.
	13	Lydia, Seth & Sam^{ll}, Child^n of Danl Jacobs; John, Dorcas, Stephen, Philip & Zechariah, Child^n of Zechariah Bunker; Sarah, Joseph & Mary, Child^n of Thomas Pinkham; all baptized at a Lect^r at ye House of Danl Jacobs.
	18	Hannah, D^r of Nathaniel Horn.
	25	Andrew, Son of Vincent Tarr.
Dec^r	9	Susanna, D^r of Joshua Perkins.

1745.

Feb	3	Samuel Hanson.
April	7	Sam^{ll}, Son of Dudley Watson.
	14	John, Son of John Wood.
	21	Tamsen, D^r of Elihu Hayes.
	28	W^m, John & Lydia, Child^n of Andrew Marshall.
	30	Eliz^a, D^r of Hezekiah Hayes, in private.
May	26	Eliz^a & Mary, Child^n of Daniel Jacobs.
		Abijah, Son of Sam^{ll} Hanson.
June	2	George, Son of Hatevil Leighton.
		George, Son of George Horn.
	9	Abigail, D^r of Shadrach Hodgdon.
		Mary, D^r of Joseph Drew.
		Abigail, D^r of Stephen Pinkham.
	23	Parnel, D^r of Tristram Coffin.
	27	Paul, Hepzibah, Lemuel & Solomon, Child^n of Joseph Twombly.
July	21	Paul, Son of Nehemiah Kimbal.
		Sarah, D^r of George Hern.
Oct^o	6	Abigail Field.
		Ichabod, Son of Dan^{ll} Horn.
	13	Timothy, Son of Wm Gerrish.
	20	Nathaniel, Son of Wm Twombly.
	27	Anna, D^r of Eph^m Wentworth.
Nov^r	3	Nathl, Son of Wm Whitehouse.
Dec^r	29	Isaac, Son of James Pinkham.

1746.
Feb 23 Sarah, Dr of Cheney Smith.
Mar 23 Mary Tuttle.
28 Ezekiel, Son of Ichabod Hayes.
May 18 Clement, Son of Jonathan Ham.
22 Baptized at ye S. W. part of ye Town:
Joseph, Son of Joseph Hicks.
Mary, Dr of James Davis.
Francis, Son of Francis Drew.
John & Eliezer, Child{n} of Nathl Davis.
Sarah, Dr of Samll Davis.
Mary, Dr of James Jackson.
Patience, Dr of Samll Jackson.
Mary, Dr of Tim{o} Moses.
Zachary, Son of Azariah Boody.
Wm Gray, Son of John Row.
John & Miriam, Child{n} of James Clements.
Martha, Dr of ———— Noble.
John, Son of David Daniel.
May 25 Suse, Dr of Wm Twombly.
June 1 Ebenezer, Son of James Kielle.
4 Abigail Millett, on a sick bed.
11 Jonathan, Son of Isaac Horn, in private.
July 11 John, Son of Eph{m} Tebbetts, in private.
15 Abigail, Dr of Richd Canney Waldron, in private.
20 Clement, Son of Danl Ham.
Augt 12 Abraham, Son of George Horn, in private.
25 Suse, Dr of Eph{m} Ham, in private.
Septr 21 Charles, Son of Arthur M{c}Danielson.
28 Sarah, Dr of Hatevil Leighton.
Octr 12 Mary, Dr of John Leighton.
Ann, Dr of John Mardin.
Eliza, Dr of Andrew Marshall.
26 Tamsen, Dr of Elihu Hayes.
Susanna, Dr of John Horn.
Decr 21 Dorothy, Dr of John Gerrish.
Joshua, Son of Richd Jones.
1747.
Feb 22 Mehetabel, Dr of John Wingate.
Mar 15 Philip, Son of Philip Eaton.

Ap^l	19	Susanna, D^r of George Hern.
	26	Jacob, Son of Wm Hanson.
May	3	Sam^{ll}, Son of Joseph Hall.
		Eunice, D^r of Vincent Tarr.
	10	Susanna, D^r of Shadrach Hodgdon.
July	19	Danl Gerrish, Son of John Wood.
		Thomas, Son of George Horn.
Sept^r	27	Danl, Son of Joshua Perkins.
		Eliz^a, D^r of Eph^m Ham.
		Moses, Son of Wm Twombly.
Nov	8	Eliz^a, D^r of Sam^{ll} Gerrish.
	9	James, Son of James Brown, in private.
	30	Anna, D^r of Sam^{ll} Wingate.
1748.		
Jan	10	W^m, Son of Cutt Shannon.
Ap^l	24	Deborah, D^r of Stephen Pinkham.
		Eliz^a, D^r of James Pinkham.
May	1	W^m, Son of Hezekiah Hayes.
	8	Sarah, D^r of Joshua Foss.
	22	Nathl, Son of Nathl Horn.
	29	Moses, Son of Wm Whitehouse.
June	12	Abigail, D^r of Jonathan Ham.
	26	Thomas Millett, Son of Benj^a Bunker.
July	3	Paul, Son of Danl Horn, jun^r.
	17	Danl, Son of James Davis.
Aug^t	7	Danl, Son of Ichabod Hayes.
	30	Joseph, Son of Joseph Drew.
Sep	13	Hannah, D^r of Eph^m Davis, in private.
	18	Eph^m Roberts, on a sick bed.
	25	Richard Pinkham.
Oct	2	Elihu, Son of Elihu Hayes.
	16	Ann, D^r of John Ham.
Nov	6	Ruth, D^r of George Hern.
	21	Kezia, D^r of Tim^o Moses, in private.
	25	Benj^a, Son of Wm Brown, in private.
Dec^r	11	Danl, Son of Wm Twombly.
1749.		
Jan	4	Saml, Son of Benj^a Heard, in private.
	22	Mary Brown.
Mar	5	Thomas, Son of Danl Ham, in private.

Ap^l	2	Hannah, D^r of Joseph Hall.
May	7	Abigail, D^r of Thomas Hayes.
	14	Dorothy, D^r of Richard Jones.
		Joshua, Son of John Heard.
June	4	Mary, D^r of Paul Gerrish, in private.
	25	Abigail, Wife of Jon^a Wentworth, & their Child Phebe.
July	16	Lucy, D^r of Cheney Smith.
Sep	17	Moses, Son of John Wood.
Oct^o	6	Joanna, D^r of Eph^m Ham, in private.
	29	Thomas, Benj^a. James & Anna, Childⁿ of Benj^a Heard.
		Bathsheba, D^r of Wm Hanson.
Dec^r	10	Lydia, D^r of Sam^{ll} Gerrish.
		Betty, D^r of Benj^a Ham.
1750.		
Jan	29	David & Soloman, Childⁿ of Joseph Daniel, in private.
		Elijah, Son of Nathl Davis, in private.
Feb	5	Elizabeth, D^r of Archelaus Mooney, in private.
Ap^l	15	Mary, D^r of Dudley Watson.
	22	Sarah, D^r of Danl Ham.
	29	Urcilla, D^r of James Pinkham.
May	6	Danl, Son of Shadrach Hodgdon.
	27	Sarah, Wife of Danl Hayes, & Eliz^a their Daugh^r.
		Sarah, D^r of Sam^{ll} Emerson.
June	24	Eph^m, Son of Stephen Evans.
July	15	Moses, Son of Ichabod Hayes.
Aug^t	12	Eliz^a, D^r of John Titcomb.
Sept^r	18	Joseph Evans, in private, sick.
	23	Eunice, D^r of Wm Gerrish.
	27	Ebenezer, Son of John Woodman, in private, sick.
	30	Timothy, Son of Nathl Young.
		Andrew, Son of Andrew Marshall.
Oct^o	14	Elizabeth Libbey.
Nov^r	7	Thomas, Son of James Davis.
		Jon^a & Benj^a, Childⁿ of Solomon Emerson.
		Thomas, Son of Paul Gerrish.
		Lydia, D^r of Eben^r Demerritt.
		Hannah, D^r of Joseph Rines.
Dec^r	26	Sarah, D^r of Elihu Hayes, in private, sick.
1751.		
Feb	14	Sarah & Ebenezer, twin Childⁿ of Benj^a Hayes, in private.

Mar	28	Phebe Evans, on a sick bed.
Ap^l	7	Mary Hanson & her Child^n, Anthony, Nabby & Betty, in priv^t.
May	5	Aaron, Son of John Wood.
June	16	Hannah, D^r of Jacob Horsum.
July	7	Dolly, D^r of Robt Hayes.
Aug^t	8	Caleb, Son of Joseph Prince.
Sept^r	8	Thomas, Son of Thomas Hayes.
Oct^r	6	Anna, D^r of Edmund Wingate.
		Abig^l, D^r of Danl Hayes.
Nov^r	17	Joseph, Son of Benj^a Heard.
		Eph^m, Son of Eph^m Kimbal.
	24	Judith Bickford.

1752.

Jan	12	Jonathan, Eliz^a & Abigail Bickford.
Feb	2	Mary, D^r of Sam^ll Gerrish.
Ap^l	26	Joanna, D^r of Wm Hanson.
May	17	Hannah, D^r of Dudley Watson.
	24	Ezra, Son of Nath^ll Young.
	28	Lydia, D^r of Jon^a Wentworth.
June	21	Molly, D^r of Stephen Evans.
	26	Susanna, D^r of Eben^r Demerritt, in private.
July	12	Sarah, D^r of James Pinkham.
Aug^t	9	Betty, D^r of Danl Horn.
		Jon^a, Son of John Thompson.
Sept^r	14	Joseph, Son of Joseph Prince.
		Francis & Zerviah, Child^n of Daniel Davis.
		Edward & Sam^ll, Child^n of Edward Woodman.
		Joseph, Son of Azariah Boody.
Oct^r	3	Mary & Isaiah, Child^n of Ezek^l Willey, in private.
	29	Aaron, Son of Ichabod Hayes.
		Abigail, D^r of Job Clements.
Nov^r	12	Sarah, Eliz^a & Hannah, D^{rs} of Andrew Gerrish.
Dec^r	13	Kezia, D^r of Hatevil Leighton, in private, sick with ye Throat Distemp^r.

1753.

Jan	6	Patience, D^r of John Ham, in priv^t, sick with ye Throat Distemp^r.
Ap^l	11	Elijah, Son of Danl Jacobs.
		The Child^n of Richd Caswell.
	15	Abra, D^r of Robt Hayes.

May	6	Sam[ll], Betty & Mary, Child[n] of Sam[ll] Tasker, deceased.
	20	Constant Davis.
June	3	Sarah, D[r] of John Titcomb.
	10	W[m], Son of W[m] Twombly.
	17	Hannah, D[r] of Cheney Smith.
		Rich[d], Son of Dan[l] Hayes.
July	6	Mercy, D[r] of Sam[ll] Heard, on her Death bed.
	10	Jethro, Betty & Kezia, Child[n] of Sam[ll] Heard, in priv[t].
		Jacob, Son of John Heard, in priv[t].
Aug[t]	5	Steph[n], Son of Nathan Foss.
		Hinkson, Son of James Marden.
Sept[r]	23	John, Son of Edmund Wingate.
	26	Dan[l] & Andrew, Child[n] of Joseph Twombly.
		Joshua & W[m], Child[n] of W[m] Twombly 3[tius].
	30	Otis Baker, Son of Dudley Watson.
		Mary, D[r] of Sam[ll] Yeaton.
Oct	7	Jonathan, Son of Eben[r] Demerritt.
Nov[r]	4	Esther, D[r] of W[m] M[c]Culloch.
	11	Lydia, D[r] of W[m] Twombly.
	18	Bathsheba. D[r] of Jacob Horsum.
		Eleanor, D[r] of Benj[a] Pearl.
	25	Jane, D[r] of Dan[l] Ham.
		Mary, D[r] of Benj[a] Hanson.
Dec[r]	9	Hannah, D[r] of Eben Hanson.
1754.		
March	17	Eleanor, D[r] of Sam[ll] Gerrish.
	20	Isaac, Son of Joseph Prince.
		Betty, D[r] of Sam[ll] Davis.
		Mary, D[r] of Timothy Moses.
		Sam[ll], Son of John Smith.
		Deborah, D[r] of W[m] Glidden.
Ap[l]	14	Tamsen, D[r] of Hezekiah Hayes.
		Sarah & Joanna, Child[n] of Sam[ll] Todd.
	21	Eph[m], Son of W[m] Hanson.
May	20	Hannah, D[r] of Sam[l] Emerson.
June	10	Margaret & James, Child[n] of George Horn, in priv[t].
	16	Deborah, D[r] of Rich[d] Jones.
July	14	Joseph, Son of Andrew Gerrish.
	21	Jon[a], Son of John Montgomery.
	28	Mary, D[r] of Eben Hanson.

Sep^t	1	Benj^a, Son of Robt Thompson.
	8	Benj^a, Son of Thomas Hayes.
	22	Eliz^a, D^r of Job Clements.
Oct^r	7	Silas, Son of Paul Harford, deceased, in priv^t.
	10	Deborah, D^r of Paul Harford, deceased, in priv^t.
	13	Joshua, Son of Hobart Stevens.
		Mary, D^r of Danl Horn.
		Joseph, Son of Steph^n Evans.
	27	Sarah, D^r of Wm Gerrish.
		Abigail, D^r of John Buswel.
Nov^r	3	Lydia & Paul, Child^n of Paul Harford, deceased.
	10	Eliz^a, Wife of Jona Pinkham & their Child^n, Hannah & Thomas.
	20	John, Son of James Davis.
		Abigail, D^r of Paul Gerrish.
		Abigail, D^r of John Tasker.
	24	Mary, D^r of James Pinkham.
Dec^r	8	John Perkins, Son of Israel Hodgdon.
	15	Sarah, D^r of James Pecker.

1755.

Feb	2	Moses Bickford, on a sick bed.
May	4	Tamsen, D^r of Ichabod Hayes.
	25	Richard, Son of Wm Shackford.
June	1	Abigail, D^r of Richd Kimbal.
	8	Sarah, D^r of Otis Baker.
	29	Cheney, Son of Cheney Smith.
		Nathl, Son of Danl Hayes.
July	13	Saml Waterhouse, Son of John Titcomb.
		John, Son of Nathl Young.
Aug^t	24	David, Son of Benj^a Hanson.
		W^m, Son of Benj^a Pearl.
Oct^r	5	Betty, Zervia, George & Danl, Child^n of Isaac Watson.
	19	Edward Winslow, Son of Moses Emerson.

1756.

Feb	4	Joseph, Son of John Tasker, jun^r.
Mar	28	James, Son of Saml Yeaton.
	31	Eben^r Chesley, on a sick bed.
Ap^l	14	Timothy, Son of Andrew Gerrish.
	27	James & Moses, Child^n of James Chesley, on a sick bed.
May	23	Dolley, D^r of John Tibbetts.

May	30	Bridget, W^m, John, Mary & Eben^r, Childⁿ of John Waldron.
June	6	Mehetabel, D^r of Sam^{ll} Todd.
	20	Susanna, Molly & Mercy, Childⁿ of Saml Ricker.
July	6	Abigail, D^r of Danl Messerve, sick.
	11	Saml, Son of Saml Gerrish.
	18	Sarah, D^r of Dudley Watson.
Aug	8	Mary, D^r of James Kielle.
	15	Joseph Roberts & his Son Ephraim.

Mary, D^r of Sam^{ll} Emerson.

22 Abigail, D^r of Eben^r Hanson.

Sept 26 Margaret, Wife of James Perkins, & their Son Ephraim.

Oct^o 17 Elijah Bunker & their Childⁿ, Martha, Betty, Esther, Abigail & Judith.

Molly, D^r of Job Clements.

Bridget, D^r of Jacob Horsum.

31 Deborah, D^r of Danl Horn.

Mary, William, Betty, Ebenezer & Stephen Wentworth, the Childⁿ of Ebenezer Horn.

1757.

Jan 2 Alexander Douglas, Son of Otis Baker.

Feb 28 Mary Waldron, on a sick bed.

Mar 20 Mercy Plummer.

May 8 John, Son of Wm Shackford.

29 Sarah, D^r of James Perkins.

June 5 Andrew, Son of Benjamin Hayes.

15 Sarah, D^r of Alexander Caldwell.

July 24 Elizabeth Nathersell.

Elizabeth, D^r of Wm Hanson.

31 Mary, D^r of Stephen Evans.

Lois, D^r of Jon^a Pinkham.

Mary, D^r of Wm Wentworth.

Augt 7 Sarah, D^r of Richd Kimbal.

14 James, Son of James Young.

Sep 18 Abra, D^r of Ichabod Hayes.

Eph^m & Benj^a, Sons of Tobias Randel.

Molly, Nanny & Eunice, Childⁿ of Jon^a Gerrish.

Oct^o 23 Abigail, D^r of Nathl Young.

Hannah, D^r of Elijah Bunker.

Novr 13 Hannah, D^r of Thomas Hayes.

Nov^r	20	Eliz^a, D^r of Danl Hayes.
		Benj^a, Son of Benj^a Hanson.
		Thomas, Son of John Waldron.
Dec^r	4	Martha, D^r of John Titcomb.
1758.		
Jan	1	James Nailer & Martha his D^r.
May	21	Mercy, Wife of Saml Lary & their Child Sarah.
June	4	Sarah, D^r of Andrew Gerrish.
Aug^t	6	Micah, Son of Sam^{ll} Emerson.
Sept^r	24	James Toby, Son of Jon^a Gerrish, baptiz^d by Mr Main.
Octob	1	Lucy, D^r of Sam^{ll} Gerrish.
	8	Mary, D^r of Daniel Ham.
		Sarah, D^r of Eben^r Hanson.
	29	Daniel, Son of James Young.
Nov^r	5	Sarah, Wife of Jon^a Bickford & their Dr Rebecca.
	19	Howard Henderson & his Child^n, Benj^a & Lovey.
1759.		
Mar	8	Silas & Mary, Child^n of Benj^a Heard, in private.
Ap^l	18	Baptiz'd at Madbury, vizt: (Names omitted in ye original.)
	22	Ichabod, Son of Wm Wentworth.
	29	Susanna, D^r of Reuben Hayes.
May	6	Jeremiah, Son of Job Clements.
	13	Deborah, D^r of Wm Shackford.
July	8	James, Son of John Leighton, deceased.
	15	Isaiah, Son of Eben^r Horn.
Sept^r	30	Jon^a, Son of Benj^a Hanson.
		John, Son of Jonathan Bickford.
Oct^b	7	Daniel, Son of Daniel Hayes.
		Mary, D^r of Richard Kimbal.
	28	Josiah Farewell, Son of Moses Howe.
Nov^r	4	——Son of John Thompson.
	11	Paul, Son of Danl Ham.
1760.		
Feb	10	Abigail, D^r of Joseph Roberts.
	24	Lydia, D^r of Dudley Watson.
Mar	30	James Chesley, Son of Ichabod Hayes.
May	25	Jon^a, Son of Jon^a Pinkham.
July	24	Mary, D^r of Hatevil Leighton.

July	27	Baptized at Rochester:
		Eliz[n], D[r] of Reuben Heard.
		Jon[a] Dana, Son of Abner Dam.
		Tristram, Son of John Richards.
		Rachel, D[r] of Eben[r] Place.
		Isaac, Son of Jethro Bickford.
		Nath[l], Son of Tristram Heard.
Aug[t]	3	John, Son of John Titcomb.
	17	Thomas, Son of Howard Henderson.
	31	Eph[m], Son of John Waldron.
Sept	28	Anne, D[r] of Patrick Malcum.
Oct[o]	5	John, Son of Tobias Randel.
		Susanna, D[r] of Elijah Bunker.
	12	Dan[l], Son of Eben[r] Demerritt.
	19	John Coffin, Son of Joseph Ham.
Nov[r]	2	Abigail, Wife of Nicolas Canada & their Child[n], Sarah, Mary & John.
1761.		
May	3	Elizabeth, D[r] of Nath[l] Young.
Sept	13	Tamsen, Wife of Otis Baker & their Child[n], viz[t]: Tamsen, D[r] of John Twombly, dec[d]; Lydia & Ebenezer, Child[n] of Otis Baker.
Nov[r]	1	Eph[m], Son of James Young.
		James, Son of Jonathan Bickford.
	15	Abigail, D[r] of Sam[ll] Emerson.
	22	Sarah, D[r] of Cap[t] Sam[ll] Gerrish.
	29	Eliz[n] Stanton, Wife of W[m] Stanton & their Child Tamsen.
Dec[r]	13	Sarah, D[r] of Moses Howe.
1762.		
April	4	Lydia, D[r] of Timothy White.
	11	Hepzibah & Martha, the D[rs] of Nath[l] Balch.
	25	Stephen, Son of Howard Henderson.
May	2	Betty, D[r] of Ichabod Hayes.
	9	Betty, D[r] of Tobias Randel.
	16	Susey, D[r] of Elijah Bunker.
June	13	Abigail Plummer.
		Abigail, D[r] of Dan[l] Hayes.
	27	W[m], Son of Eben[r] Adams.
		W[m], Son of Rich[d] Kimbal.

Aug^t	1	Deborah, D^r of Jon^a Pinkham.
	8	Tamsen, D^r of Thomas Hayes.
	22	Martha, D^r of Jon^a Gerrish.
Sept^r	19	———D^r of Wm Stanton.
		Pumphret, Son of John Whitehouse.
Oct^r	3	Sarah, D^r of Danl Ham.
	24	Sarah, D^r of John Waldron, jun^r.
Nov^r	21	Hannah, D^r of Eben^r Demerritt.
	28	Eunice, D^r of Jacob Horsum.
Dec^r	12	John, Son of Otis Baker.

1763.

Ap^l	10	Margaret Gerrish.
	24	Joseph, Son of Joseph Roberts.
May	8	Deborah, D^r of Sam^{ll} Emerson.
June	26	Sarah, D^r of John Titcomb.
July	10	Enoch, Son of Eben^r Hanson.
	17	Joanna, D^r of Joseph Hodgdon.
	31	Joseph, Son of Nathl Baich.
Aug^t	28	Job, Son of Job Clements.
		Lucretia, D^r of———Trefethern.
Sep	25	W^m, Son of Howard Henderson.
Oct^r	23	Relief, D^r of Moses Howe.

1764.

March	11	Amos, Son of Tim^o White.
April	22	Sarah, D^r of Danl Hayes.
		Abig^l, D^r of Jon^a Bickford.
May	6	Ruth Hill.
	20	Benj^a, Son of Stephen Evans.
June	17	Sam^{ll} Plummer & his Son Dodavah.
July	1	Benj^a, Son of Benj^a Hanson.
	15	Ebenezer, Son of Edward Woodman.
Aug^t	12	Ezra, Son of Richd Kimbal.
	19	W^m, Son of Nicolas Ricker.
	26	Betty, D^r of John Whitehouse.
Oct^r	14	Joanna & Lydia, Child^n of Aaron Ham.
		John, Son of Ichabod Hayes.
	15	Sarah, D^r of James Knowles of Roch^r, in private.
Nov^r	18	Wm Wentworth, Son of Thomas Heard.

1765.

Feb	13	Thomas Parks, on a sick bed.

Ap^l	21	Mehetabel, D^r of Otis Baker.
June	16	Stephen, Son of Joseph Hodgdon.
Aug^t	4	Ezek^l, Son of Nicolas Ricker.
	11	William, Elizabeth & Richard, Child^n of Thos Westbrook Waldron.
	18	Elijah, Son of Moses Howe.
Sept^r	1	Mary Chesley.
	15	John Waldron 3^d & his Daugh^r Abigail.
		Eliz^a, D^r of Joseph Roberts.
	22	Betty, D^r of Stephen Evans.
Oct^o	6	Nathaniel, Son of Jon^a Pinkham.
	20	Sarah & Lydia, Child^n of Sam^{ll} Ham.
Nov^r	3	Sarah, D^r of Aaron Ham.
		Mary, D^r of Eph^m Wentworth.
	17	Sarah, D^r of James Knowles.
1766.		
March	9	Abigail, D^r of Ebenez^r Noyes.
April	7	Ebenez^r, Son of Ebenez^r Hanson, in private.
June	8	Daniel, Son of Howard Henderson.
July	6	Mehetabel, D^r of Daniel Hayes.
Aug^t	3	Eleanor, D^r of Thos Wk Waldron.
		Otis, Son of Otis Baker.
Nov^r	9	Olive & Elijah Bunker, Child^n of Joshua Perkins, jun^r.
	23	Eliz^a, D^r of Jonathan Bickford.

BAPTISMS

BY

REV. DR. JEREMY BELKNAP

1767-1786.

RECORDS OF FIRST CHURCH, DOVER, N. H.

1767.
March 8 Sarah, D^r of Stephen Evans.
May 24 Anna, D^r of Job Clements.
July 5 Moses, Son of Richd Kimbal, baptized by Mr Pike.
   Eliz^a, D^r of John Waldron 3^d, baptized by Mr Pike.
  12 Sarah, D^r of Ebenez^r Demerritt.
  19 Hannah, D^r of John Waldron 2^d.
  29 Sam^{ll}, Son of Sam^{ll} Emerson, in private.
Augt 2 John, Son of Nicolas Ricker, in private.
Septr 13 Jonathan, Son of Eph^m Wentworth, jun^r.
  27 Hannah & Mary, D^{rs} of Elijah Bunker.
   John, Son of John Waldron 2^d.
Oct^o 4 Betty, D^r of Howard Henderson, baptiz'd by Mr Hall.
Novr 29 Mary, D^r of Joseph Hodgdon.
   Daniel, Son of Joshua Perkins, jun^r.
1768.
April 10 Sarah, D^r of Jeremy Belknap, baptiz'd by Mr Cushing,
    being ye last that ever he baptized; born April 7.
  24 James Chesley, Son of Otis Baker.
May 1 Ezek^l, Son of Daniel Hayes.
  8 Charles, Son of Thos Westbrook Waldron.
  29 Molly, D^r of Moses Howe.

June	23	Eph^m, Son of John Whitehouse, in private.
Aug^t	21	James, Son of Joseph Roberts.
Oct^r	23	Paul & Silas, Sons of John Whitehouse.
	30	William, Son of Sam^{ll} Emerson.
		Joshua, Son of Joshua Perkins.

1769.

Jan	6	James, Son of Elijah Bunker, in private.
	9	Jeremiah, Son of Eben^r Horn, in private.
Mar	19	Shadrach, Son of Eben^r Hanson.
May	2	Eph^m, Son of Eph^m Plummer, in private.
June	18	Jeremy, Son of Eben^r Demerritt.
		Samuel, Son of Sam^{ll} Ham.
		Nathaniel, Son of Richd Kimbal.
July	2	Isaac, Son of Nicolas Ricker.
Aug^t	23	Mary, D^r of Alex^r Caldwell, in private, aged 10 years.
Sept^r	10	Jeremiah, Son of John Waldron, 3^d.
	13	Richard, Son of John Wentworth, at East Town.
	15	Samuel, Son of Josiah Willey.
Oct^r	15	Benj^a, Son of Isaac Mason.
Nov^r	26	Jonathan & Thomas, Sons of Jon^a Bickford, baptized by Mr Merriam.
Dec^r	10	Joseph, Son of Jeremy Belknap, born Decr 2.
	31	Peter, Negro Servt to Thomas Hanson, baptiz'd confessing his Sins.

1770.

Jan	21	Thomas, Son of Otis Baker.
March	10	Baptized at Wolfborough at a Lecture:
		Moses & Andrew, Sons of Andrew Wiggan.
		Jane, D^r of Widow Mary Fullington.
		Samuel Conner, Son of John Sinclair.
		Jane, D^r of James Lucas.
	11	Stephen, Son of James Berry, at New Durham.
May	20	Corydon, Dinah & Rhoda, Childⁿ of Peter, Servt to Thos Hanson, & Venus, Servant to Nathl Cooper.
July	1	Ichabod, Son of Daniel Hayes.
Sept^r	2	Mary, D^r of Joseph Roberts.
	9	W^m, Son of Joshua Perkins.
	30	Enoch, Son of Job Clements.

1771

Feb	24	Abigail, D^r of Thos Westbrook Waldron.

March	10	William, Son of Saml Hodge.
April	27	Temperance, D^r of Stephen Evans, in private.
May	14	William, Son of ye Widow Sarah Titcomb, in private.
June	23	Ann, D^r of Ebenezer Hanson, baptized by Dr Langdon.
July	21	Jeremy Wheelwright, Son of Samuel Ham.
Octob^r	6	Wilmot, Son of Jonathan Bickford, bap^d by Mr Stevens of Kittery.

1772.
Jan	5	Samuel, Son of Jeremy Belknap, born Decr 31, 1771.
April	5	Moses, Son of Job Clements.
May	24	John, Son of John Wentworth.
Aug^t	2	Peter, Son of Peter, Servant to Thomas Hanson & Venus, Servant to Nathl Cooper.
Octob^r	4	Martha, Daugh^r of Nathaniel Cooper, baptiz^d by M^r McClintock.
	25	Elizabeth, Daugh^r of Stephen Evans, born ye same D.
Nov^r	19	John Smith of Durham, Æ 14, in private.

1773.
May	2	Richard, Son of John Waldron, ye 3^d.
	23	Nathaniel, Son of Daniel Hayes.
	30	Margaret, Daughter of John Wentworth.
July	4	George Jefferds, Son of Sam^{ll} Ham.
Sept^r	23	Joseph, Son of Samuel Emerson, in private.
	26	Eliza, Daugh^r of Ebenezer Demerritt.

1774.
April	3	Elizabeth, Daugh^r of Jeremy Belknap, born ye same Day.
	25	Samuel, Son of James Guppy, in private, being sick.
June	5	Lydia, Daughter of Stephen Evans, & Phillis, Daughter of Peter Hanson—Negro.
Aug^t	14	Elizabeth, Daughter of John Wentworth, Esqr, baptiz'd by Mr Adams of Durh^m.
Sept^r	4	Walter, Son of Nathl Cooper.

1775.
Jan	15	Nathaniel, Son of Jonathan Bickford.
Feb	26	William, Son of Samuel Ham.
June	25	Elizabeth Ham.
July	16	Elizabeth, Daughter of Nathaniel Ham.
Sept^r	1	Joanna, Daughter of Capt John Waldron, in private.
Octob	1	Dudley, Son of Barnabas Palmer at Rochester.
Nov	19	Josiah, Son of Capt———Smith of Newcastle.

1776.
Jan 7 Richard Canney of Newcastle, priv^t—*moriturus*.
Feb 18 Ephraim, Son of Eph^m Evans, dec^d, offered by the Grandfather, Steph^n Evans, who publickly engaged for ye Child's Christian Education.
Joseph Frost, Son of John Wentworth, Esq.
March 10 Joseph, Son of Danl Peirce of Portsmouth.
June 30 Cato, Son of Peter Hanson, Negro, baptized by Mr Tenny.
Augt 12 Mehetabel, Wife of James Chesley, on a sick bed, Æ. 68.
Octob 13 Sarah, Daughter of Jonathan Bickford.
27 Joseph, Elizabeth, Daniel, Mehetabel & Mary, Children of Benjamin Peirce.

1777.
Jan 5 John, Son of Jeremy Belknap, born Decr 30, 1776.
26 Elizabeth, D^r of Nathaniel Cooper, born ye 24th inst.
Feb 2 Ichabod Chesley, Son of Stephen Evans, born Jan. 29.
April 13 Daniel, Son of Thos Wk Waldron, Esq., baptized by Doct^r Haven.
28 Hannah Bampton, aged 90 years this day, & Sick.
May 4 Sarah, D^r of Benjamin Peirce.
25 Lydia Cook, Æ 19.
June 29 Meshech Weare, Son of John Wentworth, Esq., born June 17.
Nathaniel, Son of Nathaniel Ham, born June 28.
Septr 14 Sarah & Martha, D^{rs} of William Brock.
Novr 30 Mary Bowers, D^r of Col. John Waldron.

1778.
July 12 Judith, D^r of Jonathan Bickford.
Nov 1 Deborah Shackford, D^r of Nathl Cooper, born Oct. 24.

1779.
Feb 28 Ebenezer, Son of Samuel Ham.
June 6 Andrew Elliot, Son of Jeremy Belknap, born 4th inst.
Timothy Winn, Son of Col. John Waldron.
Thomasin, D^r of Benj^a Peirce, born ye same day.
July 25 Dorothy Frost, D^r of John Wentworth, Esq.
Decr 5 Nancy & Betsy Hamilton, Child^n of Isaac Watson.

1780.
Jany 27 Samuel Foss, Son of John Barker, at the Gore.
Feb 20 Patty, Daugh^r of Stephen Evans, Esq.

July	9	Mary, Eleanor & Ruth, Children of Ebenezer Stacey.
	16	Eunice, daugh^r of Ezra Green, born ye 15th.
		Luke Wentworth, Son of William Brock.
	30	Mary Hanson, Æ 22.
Aug^t	2	Nathaniel Horn, jun^r, Æ 27.
Sep^t	8	Samuel & Elizabeth, Child^n of Richd Kimbal.
		Mary, John, Sarah & Isaac Libbey, Children of Nathl Horn, jun^r, at a Lecture at s^d Horn's house.
	20	Mary, Sophia & Jeremy, Child^n of James Guppy, at his own house.
Oct	16	Lydia, Polly, Samuel & Betsy, Child^n of Geo. Watson, baptiz'd by Mr Buckminster.
Dec	5	Elizabeth, Lydia, Benjamin, Jonathan & Joseph, the Children of Joseph Whitehouse, at his house.
	17	Rebecca, D^r of Ebenezer Stacey.
1781.		
Mar	12	Betsy, Daugh^r of Joseph Cate of Barrington.
April	8	Gershom, Son of Jonathan Bickford.
June	3	John, Son of Benjamin Peirce.
Aug^t	19	Dudley, Son of Nathaniel Ham, born ye 11th.
Sep^t	30	Deborah, Wife of Aaron Hayes.
October	21	John Wingate, Jonathan & Paul, Children of Aaron Hayes.
1782.		
Jan^y	6	William Shackford, Son of Nathl Cooper, born ye 5th.
Feb^y	10	Hannah, D^r of Isaac Watson.
June	9	Paul, Son of John Wentworth, Esq.
July	14	Susa, Daugh^r of John Waldron.
Aug	4	Ephraim, Son of Nathl Horn, jun^r.
Nov^r	24	Lydia, Wife of Dodavah Ham, & her Children, viz: Nathaniel & John.
1783.		
Feb	1	Ruth, Daugh^r of Eben^r Stacey, in private.
April	2	Abigail & Mary, Twin Children of James Horn, in private.
May	18	William, Son of William Brock.
Aug^t	24	Reuben Hayes, Son of Ezra Green.
1784.		
Jan^y	4	Samuel, Son of Nathl Ham, born Decr 20.
		Lydia, Daugh^r of Deacon Benj^a Peirce, born Jany 1.
	18	Susanna, Daugh^r of Ebenezer Tibbetts, born ye 10th.

May	9	Lydia, Daugh^r of Aaron Hayes.
		Robert, Son of George Watson.
July	31	Judith, Daughter of Gideon Walker at Massabesick.
Octob	3	Eleanor, Daughter of Nathaniel Horn, jun^r.

1785.

Feb	20	John, Son of William Brock.
Mar	6	John, Son of Isaac Watson.
April	10	Charles, Son of Ezra Green, born March 25.
June	5	Joanna, D^r of Ebenezer Stacey.
July	3	Richard, Son of Jonathan Bickford, in private.
Nov^r	20	Four Children of Nathan Hunt of Newington, vizt: Thomas, William, Betty & Nathan.
Dec^r	18	Andrew, Son of Benj^a Peirce, born ye same day.

1786.

March	26	Charles, Son of Ebenezer Tebbetts, born ye 17th inst.
July	2	Hannah Gage.

MARRIAGES

BY

REV. DR. JEREMY BELKNAP.

1767-1776.

RECORDS OF FIRST CHURCH, DOVER, N. H.

[Rev. Dr. Jeremy Belknap's Marriages from 1777 to 1786 inclusive, are in the Dover, N. H. Records, and have already been printed in this volumn.—See pages 79-83.]

1767.
May 27 Richard Alley & Elizabeth Choate, both of Dover.
July 7 Samuel Hodge & Hannah Gerrish, both of Dover.
Decr 10 Ebenezer Clemens & Bridget Hanson, both of Dover.
 31 Enoch Chase & Joanna Balch, both of Dover.
1768.
Feb 11 Benj^a Hanson, jun^r, & Sarah Conner, both of Dover.
April 4 Samuel Heard & Elizabeth Kennicom, both of Dover.
May 5 Aaron Roberts of Sommersworth & Mary Hanson of Dover.
June 16 Benjamin Odiorne of Portsmouth & Lilly Cochran of Berwick.
July 14 Peaslee Morrill & Phebe Chatburn, both of Berwick.
 21 Daniel*Winford & Dorcas Merry, both of Sommersworth.
Augt 4 Samuel Ham of Dover & Sarah Morse of Berwick.
 31 James Lebbey & Lydia Runnells, both of Dover.
Septr 28 Daniel Heard & Anna Wentworth, both of Dover.
 29 Clement Furnell of Durham & Dorcas Tucker of Dover.
Decr 19 Reuben Wentworth of Dover & Eleanor James of Sommersworth.

*Error for Wentworth.—[ED.

1769.
Jan 2 Thomas Horn & Mary Willey, both of Dover.
Feb 2 William Hanson, jun[r], & Mehetabel Wingate, both of Dover.
March 9 Paul Harford & Anne Balch, both of Dover.
16 Nathaniel Ham & Bathsheba Hanson, both of Dover.
April 3 John Cloutman of Dover & Esther Howard of Barrington.
24 Isaac Farewell & Mary Horn, both of Dover.
May 9 George Watson & Eliz[a] Gerrish, both of Dover.
June 15 Ezekiel Hayes & Hannah Mooney, both of Dover.
July 9 Jabez Smith & Hannah Caverly, both of Barrington.
Aug[t] 2 Michael Cloudy of Portsmouth & Elizabeth Hartford of Dover.
21 Samuel Nute & Phebe Pinkham, both of Dover.
31 Samuel Hayes & Abigail Thomas, both of Dover.
Sept[r] 14 Daniel Hains & Phebe Friend, both of Dover.
Octob 4 George Horn & Catharine Wooden, both of Dover.
Nov[r] 19 Clement Pinkham of Madbury & Sarah Randal, of Dover.
22 James Butler of Berwick & Elizabeth Harford of Dover.
23 John Rendall & Abigail Twamley, both of Dover.
23 Jethro Heard & Sarah Hartford, both of Dover.
Dec[r] 3 Samuel Tibbetts, jun[r], of Wolfborough & Mary Everson of Dover.

1770.
Jan 3 Joseph Hayes & Margaret Brewster, both of Barrington.
Feb 1 Paul Kimbal & Patience Horn, both of Dover.
March 2 Daniel Fitzgerald & Elizabeth Allen, both of Kittery.
10 John Cooley & Deborah Tibbetts, both of Wolfborough.
April 3 Elisha Shapleigh of Kittery & Eliz[a] Waldron of Dover.
June 3 Moses Brown of Portsmouth & Mary Young of Dover.
15 Zechariah Bunker & Sarah Been, both of Madbury.
Aug[t] 24 Obadiah Parsons & Elizabeth Wigglesworth, both of Ipswich.
Oct[o] 6 Elisha Kingsbury of York & Molly Gowen of Berwick.
29 Tobias Warner of Portsm[o] & Agnes Caldwell of Dover.
Nov[r] 4 Samuel Smith of Durham & Deborah Randall of Madbury.
22 Isaac Roberts & Abigail Rawlings, both of Dover.
29 Ichabod Hayes of Rochester & Tamsen Hayes of Barrington.

MARRIAGES BY REV. DR. JEREMY BELKNAP, 1767-1776.

Dec.r 6 Edmond Lambert of Portsmouth & Elizabeth Holden of Dover.
31 Thomas Watson & Abigail Horn, both of Dover.

1771.
Jan 17 John Gage, 3d, & Mary Canney, both of Dover.
24 Anthony Hanson & Hannah Davis, both of Dover.
Feb.y 14 Clement Ham & Margaret Roberts, both of Dover.
16 Vere Royse & Mary Rickard, both of Portsm.
25 David Meder of Durham & Sarah Bean of Brentwood.
28 Thomas Shannon & Lillias Watson, both of Dover.
28 Ebenezer Horn of Rochester & Rebecca Pinkham of Dover.
March 21 Ebenezer Ransom & Lydia Buzell, both of Dover.
26 Shubell Mason of Sarah Bridges of York.
April 11 Thomas Cloutman of Dover & Sarah Gilman of Exeter.
11 Eleazer Davis & Sarah Cook, both of Madbury.
14 Jeremiah Gray & Joanna Hill, both of Barrington.
25 George Hanson, junr, & Judith Howard, both of Dover.
May 23 Saml Merrow of Rochester & Sarah Starbird of Dover.
June 10 Moses Bickford & Priscilla Chick, both of Rochester.
Augt 1 Nathaniel Ham & Hannah Watson, both of Dover.
Septr 19 Philip Kelley of Lee & Anne Daniels of Dover.
October 10 John McDaniels & Keziah Howard, both of Barrington.
17 Dodavah Ham of Dover & Lydia Plummer of Madbury.
17 Daniel Drew of Middletown & Hannah Layton of Rochester.
20 Howard Henderson & Eliza Ham, both of Rochester.
Novr 14 Andrew Twombly of Madbury & Lucy Young of Barrington.
Decr 31 Lemuel Ricker of Sommersworth & Dorothy Nock of Dover.

1772.
Jan 1 Wm Horn, junr, & Eliza Roberts, both of Dover.
23 Jacob Hanson & Abigl Clements, both of Dover.
March 2 Ebenezer Ham & Sarah Field, both of Dover.
26 Ephraim Bickford & Sarah Bickford, both of Dover.
April 16 Joseph Waldron & Tamasin Twombly, both of Dover.
May 24 Benjamin Tuttle & Mary Hussey, both of Dover.
June 15 William Brock of Sommersworth & Betty Mason of Dover.

June	25	Moses Whitehouse of Middletown & Betty Hanson of Dover.
July	2	William Moore & Lucretia*Winford, both of Somersworth.
	12	Stephen Austin & Abigail Saunders, both of Somersworth.
Septr	27	Thomas Thompson & Alice Watson, both of Durham.
Octobr	11	Aaron Hayes of Nottingham & Susanna Keating of Madbury.
Novr	23	John Brock & Bridget Hawsum, both of Dover.
Decr	9	Nicolas Harford & Betty Varney, both of Dover.
	10	Joseph Atkinson, Esq., of Durham & Elizabeth Waldron of Dover.
	28	Tobias Jones of Durham & Eliz^a Hall of Madbury.
1773.		
Jan	2	Simon Lord & Polly Nichols, both of Kittery.
Mar	18	Joseph Field of Falmouth & Elizabeth Hanson of Dover.
	25	Daniel Rogers of Durham & Elizabeth Hawkins of Dover.
April	29	Ephraim Evans & Sarah Morse, both of Dover.
May	5	George Horn & Mary Gerrish, both of Dover.
June	24	Jacob Daniels of Barrington & Dolly Tibbetts of Dover
Augt	19	Eben^r Jackson & Dorothy Leighton, both of Barrington.
	26	Samuel Hall & Bridget Gilman, both of East Town.
Septr	23	Ephraim Kimball of Dover & Hannah Emerson of Madbury.
	23	Abner Hodgdon & Sarah Dam, both of Rochester.
Octob	5	Asa Ricker & Abigail Rollins, both of Rochester.
	25	Richard Waldron & Betty Clements, both of Dover.
Nov	11	Timothy Young & Lydia Demerit, both of Madbury.
	15	Jonathan Door & Eunice Downs, both of Dover.
	24	Andrew Lucas of Wolfborough & Mary Rogers of the Gore.
Decr	1	Fredrick Mordant Bell & Eliz^a Gage, both of Dover.
	30	Benj^a Titcomb & Hannah Hanson, both of Dover.
1774.		
Jan	3	Enoch Jackson of Durham & Eunice Tuttle of Dover.
	13	John Remick & Susanna Perkins, both of Dover.
March	10	Eliphalet Coffin & Patience Evans, both of Dover.
	31	Isaac Watson & Mary Hogg, both of Dover.

*Error for Wentworth.—[ED.]

April	10	Edward Brown & Anna Geer, both of Barrington.
	14	John Whitehouse & Susanna Rickard, both of Dover.
Aug^t	7	Robert Rogers of Durham & Rose Hanson of Dover.
Sept^r	17	Ezekiel Perkins of Dover & Margaret Currell of Berwick.
Octob^r	13	William Horn of Somersworth & Sarah Welland of Dover.
	27	Paul Horn & Hannah Smith, both of Dover.
Dec^r	20	John Costelloe & Lydia Lord of Berwick.
	25	Jacob Garland & Mary Runnels, both of Dover.
	26	Richard, Negro Servant to Mark Hunking, Esq., of Barrington, & Julia, Negro Servant to Stephen Evans, Esq., of Dover, by Consent of their respective Masters.

1775.

March	14	Heard Roberts & Mary Watson, both of Dover.
	19	John Scribner of Wakefield & Peniel Hall of Dover.
April	4	Stephen Young of Barrington & Kezia Hanson of Madbury.
	13	Samuel Roberts & Sarah Wentworth, both of Somersworth.
	16	Thomas Hamick & Deborah Carpenter, both of Sommersworth.
June	19	Jonathan Stevens of Wells & Patience Horn of Dover.
July	22	Saml Wallingford of Sommersworth and Lydia Baker of Dover.
Aug^t	10	John Tibbetts, jun., & Lydia Gerrish, both of Dover.
	12	John Russell of Andover & Sarah Titcomb of Dover.
	24	Jacob Clark & Mary Ricker, both of Dover.
Sept^r	28	Mark Lord of Berwick & Olive Underwood of Kittery.
Octob	9	Gideon Walker of Berwick & Abig^l Bunker of Dover.
Nov	5	Duncan Campbell & Sarah Young, both of Dover.
	23	Thomas Layton & Marcy Horn, both of Somersworth.

1776.

Jan	4	George, Negro Servt of Benj^a Evans & Phillis, Negro Servt to Solomon Emerson, Esq.
Mar	10	Moses Hodsdon & Sarah Caldwell, both of Dover.
	12	Winthrop Watson & Mary Horn, both of Dover.
	21	Pumphrey Downs & Ruth Medar, both of Dover.
	24	Timothy Carswell of Northwood & Rose Tuttle of Dover.

MARRIAGES BY REV. DR. JEREMY BELKNAP, 1767-1776.

April	11	Aaron Downs of Rochester & Margaret Willey of Dover.
	21	Ebenezer Bickford of New Durham & Susanna Cook of Madbury.
	25	Daniel Nute & Lucy Tuttle, both of Dover.
June	10	Gershom Ricker & Anna Garland of Somersworth.
	17	Archibald Campbell & Deborah Young, both of Dover.
July	9	David Ham & Hannah Rennels, both of Dover.
	18	Aaron Hayes of Dover & Deborah Wingate of Madbury.
Aug^t	15	Charles Whitehouse & Eliz^a Whitehouse, both of Dover.
	28	Robert Rogers of Durham & Sarah Evans of Dover.
Sept^r	4	Thomas Clements & Alice Powers, both of Dover.
	12	Samuel Furber of Roch^r & Mary Emerson of Dover.
	30	Gershom Lord & Esther Hanson, both of Dover.
Nov^r	7	Aaron Davis of Madbury & Susanna Otis of Dover.
	18	Josiah Folsom of Rochester & Hannah Cushing of Dov^r.
Dec^r	2	Simeon Brock of Berwick & Judith Bunker of Dover.
	5	Thomas Clark of Portsm^o & Esther Tebbets of Dover.
	11	Capt Thomas Peirce of Portsm^o & Kezia Wentworth of Dover.
1786.		
Feb^y	9	*James Watson & Hannah Guppy.
April	7	Joseph Evans & Elizabeth Waldron.
June	21	Thomas Varney, jun^r, & Thomasin Roberts.
	22	John Heard, jun^r, & Abigail Waldron.

*This and the three following marriages were not recorded in the Dover, N. H. Records.—[ED.

MARRIAGES

BY

REV. JOSEPH W. CLARY.

1812-1829.

RECORDS OF FIRST CHURCH, DOVER, N. H.

1812.
April   14 James B. Varney & Sarah B. Riley, both of Dover.
Oct   4 Saml Ham & Lydia Waldron, both of Dover.
       17 George Clark & Abigail Hanson, both of Dover.
Decr 24 Danl Tracy & Abigail Watson, both of Dover.
1813.
Jany 13 Thomas Perkins and Sally Preston, both of Newmarket.
Feb   7 Robert McIntosh & Hannah Hanson of Dover.
May   9 Saml Tuttle & Anna Howard, both of Dover.
June   24 John T. Hanson & Sophia Swazey of Dover.
July   15 Winthrop Watson, Jun., & Lydia Tebbets of Dover.
Unknown   Aaron Palmer & Mary Garland.
Do   Timothy Ricker & Abigail Varney, both of Dover.
Sept   29 Lewis Wentworth and Hannah Everson, both of Dover.
Oct   16 Nathan^l Garland of Northwood and Betsy Estes of Dover.
       20 Ebenezer Coe of Northwood and Mehitable Smith of Durham.
       24 Jonathan Hayes, 2^d, of Madbury and Priscilla Hussey of Dover.
       29 John Riley, Jun., and Ann Boardman of Dover.
1814.
Feb   12 James Horn and Huldah Roberts, both of Dover.

March	8	Solomon Dinsmore of Conway and Eliza Demeritt of Dover.
	30	Capt. Paul Wentworth of Sandwich and Lydia Cogswell of Dover.
[———]		Hanson Roberts and Lydia Henderson of Dover.
Apr^l	25	Joseph Gerrish and Lydia Anderson of Dover.
May	1	Stephen Varney and Hannah Carter, both of Dover.
July	26	Married Nathaniel Swasey of North Yarmouth and Hannah Horn of Dover.
Oct	11	Married Mr. Ebenezer Smith, Junr, & Miss Hannah Richardson, both of Durham.
Nov	3	Married Mr. Miles Evans & Mrs. Eunice Church, both of Dover.

1815.

Jan^y	3	Married John Harvey, Esqr, of Northwood & Miss Dolly F. Wentworth of Dover.
Feb	22	Married Mr. John Crocket and Miss Betsey Ham, both of Alton.
	27	Married Mr. Shadrach Wingate of Rochester and Miss Sally Patten of Dover.
March	23	Married Mr. Danl Ricker, 3^d, and Miss Elizabeth Ricker, both of Somersworth.
	29	Married Mr. Archelaus Card and Miss Hannah Mace, both of Portsmouth.
April	3	Married Mr. W^m. Palmer and Miss Maria Kimball, both of Dover.
	13	Married Mr. Saml Rogers and Miss Nancy Tripe, both of Dover.
May	11	Married Mr. Reuben Twombly & Miss Hannah Clements, both of Dover.
	14	Mr. John Mann & Miss Elizabeth Hodgdon, both of Dover.
	21	Mr Aaron Watson and Miss Betsy Horn, both of Dover.
	25	Mr ——— Bradford & Miss ——— Ricker, he of Boston & she of Dover.
Aug^t	17	Noah Chick & Polly Hanson, Dover.
Sept	4	John Stephens & Lydia Hussey, Somersworth.
	7	John Holmes of Portsmouth & Priscilla Fisher.
	10	Nathan Horn & Sally Roberts, Dover.
Oct	5	John Vasey & Margaret Warner, Portsmouth.

Nov	13	Jonathan McIntire & Mary Trask, Somersworth.
	23	Wm Twombly, Wakefield, & Lydia Horn, Dover.
Decem^r	6	Josiah Akiman, [Atkinson?] Portsmouth & Ann Lock, Dover.
	7	Ezekiel Hussey, Rochester & Mercy Horn.
	7	Moses Witham, Junr, Sanford & Ann Taylor.
	11	Jonathan A. Rawson & Rebecca G. Hodgdon.
1816.		
Jany	4	Asa Swasey, Milton & Mehitable Baker.
	10	Chase W. French & Fanny Earl.
	16	Growth Palmer & Anna Garland.
Feb	15	George Butler, Berwick & Achsa Pinkham.
March	4	Benjamin Folsom, Parsonsfield & Hannah Wentworth, Somersworth.
Ap^l	4	Joseph Varney & Margaret Horn, Somersworth.
	25	Henry M. Lindsey, Wakefield & Cynthia Kimball, Dover.
May	4	Jonathan Place, South Berwick, & Clarissa Roberts, Somersworth.
	8	Gerry Rounds, Buxton, Mass. & Mary Gage.
	23	Wm Woodman & Rebecca E. Wheeler.
July	7	Ephraim Ham, Junr, Ports^o & Zoah Hillard Ham.
Aug^t	18	John Hussey & Betsy Stephens, both of Somersworth.
Sept.	26	Saml S. Coleman & Mehitable Burnham.
Oct	13	Lot Wedgwood, Ports^o & Elizabeth Wingate, Madbury.
	27	John Plumer, 3^d, Rochester & Mary Waldron.
Nov	3	Theodore Atkinson & Ann L. Tufts.
	3	Nahum Hanson & Sally Otis.
	9	Danl Bartlett, Junr, Elliot & Mary Yeaton.
	9	John Twombly & Mary Horn.
	28	Benning Wentworth & Joanna H. Leighton.
Dec	5	Danl Pike, Wolfborough & Lavina Wallingford.
	13	Hall Wentworth & Nancy Wentworth, Somersworth.
	25	Isaac Twombly & Susan Tuttle.
	26	Wm Keay, Berwick & Elizabeth Plumer, Somersworth.
1817.		
Jany	9	Thomas Jewet, South Berwick & Elizabeth Lord, Somersworth.
	20	Wm Wormwel & Christiana Twombly.
	30	Wm Hodgdon & Susan Coffin.

Feb	5	Morris Perkins & Abigail C. Paul.
Mar[h]	6	Paul Burley & Abigail Perkins.
	27	Benjamin Bailey, Westbrook, Me. & Susan Riley.
May	2	John Stocker, Boston, Mass., & Martha Trask, Somersworth.
	6	W[m] Perkins & Nancy Reade.
	12	John Tapley, Danvers, Mass. & Lydia Reade.
July	3	Hanson Hayes & Sophia Hanson, both of Milton.
Aug[t]	10	Benjamin Henderson & Ruth Tebbets.
Dec[r]	24	Moses Philpot, Somersworth, & Eliza Gage.
1818.		
Jany	1	James Lambert & Mary Foss.
Feb	11	Andrew Rollins & Sally Philpot, both of Somersworth.
March	1	Dependence Wells of Wells & Mary Hills.
May	14	Thomas Card & Sophia Neal.
	22	Jonathan Gage & Elizabeth Ham.
	25	Jeremy Wingate, Farmington & Mary Titcomb.
Aug[t]	31	Ebenezer Burton & Hannah Frost, both of Stratham.
Sept	27	Solomon Waldron & Mary Remick, both of Barrington.
Oct	9	Francis Drew & Eunice Evans.
Nov	9	Gaward Tolman & Mary W. Perkins.
	9	John Tebbets, Lisbon, Me. & Hannah Rollins, Somersworth.
	18	Nathan[l] Low, South Berwick & Mary Ann Hale.
	25	Francis Hanson & Phebe Libby.
	26	W[m] Winkley & Sarah Hussey, both of Barrington.
Dec[r]	4	Benjamin Moses & Abigail Ricker.
	31	David Sargent & Lydia W. Cushing.
1819.		
Feb	4	Henry Hodsdon, S. Berwick & Eunice Paul of Somersworth.
Ap[l]	15	Dan[l] Locke, Barrington & Susan Hayes, Rochester.
Oct	24	James Rollins, Somersworth & Sarah Wingate.
	31	Sam[l] Horn & Dorothy Scriggins.
Nov	8	James Wentworth & Eliza Paul.
Dec[r]	1	Asa Freeman & Frances Atkinson.
	9	John Roberts, 3[d], & Elizabeth Hall, Somersworth.
	10	Robert Varney & Martha Stackpole, Somersworth.
	25	Joseph Thompson & Louisa Spencer, Somersworth.
1820.		
Jan'y	9	Dan[l] Sanborn of North Hampton & Charlotte Sanborn.

Feb	14	Theodore Littlefield, Waltham, Mass. & Sophia Hanson.
March	6	Francis Cogswell, Boscawen & Elizabeth Tebbets.
	6	Jeremiah Plumer & Mercy Hobbs, Somersworth.
	22	Charles Swazey, Milton & Eunice Paul, Somersworth.
Ap^l	26	John Vazey & Dolly Pray of Portsmouth.
May	11	John Hayes & Sarah C. Gray, both of Farmington.
June	15	Gilbert Trufant, Bath, Me., & Sarah Robbins, Somersworth.
July	2	Ezekiel Hayes, Junr, & Lydia Foss.
Oct	21	Temple Nason, Berwick & Elizabeth Hobbs, Somersworth.
	30	Israel Estes & Caroline Kenney.
Nov	5	Saml Ham & Rebecca Harty.
	13	Asa A. Tufts & Hannah Phillips Gilman.
Dec^r	10	Chester Birge, Farmington, Conn. & Sarah Gerrish.
	14	Samuel Snell & Harriet Ham.

1821.

Feb	4	John Brown & Joanna Pierce.
March	11	Charles Hanson & Hannah Atwood, Boston.
May	15	Benjamin Pike, Saco, Me. & Elizabeth Wentworth, Somersworth.
July	2	Burleigh Smart of Kennebunk, Me. & Abigail Cogswell.
	22	Enoch Libbey & Martha Parsley.
Oct	11	Jeremiah Goodwin & Caroline Ham.
	23	Joseph W. Hale & Susan Emerson.
	28	Ebenezer T. Demeritt & Hannah T. Demeritt, both of Madbury.
Nov	3	Ambrose B. Paul of Somersworth & Abigail Varney.
	8	Charles Woodman & Dorothy D. Wheeler.
	29	Moses Paul & Susan Margaret Hodgdon.
Dec^r	12	Sharington A. Baker & Mary Ann Varney.
	26	Edmund Johnson of Weare & Phebe Whittier.
	27	Saml Stiles & Ruth Doe, both of Somersworth.

1822.

Jany	18	Benjamin Hanson, Junr. & Clarissa Jane Hanson.
	22	Gideon Gear, Barrington, & Pierce Hanson, Madbury.
	24	Wm P. Wingate & Eliza Chandler.
March	13	Wm P. Drew & Maria Drew.
	19	Saml Hale, Junr, & Ann Weeks, both of Barrington.
	28	Joseph Hutchings & Mary S. Brown.

June	8	John B. H. Odiorne & Abigail G. Chase.
	23	James Davis & Lydia Palmer.
July	11	George Piper & Sally Smith.
Sept	26	Danl Carlisle, Waltham, Mass., & Nancy Ricker, Somersworth.
	26	Danl Ricker & Phebe Yeaton, Somersworth.
Nov	14	Danl Trefethen, Kittery & Sally Card
	17	Nicholas Tripe & Mary Ham.
	21	Enoch Pinkham & Hannah Pinkham.
	28	Asa Perkins & Charlotte Clement.
Dec^r	4	Stephen Wiggin & Betsy Stiles of Somersworth.
	8	Thomas West & Fanny Dore.
	25	Danl Pinkham & Sophia Drew.
	29	Enoch Clark & Harriet Horn.

1823.

Jany	12	Henry Maloon & Abigail Tebbets.
March	20	Benjamin Q. Waldron, Rochester & Rosella Paul.
Ap^l	6	Charles Pishon & Sophia Ricker.
	10	Mark Hall & Ruth Ham.
	14	James M. Curtis & Ruth Leighton.
	24	Ira Haselton, Portsmouth & Abigail Palmer.
	25	James K. Jordan, Denmark, Me., & Ann Corson.
	29	Oliver Ricker & Mary Jane Roberts, Somersworth.
July	6	Joseph Meroney, Portsmouth & Lydia Spencer, Somersworth.
	27	Andrew Steel & Ann Emerson.
Aug^t	18	Oliver S. Horne & Sarah Estes.
Sept	11	Jonathan Scruton & Betsey Rogers, both of Farmington.
Oct	5	Calvin Coleman & Phebe Card.
	15	John G. Chase & Lydia Roberts, Somersworth.
	23	John G. Tilton, Newburyport & Mary Ann Hanson.
Nov	2	Oliver Libby, Elliot & Elizabeth Henderson.
	11	John A. Rollins & Mary Ann Leighton.
	20	Danl Rollins & Mary Plumer, Somersworth.
	23	Mr Nason & Eliza Warren, Dover.
	27	Sam. Hall & Sarah Tuttle.
Dec^r	14	Benjamin Carlton & Lucinda Weymouth.
	25	Seth W. Ham & Hannah C. Leighton, Somersworth.
	28	Wm Gerrish & Sally H. Hartford, Milton.

MARRIAGES BY REV. JOSEPH W. CLARY, 1812-1829.

1824.
Feb   19 John Linton & Lucinda Plumer.
       19 Thomas E. Mitchell, New Durham, & Mary Jane Ford.
       29 Joseph T. Hubbard & Sophia Burnham.
March   7 John H. Guile & Matilda Hart.
       19 Joshua Conant & Theodosia Trafton, Somersworth.
       21 Stephen Davis & Nancy H. Watson.
       25 Saml Horn & Lydia H. Blaké.
       28 Wm P. Drew, Somersworth & Lois G. Meservy.
Ap^l 13 Jeremiah H. Titcomb & Joanna W. Rollins.
May   13 Benjamin F. Lee & Lois Evans.
       15 James Pinkham & Martha Gray.
       16 Jeremiah Y. Chapman & Martha Ann Marshall.
June   29 Elijah Tuttle & Deborah Bickford.
July   25 Henry Quimby & Mehitable Waldron.
Augt 1 Horatio G. Hanson & Irena Corson.
        1 Saml Downs & Abigail Ham, Somersworth.
       15 Wm Perkins, New Durham & Abigail Twombly.
       22 Amasa Howard & Sally H. Clay, both of Somersworth.
Oct   3 Abraham Miles & Eliza H. Joy, both of Madbury.
       28 John Emery, Berwick & Abigail Horn, Dover.
Nov   22 John H. Wheeler & Mary Baker.
       28 David R. Stephens & Susan Young.
Decr 5 Edward Moulton & Elizabeth Jenks.
        9 John Smith, Junr, & Elizabeth Whitehouse.
       12 Joseph Morrill, Salisbury & Nancy A. Quimby.
       12 Warren White, Cambridge, Mass. & Lydia M. Wheeler.
       12 David Peirce & Mary Peirce.
       12 David Hix & Mary Bickford.
       20 George Clark of Berwick & Abigail Ricker.
       20 John Garvin & Rebecca Roberts, Somersworth.
1825.
Jany   2 Saml F. Gage & Martha Varney.
       10 George S. Yeaton & Elizabeth F. Taylor, both of Exeter.
       19 Thomas Scolly of Westbrook & Deborah Coffin.
       19 Jesse Gilman & Lydia Carlisle.
       23 Moses W. Straw & Sabina Stackpole, Somersworth.
       27 John Hooper, Berwick & Caroline Cushing.
Feb   4 David K. Tufts & Charlotte Smith.
       13 Thomas R. Hanson & Clarissa Dudley.

Feb	25	Stephen Coffin, Junr, & Margaret Ham, Barrington.
March	13	Guy Drake & Susan Blanchard.
	14	Calvin Chase & Eliza B. Ham.
	19	Jacob Garland & Mary Downing.
	23	Thomas Hanscom, Elliot & Abigail Card.
Apr^l	7	John Cole & Eliza Foss, Somersworth.
	14	Philip P. Tebbets & Abigail Roberts.
	17	George Kimball & Eleanor Demeritt.
	24	Stephen Palmer & Abigail Horn.
June	2	David Twombly & Lydia Coffin.
	13	Bennet Libby & Martha Huntress.
Aug^t	11	Benjamin Stokes & Sirena M. Lucas.
	16	Tristram Horn of Somersworth & Dorcas Ricker.
	22	Isaac L. Folsom & Lydia H. Titcomb.
Sep^t	11	Joseph Coleman & Dorothy Card.
	14	Saml Marcy & Mary Adaline Priest, Portsmouth.
	18	Joseph Gould & Mary Young.
	22	Joshua Ham & Susan Y. Horn.
Oct	2	James Twombly, Milton & Eunice Burrows.
	9	Ichabod Shaw, Moultonborough & Susan Buzzell, Rochester.
	13	Charles Baker, Portland & Caroline Hodgdon.
	17	John Nutter, Milton & Margaret Grieve.
	20	Benjamin Barnes & Pamelia Hanson.
	24	James Dixon, Portsmouth & Lydia Raymond.
Nov	3	James D. Green, Malden & Sarah A. Durell.
	15	Vaughan Jones, Portsmouth & Dorcas Stackpole.
	17	Henry S. Elliot & Sarah A. Cushing.
	20	Mark Hunt & Elizabeth Downs.
	24	Danl H. Watson & Susan Ham.
	24	Danl Jackson & Sophia Gage.
	24	Danl Reynolds & Sarah Watson.
Dec^r	1	Danl M. Christie & Dorothy D. Woodman.
	6	Hanson H. Wells & Eliza Garland.
1826.		
Jany	5	Thomas A. Gowen, Sanford & Rachel A. Ford.
Feb	23	Abner Locke, Barrington & Rebecca Coffin.
March	12	Stephen P. Chesley & Hannah C. Pendexter, Madbury.
Apr	5	John Furbush & Mary Parks.
	9	Eliphalet Hill & Hannah Ham, Barrington.

MARRIAGES BY REV. JOSEPH W. CLARY, 1812-1829.

Ap^l 13 Danl Horn & Sarah Watson.
July 18 Joseph Gerrish & Hannah Pierce.
  23 John H. Varney & Nancy Chase.
Augt 31 Aaron Wingate & Phebe T. Lamos, Madbury.
Nov 19 James C. Sewall & Martha Titcomb.
  23 Dearborn Lougee & Henrietta Wheeler.
  28 Joseph G. Moody, Kennebunk & Elizabeth C. Currier.
  28 Joseph S. Horn & Mary Jane Horn, both of Somersworth.
Decr 6 Alpheus Shapley, Elliot & Mary Moore.
  7 Saml H. Tebbets & Belinda Cross.
  14 Stephen Toppan & Lucy Barden.
  17 Wm E. Griffin & Elizabeth Tebbets, Somersworth.
  24 Richard Place & Christina Taylor.
  31 Silas Fisher & Tammy Cole.

1827.

Jany 3 Charles Ham & Abigail Dame Bartlett.
  10 Jonathan Pinkham & Betsy Chase.
  11 Oliver Prime & Sophronia Shaw.
  18 Sherburn Sleeper & Mary Young of York, Me.
  25 Saml Hanson, 2^d, and Clarissa Varney.
Feb 6 Lorenzo Rollins & Mary C. Waldron.
March 7 David Wilson & Mary Tebbets.
  7 Jonathan Tuck, Parsonsfield & Lois Bean.
  15 John F. Kelley & Lydia Ham.
  15 John C. Young & Lydia B. Harris, Chester.
  20 Ebenezer Gordon & Sophronia Anderson.
  29 Oliver Shapleigh, Elliot & Ann H. Odiorne.
Ap^l 9 Wm P. Wingate & Lydia G. Chandler.
  22 John Waldron 3^d & Eliza Waldron.
May 13 Ira Horn & Patience Horn, Somersworth.
  24 David Gotham & Rebecca Bishop.
June 6 Edwin Moody, Thomaston & Elizabeth Watson.
  6 Henry Folsom & Sarah Leighton.
  7 Jonathan Tebbets & Sally Randall, Rochester.
  28 Francis Kauffer & Eunice W. Page.
July 2 Nathan Clark & Mary Jane Pearson.
  16 Jacob W. Jackman & Betsy Pinkham of Madbury.
  25 Japheth D. White & Susan I Guile.

Aug^t	2	Elkanah S. Woodward & Susan J. Hussey, Somersworth.
	5	Oliver W. Johnson & Ann Trickey.
	6	Alfred Hull & Lydia Jones.
	22	Benjamin Odiorne & Martha W. Thompson. Barrington.
Sept	6	Charles Kimball & Prudence Hall.
	16	George Gray & Lydia J. Barden.
Oct	3	Danl R. Gale & Lydia Horn.
	4	Moses F. Reed & Nancy Wilson.
	22	Saml Garland & Susan Roberts, Somersworth.
	24	Leonidas V. Badger & Ann S. Stanwood.
	28	Isaac Smith & Mary Butler, Newmarket.
Nov	21	Stephen S. Stone & Sophia W. Jones.
	22	John Cook & Dorothy S. Moulton, Somersworth.
	29	Huland Dawley, Somersworth & Mary Whitehouse.
Dec^r	1	Moses Fiske & Susan F. Hurd, Somersworth.
	23	Saml Paul & Adaline F. Wentworth, Somersworth.
	23	Clark Paul & Mary Young.
	27	Henry Smith & Sally Watson, both of Barrington.
1823.		
Jany	1	Danl R. Taylor of Center Harbor & Susan T. Card.
	29	Asa Winkley, Barrington & Hannah Wingate, Madbury.
	30	Saml W. Fox & Lois Nason of Somersworth.
Feb	14	George Jenness, Rochester & Mary B. Pigeon.
	20	Saml Dame & Harriet Spencer, Somersworth.
March	20	John Corson & Eliza Jones.
	23	Jeremiah Kingman & Elizabeth Hayes, both of Barrington.
1829.		
Jany	10	Simeon Ellis & Phebe Ann May, both of Dover.

MARRIAGES

BY

REV. HUBBARD WINSLOW.

1829-1831.

RECORDS OF FIRST CHURCH, DOVER, N. H.

1829.
Jan   Mr. Lewis Stark to Miss Mary Tuttle of Dover.
Feb   11 Mr. Asa Parks to Miss Mary Pickering of Dover.
May   6 Mr. George W. Roberts of Somersworth to Miss Sally Woodhouse of Madbury.
June   16 Daniel Johnson to Miss Elizabeth Chesley, both of Dover.
           28 William Pickering Drew to Miss Eliza H. Demeritt, both of Dover.
           28 James C. Avery to Miss Nancy Rundlett, both of Dover.
July   2 William Downs to Miss Abigail Tucker, both of Somersworth.
Aug   30 Mr. James Wheeler to Mrs. Phebe Hanson, both of Dover.
Sept   20 Mr. Thomas B. Twombly to Miss Huldah T. Clark, both of Dover.
Dec   17 Mr. Isaac Benn and Miss Deborah Emerson, both of Dover.
           17 Mr. James Wood of Boston and Miss Ann Hussey of Dover.

1830.
March   3 Mr. Thomas Snell of Madbury to Mary E. Hussey of Dover.

April	27	Mr. James T. Spencer to Miss Eliza Cram, both of Somersworth.
May	20	Rev. Amos Blanchard of Lowell, Mass. to Caroline R. Draper of Dover.
	26	Daniel K. Webster to Miss Hannah Ham, both of Dover.
Sept	20	James D. Bishop to Miss Mary Ham, both of Dover.
Oct	12	Daniel Abbott to Miss Abigail Staples, both of Dover.
Nov	7	Hiram R. Roberts of Somersworth to Miss Ruth Ham of Dover.
	21	Richard Waldron of Dover to Miss Mary W. Canney of Somersworth.
Dec	1	Robert Fulton of Somersworth to Miss Susan G. Kimball of Dover.
	6	Timothy Hussey to Miss Sally F. Ham, both of Dover.
	8	Daniel W. Aspinwall to Miss Abigail P. Washburn, both of Dover.
1831.		
Jan	6	Daniel C. Gile to Miss Catharine Rogers, both of Dover.
Feb	18	Stacy Hall to Miss Sally Hayes, both of Barrington.
	18	Lucien B. Legg to Miss Mary Downs, both of Dover.
March	6	Parker Spalding to Elizabeth Danforth, both of Dover.
April	6	Jeremiah Drew to Clarissa Nute, both of Dover.
	24	Benjamin F. Hodgdon to Miss Aphia Prime, both of Dover.
May	25	Greenleaf Clark to Miss Nancy Brown, both of Dover.

DEATHS.

1773-1791.

RECORDS OF NATHANIEL COOPER.

[Printed from "Bill of Mortality, for Dover, N. H.," published in 1803.]

1773.
Feb.   21, Wife of Capt. Caleb Hodgdon.
        23, Christiana Baker, aged 84.
        26, John Field.
        28, Wife of Thomas Tuttle.
June 17, Thomas Hanson, suddenly, aged 71.
        25, John Gage, Esq., aged 71.
July 27, Deacon John Wood, aged 65.
Aug. 5, Spencer Wentworth, suddenly.
1774.
Feb.   24, Vincent Torr.
        Mrs. Waldron, aged 80.
Mar. 12, Mrs. Hanson.
April 7, Deacon Thomas Hayes, aged 59.
June 23, Mother of James Varney.
Aug. 12, Child of Daniel Heard.
Nov. 15, Joseph Hanson, aged 18.
Dec. 8, Wife of James Young.
1775.
Jan.   1, Daughter of James Calef, aged 5.
        8, Silas Hanson, aged 48.
Aug. 4, Child of James Calef, aged 2.
Sept. 1, Wife of Capt. John Waldron.
Dec. 2, Daughter of John Peirce, aged 3.

1776.
Jan. 12, Richard Canney.
 16, Frederic Bell, infant.
 18, Wife of Capt. Alex'r Caldwell.
Feb. 11, Joseph Bickford, apoplexy.
 12, Wife of John Horne, aged 92.
 24, Ephraim Wentworth.
 25, Son of Enoch Hoag.
Mar. 10, Mrs. Parks, old age.
 Mrs. Willand, old age.
 Jonathan Merrow.
 18, Widow Christina Watson, aged 61.
 23, Capt. Sam'l Gerrish.
 Catharine Foss.
April 4, James Nute.
 Mercy Punkin.
 9, John Ham, aged 15.
 18, Widow Hanson.
 26, Child of Mr. Yeaton.
 29, Joseph Conner, old age.
May 3, Capt. Shadrach Hodgdon, aged 46.
 6, Mrs. Young.
 10, Lieut. William Hanson, aged 48.
 11, John Cromwell and Wife.
 14, William Horn.
 Child of Josiah Folsom.
June Joseph Austin and his two Sons.
 10, Daughter of Richard Kimball, aged 19
 19, Wife of Benj. Evans.
 22, Daughter of Joseph Austin.
Aug. 21, Wife of James Chesley.
Oct. 3, Child of Thomas Ham.
Nov. 2, Doctor Moses How, bleeding, aged 48.
 21. Child of Jonathan Gage, infant.
 30, Ebenezer Varney.
1777.
Jan. 5, Wife of James Keille, old age.
 26, Widow Estes, old age.
Feb. 12, Child of Zaccheus Hanson.
 18, Tabitha Jenkins, old age; she was a Preacher among the Friends.

April	7, Daniel Horn, old age, aged 88.
	29, Child of Sam'l Ambrose, infant.
	Child of Daniel Randall, infant.
May	7, Mrs. Bampton.
June	5, Child of John B. Hanson, Esq., aged 2.
Sept.	6, Child of John Tebbets, Jun., aged 2.
	12, Child of Ichabod Horne.
	20, Child of Jo. Waldron.
	25, Richard Eystick; he was a prisoner taken by the ship Oliver Cromwell.
Oct.	2, Son of Paul Pinkham.
	10, James Chesley, aged 71.
	14, Widow Horne, aged 83.
	Three children of Jona. Bickford.
Nov.	17, Child of William Foss.
1778.	
Jan.	10, Thomas Ransom.
	20, William Hussey.
	24, James Edgcomb.
Feb.	20, Widow Garland.
Mar.	25, Sam'l Ambrose.
June	1, Wife of John Kimball.
July	4, John Waldron, aged 80.
Sept.	11, Nathan'l Allen, aged 60.
Oct.	10, Child of Isaac Watson.
	Mother to James Calef.
	28, Child of Jo. Burnham, aged 3.
Nov.	5, Mrs. Tuttle.
	15, John Horne.
	16, Child of James Calef.
1779.	
May	7, Widow Hannah Hayes.
June	21, Negro Boy of John Wentworth, Esq., drowned.
	Benj. Varney, killed by limb of a tree.
July	20, ——Allen.
Sept.	17, Child of Col. Evans, aged 3.
	20, Wm. Twombly.
Oct.	29, Child of Thomas Shannon.
Dec.	27, Lois Todd.
	Isaac Young.

1780.
Jan. 29, Son of Thomas Shannon, aged 5.
April 4, William Foss, aged 16.
Mrs. Powers.
May 3, Nancy Waldron.
June 12, Child of Wm. Waldron.
24, Peter Cushing, suddenly.
26, Child of Samuel Ham.
July 17, Child of Geo. Watson, infant.
Oct. 7, Child of Doctor Green, infant.
Nov. 10, ——Roberts, aged 50.
Dec. 10, Joseph and Nathan Varney.
13, Wife of Solomon Hanson.
20, Love Canney.
Child of Richard Waldron.

1781.
Jan. 16, Ahijah Hanson.
Feb. 15, Wife of Isaac Horne.
25, Daniel Evans.
Mar. 5, Benjamin Ham, aged 88.
April 6, Child of Capt. James Calef, infant.
10, Child of Capt. James Calef, aged 2.
13, Wife of Thomas Hanson.
Aug. 3, Benj. Libbey, aged 88.

1782.
Jan. 4, Widow Martha Hanson.
16, John Tebbets, aged 78.
19, Paul Varney.
Feb. 8, Wife of Joseph Peasley.
9, Lieut. Moses Wingate, aged 84.
March Mother of Jona. Bickford.
May 4, Wife of Nehemiah Kimball.
14, Widow Tamson Tibbets.
June 17, Child of William Watson, infant.
July 25, Child of Ichabod Tebbets, aged 4.
Sept. 30, Hope Scammond.
Oct. John Conner, Isaac Roberts } drowned.
& son of Richard Kimball }
Nov. 14, Joseph Hall, aged 80.
Dec. 6, Ebenezer Hanson.
9, Molly Hanson.

1783.

Jan.	Ebenezer Stacey's child.
Feb.	4, Child of Marble Osborne.
Mar.	19, George Horn.
	19, Child of Anthony Hanson.
	29, Child of Widow Cole.
April	14, Child of Isaac Watson.
	22, Child of Jona. Hanson.
May	16, Child of Nathaniel Horn, Jr.
	21, Timothy Tebbets, aged 1.
	28, Child of David Ham.
July	24, Wm. Wells.
Aug.	20, Widow Varney.
	21, Mary Twombly.
Sept.	24, Wife of Th. W. Waldron, Esq.
Nov.	6, Timothy Robinson, found dead in the street.
	25, John Conner, aged 48.

1784.

Jan.	9, John Hanson.
Feb.	16, Child of Wm. Waldron.
April	6, Daughter of Sam'l Ricker.
May	4, Molly Kimball.
June	11, Widow Young.
	18, Elijah Drew.
Oct.	13, Wife of Joseph Belknap.
	28, Widow Joanna Watson.
Nov.	10, Benj. Roberts.
	26, Child of James Calef, infant.
	27, Two children of Isaac Horn, Jun., infants, and his wife's son.
Dec.	17, Child of James Calef.
	29, Mrs. Estes.

1785.

Jan.	1, Widow Goodwin.
	4, Widow Heard.
	18, Widow Wood.
	31, Benj. Watson.
Mar.	Child of George Ricker.
	Wm. Robinson.
	Girl at Joseph Waldron's.

April	3, Thos. W. Waldron, Esq.
	9, Dinah Waldron, drowned, suicide.
	23, William Dore, aged 78.
May	17, Child of Joseph Waldron, infant.
	26, Lydia Russel.
June	28, Wife of Job Clements, Jun.
Aug.	4, Son of Widow Conner.
	5, Child of Th. Footman.
	16, Stephen Henderson.
	Wife of John Ham.
Sept.	10, Alexander Caldwell.
Oct.	7, Sam'l Emerson.
	24, Wife of Marble Osborne.
Nov.	8, Wife of Aaron Roberts.
	21, Mr. Ellis, mortification; fell from a pier of the bridge and broke his thigh and died.
Dec.	22, Wife of Joseph Hall.

1786.

Jan.	21, Daniel Horne.
	Child of John Hill.
April	Child of Joseph Waldron.
	15, Daniel Plummer, drowned.
July	Loath Henderson.
Sept.	11, Daughter of Capt. T. Shannon.
	18, Daughter of Capt. T. Shannon.
	18, Child of Paul Gerrish.
Sept.	Three children of John Leighton.
	21, Capt. John Tebbets, at sea.
	28, Child of Daniel Heard, aged 2.
Oct.	19, Child of Ichabod Tebbets.
	Woman at Andrew Torr's.
	Daughter of Capt. Guppy.
	29, James Young.
Nov.	1, Daughter of Capt. Guppy, infant.
	12, John Horn.
	22, Daughter of William Ham, aged 8.
	23, Daughter of Moses Roberts.
	27, Wife of Solomon Loud.
Dec.	3, Wife of Paul Horn.
	18, Child of John Titcomb, aged 4.
	21, Nehemiah Kimball, aged 82.

1787.
Jan.   10, John Wentworth, Esq., consumption, aged 40.
Feb.   3, Son of Richard Tripe, aged 10.
        12, Child of Nathaniel Watson.
        James Young, aged 69.
        16, Daughter of Amos Howard.
Mar.   5, Wife of Benjamin Canney.
        18, Widow Smith.
        19, Samuel Hodge, aged 79.
        23, Widow Titcomb, aged 94.
        Eleazer Hodgdon, aged 60.
        29, Wife of Capt. James Libbey.
        30, Stephen Varney.
        31, Daughter of Solomon Perkins.
April   3, Deborah S. Cooper, aged 8.
        5, Two children of Ebenezer Tuttle.
        13, Lieut. Jonathan Hayes.
        15, Child of Thomas Footman.
        Child of Daniel Heard.
        23, Child of Capt. Enoch Chase.
May   12, Widow Chesley.
        14, Daughter of Moses Sawyer.
        20, Widow Church.
June   14, William Hanson, aged 83.
        17, William Young.
        28, Amos Peasley.
        30, Child at Col. Baker's.
Aug.   21, Moses Randell.
Sept.   14, Wife of George Hanson.
        Child of Elijah Perkins.
        21, Child of Richard Kenney.
        30, Child of James Horn.
Oct.   11, Child of George Watson.
        22, Benjamin Hanson.
        23, Elijah Tuttle.
1788.
Jan.   6, Widow Russell.
        8, Wife of John Friend.
Feb.   1, Child of John Gage, Jr.
        10, Child of Mr. Toppan, aged 2.

June	3, Elisha Thomas, executed for murder.
	26, Wife & Child of Nath'l Horne.
Aug.	17, Widow Elizabeth Libbey, aged 84.
Nov.	24, Elijah Estes.
Dec.	17, John Burnham Hanson, insane, was found dead in the river.

1789.

Jan.	Mr. Austin.
	30, Ichabod Varney.
Feb.	5, Widow Wentworth.
June	1, Son of James Horn, aged 18.
Sept.	23, Isaac Horn.
	28, Widow Coffin, aged 86.
Nov.	11, Child of Janvrin Fisher, aged 1.

1790.

Feb.	16, Mrs. Todd.
May	10, Child of Charles Clapham, infant.
	Child of Joshua Varney.
	Ensign Samuel Heard's son, drowned.
	20, James Kellie, aged 82.
	29, Child of Benjamin Hayes.
	30, Child of Ebenezer Hanson.
July	8, Child of Gershom Lord.
Aug.	5, John Perkins.
	James Tuttle.
	25, Ambrose Bampton, supposed to weigh 400 pounds.
Sept.	15, Child of James Remick.
	23, Child of Capt. William Twombly, aged 4.
Oct.	24, Col. Jonathan Wentworth.
	Child of Richard Kenney.
	29, Caleb Estes.
	Sarah Austin.
Dec.	3, Son of Widow Anderson.
	Child of Ebenezer Tebbets.
	28, Child of George Watson.
	29, Child of Thomas Merrow.

1791.

Jan.	7, Child of Otis Watson.
	23, Child of Doct. Ezra Green.
	Child of James Watson.
	27, Child of Capt. Wm. Twombly.
	Child of John York.

Feb.	6,	Two children of Samuel Estes.
March.		Peter Hanson, negro.
		Child of Capt. James Libbey.
	20,	Wife of Richard Kenney.
May	17,	Charles Waldron.
Oct.		Child of Ichabod Tebbets.
Nov	15,	Mother of Richard Kenney.
		Deacon Shadrach Hodgdon, aged 82.

DEATHS.

1792-1802.

RECORDS OF DEA. BENJAMIN PEIRCE.

[Printed from "Bill of Mortality, for Dover, N. H.," published in 1803.]

1792
Mar. 19, Deacon Ephraim Kimball.
29, Abraham Preble.
April 3, Phillis Hanson.
Aug. 18, Richard Kimball.
Sept. 19, Widow Lydia Marshall, old age, aged 85; who n the course of her life assisted at the birth of more than one thousand children.
24, Mrs. Stackpole, old age, aged 101.
Child of Mr. Guppy, infant.
Oct. 17, Child of John Titcomb.
Nov. 14, Capt. Howard Henderson, palsy, aged 82.
24, Wife of James Smith, child bed, aged 26.
28, Child of Doct. Green.
Dec. 18, Nathan Varney.
1793.
Jan. 12, Widow Bickford, aged 85.
19, Abigail Tuttle, aged 85.
19, Mary Clark, aged 26.
20, Wife of Nathan Varney.
Feb. 25, Child of B. Ham.
27, Mrs. Abigail Cooper, fever, aged 57.
Mar. 18, Benjamin Dean, fever, aged 31.

April   20, William Hussey.
May   17, Child of J. Hodgdon.
June   Elijah Hodgdon, at sea, aged 28.
        8, Mary Varney, aged 20.
        23, Judith Varney, old age, aged 83.
        28, Child of Col. Titcomb, fever, aged 2.
July   6, Anna Jenks, consumption, aged 32.
        12, Mrs. Place, consumption.
Aug.   1, Mrs. Mellen, consumption, aged 21.
Sept.   18, William Waldron, fever.
        24, Child of Edward Sise, sore throat, infant.
Oct.   6, John Lindsey, consumption.
Nov.   29, Mr. Todd.
Dec.   6, Child of Samuel Roberts, infant.

1794.
Feb.   18, Wife of J. Hartford, consumption, aged 72.
        19, John Heard.
            William Foss, consumption, aged 23.
May   10, Col. J. Rawson, consumption, aged 35.
        13, Joshua Wingate, Jr., fever, aged 30.
June   17, Mrs. Gould.
        19, Mary Hoag, aged 36.
July   4, Child of M. Read, aged 3.
        15, Child of Doct. Ezra Green.
        18, Mrs. Farewell.
Aug.   15, Child of Andrew Torr, aged 12.
        22, Child of Wm. Hodge, aged 7.
Oct.   11, John Waldron.
        15, Ichabod Hayes, fever, aged 76.
Dec.   19, Child of B. Kelley, aged 2.

1795.
March   4, Nathaniel Cooper, consumption, aged 53.
        5, Capt. Thomas Young, consumption.
        6, William Ricker.
        24, Stephen Young, consumption, aged 30.
        25, Henry Duplesis, consumption, aged 37.
        26, Miriam Hanson.
        30, Elizabeth Hayes, old age, aged 73.
July   6, Sarah Fisher.

Aug. 18, Isaac Nute, mortification.
22, Child of Doct. Green.
Oct. Wife of William Waldron, palsy, aged 35.
Nov. 29, Child of Ezra Young.
Dec. 27, Thomas Hanson, jaundice.

Dates Un-known.
- Isaac Horn's wife, child bed, aged 37.
- William Willand, mortification, aged 56.
- George Baker.
- Child of Ichabod Ham.

1796.
Jan. 11, John Tuttle, old age.
12, Rebecca Kenney.
Widow Roberts.
14, Widow Nute.
Feb. 7, Paul Nute.
9, Col. Joshua Wingate, pulmonic fever, aged 71.
Corodon's child, infant.
Mar. 19, Widow of Deacon Hodgdon.
Child of Widow Estes, aged 13.
22, Mercy Smith, consumption, aged 54.
Mrs. Ewers, old age.

Dates Unknown.
- Peggy Pumpkin, consumption, aged 24.
- Dover Gage's child.

June 27, Child of Doctor Green, infant.
29, Eunice Hanson, fit, aged 27.
July 1, Phillip Cromwell, consumption.
5. John Clements.
9, Child of John Titcomb, diarrhea, aged 5.
9, Betsy Comwell, fever.
Aug. 5, Lydia Gray, throat distemper, aged 4.
12, Patience Mann, throat distemper, aged 17.
14, Nabby Gray, throat distemper, aged 6.
28, Ephraim Plummer.
29, Child of B. Ham.
Sept. 4, Child of Jona. Plummer, throat distemper, aged 4.
10, Son of Paul Pinkham.
Nov. 22, Paul Hussey, pulmonic fever, aged 66.
Dec. 17, Robert Gray, Jr , pulmonic fever, infant.
1797.
Jan. 4, Abigail Ham.

Jan.	10, Aaron Roberts, old age, aged 84.
	12, Susanna Lamos, consumption, aged 23.
Feb.	5, William Gage, old age.
April	26, Child of William Jackson, infant.
May	17, Peace Purington, consumption, aged 17.
	Samuel Emerson, aged 44.
	30, Child of Daniel Libbey.
June	3, Child of John Gage.
	28, Child of Daniel Libbey.
Aug.	30, Joseph Belknap, old age, aged 81.
	Joseph Evans, consumption.
Sept.	11, Elizabeth Ladd, dysentery, aged 31.
	18, Child of Nathaniel Watson, canker rash, aged 1,
	21, Wife of Benjamin Kelley, pulmonic fever, aged 25.
Oct.	28, Child of David Boardman.
	Henry Trefethern, consumption, aged 63.
Nov.	3, Susanna Footman, consumption, aged 38.
	Silas Tuttle, consumption.
	13, Jeremy Drew, consumption, aged 22.
Dec	Ebenezer Tuttle, consumption, aged 57.
	31, Wife of John Kelley, palsy, aged 58.

1798.

Jan.	3, Benjamin Ham, suddenly, aged 33.
	8, Mr. Everson, old age.
	9, Nathaniel P. Cogswell, consumption.
	11, Sarah Henderson, consumption.
	25, Mrs. Horn.
	30, Child of Tobias Tuttle.
Feb.	10, Wife of Miles Evans, mania, aged 50.
	Peter Mann, perished in the cold, aged 31. He left his own house (being maniacal) 15th February about 7 o'clock in the evening, and travelled about two miles and perished in the snow with the cold. He was found in the field of Ezra Young 10th of April.
	16, Anna Dame, aged 73.
Mar	16, Wife of Jedediah Varney, consumption, aged 64.
April	1, Child of Joseph Smith, infant.
May	Joseph Stackpole, at sea, aged 28.
	16, Maul Hanson.
July	29, Mary Cushing, fever, aged 81.

Aug.	11, Child of Ezra Kimball, worms, aged 2.
	11, Isaiah Gould, consumption, aged 43.
	24, Sally Horne, consumption, aged 21.
	28, Joseph Hanson, old age, aged 84.
	28, John Fernald, yellow fever, aged 20.
	30, Moses Little, Esq., yellow fever, aged 60.
Sept.	3, Child of William Hale.
	8, Joseph Young, drowned, aged 40.
	12, Child of Ichabod Horn, premature, infant.
	16, Child of N. W. Ela, dysentery, aged 2.
	25, Child of Ezra Kimball.
	27, Col. Janvrin Fisher, yellow fever.
	27, Child of Israel Hodgdon, consumption, aged 2.
Oct.	3, Child of Daniel Libbey.
	22, Child of Ebenezer Baker.
Nov.	11, Child of Douglas Stackpole.
	11, Child of Joseph Roberts, swelling in the throat, aged 2.
	14, Cæsar Gage, drowned, aged 21.
Dec.	29, Daughter of Jo. Whitehouse, consumption, aged 30.

1799.

Feb.	11, Widow M. Hanson, fever.
Mar.	6, Amos Howard, palsy, aged 78.
	17, Mrs. Purington, consumption, aged 65.
	29, Widow Dore, old age.
April	8, Asa Tufts, putrid bilious fever, aged 34.
	14, Lydia Ransom, consumption.
	26, Polly Gage, consumption, aged 31.
	Jacob Sawyer, dropsy, aged 79.
	27, Zaccheus Purington, Jun., consumption, aged 24.
May	Meshech Wentworth, at sea, aged 21.
	4, Col. Benjamin Titcomb, consumption, aged 56.
July	8, Moses Hodgdon, consumption, aged 27.
	14, Barbary Jourdan, consumption, aged 34.
	19, Wife of Col. Waldron, consumption.
Aug.	18, Master Moses Hodgdon.
Sept.	1, James Horn.
	John Hanson.
	22, Joseph Peirce, bilious fever, aged 31.
	25, Jedediah Varney, dropsy, aged 67.
Oct.	19, Capt. John Gage, fit, aged 70.

DEATHS, 1792-1802.

Oct. 30, Child of Jonathan Lamos.
Nov. 13, Job Clements, pulmonic fever, aged 75.
Joshua Perkins, Jun., at sea, aged 33.
John Watson, at sea, aged 18.
23, Molly Willand, putrid fever, aged 33.
29, Charlotte Paul, fever, aged 28.

1800.
Jan. 3, Josiah Folsom, consumption, aged 21.
6, Anna Purington, consumption, aged 22.
7, Elizabeth Clements, jaundice, aged 70.
10, Col. Theophilus Dame.
23, Widow Jefferds, fever, aged 77.
25, William Watson, mortification, aged 67.
Molly Leighton, consumption.
Feb. 3, Deborah Wingate, old age, aged 79.
4, John Gage, consumption, aged 44.
21, Samuel Place, consumption.
27, Ezekiel Heard, fever, aged 27.
Mar. 4, Mrs. Wingate, old age, aged 97.
10, Paul Robinson, consumption.
April 3, Child of J. Smallcorn, fit, infant.
4, W. In. Lad at Capt. Riley's.
9, Stoughton Austin, fever.
May 7, Nahum Sawyer, drowned, aged 21.
9, Child of John Heard.
17. Nicholas Drew, consumption, aged 22.
22, Child of J. M. Currier, premature, infant.
23, Sarah Varney, rickets, aged 2.
28, —— Eliot, accident, aged 6.
June 7, Capt. S. Gerrish, consumption, aged 42.
Jonathan Nute, consumption, aged 25.
Jeremiah Perkins, at sea, aged 21.
July 18, Lieut. Clement Meserve, fever, aged 84.
30, Wife of Ensign Heard, fever, aged 58.
Aug. 17, Widow Sarah Hanson.
17, Samuel Hartford, at sea, aged 26.
Sept. 17, Child of Mrs. Gerrish.
19, Child of Jo. Smith, pulmonic fever, aged 2.
Oct. 5, Child of Samuel Ricker, fever, aged 2.
8, George Watson, consumption, aged 52.

Oct.   14, Jonathan Gage, fever, aged 66.
Nov.   6, Caleb Hodgdon, Jr., consumption, aged 33.
       15, Samuel Ricker, old age, aged 75.
       18, Child of Heard Horn, fever.
       18, Lydia Libbey, malignant fever.
       24, Daughter of Ezekiel Hayes, consumption.

1801.
Jan.   3, Widow Roberts.
       18, Widow Evans, palsy, aged 83.
       21, Child of William H. Clark, consumption, infant.
Feb.   17, Lydia Willand, putrid fever.
       26, Sarah Hanson, putrid fever, aged 63.
Mar.   28, Sarah Canney.
       29, Widow Dorcas Hodgdon, old age, aged 80.
April 8, Child of Tamesin Row, infant.
       9, Child of John Tibbets, quinsy, aged 3.
       26, Tamesin Row.
       28, James Ham, accident, aged 32.
May   7, Capt. J. Leavitt, dropsy, aged 50.
       7, Abra Hayes, consumption.
June   8, Richard Hanson, consumption, aged 49.
       28, Mary Bragg, consumption, aged 59.
July   7, William Randall, bilious fever, aged 20.
       Child of E. Gilman, infant.
       14, Daniel Libbey, consumption, aged 39.
Aug.   11, Wife of E. Gilman, bilious fever, aged 21.
       24, Uriah Goodwin, consumption, aged 5.
       27, Clement Meserve, Jr., drowned, aged 21.
       31, Lydia Gray, consumption.
Sept. 14, James Chase, bilious fever, aged 31.
       Jane Kenney, bilious fever, aged 29.
       15, Joshua Hartford, consumption, aged 32.
       21, Rebecca Libbey, bilious fever, aged 2.
       21, Lydia Peirce, bilious fever, aged 18.
Oct.   3, Child of Wm. Neil, fever, aged 2.
       13, Ezra Kimball, Jr., bilious fever, aged 38.
       23, Nancy Hanson, bilious fever, aged 16.
       27, Col. Otis Baker, bilious fever, aged 75.
       27, Peggy Wentworth, bilious fever.
       27, ——Stimpson, fever.

Oct.	29, Nicholas Ricker, bilious fever.
	30, Elijah Jenkins, bilious fever, aged 77.
Nov.	1, Widow Meserve, fever, aged 66.
	6, Tammy Baker, bilious fever.
	Jotham Nute, palsy.
	23, N. W. Ela, quinsy, aged 2.
	27, Widow Horn, old age.
	28, Tamesin Gage, fever.

1802.

Jan.	8, Child of J. Sawyer, fever, infant.
	12, Ebenezer Woodman, fit, aged 34.
	17, Child of David Twombly, whooping cough, infant.
Feb.	2, Child of Stephen Roberts.
	13, Joanna Drew, bilious fever, aged 17.
	25, Col. Thomas Watson, pulmonic fever, aged 60.
March	1, Child of Israel Hanson, fever, infant.
	2, Sally Walker, aged 22.
	13, Child of Jo. Roberts, infant.
	19, Ephraim Hanson, accident, aged 15.
	26, Elizabeth Hanson, consumption, aged 62.
	David Boardman, at sea, aged 34.
	John Kimball, at sea, aged 23.
April	7, Joseph Gage, consumption, aged 37.
May	7, Sarah Sawyer, dropsy.
	24, J. Guppy, bilious fever, aged 23.
	25, Elsie Rogers, fever, aged 73.
	27, Child of Thomas Young, fever, aged 4.
	30, Widow Hanson, cancer, aged 84.
June	7, Thomas Goudy, old age, aged 71.
	19, Child of J. Stickney, fit, aged 4.
	26, Widow Young.
July	1, Hannah Nute.
	11, John Friend, yellow fever, aged 52.
	12, Moses Gage, palsy, aged 70.
	28, Jabez Davis, fit.
Aug.	21, Widow Bampton, old age, aged 82.
	24, Child of George Young, dysentery, infant.
Sept.	3, Child of E. Chase, Jr., fever, aged 2.
	12, Eliphalet Ladd, bilious fever, aged 33.
Oct.	3, Daniel Varney, mortification, aged 76.

Oct. 18, Child of J. Baker, mortification, aged 1.
     29, Child of Benjamin Carter, consumption, aged 5.
     31, Child of G. Ricker.
Nov. 4, Child of George Ham, dysentery.
     11, Child of Jeremiah Ricker, premature, infant.
     12, Child of G. Ham, aged 6.
     James Varney, jaundice, aged 72.

MEMBERS

OF

FIRST CHURCH.

1718-1850.

RECORDS OF FIRST CHURCH, DOVER, N. H.

[Arranged according to the date of their admission. There is no list of members prior to 1718. Marriage subsequent to union with the church is put in parenthesis, with letter m.]

1718.
Mar. 30, William Waldron, afterwards minister in Boston.
        Abra, wife of Paul Wentworth.
        Elizabeth, wife of Jonathan Cushing, pastor.
May 25, Paul Gerrish.
Aug. 31, Gershom Downs.
Oct. 19, Abigail Hayes.
1719.
Sept. 20, Martha Wentworth ; dismissed to Somersworth church.
1720.
Oct. —, Gershom Wentworth ; dismissed to Somersworth church.
Nov. —, Ann Evans.
1721.
Sept. —, Tristram Coffin and his wife.
1722.
June 3, Maturin Ricker ; dismissed to Somersworth church.
        Joseph Twombly.
        Elizabeth Twombly.
1723.
Mar. 3, Mary, wife of Wm. Chamberlain ; dismissed to Rochester church, July 2, 1749.

Nov. 24, Col. James Davis and Elizabeth, his wife.
Thomas Starboard.
Edward Peavey; dismissed to Berwick church.

1725.
May 9, Jane Heard, widow of Tristram, (m. Benjamin Hayes.)
Oct. 3, Benjamin Faust; dismissed to Rochester church, Aug. 22, 1732.
Mary, wife of Paul Gerrish.
Hannah, wife of Job Clements.

1726.
Mar. 20, Thomas Nock: dismissed to Somersworth church.
Elizabeth Hanson.

1727.
May 21, James Davis, Jr.

1728.
Mar. 10, James Cushing.
Daniel Titcomb.
Aug. 11, James Heard and Deborah, his wife.
Mary, wife of Edward Peavey; dismissed to Berwick church.

1729.
Mar. 23, Tamson, wife of John Hayes.
Ruth, wife of James Davis, dismissed and recommended from the church in Haverhill.
June 22, Elizabeth Wentworth, widow; dismissed to Somersworth church.
Sept. 14, Abigail, wife of Joseph Richards; dismissed to Rochester church Aug. 20, 1732.

1730.
Mar. 22, Joseph Ricker and Elizabeth, his wife; both dismissed to Somersworth church.
Aug. 9, Sarah, wife of Gershom Wentworth; dismissed to Somersworth church.
Mary, wife of William Wentworth; dismissed to Somersworth church.
Sept. 5, Sarah, wife of Peter Hayes.

1731.
July 2, Joseph Hall and Peniel, his wife.
Nov. 5, Mary, wife of Daniel Horne.

1733.
Apr. 1, Rebecca Hanson.

Sept. 2, Elizabeth, wife of John Horn.
Abigail Hayes.

1735.
May 11, John Gerrish and Margery, his wife.
Christine Baker, recommended from the church at Mendon.
Oct. 26, Elizabeth Gerrish, (m. John Wood.)

1736.
April 4, Dorothy, wife of Joshua Perkins.
Nov. 14, Dorothy, wife of Derry Pitman of Durham.
Christine, wife of Dudley Watson.

1738.
June 25, Ruth Hanson, (m. George Hern.)
Aug. 6, Elizabeth, wife of Joseph Bickford.

1740.
Aug. 24, Ephraim Wentworth and Martha, his wife.
Oct. 5, John Wood, dismissed and recommended from the First Church in Cambridge.

1741.
Apr. 26, Mary Tebbetts.
July 19, Samuel Hale; dismissed to the South Church in Portsmouth.
Aug. 30, Mary, wife of Dr. Moses Carr.
Oct. 11, Kezia, wife of Spencer Wentworth; afterwards wife of Thomas Peirce.

1742.
Mar. 28, John Wingate.
William Hanson.
Daniel Hayes.
Hezekiah Hayes; dismissed to the church at Barrington.
Benjamin Hayes; dismissed to the church at Barrington.
Mehitable Hayes.
Daniel Ham and Sarah, his wife.
Clement Ham.
Elizabeth Twombly, (m. Benj. Pearl of Barrington.)
Hannah Perkins.
Sarah, wife of John Roberts.
May 9, Shadrach Hodgdon.
Esther Horn.
Hannah, wife of Thomas Hayes.
Mary Weymouth; turned Quaker.

June 20, Ichabod Hayes and Elizabeth, his wife.
Reuben Hayes.
Esther Bickford.
Charity Heard.
Elizabeth, wife of John Mills.
Hannah Leighton, Barrington.
Mercy Watson, (m. Benjamin Hanson.)
Aug. 1, Patrick Manning; dismissed to the church in Berwick, May 29, 1743.
George Horn and Mary, his wife.
Ursilla, wife of Richard Jones.
Joseph Evans, 3d.
Abra Hayes, (m. John Montgomery.)
Mary, wife of John Waldron, Sen.
Sept. 12, Judith Horn, (m. Henry Buzzell.)
Margaret Horn.
Oct. 24, Stephen Evans.

1743.
Apr. 17, Joseph Hayes.
George Hern.
Bridget Horsum.
Elizabeth Hubbard, (m. —— Weymouth, Kittery.)
May 29, Elizabeth Heard.
Deborah, wife of Joseph Bickford.
Nov. 13, Samuel Heard.
Lois, wife of Vincent Tarr.

1744.
Mar. 18, Mary Wentworth.
Sept. 9, Elizabeth Bickford, (m. Ebenezer Young, Barrington.)
Oct. 21, Mary Titcomb, (m. Edward Woodman.)

1745.
Apr. 14, William Demeritt.
Eunice Smith.
May 26, Joanna Gerrish.
1746.
June 29, Ezekiel Wentworth and Elizabeth, his wife.
Oct. 5, Deborah Ham.
1748.
Oct. 9, William Faus.

1749.
Sept. 24, Lucy, wife of Samuel Gerrish; afterwards, wife of James Bracket.

1753.
The following six persons were from the Durham church:
Apr. 22, Hubbard Stevens.
Joseph Bickford.
June 17, Jonathan Thompson and Sarah, his wife.
Joseph Atkinson.
Benjamin Bickford.

1755.
July 13, Joanna Watson.

1756.
June 13, Abigail Hayes, (m. Nathaniel Cooper.)
July 25, Judith, wife of Elijah Bunker; dismissed and recommended to the church in Sanford, Oct. 9, 1791.
Oct. 24, Otis Baker; died Oct. 27, 1801, aged 75.

1757.
July 31, Elizabeth Nathersell, (m. Samuel Heard, Jr.)
Hannah, wife of Ebenezer Demerritt.

1761.
Apr. 19, Susanna Wood.

1762.
May 2, Joanna, wife of Nathaniel Balch.

1763.
Oct. 16, Elizabeth, wife of Benjamin Libbey, Sen.

1764.
Apr. 22, Elizabeth Wood, Jr.
July 15, John Woodman.

1767.
Feb. 16, Jeremy Belknap, dismissed and recommended from South Church, in Boston.
Samuel Hodge, recommended by Mr. Davidson of Londonderry.

1768.
June 12, John Waldron, 3d, and Joanna, his wife.
Sarah Brown.
Nov. 20, Deborah, wife of James Kielle.

1769.
Mar. 12, Thomas Hayes.

May	10, Nehemiah Kimball.
	Benjamin Evans.
	Jonathan Bickford.
	Lydia, wife of Daniel Horn, Jr.
	Elizabeth, wife of Joseph Roberts.
	Sarah, wife of Jonathan Bickford.
June	18, Moses Emerson, from the church in Milton.
	Sarah Wingate, from Dr. Cooper's church in Boston.
	Ephraim Kimball and Sarah, his wife.
Sept.	10, Mary Young, widow.
Oct.	8, Dorcas, wife of Eleazer Hodgdon.
	Elizabeth, wife of Isaac Mason.
	Sarah Elliot.
Dec.	31, Peter, servant of Thomas Hanson.

1770.
Oct. 7, Mary, wife of Nehemiah Kimball.

1771.
Dec. 29, Margaret, wife of John Wentworth, from the church in Newcastle.
Mary Hodge, recommended by Mr. McGregor of Londonderry.

1773.
May 9, Dorothy, wife of Samuel Emerson.

1775.
June 25, Elizabeth Ham.
July 2, Hannah, wife of Nathaniel Ham; died Feb. 6, 1842, in Madbury, aged 90 years.

1776.
Feb. 4, Lydia, wife of Timothy White.
July 14, Abigail Belknap.
Oct. 13, Mary, wife of Benjamin Peirce.

1777.
Apr. 6, Ezra Green; dismissed to Unitarian Society in Dover, Feb. 1829.

May 25, Lydia Cook.

1780.
Mar. 5, Benjamin Peirce; died Sept. 12, 1823, aged 80 yrs. and 6 mos.
July 30, Mary Hanson.
Aug. 2, Nathaniel Horn, Jr. and Mercy, his wife. He died June 16, 1832, aged 78 yrs. 2 mos. and 13 days.

Oct.	1, Anna, wife of Richard Kimball.
	Elizabeth, wife of George Watson.
Dec.	3, Joseph Whitehouse and Susanna, his wife.

1781.

Sept.	30, Deborah, wife of Aaron Hayes.

1782.

Nov.	24, Lydia, wife of Dodavah Ham.

1786.

July	2, Hannah Gage, (m. Jonathan Rawson.)

1787.

June	3, Jonathan Calf of Chester.
July	4, Susanna, wife of Ezra Green; dismissed Feb. 1829, to Unitarian church, Dover; died Feb. 14, 1836, aged 77.
Sept.	2, Theophilus Dame.

1790.

——	— Sarah, daughter of William Hanson.

1791.

Oct.	2, Anna, wife of Samuel Shackford.
Nov.	4, Phineas Wentworth.
Dec.	4, Henry Mellen.

1792.

Jan.	22, Nathaniel Cooper.
	29, Sarah, wife of William J. Fiske.
	Ezra Young and Elizabeth, his wife.
Aug.	5, Molly, wife of Reuben Ricker.

1793.

May	4, Lydia, wife of Ephraim Ham.

1794.

May	1, Abigail, wife of John Kelley.
	19, John Wheeler and Rebecca, his wife, on the halfway covenant.
Oct.	1, Mary, wife of Ezra Kimball.

1795.

Oct.	4, Philemon Chandler.

1797.

July	15, Lydia, wife of Amos Cogswell.

1799.

Sept.	1, Elizabeth Dean.

1800.

Nov.	27, Judith, wife of Joseph Smith.

Dec. 3, Sarah, wife of Ichabod Horn.
William Blake and Elizabeth, his wife.
Abigail Folsom.
Joseph Swan; removed to Charlestown, Mass., 1810.
Oliver Crosby and Harriet, his wife. He died July 30, 1851, aged 82; she died March, 1843.
John W. Hayes; dismissed to Congregational church, Haverhill, Mass., Dec. 8, 1839.
Anna Robinson; died March 13, 1850, aged 82.

1802.
Oct. —, Sarah, wife of Amos White; died August 3, 1845, aged 66.
——— Mary, wife of Ebenezer Baker; died Sept. 15, 1851.
——— Mrs. Hannah Hanson, daughter of Stephen Patten.

1804.
——— Aaron Hayes.

1808.
Oct. 23, Sarah, wife of John Titcomb; died April 25, 1857.

1809.
July 16, Widow Mary Kimball; died April 29, 1848, aged 78.
Sept. 11, Lydia, wife of Jonathan Trickey.
Nov. 4, Deborah Green, daughter of Deacon Ezra Green; dismissed Feb., 1829 to Unitarian society, Dover.

1810.
——— Abigail, widow of Otis Legg; died Sept. 1846.

1811.
——— Sarah Green, daughter of Deacon Ezra Green; died Nov. 2, 1874, aged 86.

1812.
May 7, Rev. Joseph W. Clary.
Sept. 12, Abigail Tibbetts; died April 2, 1860.
Nov. 6, Mary, wife of Israel Twombly.
Lydia Hayes, (m. John Nutter of Milton, May 16, 1833;) died at Rochester, Feb. 21, 1850.

1813.
Nov. 7, Mary Perkins, (m. Moses Perkins;) died Jan. 27, 1873, aged 81.

1814.
Aug. —, Maria Kimball, (m. William Palmer;) died Jan. 8, 1866.
Elizabeth Hodgdon, (m. John Mann;) died Jan. 30, 1868, aged 76.
Eunice Green; died March 25, 1839, aged 39.

MEMBERS OF FIRST CHURCH, 1718-1850.

Nov. —, Clarrissa Wheeler, died at Medford, Mass., May 25, 1847.
1815.
April 2, Mary Tuttle.
June —, Elizabeth, wife of John Wheeler; died June 5, 1857.
Sept. 15, Israel Twombly; died in Illinois near 1855.
Oct. —, Anna Hanson; died Nov. 3, 1856.
—— Anna, wife of Rev. J. W. Clary.
—— Abigail Cogswell.
—— Lydia Prentice, dismissed.
—— Eliza Hodgdon.
—— Wife of George Ricker.
1816.
Oct. —, Delia, wife of Edmund Paul, (m. Dec. 24, 1840, Nathaniel Hobbs of North Berwick, Me.)
—— Lydia Horne.
1817.
May 4, Eliza Perkins.
Izetta Kenney.
Esther Blake.
1818.
June 7, Rebecca S. Footman; died Dec. 31, 1874, aged 85.
Dec. 6, Peter Cushing, 2d; died June 6, 1874, aged 78.
Susan M. Hodgdon, (m. Moses Paul;) died Mar. 29, 1891, aged 93.
Abigail Horn, (m. Job Emery of Somersworth;) dismissed March 15, 1840, to the church in Somersworth.
Dexter Brewer; removed to Westbrook, Me.
Frances Atkinson, (m. Asa Freeman;) died Sept. 5, 1883, aged 86.
1819.
Nov. 7, Rachel Corson, (m. Henry Seavey.)
May —, Asa Freeman; died Dec. 8, 1867.
—— Olive, wife of Daniel Watson; removed to Portsmorth.
1822.
July 7, Sarah Twombly; died Jan. 10, 1852, aged 91.
1823.
Jan. 26, Ann Louisa, widow of Theo. Atkinson; dismissed to St. Thomas church Dover, Feb. 11, 1840.
Sally Pierce; died Aug. 18, 1862.
Olive W. Brown; dismissed to Baptist church Portsmouth, June 25, 1834.

MEMBERS OF FIRST CHURCH, 1718-1850.   215

Jan.   26, Deborah Palmer, (m. Ebenezer Buzzell;) dismissed Aug. 13, 1848.
        Asa Alford Tufts and Hannah Philips Tufts, his wife; he was dismissed to St. John's church Portsmouth, Aug. 4, 1839, she was dismissed to St. Thomas church Dover, Feb. 11, 1840.
        John Hancock Wheeler; died Aug. 21, 1867.
Mar.   —, Mary Pierce; died Sept. 10, 1850.
        Thomas R. Hanson; dismissed to the church in Amesbury, Mass., Nov. 17, 1831.
        Clarissa Dudley, (m. Thomas R. Hanson;) dismissed to church in Amesbury, Mass., Nov. 17, 1831.
April 6, Lydia Gray Chandler, daughter of P. Chandler, (m. Wm. P. Wingate;) died Jan. 1, 1871, aged 70.
June   12, Moses Paul; died July 9, 1860.
        Samuel Prescott; excommunicated Aug. 4, 1842.
        Sarah, widow of James Chesley Baker; died June 27, 1833, aged 55.
        29, Elizabeth Hale, (m. Hon Jer. Smith;) dismissed to Exeter, Aug. 20, 1834.
Aug.   30, John Gould and Mary, his wife, from the church in Exeter.
1824.
July   4, Lydia, wife of Capt. Wm. Twombly; died June 30, 1857.
        Lucy, widow of Ezekiel Hayes; died at Portland, 1840.
Sept. 3, Dolly Wentworth, (m. Thos. J. Roberts, Oct. 14, 1832;) died March 25, 1858.
        5, David Sargent; died at Somersworth in 1866.
        Jane, wife of Nathaniel Horn; died Sept. 3, 1851, aged 90;
        Sophia, daughter of Nathaniel Horn; died April 18, 1879, aged 81.
        Betsy, daughter of Nathaniel Horn; died Oct. 2, 1851.
        Mercy, widow of Ezekiel Hussey, (m. John B. Sargent;) died June 10, 1852.
        Dorcas Downs, (m. Moody Haskell of Burlington, Vt.)
1825.
Aug.   7, John Pratt and Hannah, his wife, by letter from the church in Malden, Mass.; dismissed to the Episcopal church in Saco, Me., Oct. 3, 1832. She died at Saco, April 15, 1833, aged 52.
1826.
Feb.   13, Jonathan H. Cushing; died March 22, 1836, aged 50.

Dec. 3, Jonathan Young; died Jan. 7, 1843.

1827.
Jan. 7, Lydia, wife of Wm. Twombly, Jr.; dismissed to First church, Lowell, Mass., Aug. 26, 1849.
Elizabeth Pearl Hammott.
Mary Ann, wife of John Tilton; dismissed to First Presbyterian church in Newburyport, Mass., Dec. 4, 1831.
Sally Leighton; dismissed to the church in Lincoln, Me., July 10, 1831.

Nov. —, John Robinson; admitted by letter from England.

1828.
Jan. 6, Harriet Patten; dismissed to the First Presbyterian church, Newburyport, Mass., Dec. 4, 1831.

1829.
Mar. 1, William Woodman; died Jan. 30, 1865, aged 85.
Joshua Patten; died May 10, 1847, aged 74.
Henry Dearborn; dismissed to Milton, N. H., May 22, 1836.
Daniel Pierce; died Jan. 19, 1850.
Lydia W., wife of David Sargent; died Jan. 5, 1858.
Hannah Whidden, (m. James E. Macy Sept. 8, 1846;) dismissed Oct. 10, 1866, to the Methodist church, Dover.
Mary H. Cushing; died Jan. 26, 1853.
Hannah C., wife of Lemuel Draper; dismissed to New York City, Sept. 11, 1836.
Caroline R. Draper, (m. Rev. Amos Blanchard;) dismissed to Lowell, Mass., about 1831.
Abigail Vincent; died at Portsmouth, Aug. 29, 1865, aged 84.
John P. Sargent and Lucy, his wife; she died Oct. 8, 1835; he died Feb. 8, 1855.
James L. Foot; dismissed to Lowell, Mass., about 1830.
Mehitable, wife of Bradley Osgood; died Apr. 19, 1880, aged 85 years, 9 months.
Sophia, wife of Samuel Wyatt; died Dec. 31, 1857, at Georgetown, Mass.
Hammon Hutchinson; died Mar. 9, 1867.
Sophia W., wife of Stephen Stone; dismissed to Bowdoin St. church, Boston, Mass., Nov. 20, 1834.
Mary Stanwood; dismissed to the church at Somersworth, June 1, 1832.

Mar. 1, John G. Tilton; dismissed to the First Presbyterian church, Newburyport, Mass., Dec. 4, 1831.
Eliza Leighton; dismissed to the church in Lincoln, Me., July 10, 1831.
Solomon Childs and Lucinda, his wife; both dismissed to the church in Henniker, N. H.
Mary Childs, daughter of Solomon; dismissed May 17, 1840, to Henniker.

May 10, Sarah Lord, (m. Josiah Winn;) dismissed Dec. 1, 1844, to New Sharon, Me.
Sarah Ann, wife of Joseph Hanson; dismissed to Franklin Church, Boston, Mass., Dec. 20, 1835.
Capt. Isaac A. Porter and Mary K., his wife; both dismissed to Belknap Church, Dover, Aug. 31, 1856.
Lucy Barnes; dismissed to Lowell, Mass., July 7, 1836.
Sarah Wentworth; dismissed May, 1831, to church in Somersworth.

July 5, Mehitable Libby, widow; died Jan. 29, 1842.
Abigail Dame, wife of Charles Ham; died Nov. 29, 1890.
Clarissa M. Ham, (m. Moses Hussey;) died Dec. 2, 1873.

Sept. 13, Abigail Tibbetts; dismissed to Barrington, Sept. 24, 1838.
Dorcas Stacey.
Mary Burrows, (m. John Dame Sept. 8, 1831;) died Sept. 30, 1841, aged 28.
Elizabeth L., wife of George L. Foss; dismissed July 21, 1842, to Strafford.
Mary Ann Peirce, (m. Eben H. Berry in 1840;) dismissed Feb. 12, 1862.
Hannah Colby; died at Newfield, Me., June, 1831.
Enoch L. Childs, dismissed to church in Yale College, Oct. 16, 1831.
Armenia Goodwin, (m. Solomon Perkins of Exeter;) dismissed to church in Exeter, Oct. 29, 1843.

Dec. 7, Mary, wife of Joseph Smith; died Jan. 21, 1868.

1830.
Jan. 3, Zebediah Wyman and his wife; both dismissed to church in Woburn, Mass., Nov. 24, 1831.
Mehitable Pray.
Andrew Peirce and Abigail Smith Peirce, his wife. He died Sept. 4, 1862, aged 76; she died Mar. 5, 1875, aged 86 years, 8 mos.

Jan. 3, John Tapley; died Aug. 28, 1831.
John S. Meserve; dismissed to the church at Lamprey River, Dec. 20. 1832.
Robert H. Cushing; died May 24, 1877, aged 78 years, 9 months.
Priscilla, wife of Samuel Watson, Jr.; dismissed Apr. 30, 1861, to Lawrence, Mass.
Elizabeth, wife of Barnabas H. Palmer; dismissed to South Berwick, Me., April 16, 1837.
Alice Abbott; dismissed to Salem, Mass., April 1, 1833.
Esther P., wife of Joshua Banfield; dismissed Jan. 9, 1868, to Hampton.
Mary B., wife of John H. Wheeler; died Dec. 5, 1866, aged 68.
Mary Jane Gilman, died July 14, 1832.
Mary Ann Varney.
Betsey Peirce; died May 24, 1856, aged 87.

Mar. 7, Susan C. Gilman; dismissed to Rev. Mr. Maltby's church, Bangor, Me., May 22, 1836.
Lydia H., wife of Sam'l Horne, 2d; dismissed to Woburn, Mass., Oct. 26, 1856.
Rachel Peirce, (m. Josiah Hall Nov., 1832;) dismissed to Laconia, Mar. 10, 1862.
Charles C. P. Moody; dismissed to the church at Somersworth, Oct. 3, 1832.
Jeannette Pray; died March 20, 1835.
Paulina Hasty; dismissed May 31, 1842, to John St. church, Lowell, Mass.

May 2, Nelson Swift Johnson.
Wm. Cutter Draper; dismissed to Bleeker St. church, New York, N. Y., Sept. 10, 1834.
Eliza Ann Wilson.
Frances Evans, (m. Charles C. P. Moody in 1831;) dismissed to the church at Somersworth, Oct. 3, 1832.
Mary Jane Ham.
Mary Young, (m. Charles Hazeltine of Newburyport, Mass., July 4, 1842.)
Elizabeth Wentworth, (m. James Smith, Springfield, Mass.)
Mary Nute.
Mary S. Williams; dismissed and recommended Sept. 26, 1830.

May   2, Martha Winslow.
        Abigail Rollins; died at Vassalborough, Me., May, 1834.
        Sarah, wife of Abel C. Smith; died Feb. 24, 1861, in Lawrence, Mass.
        Susan Ward Winslow, wife of Rev. H. Winslow; dismissed to the Bowdoin St. church in Boston, Oct. 3, 1832.
        Artemas Rogers and Abigail, his wife; she died Dec. 21, 1838, aged 43.
        Oliver Washburn; dismissed to the church in Lowell, Mass. Nov. 6, 1831.
        Margaret, wife of James L. Foot; dismissed to Lowell, Mass.
July 18, Charles Dame; dismissed to Cong. church, Falmouth, Me., Oct. 18, 1840.
        Catherine Barstow, (m. ——— Magoon;) dismissed to the church in Kingston, Nov. 20, 1834.
        Elizabeth Allen; dismissed to Cong. church, Dexter, Me., Aug. 20, 1834.
        Sally Bodge, died May 9, 1833, aged 22.
        Sarah W. Johnson, (m. Christopher Palmer Oct., 1842;) died Jan. 12, 1886, aged 77.
        Eliza W. Warren, (m. Samuel Foss;) dismissed to Milton, N. H., March 30, 1837.
        Sarah Hartford, (m. John Littlefield of Strafford;) died in Dover, Feb. 1, 1863.
        Mary, wife of John Twombly; dismissed to Belknap Church, Dover, Aug. 31, 1856.
        Drusilla B. Pendexter, (m. William B. Glidden of Tuftonborough, Sept., 1833.)
        Louisa Perkins, (m. Stephen Willey June 2, 1832;) died Dec. 5, 1872, aged 69.
        Lydia, wife of James Dixon; dismissed to Belknap Church, Dover, Aug. 31, 1856.
        Elizabeth Watson, daughter of Capt. Samuel Watson; died Sept. 1, 1872, aged 66 years, 8 months.
        Palfrey W. Downing; excommunicated July 21, 1842.
        Sarah A. Stevens; dismissed to the Baptist church in Lowell, Mass., Nov. 11, 1832.
Sept. 5, Orin M. Payson; dismissed May 5, 1854, to North Church, Portsmouth.

Nov. 14, Sarah Jane Hall; dismissed to Newton, Mass., Sept. 2, 1833.
Nancy Morrill, (m. Walter Ham, July, 1840.)
Elizabeth Ricker.
Diana, wife of William B. Hayes; dismissed to Cong. church, Tuftonborough, N. H.. Aug. 25, 1839.
Jane, wife of Jeremiah Legg; died Oct., 1854, in Chelsea, Mass.
Elizabeth G. Watson, daughter of Samuel Watson, Jr.; dismissed April 30, 1861, to Central Church, Lawrence, Mass.
Huldah, wife of Thos. B. Twombly; died Sept. 17, 1889, aged 80.
Mary Young; died May 9, 1843.
Asa Farnsworth and Elizabeth his wife; both dismissed to Essex St. church, Boston, Mass., Sept. 12, 1841.
——, ——, Rebecca, wife of John Adams; dismissed to Methuen, Mass.

1831.
Jan. 1, Thomas Cushing, received on his death bed and died two weeks after.
John Caldwell; dismissed May, 1831, to church in Haverhill, Mass.
Martha Morse; dismissed and recommended to the church at Kennebunk, Me., June 1, 1832.
Hannah S. Horne, daughter of Benjamin Horne; died Mar. 11, 1875, aged 64.
Sarah Ann Stevens; died Feb. 6, 1833.
Apr. ——, Sophia M., wife of John Williams; dismissed to New Church, Boston, Mass., Nov. 29, 1842.
May 22, Hannah, wife of William H. Clarke; died April 12, 1843, aged 83.
Nancy, wife of William Cushing; died at Somersworth, Nov. 19, 1839.
Elizabeth Webster.
Sarah H. Hussey; dismissed to the Congregational church, Augusta, Me., Sept. 1, 1839.
Statira Ann, wife of William Frye; removed to Saco, Me.
Caroline Doe, (m. Jonathan Morrill;) died Feb. 25, 1843.

May 22, Almira Melcher; died Mar. 9, 1891.
Rebecca Elizabeth, wife of William Woodman; died Jan. 27, 1866.
July 10, Mary Kelley, from the Congregational church in Portland, Me.
Eliza Jane Kelley, (m. Ira Oliver;) dismissed to Salisbury, N. H., April 18, 1839.
July 31, Mary Barnes; dismissed to Congregational church, Taunton, Mass., Nov. 20, 1834.
Sarah, Wife of Stephen Hodgdon; dismissed to Lowell, Mass., May 1, 1836.
Daniel Hussey; dismissed to Belknap Church, Dover, Aug. 31, 1856.
John B. Nealley; dismissed to South Berwick, Me., Dec. 31, 1835.
William S. McCollister; died Jan. 13, 1868.
Ebenezer Faxon; died Dec. 14, 1875, aged 73.
Charles L. Ricker; excommunicated Aug. 4, 1842.
William Plaisted Drew; died Oct. 25, 1868, aged 74.
Daniel R. Gale; excommunicated July 21, 1842.
Rufus Flagg; excluded from the church Nov. 4, 1842.
John H. Gile; dismissed to Saco, Me., Dec. 2, 1833.
Martha, wife of Samuel Gage; (m. Samuel Willey, Oct. 15, 1834;) died Mar. 30, 1874, aged 74.
Mary Leighton.
Eliza, wife of Joshua Jones; dismissed to Allen St. church, New York, N. Y., Sept., 1838.
Elizabeth, widow of John P. Gilman; died June 8, 1832, aged 65.
Lydia, wife of Joseph Pendexter; died May 20, 1880, aged 85.
Elizabeth, wife of John N. Watson; died Apr. 22, 1870, aged 67.
Mary Ann, widow of James P. Plumer, (m. May 14, 1836, Richard Goodwin;) dismissed May 10, 1840, to Salem St. church, Boston, Mass.
Samuel M. Horne; dismissed to Belknap Church, Dover, Aug. 31, 1856.
Maria, wife of William Plaisted Drew; died Sept. 13, 1867, aged 69.

July 31, Lucy, wife of Wells Waldron; died July 29, 1853, aged 49.
Abigail, wife of Daniel Hussey; dismissed to Belknap Church, Dover, Aug. 31, 1856.
Lucy, wife of Rufus Flagg; died Oct. 19, 1842.
Susan Roberts, widow.
Elizabeth Bogle, widow; died Sept. 25, 1832.
Mary Ann Doe; dismissed to the Congregational church, Meredith Bridge, N. H., Jan. 5, 1844.
Abigail B. Drew, (m. Elijah Jenkins of New Durham;) died Jan. 28, 1860.
Martha Trickey; dismissed to Congregational church in Saco, Me., July 2, 1832.
Hannah Ricker.
Hannah McKenney; dismissed to church at Somersworth, May 1, 1833.
Mary, wife of James Bishop.
Eliza Kimball, (m. Charles Kimball;) died Sept. 27, 1883, aged 82.
Sally Bickford, (m. Increase French, Exeter, Me.)
Esther Bickford, (m. 1st, John Cook, 2d, Daniel Card;) died July 3, 1885, aged 76.
Abigail Wingate; dismissed March 7, 1847, to the Congregational church, Norway, Me.
Mary Reade; died Jan. 24, 1846, aged 65.
Hannah S. Canney; died Feb. 19, 1870, aged 81.
Lucy Ann Green; died at sea Aug. 5, 1834.
Maria J. Drown, (m. John B. Nealley;) died June 8, 1832, aged 21.
Jane Walsh, (m. Samuel Wentworth of Somersworth.)
Mary T. Smith; dismissed to Congregational church, Kennebunk, Me., June 1, 1832.
Charlotte Porter; dismissed to Second Congregational church in Concord, May 2, 1847.
Elizabeth Newcomb; dismissed to Congregational church, Saccarappa, Me., Aug. 15, 1840.
Dorcas T. Pease; dismissed April 12, 1835, to Wilton, Me.
Sept. 11, Eunice, wife of John L. Evans; died Feb. 6, 1852, aged 77.
Lois, wife of Benjamin F. Lee; died Dec. 2, 1867, aged 67 years, 7 months.
Dorothy S., wife of John Cook; died June 16, 1836, aged 30.

Sept. 11, Susan Caverly; died Jan. 28, 1833, aged 21.
      Mary V. Sawyer; died Mar. 14, 1860, aged 51.
      Abigail T. Gilman; dismissed Oct. 18, 1840, to the church in Tamworth, N. H.
      James Dixon, (a colored man;) excluded Nov. 4, 1842.
Nov. 6, Mrs. Sarah Swanton, from the Congregational church, Woburn, Mass.; and dismissed to the same church May 12, 1835.
Nov. 20, Eli French; dismissed to Bleeker St. church, New York, N. Y., July 13, 1834.
      John Cook, 2d; died Mar. 14, 1851.
      Eliza Gilman, (m. 1st, Gardner Ruggles, 2d, Wells Waldron;) dismissed to Barre, Mass., March 29, 1835.
      Ann Robinson; dismissed to the church in Mount Vernon Place, Boston, Mass.
      Almira Paul, (m. Hammon Hutchinson in Nov. 1832;) died Mar. 1, 1851.

1832.
June 1, Harriet, wife of Lurandus Beach; dismissed to Wolcotville, Conn., June 16, 1836.
July 25, Edmund James Lane, from the Congregational church, Durham; died Feb. 28, 1884, aged 81 years, 8 months, 22 days.
Nov. 11, Esther D., wife of Arlo Flagg, from the Congregational church in Keene; dismissed to Belknap Church, Dover, Aug. 31, 1856.
      Johnson Hill.
      Wells Waldron; died Nov. 10, 1881, aged 76.
      Sophia, wife of Dr. Alfred Upham; dismissed to Rochester, April 7, 1834.
      Jerusha S. Kenniston; dismissed Feb. 7, 1847, to Old South Church, Boston, Mass.
      Lydia Pinkham, widow of Samuel; died Apr. 13, 1880, aged 90.
      Lydia, widow of John Tapley; died Dec. 15, 1859.
      Mary Ann Roberts; dismissed to the First Congregational church, Lowell, Mass., April 9, 1837.
      Eliza Choate, (m. ——— Moody;) removed to Tamworth.
      Priscilla Winn; died Oct. 16, 1868.
      Aaron Watson; died May 25, 1856, aged 75.

Nov. 11, John Langdon Cook; dismissed Dec. 22, 1844, to Kennebunk, Me.

Dec. 16, Daniel L. Norris and Sophia Ann, his wife, both from the Congregational church in Raymond, N. H.; he was excommunicated March 26, 1835; she was dismissed Dec. 10, 1854, to Raymond.

1833.

July 10, William Hillhouse Alden; excommunicated May 15, 1846.
Elizabeth, wife of Rev. A. Alden; died July 14, 1852.
Mary, wife of Col. Nathaniel Gilman, from the Centre Congregational church in Gilmanton, N. H.; dismissed to Bangor, Me., May 22, 1836; readmitted Feb. 18, 1840.
Sarah A. Carr, daughter of Benjamin Hanson's widow; dismissed to Lamprey River, Aug. 14, 1835.
Lavina Treadway; died March 2, 1843.
Caroline G. Willey.
Hester Ann Butler; dismissed to John St. church, Lowell, Mass., Aug 30, 1842.

Sept. 5, Stephen Willey, from the church in Dunstable; died May 1, 1838, aged 36.

8, Mary Ann D. Huckins.

29, Harriet Eliza, wife of Dr. C. Wood; dismissed to Presbyterian church, Charleston, S. C., March 4, 1838.

Nov. 3, Mrs. Mary Gordon, from the church in Pembroke, N. H.; dismissed June 27, 1841, to Waterbury, Conn.
Mary Elizabeth, wife of Rev. D. Root, from the North Church in Portsmouth, N. H.; dismissed June 27, 1841, to Waterbury, Conn.

1834.

Jan. 5, Jane Paul, widow; dismissed to the church at North Bridgewater, Sept. 2, 1838.
Elizabeth B. Parker, widow; died of apoplexy April 15, 1836, aged 73.
Rebecca, wife of Simeon Hartford; dismissed to South Berwick, Me., April 17, 1837.

Mar. 2, John Dame; died August 20, 1839.
Mary Rollins, (m. Oct. 19, 1835, Isaac C. Pray of Boston, Mass.;) dismissed to Rev. Mr. Roger's church in Boston, Mass., Nov. 24, 1836.
Caroline Heard.

March 3, Esther Main, widow; died April 29, 1834.
May 4, Dr. Arthur L. Porter; dismissed Nov. 29, 1835, to the First Presbyterian church in Detroit, Mich.; died April 1845.
Hosea Sawyer; excommunicated May 15, 1846.
Mary, wife of Francis Cogswell; dismissed to Christ's Church, Andover, Mass., March 9, 1845.
Sarah, wife of Samuel Blake; dismissed Jan. 30, 1844, to Amesbury, Mass.
Hannah Haynes; dismissed Nov. 30, 1841, to Tabernacle Church, Salem, Mass.
July 6, Thomas G. Morse and Eliza J., his wife. She died Nov. 23, 1845; he died in Detroit, Mich., March 3, 1858.
Mary B. Brown; dismissed January 6, 1840, to the Congregational church at Sanbornton, (m. Otis Stackpole.)
Mary G. Smith, (m. Joseph Pickering April, 1845;) dismissed to Congregational church in Barnstead, Feb. 8, 1846.
John Wheeler; died April 3, 1840, aged 70.
Arlo Flagg; dismissed to Belknap Church, Dover, Aug. 31, 1856.
Lurandus Beach; dismissed to Wolcotville, Conn., June 16, 1836, readmitted in 1837.
Samuel Blake; dismissed January 30, 1844, to Amesbury, Mass.
William Hanson Clarke; died Feb. 19, 1844, aged 76.
Alfred Metcalf Clarke; died at Wolfeborough, N. H., August 18, 1855.
Oliver Cromwell Demeritt; dismissed to Durham church, April 9, 1837.
Israel Estes; died Oct. 22, 1864, aged 80.
William Pitt Wingate; died Feb. 26, 1880, aged 90 years, 7 months.
Abigail, wife of Philemon Chandler; died Jan. 27, 1862.
Hannah, widow of Jonathan Cushing; died Sept. 16, 1853.
Caroline, wife of Israel Estes; died Aug. 13, 1868, aged 72.
Elizabeth, wife of Nathaniel Garland; dismissed to the church in Northwood, May 15, 1846.
Lydia, widow of Samuel Ham; died June 1, 1883, aged 95.
Elizabeth, widow of Joseph Hussey; died Dec. 9, 1852.
Mary, wife of Ebenezer Jackson; died at Durham, May 11, 1843.

July 6, Lydia, wife of John F. Kielle; died April 26, 1876.
Rebecca, wife of Robert C. Miller; died in Portland, Me., April 10, 1868.
Eliza, widow of Joseph Nason, (m. in 1843 William Halligan;) died Oct. 7, 1863, aged 66.
Elizabeth, widow of Enoch Pinkham; died Nov. 14, 1868.
Elizabeth Crocker, wife of Dr. Arthur L. Porter; dismissed Nov. 29, 1835, to the First Presbyterian church in Detroit, Mich.
Tamson, wife of James Richardson; died Feb. 11, 1846, aged 62.
Mary, wife of Daniel Rollins.
Mary C., wife of Lorenzo Rollins; died Nov. 29, 1847, aged 41.
Hannah, wife of Thomas Warren; died Oct. 6, 1851.
Abigail, wife of Jonathan Young; died June 24, 1836, aged 55.
Ruth, wife of John Young; died March 30, 1844, aged 56.
Eliza, daughter of Amos Burrows, (m. Jan., 1855, Samuel Howard;) died Sept. 23, 1878, at West Dedham, Mass., aged 64.
Mary Clark, (m. J. H. Cushman:) dismissed to St. Johnsbury, Vt. May 8, 1842.
Eliza, daughter of Jonathan Cushing, (m. Thomas Bickford July 28, 1857;) died July 3, 1887.
Mehitable Dame; dismissed to Belknap Church, Dover, Oct. 26 1856.
Comfort Boody Howe; removed to Charlestown, Mass.
Jane Hussey, (m. Joseph Littlefield;) dismissed to Belknap Church, Dover, Aug. 31, 1856.
Sarah, daughter of Michael Reade; died Oct. 17, 1853.
Martha Rankins; dismissed to the church in Wells, Me., Nov. 3, 1834.
Mary Snell; died Feb. 18, 1843.
Hannah Tibbetts; dismissed April 28, 1844, to Alfred, Me.

Sept. 7, Sarah Sargent, (m. John Gould:) dismissed Oct. 27, 1857, to the Franklin St. Baptist church, Dover.
Susan Carr; died in Rollinsford, Jan. 1, 1864.
Mahala Kimball, (m. in 1845, William H. Davis;) died Feb. 2, 1874.

Sept. 7, Mary Ann Porter, (m. Capt. Joseph E. Estabrook July, 1836;) dismissed to the Second Congregational church in Concord, March 7, 1847.

Susan Goodwin, (m. ——— White of Exeter;) dismissed to First Church, Exeter, May 21, 1843.

Eliza Young; dismissed to Belknap Church, Dover, Aug. 31, 1856; died March 21, 1872, aged 78.

Hannah Smith Young; dismissed to Belknap Church, Dover, Aug. 31, 1856.

1835.
Feb. 15, Mrs. Ann Laird, from the church at Uxbridge, Mass.

Mrs. Jemima Stevens; dismissed to Saco, Me., June 14, 1835.

March 1, Jeremiah Mason; dismissed to the church in Somersworth, Nov. 24, 1836; died March, 1838.

Susan, widow of Joshua Ham; died Nov. 4, 1872, aged 77.

Hannah Rogers Draper, (m. Eli French in 1835;) dismissed to Rev. Erskine Mason's church in New York, N. Y.. Sept. 11, 1836.

March 19, Caroline Curtis, from the church at Somersworth; (m. John J. Hodgdon Sept. 26, 1836;) dismissed to South Berwick, Me., June 7, 1857.

June 17, Dr. Nathaniel Low and Mary Ann, his wife, from the church in South Berwick, Me. He died April 2, 1883, aged 90 yrs., 9 mos.; she died Oct. 7, 1882, aged 83 yrs., 10 mos.

Benjamin Odiorne and Martha, his wife; both dismissed to the church at Barrington, May 12, 1836.

Mrs. Sarah Gowell; dismissed to the Appleton St. church, Lowell, Mass., June 30, 1839.

July 12, Lydia, wife of James Davis.

Sarah Ann, wife of Henry Elliot; died April 10, 1887, aged 83 yrs., 2 mos., 7 days.

Nancy, widow of Stephen Davis; died Jan. 24, 1842.

Hannah, wife of Dr. Jabez Dow; died April 25, 1864, aged 84.

Hannah, wife of Ephraim Ham, Jr.; died June 1, 1849, aged 84 yrs., 2 mos. and 12 days.

Mary Tripe; died Dec. 28, 1863.

Aug. 14, James Ladd & his wife; both dismissed to North Church, Portsmouth, Jan. 21, 1836.

Aug. 14, Charlotte A., wife of Washington Williams; dismissed to South Church, Concord, Nov. 28, 1841.
Sally Ricker, (m. Asa Wiggin of Brookfield, in 1842;) dismissed Nov. 25, 1849.
23, Ebenezer Jackson; died Nov. 16, 1840.
Abigail, wife of Amos Burroughs; died July 5, 1837.
Nancy Elizabeth, wife of Richard P. Sayward; died at North Berwick, Me., Aug. 28, 1844, aged 34 yrs.
Mary Little Osborne; dismissed to New Church, Boston, Mass., Nov. 29, 1840; died at Boston, Feb. 8, 1881, aged 92.
Angeline Tuttle.
Charlotte King Atkinson Richardson, (m. John Nesmith;) died Dec. 20, 1870, aged 61.
Martha Fitch Williams; dismissed to New Church, Boston, Mass., Nov. 24, 1842.
Abigail Ann Varney, (m. June 14, 1848, Nahum Wentworth of Somersworth, now Rollinsford;) dismissed to Belknap Church, Dover, Aug. 31, 1856.
Mary Bagley Sargent; dismissed to Amesbury, Mass., March 4, 1838.
Sally Rollins Philpot, (m. John H. Kimball in 1842;) dismissed May 29, 1843, to South Trenton, N. J.
Harriet T. Flagg, (m. Oct. 7, 1847, Abner C. Griffin of Boston, Mass.)
Emma Wallace, (m. ———— French;) dismissed to Congregational church, Pittsfield, Jan. 26, 1840.
Mary Esther Woodman; excommunicated May 5, 1844.
Mary Thompson Perkins, (m. Samuel H. Mathes.)
Sarah Jane Hanson; dismissed to Franklin Church, Boston, Mass., Dec. 20, 1835.
Drusilla Ellen Horne, (m. ———— Putnam.)
Hannah Giles, (m. Charles Tredick.)
Eliza Ham, (m. Oliver K. Hayes;) died March 25, 1892.
Olive Furber Garland, (m. April 30, 1843, Dr. Thomas Tuttle of Northwood;) dismissed May 15, 1846.
Mercy Plumer Perkins, (m. Edward D. Boylston of Amherst, Aug. 12, 1841;) dismissed to Congregational church, Somersworth, May 26, 1844.
Emily W. Clark; dismissed to Belknap Church, Dover, August 31, 1856.

Aug. 23, Susan Garrison Adams; dismissed to Methuen, Mass.
Cynthia Verrill Dinsmore, (m. ———— Newman;) dismissed to Winthrop, Me., June 24, 1842.
Lydia Sherburne Davis.
Elizabeth Ham Walsh, (m. George Whitehouse of Portsmouth;) joined the Unitarian society in Portsmouth, May 2, 1859; died at Dover March 15, 1878.

Nov. 1, Susan Webster; dismissed to the Congregational church, Newburyport, Mass., Aug. 25, 1839.
20, John S. Meserve; dismissed to Lamprey River, May 12, 1836.
Joseph H. Warren; dismissed to Lamprey River, May 12, 1836.
Sarah C. Hill; dismissed to Lamprey River, May 12, 1836.
Olive, wife of Ebenezer Faxon; died June 21, 1879, aged 71 yrs., 4 mos.
Mary L. Mason; dismissed to Congregational church, Lowell, Mass., April 26, 1840.
29, Abigail, wife of Alfred M. Clark, from South Berwick, Me.; died July 9, 1887.

1836.
Jan. 3, Elizabeth Barker, wife of Edmund James Lane; died April 23, 1838, aged 40.
June 16, Asenath, wife of Samuel W. Cushing, from the church in Tamworth, died Sept. 15, 1861.
Oct. 21, Elizabeth P. Lamson; dismissed to John St. church, Lowell, Mass., July 21, 1842.
Dec. 17, Mary, wife of Benjamin Haselton; dismissed to North Church, Portsmouth, June 30, 1840.

1837.
Nov. 1, Nancy, wife of John Wallis; dismissed to Belknap Church, Dover, Aug. 31, 1856.
Lurandus Beach and Harriet, his wife, readmitted by letter; both excluded from the church, Nov. 4, 1842.
Dec. 20, Deacon John Osgood; dismissed to the church at Gilmanton Iron Works, Nov. 17, 1844.
31, John Riley Varney; dismissed to the Congregational church at Hanover, Jan. 3, 1862, afterwards readmitted.

1838.
Jan. 7, John Osborne Peirce; died May 2, 1869, at Charlestown, Mass., aged 48.

Jan. 7, Alpheus Augustus Hanscom; dismissed to the church in Elliot, Me., March 1, 1840.
Stephen Greeley Horne; died at Gilmanton, March 21, 1840, aged 18 yrs., 3 mos.
Charles Augustus Tufts; dismissed Feb. 11, 1840, to St. Thomas Episcopal Church, Dover.
Sarah Snell, widow; died Sept. 22, 1862, aged 88 yrs., 6 mos.
Elizabeth Watson, (m. Winthrop Watson;) died in 1869 at Rochester.
Mary Riley Varney, (m. Capt. John B. Haley of Portsmouth, Oct. 1, 1846;) dismissed to North Church, Portsmouth, Feb. 22, 1849.
Caroline Elizabeth, daughter of Israel Estes, (m. Feb. 5, 1845, Samuel Gerrish;) died in Dover, Feb. 28, 1858.
Clarissa Matilda Nute; excluded May 7, 1862.
Lydia Abigail Cushing, (m. Benjamin Collins Jan. 28, 1847.)
Susan Elizabeth Bailey, (m. Hazen K. Riley Nov. 7, 1842;) dismissed Aug. 24, 1849, to the Old South Church, Boston, Mass.
Julia Adelaide Bailey, (m. James Drew of South Boston, Mass;) dismissed to Berkley St. church, Boston, Mass., May 22, 1866.
Sarah Elizabeth Wingate; died August 30, 1841, aged 17.
Lydia Margaret Jackson; died April 12, 1839, aged 17.
Catherine Evans, daughter of Isaac A. Porter; dismissed to Belknap Church, Dover, Aug. 31, 1856.
Lydia Ann Richardson, (m. John Nesmith;) died Jan. 19, 1854.
Sophronia Wallace; dismissed to Chapel Church, Andover, Mass., July 18, 1876.

March 4, Harriet Boardman, wife of William H. Alden; dismissed to the Congregational church, Westville, Conn., Jan. 15, 1871.

18, Elizabeth L. Root; dismissed June 27, 1841, to the church at Waterbury, Conn.; died at Guilford, Conn., Aug., 1845.
Ann T. Wilbur, (m. —— Wood;) dismissed to Congregational church, Harmon, Ohio, Aug. 6, 1861.

25, Sophia Smith, (m. Nov. 7, 1843, John T. Rogers of Whitehall, N. Y.;) dismissed May 26, 1844, to the Presbyterian church, Whitehall.

April 23, John Leighton Evans; died June 14, 1848, aged 75.
Hannah Winn; died at Ashland, Mass., Aug. 14, 1869, aged 51.
Mary Ellen, daughter of Asa Farnsworth; dismissed Sept. 12, 1841, to the Essex St. church, Boston, Mass.

Sept. 2, Hannah P. Palmer, (m. Joseph Daniels of Barrington;) dismissed to the Congregational church, Barrington, June 21, 1870.
Hannah Wadleigh, widow; died at Weare, May 18, 1854.
Lydia, daughter of William Kimball, (m. Capt. John Smith;) died Oct. 1, 1882.
Lydia P. Blake, (m. Samuel Baker;) dismissed Jan. 30, 1844, to the church at Amesbury, Mass.; afterwards readmitted.
Charlotte M., daughter of William Palmer; died Aug. 20, 1891, aged 71.

Dec. 1, Israel E. Cheney and Sarah, his wife; both dismissed to John St. church, Lowell, Mass., Sept. 15, 1843.

1839.
May 12, Sarah, wife of Oliver Carter, by letter from Somersworth.

1840.
Feb. 18, Sarah Palmer, widow; dismissed August 1, 1841, to the Congregational church, Derry.
Lydia A. Peirce, (m. Oliver P. Hayes April, 1841;) died Feb. 25, 1842.
Sarah Jacobs, widow; died in Providence, R. I., March 29, 1875.
Mary, wife of Nathaniel Gilman, from Bangor, Me.; dismissed June 19, 1864, to South Church, Concord; died May, 1874.
Rebecca Palmer, (m. Deacon John W. Hayes of Barrington, Dec. 25, 1842;) dismissed to Barrington, Aug. 17, 1845.
Martha, wife of Parkman Burley; died July 3, 1889, aged 78.
Daniel Hanscom; dismissed Aug. 13, 1848, to Elliot, Me.

March 1, Jedediah Cook; died Jan. 26, 1876.
James Stewart; dismissed Sept. 20, 1840, to the Congregational church, Pawtucket, R. I.
Lydia Leonard Tasker.

March 1, Abigail, daughter of John P. Sargent; died Dec. 6, 1855, in Georgetown, Illinois.

Susan B., daughter of John P. Sargent; dismissed Sept. 12, 1858, to the Presbyterian church, Danville, Illinois.

May 3, Judith P. Wallace; died March 2, 1841, aged 63.

Jane McNorton; excluded May 7, 1862.

William Cook and Mary, his wife; he died July 4, 1850; she was dismissed April 12, 1857, to the Lawrence St. church, Lawrence, Mass.

Mehitable B., wife of Joseph Dame, 2d; dismissed to Belknap Church, Dover, Aug. 31, 1856.

George W. Allen and Mary, his wife; he died Sept. 8, 1868; she died March 28, 1875, aged 63.

Harriet F., wife of Rev. Jeremiah S. Young; dismissed Feb. 23, 1845, to South Church, Andover, Mass.

William L. Chandler and Mary, his wife; he died June 18, 1887, aged 82 years, 1 month.

James R. Stewart and Jane, his wife; both dismissed June 22, 1841, to the Congregational church, Pawtucket, R. I.

Jonathan Morrill; dismissed to Belknap Church, Dover, Aug. 31, 1856.

Amos, son of John P. Sargent; died Aug. 10, 1848, aged 29.

Nathaniel Twombly.

July 5, Ezra Haskell and Emily, his wife; both dismissed to Belknap Church, Dover, Aug. 31, 1856; he died March 28, 1858, aged 77 years, 15 days.

Isaac Hayden and Abigail, his wife; she died in Lawrence, Mass., in 1855.

Stephen Palmer Blake and Elizabeth Mary Ann, his wife; both dismissed to the church in Barrington, May 8, 1842.

Sophia, daughter of Samuel Blake; dismissed Jan. 30, 1844, to Amesbury, Mass.

Abraham Folsom and Abigail Smith, his wife; both excluded Nov. 4, 1842.

Jacob Clarke and Susan, his wife; both dismissed to Belknap Church, Dover, August 31, 1856.

Michael Whidden and Eliza, his wife; he died Aug. 28, 1851, aged 68; she died April 7, 1857, aged 79.

Charles Paul and Lois, his wife; both dismissed to Belknap Church, Dover, Aug. 31, 1856.

July 5, Joshua Banfield; dismissed Jan. 8, 1868, to the Congregational church, Hampton.
Josiah Hall; dismissed April 10, 1862, to the Congregational church, Laconia.
Francis Cogswell; dismissed to Christ Church, Andover, Mass., March 9, 1845.
Samuel Hanson Mathes; dismissed to Belknap Church, Dover, Aug. 31, 1856.
Dr. James Wellington Cowan; died July 21, 1848, aged 35.
Oliver Peabody Hayes.
Elijah Hussey Hayes; dismissed to F. W. Baptist church, Effingham, May 31, 1842.
George Burns Wallace; died at Portsmouth, 1861.
Abel Whitton; dismissed to Garden St. church, Boston, Mass.
Richard Nutter Ross.
Capt. Leonard, son of Samuel Horne; murdered in the street at Leavenworth, Kansas, Nov. 9, 1861.
Lafayette Varney; died March 12, 1875, in Chicago, Illinois, aged 49.
John Henry Wilkinson.
Thomas Nute; excluded Dec. 28, 1886.
James Munroe Gordon; dismissed Aug. 1, 1841, to Presbyterian church, Brooklyn, N. Y.
George Franklin Parmenter.
Oliver Perry Hussey; dismissed to John St. church, Lowell, Mass., May 31, 1842.
James Madison Horne and Mary, his wife; both dismissed Jan. 31, 1865, to Central Church, Lawrence, Mass.
Phebe, wife of Simon Ross; died Sept. 19, 1876, in Pittsfield, Mass., aged 82 years, 9 months.
Mary Barrows, (m. ——— Tibbetts;) died Sept. 29, 1870, aged 62.
Joanna Horne, widow; dismissed to Belknap Church, Dover, Aug. 31, 1856.
Tamson, wife of William Kimball; died May 18, 1874, at Portsmouth, aged 84.
Sarah, wife of Oliver S. Horne; died Sept. 21, 1882, aged 81.
Mahala, wife of Moses Bickford.

July 5, Verona, wife of Capt. Leonard Shepard; dismissed to Belknap Church, Dover, Feb. 27, 1859.
Abigail Stevens, wife of Josiah C. Burnham; died April 2, 1858, in Warwick, Mass.
Mary Ann Hayes; dismissed Sept. 22, 1844, to John St. church, Lowell, Mass.
Elizabeth Wingate Nason, (m. Alpha Knight of Boston, Mass., in 1843;) died March 9, 1846, at Boston.
Sophia Parker, daughter of Daniel Hussey; suspended May 5, 1844.
Susan Ela, daughter of Capt. George Young; died May 28, 1857.
Harriet Boardman, daughter of Capt. George Young, (m. Jacob Jewett Smith of Rowley, Mass., in Oct., 1859;) dismissed to First Church, Rowley, June 20, 1877.
Lydia Neal Pinkham; excluded Dec. 22, 1846.
Dorcas Winn, (m. Richard Nutter Ross, Dec. 28, 1840.)
Abigail Henderson; dismissed July 16, 1843, to Broome St. church, New York, N. Y.
Caroline McDuffee, (m. Franklin Varney;) dismissed to Belknap Church, Dover, August 31, 1856.
Mary McDuffee; died at Rochester in 1852.
Olive Willard Wallace, (m. Arthur F. L. Norris, of Manchester, in 1846.)
Mary Ann Lee, (m. Edward J. Pinkham, Oct. 7, 1844;) dismissed to the Congregational church, Somersworth, July 19, 1857.
Susan Hanson Hodgdon; died May 28, 1843.
Rosilla Wentworth, (m. Horace C. Smith;) dismissed to South Newmarket, August 19, 1873.
Hannah Caverly; dismissed to Belknap Church, Dover, August 31, 1856.
Betsey Jackson Parsley, (m. Robert S. Webster;) dismissed to Barnstead, Nov. 21, 1847.
Susan Amanda Nason, (m. Abraham Burnham Sanders Nov. 28, 1848;) dismissed to Winthrop Church, Charlestown, Mass., May 27, 1852.
Mary Elizabeth Nason, (m. George K. Warren, of Wolfeborough, May 25, 1853;) dismissed to Wolfeborough, June 17, 1854; died Dec. 14, 1856.

July 5, Maria Brock, (m. Thomas Nute Sept. 3, 1843;) died April 12, 1886, aged 69.
Martha Abigail Drew, (m. Nathaniel Twombly June 13, 1843.)
Dorothy Young; (m. Joseph P. Adams April, 1842;) died Jan. 10, 1879.
Mary Elizabeth, daughter of Samuel Horne, (m. George Batchelder of Reading, Mass., in 1849;) dismissed to the Congregational church in Mount Vernon, March 13, 1866.
Lucy Ann, daughter of John P. Sargent, (m. William H. Lamm of Danville, Illinois;) dismissed to the Presbyterian church in Danville, Sept. 12, 1858.
Mary Elizabeth Quimby, (m. Charles T. Bedell June 20, 1846;) dismissed to Lawrence St. church, Lawrence, Mass., June 24, 1859.
Sarah Ann Ladd, (m. ——— Farnham of Somersworth.)
Jane Watson, (m. George Burns Wallace Nov. 2, 1843.)
Lucy Watson, (m. Thomas Horne;) dismissed to the Congregational church in Rochester, Oct. 25, 1861.
Olive, daughter of Joshua Ham, (m. Joseph Delaney March 9, 1854;) died Nov. 26, 1857, aged 39.
Sally Baker, daughter of Joshua Ham; died single Sept. 27, 1890, aged 82 yrs., 8 mos.
Ann Elizabeth Brown; left without letter and joined the Universalist church, Dover.
Lavina Powers Davis, (m ——— Locke of Wenham, Mass.)
Sarah Caroline Brown.
Sarah Elizabeth Henderson, (m. William Wastfall;) died in New York, N. Y., near 1854.

Sept. 6, John Bowen Sargent; died June 3, 1864, aged 64.
Salome Reed Wallace, (m. Joseph A. Perkins of Manchester, July, 1845.)
Elizabeth Quimby, widow; died June 10, 1877, in Lawrence, Mass., aged 86.
Sarah, wife of Capt. George Young; died Sept. 19, 1849, aged 70.
Mary, wife of Clark Paul; dismissed to North Bridgewater, Mass., May 5, 1857.
Mary Elizabeth, wife of John A. French; residence in 1894 at Minneapolis, Minn.

Oct. 30, Rev. Jeremiah Smith Young; dismissed Feb. 25, 1845, to South Church, Andover, Mass.

Benjamin Franklin Babb and Mary, his wife; he died Oct. 29, 1851; she died May 29, 1858.

Catherine, wife of Ezra Young, (m. John G. Palmer;) dismissed April 11, 1860, to Washington St. F. W. Baptist church, Dover.

Nov. 1, John Horne Kimball; dismissed May 29, 1843, to South Trenton, N. J.

Joseph Potter Adams; was killed in felling a tree in Illinois, Sept. 1859.

Susan Hall Jenness; dismissed Dec. 16, 1849.

1841.
Jan. 3, William Hodgdon, son of Horatio G. Hanson; excluded May 15, 1846.

Angelina Hall, (m. George W. Jackson July 30, 1842.)

Sarah Thing, widow, from Brentwood; died at South Berwick, Me., in 1850.

Oliver Libbey and Elizabeth, his wife; he was supposed to have been murdered in the West about 1858; she died June 5, 1871, at Dover, aged 70 years, 5 mos.

March 7, Sally B., wife of Tobias Bunker; died in Durham, May 16, 1854, aged 41.

April 4, Robert Rogers; died April 21, 1841, aged 66.

July 4, Daniel Pinkham and Sophia, his wife; he died March 6, 1885, aged 87 years, 9 months; she died August 22, 1878, aged 78 years, 6 months.

Charles Evans; dismissed to Bowdoin St. church, Boston, Mass., Jan. 5, 1844.

John Colby; dismissed March 6, 1857, to Hampton.

Nov. 4, Martha W. Sanders, from Saco, Me.

1842.
July 3, Mary B., wife of Col. Otis Stackpole, readmitted from Sanbornton; died in Madbury April 8, 1880, aged 76 years, 7 months.

William Henry Crane and Fanny Elizabeth, his wife; both dismissed to Seekonk, Mass., April 28, 1843.

Ivory Paul and Judith Smith, his wife; he died July 8, 1878, aged 73.

Abigail, wife of John Evans; died Oct. 25, 1857, aged 65.

July 3, Hazen Kimball Riley; dismissed August 21, 1849, to South Church, Boston, Mass.

Russell Hodgdon; excluded May 7, 1862.

Lucy Kent, daughter of Deacon Isaac A. Porter; died March 11, 1849, aged 21.

Mary Elizabeth Tapley, (m. Joseph W. Welch July 13, 1848.)

Sarah Ann, daughter of Wells Waldron, (m. Eleazer Davis April 12, 1861;) dismissed May 27, 1852, to the Methodist Episcopal church, Dover.

Louisa Hadley, (m. William Heddle of Laconia, in 1847;) dismissed to church in Sandwich, Oct. 10, 1866.

Phebe Tuttle Pinkham, (m. Charles Thompson April, 1845;) died May 9, 1848, aged 36.

Susan E., daughter of Benjamin Colby, (m. John Littlefield in 1850;) dismissed to Belknap Church, Dover, April 8, 1869.

Harriet Elizabeth Darling; died in Illinois, near 1852.

Nov. 4, Eliza Tucker; died March 11, 1848, aged 58.
1843.

March 5, Lucinda Pease Leavitt; was residing at Wheeling, Va., in 1857.

Moses Gage; excluded Dec. 28, 1886.

Henry Tasker.

William Allard; died April 12, 1863.

Ezekiel Hussey, son of John Bowen Sargent; dismissed to Lowell, Mass., Jan. 1, 1847.

George Washington, son of John Bowen Sargent; dismissed to Raymond, Dec. 29, 1859.

Rebecca Kendall, widow, (m. Rev. George O. Cotton of Wolfeborough, March 6, 1844.)

Eliza H., wife of Josiah P. Whidden; dismissed to Rollinsford, Aug. 26, 1849.

Clarissa, wife of Moses Nute; dismissed Sept. 5, 1847, to Lowell, Mass.

Eliza C., daughter of William P. Wingate, (m. Aaron P. Wingate of Rochester, Jan. 22, 1849;) dismissed Dec. 2, 1849.

Jerusha A. Sceggell; dismissed to Ossipee Centre church, Ossipee, Nov. 26, 1865.

March 5, Olive Kimball, (m. —— Flanders of Newburyport, Mass., Nov., 1845.)
Lydia Philpot, (m. Lorenzo Gilman in 1848;) died Feb. 21, 1892, aged 69.
Fidelia Abbott Goodwin; dismissed to Rumford, Me., March 4, 1844.
Susan Young Brock, (m. John H. Winkley of Barrington.)
Abigail, daughter of Winthrop Watson, (m. Joshua Watson.)
Ann Sise; died April 17, 1873, aged 76.
Martha Whiting Boyd; dismissed to the Lawrence St. church, Lawrence, Mass., Sept. 11, 1859.

April 30, Otis Stackpole; died in Madbury, Nov. 12, 1880, aged 82 yrs., 10 mos.
Henry Mills, son of Ezra Haskell; dismissed to College Church, New Haven, Conn., Jan. 25, 1846.
Joseph Horne Littlefield; dismissed to Belknap Church, Dover, Aug. 31, 1856.
Gustavus Hodgdon, son of John Mann; died March 12, 1848.
John Joseph Hodgdon; dismissed to South Berwick, Me., June 7, 1857; died Nov. 24, 1862.
Hannah Evans; died June 23, 1849, aged 59.
Clarissa Jane, daughter of David Sargent; died July 26, 1857, aged 30.
Louisa Maria Falls.
Betsey Wiggin Haynes, (m. Alonzo F. Tibbetts of Wolfeborough, July 29, 1848;) dismissed April 29, 1859, to Wolfeborough.
Lydia Jane, daughter of James Kimball; died Jan. 24, 1845, aged 32.
Betsey Emerson.
Sarah Jane Hayes; afterwards resided in Augusta, Me.
Mary Jane Bunker, (m. Samuel W. Farnham of Newburyport, Mass., in 1847;) dismissed to West Newbury, Mass, Nov. 11, 1881.
Ann, widow of Capt. John Riley; died Feb. 17, 1874, aged 84.
Ann Boardman Riley, (m. Abel Whitton;) dismissed to Newburyport, Mass., Jan. 5, 1845.
Mary, daughter of Capt. John Riley, (m. John Q. A. Smith June 8, 1852;) dismissed June 18, 1854, to Broadway Church, Chelsea, Mass.

April 30, Abby Waldron Riley, (m. Gilbert T. Sewall of New York, N. Y., Dec. 28, 1847;) dismissed to St. Thomas Episcopal Church, Dover, May 9, 1858.

Elizabeth McNeal Clarke, (m. Henry Tasker June 10, 1847.)

Mary Henderson, (m. Joseph Ayers of Barrington, Feb. 4, 1855;) dismissed to Barrington Aug. 30, 1870.

1844.
July 23, Elizabeth Ann, wife of William Allard, from Augusta, Me.; died Feb. 1, 1868, aged 60.

1845.
Sept. 26, Hannah, wife of M. M. Haines, readmitted from Salem, Mass.; died Nov. 29, 1848.

Dec. 24, Rev. Homer Barrows and Sarah M. W., his wife; both dismissed Oct. 24, 1852, to Wareham, Mass.

Martha Farnham, widow, from South Berwick, Me.; died at Wakefield, Mass., May 9, 1874, aged 84.

1846.
June 23, Nathaniel Hills and Mary Ann, his wife; both dismissed to Durham, Aug. 13, 1848; both were afterwards readmitted.

1847.
July 4, Abigail Brown, widow, from Rochester; dismissed to Rochester, Oct. 23, 1849.

Sept. 5, Joseph W. Welch, from Derry; died Oct. 25, 1877, aged 60 yrs., 10 months.

Nov. 7, Olive W. Brown, from Portsmouth; died Dec. 23, 1878, aged 83 yrs., 10 mos.

1848.
Jan. 2, Mehitable, widow of Moses Ham, from Danville, Vt.; died Jan. 9, 1852, aged 76.

Sarah Jane, daughter of Moses Ham, from Danville, Vt.; died, single, Jan. 14, 1873, aged 65.

March 5, Julia A., wife of Amos Sargent, (m. Joseph L. Grant April 1851;) dismissed to Belknap Church, Dover, Aug. 31, 1856.

May 7, Esther Gilman, widow, from Tamworth, m. (John Bowen Sargent Oct., 1853;) died Sept. 12, 1872, aged 63.

July 2, Caroline Wentworth, (m. Edward M. Morse of Paradise, Nova Scotia, Sept. 2, 1860;) dismissed to Paradise, N. S., Oct. 8, 1872.

Sept. 1, Betsey Grant, widow, from Ossipee; died Jan. 1, 1851, aged 50.
Joseph L. Grant, from Ossipee; died in Charlestown, Mass., June 4, 1855.
Mary J. Thompson.
Hannah Coffin, widow, from Newburyport, Mass.; dismissed to First Presbyterian church, Newburyport, Sept. 4, 1857.

Nov. 3, Abraham Burnham Sanders, from Epsom; dismissed May 27, 1852, to Winthrop Church, Charlestown, Mass.; died in Dover, Sept. 14, 1854.

1849.
Jan. 5, Lucy Maria Tucker, from Concord, (m. Capt. ——— Arthur of Boston, Mass;) dismissed to Philips Church, Boston, Oct. 28, 1854.

May 6, Irena Young; dismissed to Belknap Church, Dover, Oct. 26, 1856.
Dr. Thomas J. W. Pray, from Somersworth; died Dec. 9, 1888, aged 69.

July 1, Frances Williams, widow, from Exeter; dismissed to Belknap Church, Dover, Aug. 31, 1856.
Richard Kimball and Elizabeth W. H., his wife; he was from Rochester, and she was from Portland, Me.; she died March 22, 1873, aged 63; he died March 2, 1881, aged 83.

Sept. 2, Elizabeth Mathes, (m. John Wentworth of Rollinsford, April, 1853.)

Nov. 4, Mary Frances, daughter of William P. Wingate; died Sept. 29, 1855, aged 20.

1850.
March 3, Elizabeth P., wife of Joseph P. Nute, from Medway, Mass.; died in East Medway, Mass., April, 1869.
Alonzo Hall, son of George Quint; dismissed to Mather Church, Jamaica Plain, Mass., Dec. 25, 1856.
John McMillan; dismissed to Lynn, Mass., Feb. 12, 1862.
John Mack; died April 24, 1890.
Edwin Grant; dismissed to Charlestown, Mass., Nov. 25, 1855.

July 7, Mary, wife of Samuel Davis, from Barrington.

Sept. 1, Mary Ann Chandler; died single, Sept. 28, 1884, aged 85 yrs., 4 mos.

BAPTISMS

BY

REV. ROBERT GRAY.

1787-1800.

RECORDS OF FIRST CHURCH, DOVER, N. H.

1787.
April   8, Deborah Shackford, daughter of Ezra and Susanna Green.
Aug.   8, Elizabeth Brooks, daughter of John and Mary Waldron.
Sept. 26, George, son of George and Elizabeth Watson.
1788.
Aug.   24, Abigail, daughter of Ebenezer and Rebecca Tebbets.
Sept. 28, Peter, son of Robert and Lydia Gray.
Oct.   26, Sarah, daughter of Ezra and Susanna Green.
1789.
June   24, Solomon, son of Ephraim and Hannah Kimball.
       29, Daniel, son of Joseph and Susanna Whitehouse, and Reuben, David and Jacob Kittredge, their sons.
Sept.   6, Sarah, daughter of William Hanson.
1790.
July   18, George, son of George and Elizabeth Watson.
Oct.   3, Abigail, daughter of Robert and Lydia Gray.
1791.
July   12, Martha, daughter of Ezra and Susanna Green.
1792.
Feb.   5, Jonathan, son of Ezra and Elizabeth Young.
       25, Polly, daughter of Ezra and Elizabeth Young.
April   1, Susanna, daughter of Jonathan and Sarah Fisher.
June   22, Sarah, wife of Jonathan Fisher.

BAPTISMS BY REV. ROBERT GRAY, 1787-1800.

Sept. 2, Jeremy, Mary, Betsey, Isaac, Abigail and Timothy, children of Reuben and Molly Ricker.
Oct. 7, Lydia, daughter of Robert and Lydia Gray.
15, Eunice, daughter of Ezra and Susanna Green.
Nov. 11, James, son of Ezra and Elizabeth Young.

1793.
March 3, Lucy Cutts, daughter of George and Elizabeth Watson.
May 4, Joshua, son of Ephraim and Lydia Ham.

1794.
April 27, Caroline, daughter of Ebenezer and Rebecca Tebbets.
May 19, Rebecca Elizabeth, daughter of John and Rebecca Wheeler.
Aug. 24, Elizabeth, daughter of Robert and Lydia Gray.
Oct. 1, Maria, daughter of Ezra and Mary Kimball.

1795.
June 4, Martha, daughter of Ezra and Susanna Green.

1796.
July 6, Sophia, Elizabeth, Francis, Abigail and Lydia, children of Amos and Lydia Cogswell.

1797.
Aug. 10, Eliza, daughter of Philemon and Betsey Chandler.
25, Isaac Hasey, son of Ezra and Mary Kimball.
Sept. 14, Samuel, son of Ezra and Susanna Green.
16, Robert, son of Robert and Lydia Gray.

1798.
Jan. 17, Martha Tufts, daughter of Robert and Lydia Gray.
March 14, Dorothy Dix, daughter of John and Rebecca Wheeler.

1799.
——— ——, Eliza, daughter of Ezra and Elizabeth Young.
Feb. 5, Nancy Walker, daughter of Samuel & Anna Shackford.
Mar. 24, John Prentice, son of Henry and Martha Mellen.
July 21, Walter Cooper, son of Ezra and Susanna Green.
Sept. 1, Eliza Ann and Nathaniel Benjamin, children of Elizabeth Dean.

1800.
April 20, Caroline Margaret, daughter of Abraham and Mary Duncan.
Aug. 14, Lydia and Sally, daughters of Reuben and Molly Ricker.
Sept. 6, Abigail Gray, daughter of Ezra and Mary Kimball.
Oliver Crosby, son of Robert and Lydia Gray.
Oct. 10, John, son of John and Rebecca Wheeler.
Nov. 17, Martha Wentworth, daughter of Henry and Martha Mellen.

MARRIAGES.

1835-1850.

RECORDS OF ST. JOHN'S METHODIST EPISCOPAL CHURCH, DOVER, N. H.

[Marriages other than those found in Dover, N. H. Records, pages 87-105.]

MARRIAGES BY REV. JARED PERKINS.

1835.
Aug. 23, Mr. Ambrose Brown to Miss Grace F. Burley, both of Dover.
Nov. 17, Mr. Edmund Coffin of South Berwick, Me., to Miss Olive T. Frost, of Somersworth, N. H.

1837.
Feb. 16, Mr. John C. Ingalls of Rochester, N. H., to Miss Emily T. Colby, of Danville, N. H.
May 4, Aaron B. Smith, M. D., of Tuftonborough, N. H., to Miss Harriet M. Leavitt, of Dover.
" 14, Mr. John Ham to Mrs. Martha Drew, both of Dover.
" 31, Mr. John S. Vickery to Miss Mary A. Cook, both of Dover.
June 15, Mr. Joseph C. Quimby to Miss Sally C. Leighton, both of Dover.

MARRIAGES BY REV. ELEAZER SMITH.

1837.
Sept. 10, Mr. Michael E. Courson of Rochester, N. H., with Miss Mary Butler, of Berwick, Me.
" 18, Mr. Wm. H. Willey, of Wakefield, with Miss Mercy Ann Roberts, of Albany, N. H.
" 27, Mr. Frederick Beach, of Somersworth, with Miss Susan Crook, of same place.

Oct. 1, Mr. Elmer D. Chapin, of Greenfield, Mass., with Miss Clarissa Betton, of Dover.

" 4, Mr. Azro P. Cutting, of Strafford, Vermont, with Miss Eliza R. Legg, of Dover.

" 8, Mr. Daniel Murray with Miss Margaret Dore, both of Dover.

" 22, Mr. Ebenezer Downing with Miss Dorothy Gray, both of Somersworth.

" 29, Mr. James Adams, of Newmarket, with Miss Mary Jane Furber, of Dover.

Nov. 13, Mr. Samuel L. Wiggin with Miss Harriet S. Bruce, both of Dover.

" 23, Mr. Oliver P. Spinney with Miss Nancy Ann Whitehouse, both of Dover.

MARRIAGES BY REV. SILAS GREEN.

1838.
Sept. —, Mr. James Peirce to Miss Naomi Dearborn, both of Dover.

" 24, Mr. Theodore Lord to Miss Eliza J. Card, both of Dover.

Nov. 11, Mr. Amos Swinerton to Miss Betsey Harriman, both of Somersworth.

Dec. 25, Jethro Furber to Miss Susan Ellison.

" 29, Mr. Mark Coleman to Miss Mary J. Sanders, both of Dover.

1839.
Feb. 20, Mr. John H. Ham to Miss Caroline B. Lewis.

" 27, Mr. Lucien B. Legg to Miss Sarah Ann McDuffee.

March 12, Mr. Samuel Winkley to Miss Lydia Foye.

" 17, Mr. John Cater to Miss Mary Leighton.

" 24, Mr. Oliver Guppy to Miss Betsey W. Drew.

April 4, Mr. Ebenezer P. Swain to Miss Susan C. Wingate.

" 29, Mr. Jonathan Wentworth to Miss Betsey Leighton.

May 5, Mr. Daniel Vickery to Miss Sarah A. Pinkham.

" 19, Mr. Robert Walker, of Denmark, Me., to Miss Martha Jane Gentleman, of Dover.

" 19, Mr. Daniel Hayes to Miss Hannah Warren, both of Dover.

" 20, Albee Hanson, of Milton, to Miss Mary A. Pray of Dover.

June 8, Mr. J. Hanson to Miss L. Scruton.

" 20, Mr. Artemas Rogers to Miss Sabra Osgood.

" 26, Mr. Abram Smith to Miss Mahala C. Hill, both of Dover.

MARRIAGES, M. E. CHURCH RECORDS, 1835–1850.

July	17, Mr. Thomas Tuttle to Miss Hope Twombly, both of Dover.
Aug.	17, Mr. William Pike to Miss Rhoda Emery.
Sept.	1, Mr. John Ricker, of Greenland, to Miss Pamelia Peavey, of Dover.
"	19, Mr. Freeman Otis to Miss Mary Stackpole, both of Dover.
"	30, Mr. Herman Chase to Miss Content A. Shapleigh.
Oct.	20, Mr. Jeremiah Gray to Miss Betsey Cook, both of Dover.
"	24, Mr. Oliver K. Hayes, of Madbury, to Miss Eliza Ham, of Dover.
Nov.	10, Mr. Timothy E. Meader to Mrs. Miriam H. Trickey.
"	25, Mr. Lyman Allen to Miss Emily Piper, both of Dover.
Dec.	22, Mr. James M. Jackson to Miss Mary Jane Blaisdell.
1840.	
March	17, Mr. Alfred Hall, of Barnstead, to Miss Mary Ann Otis, of Dover.
"	30, Mr. John Skinner to Miss Elizabeth M. Emerson, both of Dover.
May	28, Mr. William Beck to Miss Elizabeth Hobbs, both of Dover.
June	6, Capt. Daniel Trefethen to Miss Hannah Card, both of Dover.
July	15, Mr. William Robinson to Miss Ann Peirce, both of Dover.

MARRIAGES BY REV. ELIHU SCOTT.

1840.	
Oct.	29, Mr. John F. Woodes to Mrs. Mary Hall, both of Dover.
1841.	
Jan.	10, Mr. James G. Chesley and Miss Mary Brock, both of Dover.
"	21, Mr. Ivory Jones and Miss Harriet Parsons, both of Somersworth.
Feb.	14, Mr. Andrew W. Shute and Miss Lydia Moulton, both of Durham.
April	11, Mr. Joseph Winkley and Miss Mary Cater, both of Barrington.
"	17, Mr. Oliver P. Burley and Miss Mary J. Demeritt, both of Dover.
"	29, Mr. William Card and Miss Martha Ann Roberts, both of New Durham.

MARRIAGES, M. E. CHURCH RECORDS, 1835–1850.

May	20,	Mr. Charles G. Frye and Miss Elizabeth M. Hall, both of Somersworth.
June	10,	Mr. John Hubbard and Miss Abigail B. Spencer, both of Somersworth.
"	20,	Mr. Moses Gage to Miss Betsey Hussey, both of Dover.
July	11,	Mr. James L. Huntress to Miss Sarah H. Langley, both of Newmarket.
"	13,	Elder Lemuel Goodwin to Miss Ann Downs, both of Dover.
Aug.	25,	Mr. William Ricker to Eliza Daniels, both of Dover.
Sept.	8,	Mr. Derrick W. Chapin to Miss Sarah C. Drew, both of Dover.
Oct.	28,	Mr. John M. Smith and Miss Comfort York, both of Newmarket.
Dec.	12,	Mr. Charles E. Thompson, of Rochester, to Miss Sarah A. Cater, of Barrington.
"	16,	Mr. Abraham Eddy, of Portsmouth, to Miss Dorcas Bracy, of Kittery, Me.
"	23,	Mr. Israel T. Hanson to Miss Mary Horne, both of Dover.

1842.

Jan.	6,	Mr. George W. Gray to Miss Sally Weare, both of North Berwick, Me.
March	1,	Mr. Calvin Dame to Miss Elizabeth P. Litchfield, both of Somersworth.
"	31,	Mr. John H. Hersom, of Lebanon, Me., to Miss Mary J. Barnes, of Somersworth.
April	12,	Mr. John M. Stanton to Miss Emily W. Merrill, both of Somersworth.
May	22,	At Rochester, Mr. Daniel Wentworth to Miss Betsey H. Roberts, both of Rochester.
June	2,	At Dover, Mr. Mark S. Richardson, of Andover, Mass., to Miss Mary Ann Jenness, of Dover.

MARRIAGES BY REV. ELIJAH MASON.

1842.

Sept.	4,	Mr. John Cate, of Barrington, to Mrs. Lavina Pott, of Dover.
"	11,	Mr. George Freeman to Miss Julia A. Watson, both of Dover.

MARRIAGES, M. E. CHURCH RECORDS, 1835–1850.   247

Sept. 25, Mr. Moses Whittier to Miss Deborah Burnham, both of Dover.
Oct. 11, Mr. Thomas B. Guppy to Miss Emeline Pinkham, both of Dover.
Nov. 22, Mr. Peter Lew to Miss Eunice F. Richardson, both of Dover.
" 26, Mr. George A. Adams to Miss Mary Parshley, both of Dover.
Dec. 22, Capt. Henry Card to Miss Sarah Ann Cate, both of Dover.
" 22, Mr. Daniel Moulton to Miss Elizabeth Drew, both of Dover.

1843.
Jan. 29, Moses P. Horn to Miss Nancy Bragdon, both of Dover.
Feb. 5, Mr. James Dennis, of Newmarket, to Miss Nancy Swain, of Dover.
" 9, Mr. Ethan Streeter to Miss Julia Ann Drew, both of Dover.
" 26, In Madbury, Mr. Curtis Tasker to Miss Emeline L. Joy, both of Madbury.
March 2, Mr. Enoch T. Coleman to Miss Abby H. Gray, both of Dover.
May 3, Mr. James Ellison, of Exeter, to Miss Tamson Parshley, of Strafford.
" 31, Mr. Samuel Hussey to Miss Susan Horn, both of Dover.
June 18, Mr. Stephen Brock to Miss Nancy Brock, both of Dover.
July 13, Jeremiah Hanson to Sarah D. Pike, both of Dover.
" 13, Josiah P. Vickery to Miss Julian Haines, both of Dover.
Aug. 2, Wm. J. Chesley, of Durham, to Miss Hannah Jane Jenkins, of Madbury.
Sept. 19, Mr. James Seavey, of Rye, to Miss Eliza H. Whidden, of Dover.

MARRIAGES BY REV. JACOB STEVENS.

1844.
Aug. 22, Mr. James Drew, of Dover, to Miss Caroline Whitehouse, of Rochester.
" 25, Mr. Calvin Rollins, of Somersworth, to Miss Rebecca Thompson, of Dover.
Sept. 15, Mr. Samuel R. Preston to Miss Sarah Blaisdell, both of Dover.
" 26, Mr. Joseph Nute to Miss Hannah C. Tuttle, both of Dover.

"	28 Mr. William H. S. Cloggston to Miss Eunice A. Hayes, both of Dover.
Oct.	6, Mr. James D. Andrews to Miss Priscilla F. Packard, both of Somersworth.
"	6, Mr. Milo A. Humphrey to Miss Lucinda Andrews, both of Dover.
"	20, Mr. William Hanson to Miss Susan Spurling, both of Dover.
"	27, Mr. Amasa S. Rogers to Miss Ann Dame, both of Dover.
Nov.	6, Mr. Isaac Smith to Miss Nancy Oates, both of Dover.
"	17, Mr. George W. Gray to Miss Mary E. Chamberlin, both of Dover.
Dec.	25, Mr. Edwin Wentworth, of Somersworth, to Miss Sarah Ham, of Dover.

1845.

Feb.	25, Mr. Jacob K. Young to Miss Rebecca Jane Gove, both of Dover.
March	31, Mr. Charles Smith to Miss Margaret Young, both of Dover.
April	20, Mr. J. Henry Crane, of Charlestown, Mass., to Miss Martha D. Crockett, of Dover.
"	24, Mr. Nathaniel Demeritt to Miss Alice George, both of Dover.
May	4, Mr. William Spinney to Miss Abigail M. Bickford, both of Somersworth.
"	11, Mr. John Lord, of Berwick, Me., to Miss Olive Hatch, of Dover.
June	26, Mr. Timothy E. Rollins, of Camden, N. J., to Miss Caroline S. Watson, of Dover.
July	20, Mr. Lorenzo Hanscom to Miss Maria Newbegin, both of Somersworth.
"	24, Mr. Henry P. Preston to Miss Mary L. Drew, both of Dover.
Aug.	5, Mr. John W. Putnam to Miss Ellen D. Horne, both of Dover.
"	13, Mr. Israel P. Quimby to Miss Betsey Hall, both of Dover.
"	28, Mr. Oliver Fernald, of Berwick, Me., to Miss Mary A. Evans, of Somersworth.
Sept.	4, Mr. James Hurd, of S. Berwick, Me., to Miss Lucy H. Greward, of Somersworth.

Sept. 16, Mr. Andrew Webster, of Somersworth, to Miss Sophia C. Walker, of S. Berwick, Me.
" 18, Mr. Samuel B. Amazeen to Miss Lucinda S. Frost, both of Newcastle.
Nov. 27, Mr. Tappan Roby to Miss Louise Nelson, both of Dover.
" 28, Mr. Ward E. Gilman to Miss Eliza Dorr, both of Dover.
1846.
April 2, Mr. Seth Watson, of Dover, to Mrs. Ann W. Berry, of Saco, Me.
" 11, Mr. Asa F. Crosby to Miss Sarah A. Aspinwall, both of Somersworth.
" 12, Mr. Eleazer Davis, Jr., of Alton, to Miss Ann P. Waldron, of Dover.
May 4, Mr. Newell C. Davis to Miss Mary A. Emerson, both of Dover.

MARRIAGES BY REV. SAMUEL KELLEY.

1846.
June 6, Mr. John M. Kimball, of Plaistow, N. H., to Miss Judith A. Horn, of Dover.
Sept. 6, Capt. James Wentworth to Miss Mary Ann Tuttle, both of Dover.
Oct. 26, Mr. Walter Sargent to Miss Lydia A. Wheeler, both of Somersworth.
Nov. 5, Mr. Joseph W. Bennett, to Miss Susan Twombly, both of Dover.
" 7, Mr. Elias Varney, Jr., to Miss Eliza A. Foss both of Barrington.
" 18, Mr. Daniel E. Emerson to Miss Elizabeth R. Roberts, both of Dover.
" 21, Mr. Joshua B. Nute to Miss Lucy C. Ham, both of Dover.
" 22, Mr. James Tuttle to Miss Mercy Hussey, both of Dover.
Dec. 7, Mr. George W. Stevens to Miss Eliza Libbey, both of Dover.
1847.
Jan. 1, Mr. William H. Gray to Miss Clara D. Woodes, both of Dover.
Feb. 17, Mr. Temple Lord, of Somersworth, to Mrs. Sylvina P. Andrews, of South Berwick, Me.
March 21, Mr. William Kimball, 2d, to Miss Hannah S. Twombly, both of Dover.

April	4,	Mr. Aaron H. Freeman to Miss Sarah F. Berry, both of Dover.
"	12,	Mr. Gustavus Thompson to Miss Love S. Mathes, both of Dover.
"	29,	Mr. John W. Leighton to Miss Susan C. Bennett, both of Farmington.
May	30,	Mr. David F. Littlefield to Miss Mary D. Ham, both of Dover.
June	5,	Mr. Robert C. Fernald to Miss Eunice Lord, both of Somersworth.
"	20,	Mr. John S. Watson, of Somersworth, to Miss Joanna M. Davis, of Somersworth.
"	23,	Mr. Miles Chesley, Jr., to Miss Maria Augusta Hurd, both of New Durham.
"	27,	Mr. William Patten to Miss Lucy Ham, both of Dover.
"	28,	Mr. James M. Downs to Miss Caroline M. Pillsbury, both of Dover.
July	4,	Mr. Joseph Wentworth to Miss Frances Amazeen, both of Farmington.
Aug.	1,	Mr. Joseph G. Hills to Miss Ellen Perkins, both of Dover.
Sept.	12,	Mr. Franklin Freeman to Miss Hannah S. Dame, both of Dover.
"	16,	Mr. Edward Morrill to Miss Sarah J. Moulton, both of Dover.
Nov.	14,	Mr. William Banton, of Lagrange, Me., to Miss Caroline A. Willey, of Dover.
"	24,	Mr. Elias Stratton, of Cambridge, Mass., to Miss Sarah A. Smith, of Dover.
Dec.	1,	Mr. George W. Mitchell to Miss Clara A. Kimball, both of Dover.

1848.

Jan.	16,	Mr. James M. Ryan to Miss Martha Ann Young, both of Dover.
"	16,	Mr. Seth Watson, of Biddeford, Me., to Miss Isabella G. Roberts, of Dover.
Feb.	2,	Mr. Francis A. Shorey to Miss Susan W. Gellett, both of Somersworth.
"	3,	Mr. Eugene De Jean to Miss Lydia Ann Ricker, both of Newburyport, Mass.

MARRIAGES, M. E. CHURCH RECORDS, 1835–1850.

Feb. 6, Mr. Charles Trefethen to Miss Elizabeth Neal, both of Dover.
April 15, Mr. Merrill D. Palmer to Miss Eveline L. Varney, both of Dover.
" 23, Mr. Levi Clark, of Berwick, Me., to Miss Hannah P. Downs, of Dover.
" 30, Mr. Abram M. Drake, of Dover, to Miss Mercy Bennett, of Farmington.
June 4, Mr. John S. Calef to Miss Rebecca W. Page, of Rochester.

MARRIAGES BY REV. CHARLES N. SMITH.

1848.
July 13, Mr. Ephriam M. Jones to Miss Adelia A. P. Moulton, both of Dover.
Aug. 6, Mr. Jeremiah P. Burnham to Miss Mary J. Canney, both of Dover.
Sept. 6, Mr. Stephen S. Henderson to Miss Olive J. Tibbetts, both of Somersworth.
" 10, Mr. John M. Smith to Miss Priscilla B. Preston, both of Dover.
Oct. 1, Mr. George P. Bennett to Miss Abigail Straw, both of Dover.
" 15, Hon. Thomas E. Sawyer to Miss Elizabeth Moody, both of Dover.
" 16, Mr. Jeremiah Emerson, of Wolfboro, to Mrs. Phebe Dame, of Dover.
" 19, Mr. John Pray to Miss Sarah E. Pinkham, both of Dover.
Nov. 5, Mr. William Q. White to Miss Mary Prescott, both of Dover.
" 5, Mr. Ralph Brock, of Dover, to Mrs. Elizabeth Demeritt, of Madbury.
" 6, Mr. Federal B. Ham, of Lawrence, Mass., to Miss Caroline E. Heath, of Newmarket.
" 19, Mr. Ezekiel Stanton to Miss Esther Jenness, both of Dover.
1849.
Jan. 8, Mr. William C. Leavitt to Miss Nancy W. Johnson, both of Dover.
" 28, Mr. Alfred S. Sayles to Miss Mary A. Tarr, both of Dover.
March 8, Mr. Reuben Twombly to Miss Mary G. McLucas, both of Dover.

March	22, Mr. Ambrose Brown to Miss Mary G. Stebbins, both of Dover.
April	8, Mr. F. Cram, of Lawrence, Mass., to Miss Susan P. Colbath, of Dover.
"	8, Mr. William H. Hill to Miss Martha J. P. Davis, both of Dover.
"	26, Mr. Charles Osborne to Miss Lucy Ann Quimby, both of Dover.
May	19, Mr. Albion Goodwin to Miss Clara Sanborn.
"	27, Mr. Ralph Brock, Jr., to Miss Ann S. Beal, both of Dover.
July	15, Mr. Jefferson Lord to Miss Tamson P. Church, both of Biddeford, Me.
"	22, Mr. Joseph Burnham to Miss Harriet Boutwell, both of Exeter.
"	24, Mr. Phineas Merrill, of Lawrence, Mass., to Miss Almira H. Caverly, of Dover.
Aug.	12, Mr. Tobias Stackpole to Miss Eliza Osgood, both of Dover.
Oct.	18, Mr. William H. Lewis to Miss Lydia J. Emerson, both of Dover.
Nov.	1, Mr. Israel P. Church to Miss Lydia S. Brown, both of Dover.

1850.

March 18, Mr. William S. Stevenson to Miss Mary L. Peirce, both of South Hampton.

MARRIAGES.

1839-1850.

RECORDS OF ST. THOMAS' EPISCOPAL CHURCH, DOVER, N. H.

[Marriages other than those found in Dover, N. H. Records, pages 87-105.]

MARRIAGE BY REV. THOMAS R. LAMBERT.

1839.
Sept.   17, Mr. George Briggs, of Boston, Mass., to Caroline Young, of Dover.

MARRIAGES BY REV. WILLIAM HORTON.

1840.
Jan.   16, Mr. Richard P. Harper to Miss Love Stevens.
Aug.   12, Mr. Thomas S. Spear to Miss Abbie P. Pickering, both of Portsmouth.

1841.
Sept.   11, Mr. Samuel Rowell, of Amesbury, Mass., to Miss Lydia J. Neale, of North Berwick, Me.
 "   16, Mr. Edward Cocking, of Providence, R. I., to Miss Elizabeth Twombly, of Dover.

1842.
July   7, Mr. William Pinkham, 2d, to Miss Betsey S. Gilman, both of Dover.
Sept.   29, Mr. Edward Appleton, of Boston, Mass., to Miss Frances Anne Atkinson, of Dover.
Dec.   21, Mr. William L. Howcroft to Miss Judith E. Tibbetts, both of Dover.

1843.
Nov.   7, Mr. John F. Rogers, of Whitehall, N. Y., to Miss Sophia Smith, daughter of Joseph Smith, Esq., of Dover.

MARRIAGES, ST. THOMAS' CHURCH RECORDS, 1839–1850.

Nov. 7, Mr. Charles Hovey, of Lowell, Mass., to Miss Catharine Smith, daughter of Joseph Smith, Esq., of Dover.

" 15, At St. Thomas' Church, Mr. John M. Hill, of Concord, N. H., to Miss Elizabeth L. Chase, of Boston.

1844.
Jan. 18, At St. Thomas' Church, Henry Hough to Eliza Drew, both of Dover.

Feb. 15, At Newmarket, Nathan B. Chase, M. D., to Sarah Elizabeth Branscomb.

July 7, Dr. John H. Paul to Miss Mary Ann Paul.

" 28, Abel Whitton, of Newburyport, Mass., to Ann B. Riley, daughter of Capt. Riley, of Dover.

Oct. 31, Mr. Daniel S. King to Miss Anasatsia Prestwitch.

1845.
Feb. 5, Mr. Samuel Gerrish, of Boston, Mass., to Miss. Caroline Elizabeth Estes, of Dover.

April 3, Mr. Charles A. Fiske, of Boston, Mass., to Miss Abby Waldron, of Boston, Mass.

" 16, Mr. James M. Flagg and Miss Jane Mary Estes, both of Dover.

Sept. 4, Mr. Samuel B. Swett, of Exeter, N. H., and Miss Mary Sheafe Lowe, of Dover.

Oct. 23, Dryden Smith. M. D., and Miss Emily Webster.

1846.
Sept. 9, Mr. Edwin Bartholomew and Miss Sarah M. Gerrish, both of Dover.

1847.
Jan. 21, Mr. Geo. S. Woodman, of Dover, and Miss Maria Chase, of Somersworth.

April 6, Being Tuesday after Easter, Rev. Newton Epaphroditus Marble, of Taunton, Mass., to Miss Sarah Huntington Freeman, eldest daughter of Asa Freeman, Esq., of Dover.

June 1, James A. Abbott, Esq., of Boston, Mass., to Miss Hannah Kittridge, only daughter of the late Dr. Jacob Kittridge, of Dover.

MARRIAGES BY REV. THOMAS G. SALTER.

1848.
Feb. 14, John Shaw and Deborah Elliott, both of Portsmouth.

June 5, David Howcroft and *Mrs. Anne Guy, both of Dover.

*The publishment says Miss Anne Guy.—[ED.

Sept.	13, John Nesmith, of Dover, and Miss Lydia Ann Richardson, of the same town.
Nov.	8, Joseph S. Brown, of Lowell, Mass., and Sarah F. E. Hardy, of Dover.
"	23, Charles H. Kingman and Mary L. Hanson, both of Madbury.

1849.

Jan.	13, John Chapman and Mary Higgs, both of Rochester.
Feb.	4, Ralph Hough and Sarah Delaney, both of Dover.
Aug.	14, William G. Keay and Olive J. Emery, both of Dover.
"	30, John H. Wentworth, of Rollinsford, and Mary J. Stackpole, of Somersworth.

1850.

Jan.	30, James McLaughlin, of Portland, Me., and Mary M. Souther, of Portsmouth, Virginia.
May	16, James H. Davis and Margaret J. Bickford, both of Dover.
Dec.	16, Dr. A. W. Pike, Jr., and Abby A. Freeman, both of Dover.

MARRIAGES,

1829-1850.

RECORDS OF FIRST UNITARIAN SOCIETY, DOVER, N. H.

[Marriages other than those found in Dover, N. H. Records, pages 87-105.]

MARRIAGES BY REV. SAMUEL K. LOTHROP.

1829.
    Aaron Wingate March to Ann Tredick.
    John Plumer to Mary Tasker.
    William Gerrish to Abigail Watson.
    William Hughes to Sarah Jones.
    *Woodbury T. Prescott to Frances E. Bangs.
    William Drew to Sarah Wingate.
    Daniel Curtis to Elizabeth Swan.

1830.
    Andrew Hall to Betsey Young.
    William Fry to Mary Galloway.
    Edward F. Gerrish to Fanny P. Tuttle.
    Moses Davis to Nancy B. Tuttle.
    George Laird to Abigail Goodrich.
    Leonard Davis to Hannah Bailey.

1831.
    George Meserve to Sarah P. Nute.
    Samuel Dunn to Rose Tuttle.
    William Hale, Jr., to Martha Hale.
    James Bartlett to Jane M. Andrews.
    Jeremiah Smith to Elizabeth Hale.
    †William Kielly to Mary Haskell.
    True Seavey to Sarah Ann F. Trussell.

*Publishment says Frances E. Banks.—[ED.
†Date of certificate of publishment, Sept. 16, 1832.—[ED.

1832.
>
> Francis Winkley to Olive Hanniford.
> Ebenezer Meserve to Lucretia Rogers.
> Silas McIntire of Dover to Caroline Simpson of Durham.
> Leonard M. Hough to Rhoda Buzzell.
> Abraham Folsom to Abigail S. Peirce.
> Charles C. Ayer to Ellen M. Melcher.
> Richard Kimball to Margaret J. Pendexter.
> Jonathan Horn to Sarah Twombly.
> Shubael Varney to Rebecca Paul.
> Robert Plumer to Susan R. Watson.
> Ira Christie to Ann Collier.

1833.
>
> George Gilman to Susan G. Plumer.
> Ira Allen to Hariet S. Locke.
> John Tucker to Eliza Hussey.
> Isaac Gear to Mary Hill.
> Samuel B. Nichols to Ann Augusta Perkins.
> Joseph B. Upham to Sarah C. Currier.
> Henry R. Reed to Elizabeth S. Victor.
> William Bailey to Maria Occleston.
> Nathaniel Drew to Sabrina Spurling.
> Isaac Meader to Nancy Berry.
> Nathaniel R. Long to Caroline Smith.
> Robert Perkins to Dolly M. Prescott.
> John Fogg to Sarah R. Sankey.
> William R. Thomas to Mary E. Smith.
> Thomas W. Kittredge to Adeline Tredick.

1834.
>
> Frederick B. Hurd to Sarah Hooper.
> Ai Remick to Mary P. Drew.
> Benjamin Kingsbury to Sarah V. Ham.
> Winthrop A. Marston to Mary C. Waldron.
> George Norton to Leonora F. Leighton.

MARRIAGES BY REV. EDGAR BUCKINGHAM.

1838.
May 22, Elihu H. Palmer to Nancy M. Drew.
June 10, Elisha Merrow to Maria Merrow.
July 5, Samuel H. Henderson to Sarah Ann Guppy.

Oct. 2, Elijah Wadleigh to Charlotte King Atkinson Copp.
Dec. 6, Albert Chamberlin to Philenia G. Collins.
1839.
May 20, George Norton to Hannah E. Leighton.

MARRIAGES BY REV. JOHN PARKMAN.

1840.
Oct. 17, John G. Parshley to Betsey R. Hayes.
" 20, John Meserve to Jane Dunn.
Dec. 24, James Whitehouse to Elizabeth A. Peaslee.
1841.
Aug. 17, William Pickering Libbey to Maria Louisa Bridge.
1842.
*John F. Long to Olive G. Philpot.
Oct. 13. John H. Wiggins to Nancy D. Wiggin.
Nov. 2, Henry W. Smith to Clara Augusta Jackson.
" 17, Tobias W. Roberts to Mary F. Smith.
Dec. 7, James M. York to Catharine Dockham.
" 7, Eri Pinkham to Eliza J. Jones.
1843.
March 2, Thomas Henderson to Olive Bickford.
May 16, Luther C. Kimball to Abby J. Hanson.
June 28, Smith Clarke to Abigail Henderson of Somersworth.
1844.
April 25, John T. Gibbs to Anna T. March.
1845.
Aug. 22, Thomas C. Robinson to Pamelia Pearl.
Sept. 30, King Colbath to Emily Guppy.
1846.
May 4, George W. Lane to Eliza A. S. Dexter.
" 21, Joseph Y. French to Elizabeth R. Parshley.

[Marriages solemnized by the Rev. Mr. Thompson and Rev. Wm. P. Tilden, during the absence of Rev. John Parkman, in the years 1846 and 1847, were not recorded in the records of the Society.]

1848.
July 6, Joseph A. Peirce to Anne Elizabeth Drew.
" 23, John B. Wood to Mary A. Gerrish.
Oct. 12, Joseph Ballou to Sarah A. Proudman.

*Certificate of publishment May 30, 1842.

MARRIAGES.

1843-1850.

RECORDS OF ST. MARY'S CATHOLIC CHURCH, DOVER, N. H.

[Marriages other than those found in Dover, N. H. Records, pages 87-105. The record from which the following marriages were taken is that now used by the Church, and is said to be a copy of the original record; but it is evident that it contains several errors.]

1843.
June   22, Michael Bennett and Catherine Haughey.
Nov.   13, Patrick Garr and Mary Garr.
"   30, Michael Donovan and Julia Clifford.
"   31, *Richard Hines and Mary Agnew.
         †John Cocklin and Mary McCabe.
         Peter Flynn and Mary Preston.

1844.
Feb.   6, Andrew McGuinness and Catherine Ward.
May   11, Philip Cassily and Mary Ward.
"   12, Owen Sullivan and Bridget McEvoy.
"   16, Patrick Doran and Phebe Hughes.
"   27, James Mullen and Alice McBennett.
"   30, Michael Agnew and Ann Rodgers.
         Daniel Allen and Ellen Spelan.
         ‡Henry Hughes and Bridget Marlow.
June   8, Thomas Synnot and Mary Rossiter.
Aug.   10, Joseph Lane and Mary Morrison.
"   11, Thomas Grimes and Bridget Gorman.
         Patrick Lyons and Ann Walsh.
         Edward Goodwin and Catherine Printy.
         ‖Edward Mulligan and Ann Haughey.

*Date of certificate of publishment, May 27, 1849.
†Date of certificate of publishment, May 30, 1849.
‡Date of certificate of publishment, May 18, 1848.
‖Date of certificate of publishment, Sept. 12, 1848.

Oct.	4,	*James Hughes and Margaret McClosky.
"	8,	†John Gilligan and Catherine McMullen.
		Peter Murphy and Bridget Haughey.
"	13,	‡Robert O'Brien and Ann Halpin.
		‖James Dyer and Catherine Feeney.
Nov.	28,	Patrick Wade and Joanna Shay.
		§Richard Doherty and Grace Doherty.
		Thomas McBennett and Mary Cluncart.

1846.

Patrick Harrington and Margaret Buckley.
Edmund Flynn and Mary Kelly.
James York and Mary Cahill.
Anthony Donahoe and Mary O'Donnell.

Feb.	25,	James Hynes and Mary Whelan.
		Joseph Ellingworth and Mary Bryne.
		Patrick Filierty and Mary Filierty.
July	27,	Moses Fiske and Sarah Huntress.
Aug.	2,	**James McMullen and Margaret Rodgers.

1847.

James Malone and Rose McNally.

May	28,	James Hughes and Jane Hughes.
Oct.	4,	John O'Donald and Mary Ann Smith.
		Felix Hughes and Alice Moon.

1848.

James Danvers and Ellen Cunningham.
James Waters and Agnes McNally.
Timothy Flannigan and Hannah Cassidy.
John Kelly and Abby Moon.
Mark Burns and Catherine Lawler.
Patrick Mullen and Elizabeth McKone.

1849.

John Hughes and Ellen McClosky.

Jan.	19,	††Daniel Buckley and Mary Kelly.
"	19,	John Clinton and Julia McCarty.
May	3,	Dennis Harrington and Ellen Murphy.

*Date of certificate of publishment, Oct. 1, 1848.
†Date of certificate of publishment, Oct. 7, 1848.
‡Date of certificate of publishment, Oct. 9, 1848.
‖Date of certificate of publishment, Oct. 28, 1848.
§Date of certificate of publishment, Nov. 28, 1848.
**Date of certificate of publishment, July 31, 1847.
††Date of certificate of publishment, April 13, 1849.

May	3,	William Tierney and Bridget Hackin.
"	9,	John Cody and Julia Regan.
		*Thomas Horan and Ellen Harrigan.
Sept.	3,	William Slattery and Bridget Donahoe.
		†Patrick McManus and Catherine McGuinness.
"	13,	Timothy O'Connell and Hornora McCarty.
Oct.	4,	Michael Hughes and Mary Murray.
		Patrick Flynn and Mary Kane.
"	24,	James Hoy and Catherine Gafney.
"	24,	James Kay and Margaret O'Brien.
"	28,	John Campbell and Ann Hoffy.
Nov.	6,	Edward Hughes and Catherine Murphy.
		‡Dennis Brennan and Sarah Brennan.
"	6,	James Kelley and Margaret Rand.
		Michael Mahon and Hannah Kilminton.
		Thomas Moore and Lucy Walsh.
		John Sullivan and Margaret Noonan.
		Owen Hughes and Catherine Nooney.
		Peter Grimes and Eleanor Kelley.
		Arthur McKone and Mary Ackley.
		Patrick Lawler and Catherine James.
		James Fawley and Bridget Kernan.
		Owen Rodgers and Mary Ward.
		Patrick Kivel and Bridget Donahoe.
		Thomas Flynn (or Finn) and Mary McCarthy.
		Patrick Bean and Mary Devitt.

1850.

Feb.	6,	James Mullen and Mary Ann Connors.
		Charles McCarty and Ellen Murphy.
		Jeremiah Buckley and Mary Burtell.
April	12,	Samuel Jones and Ellen Buckley.
"	18,	Leonard M. Hauck and Margaret Harrigan.
"	26,	Hugh McIntyre and Susan Reynolds.
May	2,	Richard Knott and Ellen Hughes.
"	2,	Thomas Agnew and Bridget Haughey.
"	7,	Patrick Collins and Bridget McNulty.
"	7,	Patrick Conerty and Alice McKone.

*Publishment says Thomas Moran, date of certificate, July 8, 1849.
†Date of certificate of publishment, Sept. 29, 1849.
‡Date of certificate of publishment, Nov. 24, 1849.

May	9, James Dilhanty and Margaret Joyce.
"	12, Patrick Henry and Margaret Keating.
	Michael Derrigan and Mary Ann Howard.
"	19, Dennis McCarthy and Mary Kane.
"	20, Harry Fagan and Ellen Donnelly.
"	20, John Bellew and Bridget Walsh.
June	9, John Carberry and Elizabeth Morgan.
"	20, Michael Dolan and Maria Walsh.
July	16, William Quinn and Hannah Crowley.
"	16, John Harold and Margaret Doherty.
	Jeremiah Murphy and Margaret McCarthy.
	John Ryan and Maria Scully.
	John Flannigan and Eliza Burns.
Aug.	10, Thomas Connolly and Ann McDermott.
	Thomas Burns and Eliza Bean.
	Thomes Morgan and Mary McShane.
	Alexander Cross and Joanna O'Donnell.
"	15, Thomas Kennedy and Mary Minehan.
Oct.	24, Charles Mullen and Isabella Mitchell.
"	24, Michael Cunningham and Mary Velden.
"	25, Patrick Mooney and Alice Trainor.
"	25, James Cawley and Elizabeth Brennan.
Nov.	7, John Merrill and Joanna Gahan.
"	27, James Kelly and Bridget Lane.

INDEX.

INDEX OF PERSONS.

Abbott, Alice, 218
    Daniel, 187
    Henry G., 104
    James A., 254
    Jane, 76
    John, 100
    John Sullivan, 76
    Mary Ann, 76
    Samuel, 76
    William. 89
Ackley, Mary, 261
Adams,——140, 166
    Drusilla, 97
    Ebenezer, 161
    Ezekiel, 99
    George A., 247
    Hugh, 43
    James, 244
    Jane, 99
    John, 91, 94, 220
    Joseph P., 235
    Joseph Potter, 236
    Rebecca, 220
    Sarah, 119
    Susan Garrison, 229
    William, 161
    William S, 101
Agnew, Mary, 259
    Michael, 259
    Thomas, 261
Aiken, John, 80
Akiman, Josiah, 178
Alden, A., 224
    Elizabeth, 224
    Harriet Boardman, 230
    William Hillhouse, 224, 230
Alkins, Robert, 128
Allard, Elizabeth Ann, 239
    Grace, 131
    William, 237, 239
Allen, ——, 190
    Ann, 130
    Daniel, 259
    Edward, 2
    Elizabeth, 130, 171, 219
    George W., 232
    Ira, 257
    Jacob, 2, 30, 130, 134
    James, 96
    Joseph, 30
    Leah, 130
    Lyman, 245
    Martha, 2, 30
    Mary, 130, 134, 232
    Nathaniel, 190
    Rachel, 129
    Sarah, 83
Alley, Daniel, 48
    Elizabeth, 21, 45, 48
    Ephraim, 48
    John, 6, 45, 48
    Martha, 45
    Phebe, 45

Alley, Richard, 170
    Samuel, 6, 21, 45, 48
    Sarah, 45
    Thomas, 45, 48
Amazeen, Frances, 250
    Samuel B., 249
Amblar, Abraham, 8
    Elizabeth, 8, 34
    Hannah, 8
    John, 8, 34, 131
    Joseph, 8
    Mary, 8
Ambrose, Samuel, 190
Anderson, ——, 195
    Lydia, 177
    Sophronia, 184
Andrews, Ann Sinclair, 64, 65
    Edmund Charles, 64
    Edward, 132
    Elizabeth Neal, 64
    George, 64, 65
    James D., 248
    Jane Margaret, 64, 256
    Lucinda, 248
    Sylvina P., 249
    William Neal, 65
Appleton, Edward, 253
Armstead, John E., 96
Arthur, ——, 240
Ash, Benjamin, 142
    Eleanor, 142
    Hannah, 27
    Judith. 133, 142
    Mary, 133, 142
    Thomas, 142
Aspinwall, Daniel W., 187
    Sarah A., 249
Atkinson, Abigail, 66.
    Ann Louisa, 214
    Charlotte King, 66
    Elizabeth, 106, 122
    Frances, 66, 179, 214
    Frances Anne, 253
    George, 58
    John Pickering, 66
    Joseph, 173, 210
    Mary, 106
    Susanna Sparhawk, 66, 86
    Theodore, 66. 106. 178, 214
    William King, 66
Atwood, Hannah, 180
Austin, ——, 195
    Anne, 32
    Catherine, 32, 35, 41
    Joseph, 35, 189
    Nathaniel, 32, 35
    Phebe, 32
    Rebecca, 35
    Sarah, 32, 35, 88, 195
    Stephen, 173
    Stoten, } 101, 202
    Stoughton, }
    Thomas, 35

INDEX OF PERSONS.

Avery, James C., 186
    Thomas, 130
Ayer, | Charles C., 257
Ayers, | Clara, 103
    Edward, 112
    Elizabeth, 112
    Joseph, 230
    Maria, 102
    Richard, 94
    Ruth, 39, 46
    William, 131
Babb, Benjamin Franklin, 236
    Mary, 236
    Mary Ann, 93
Badcock, Nicholas, 107
Badger, Elizabeth, 111
    Leonidas V., 185
Bailey, Benjamin, 179
    Hannah, 256
    Julia Adelaide, 230
    Susan Elizabeth, 230
    William, 257
Baker, ——, 194
    Alexander Douglass, 159
    Charles, 183
    Christina, 188, 208
    Ebenezer, 161, 201, 213
    General S., 96
    George, 199
    J., 205
    James Chesley, 164, 215
    John, 162
    Lydia, 161, 174
    Mary, 182, 213
    Mehitable, 163, 178
    Otis, 58, 158, 159, 161, 162, 163, 164, 165, 203, 210
    Samuel, 231
    Sarah, 158, 215
    Sharington A., 180
    Sophia, 96
    Tamson, 161, 204
    Thomas, 165
    William P., 96
Balch, Anne, 171
    Hepzibah, 161
    Joanna, 170, 210
    Joseph, 162
    Martha, 161
    Nathaniel, 161, 162, 210
Ballou, Joseph, 258
Bampton, ——, 190, 204
    Abigail, 147
    Anna, 147
    Ambrose, 146, 195
    Elizabeth, 140
    Hannah, 140, 167
    Mary, 147
Bangs, Frances E., 256
Banfield, Esther P., 218
    Joshua, 218, 233
Banks, Francis E., 256
    Jeremiah, 84
Banton, William, 250
Barden, Lucy, 184
    Lydia J., 185
Barefoot, ——107, 118, 123
Barker, John, 167
    Samuel Foss, 167
Barnes, Benjamin, 183
    Elizabeth, 131
    Henry, 100
    Lucy, 217
    Mary, 221
    Mary J., 246
Barrows, Elkanah, 92
    Homer, 239

Barrows, Mary, 233
    Sarah M. W., 239
Barsham, Annabel, 107
    Dorothy, 107
    John, 107
    Mary, 107
    Mehitable, 107
    Sarah, 107
    William, 107
Barstow, Catherine, 96
    Catherine H., 219
Bartholomew, Edwin, 254
Bartlett, Abigail Dame, 184
    Daniel, 178
    James, 256
    John, 81
Bassford, Mary, 38, 39
Batchelder, George, 235
Beach, Frederick, 243
    Harriet, 223, 229
    Lurandus, 223, 225, 229
Beal, Ann S., 252
    Sarah, 96
Bean, Eliza, 262
    Lois, 184
    Mary, 102
    Patrick, 261
    Peniel, 40
    Sarah, 171, 172
    Sarah C., 97
Beard, Bridget, 133
    Esther, 131
    Hannah, 106
    Hester, 131
    Joseph, 130, 133
    Mary, 106, 128
    Samuel, 133
    Thomas, 106
    William, 106
Beck, William, 245
Bedell, Charles T., 235
Beede, Cyrus, 83
    Samuel, 98
Belknap, Abigail, 211
    Andrew Elliot, 55, 167
    Elizabeth, 55, 166
    Jeremy, 52, 54, 55, 58, 78, 79, 82, 164, 165, 166, 167, 170, 210
    John, 55, 167
    Joseph, 55, 165, 192, 200
    Ruth, 54, 55
    Samuel, 55, 166
    Sarah, 54, 164
Bell, Benjamin, 108
    Elizabeth, 81, 108
    Frederick, 189
    Frederick Mordant, 173
    Meshech, 108
    Rachel, 107
    Shadrach, 107
    Thomas, 108
Bellew, John, 262
Benmore, Philip, 107
    Rebecca, 107
Benn, Isaac, 186
Bennett, Benjamin, 81
    George P., 251
    John, 81
    Joseph W., 249
    Mercy, 251
    Michael, 259
    Rachel, 89
    Ruth, 118
    Susan C., 250
Berry, Abigail, 107
    Ann W., 249

INDEX OF PERSONS. 267

Berry, Deliverance, 130
　　　Ebenezer H., 217
　　　Elizabeth, 107
　　　Enoch, 96
　　　Frederick, 107
　　　James, 165
　　　Jane, 107, 129
　　　Jeremiah, 107
　　　Judah, 107
　　　Nancy, 257
　　　Nathaniel, 93, 107, 129
　　　Richard, 102
　　　Sarah, 98, 111
　　　Sarah F., 250
　　　Stephen, 107, 165
　　　William, 107, 129
Betton, Clarissa, 214
Bickford, ——, 197
　　　Aaron, 69
　　　Abigail, 156, 162
　　　Abigail M., 248
　　　Andrew, 79
　　　Anna, 5, 140
　　　Benjamin, 106, 210
　　　Bridget, 5
　　　Deborah, 69, 182, 209
　　　Dodavah, 5
　　　Ebenezer, 175
　　　Eliakim, 5
　　　Elizabeth, 34, 81, 134, 148, 156, 163,
　　　　208, 209
　　　Ephraim, 69. 151, 172
　　　Esther, 209, 222
　　　Gershom, 168
　　　Hannah, 69, 106
　　　Hannah S., 96
　　　Henry, 34, 148
　　　Isaac, 161
　　　James, 161
　　　Jethro, 5, 161
　　　John, 5, 34, 106, 129, 134, 140, 160
　　　Jonathan, 48, 156, 160, 161, 162,
　　　　163, 165, 166, 167, 168, 169, 190,
　　　　191, 211
　　　Joseph, 5, 34, 69, 140, 142, 143, 147,
　　　　150, 151, 189, 208, 209, 210
　　　Judith, 156, 167
　　　Lemuel, 5
　　　Mahala, 233
　　　Margaret J., 255
　　　Martha, 34
　　　Mary, 5, 69, 131, 142. 182
　　　Moses, 158, 172, 233
　　　Nathaniel, 166
　　　Olive, 258
　　　Peirce, 5
　　　Phebe, 104
　　　Rebecca, 144, 160
　　　Richard, 169
　　　Sarah, 69, 140, 143, 144, 160, 167,
　　　　172, 211, 222
　　　Susanna, 5, 69
　　　Temperance, 106
　　　Thomas, 34, 69, 144, 147, 165, 226
　　　Wilmot, 166
Birge, Chester, 180
Bishop, James, 79, 222
　　　James D., 187
　　　Maria, 91
　　　Mary, 222
　　　Rebecca, 184
Blackden, Charles, 142
　　　John, 140, 142
　　　Mary, 140
Blaisdell, Eliza, 104
　　　Mary Jane, 245
　　　Sarah, 247

Blake, Abigail, 68
　　　Dorothy, 107
　　　Elizabeth, 68, 213
　　　Elizabeth Mary Ann, 232
　　　Esther, 214
　　　Frances, 107
　　　John, 107
　　　Lydia, 68
　　　Lydia H., 182
　　　Lydia P., 231
　　　Mary, 89
　　　Samuel, 84, 225, 232
　　　Sarah, 225
　　　Sophia, 232
　　　Stephen Palmer, 232
　　　William, 68, 85, 213
Blanchard, Amos, 187, 216
　　　Elizabeth, 131
　　　Susan, 183
Boardman, Abigail, 61
　　　Anna, 61, 176
　　　Benjamin, 89
　　　David, 61, 200, 204
　　　Harriet, 61
Bodge, Jacob, 90
　　　Mary, 84
　　　Samuel, 79
　　　Sarah, 219
Bogle, Elizabeth, 222
Bolo, Hannah, 84
　　　Lucinda, 94
Boody, Azariah, 151, 153, 156
　　　Joseph, 156
　　　Mary, 58
　　　Moses, 130
　　　Robert, 151
　　　Zechariah, 153
Boutwell, Harriet, 252
Bowen, Harriet, 99
Boyd, Martha Whiting, 238
Boylston, Edward D., 228
Brackett, Eleanor, 116
　　　Elizabeth, 90
　　　James, 80, 210
　　　Jane, 114
Bracy, Dorcas, 246
Bradford, ——, 177
Bragdon, John, 82
　　　Nancy, 247
Bragg, Abigail, 84
　　　Mary, 203
Branscomb, Sarah Elizabeth, 254
Brawne, Eleanor, 131
　　　Elizabeth, 131
　　　George, 107, 130
　　　Mary, 107
　　　Michael, 107
Brennan, Dennis, 261
　　　Elizabeth, 262
　　　Sarah, 261
Brew, Elizabeth, 147
　　　Frances, 147
　　　Jonathan, 147
Brewer, Dexter. 214
Brewster, Margaret, 171
Bridge, Aaron, 105
　　　Maria Louisa, 258
　　　Mary, 75
　　　Matthew, 75
　　　Matthew Harrington, 75
　　　Samuel Ingersoll, 75
Bridges, Sarah, 172
Briggs, George, 253
Brierley, Benjamin, 103
Brock, Benjamin, 36
　　　Hannah, 180
　　　Hannah N., 102

INDEX OF PERSONS.

John, 169, 173
Luke Wentworth, 168
Maria, 235
Martha, 167
Mary, 36, 148, 245
Nancy, 247
Ralph, 251, 252
Sarah, 167
Simeon, 78, 175
Sophia, 102
Stephen, 247
Susan Young, 238
William, 167, 168, 169, 172
Brooks, Elizabeth, 241
John, 241
Mary, 241
Brown, Abial, 107
Abigail, 65, 239
Alice, 65
Ambrose, 243, 252
Amos, 65, 97
Ann Elizabeth, 235
Anna, 65
Benjamin, 86, 154
David Sands, 65, 77
Edward, 77, 174
Elizabeth, 79
George Thornton, 77
Hannah, 82, 112
Isaac, 82
Jacob, 107
James, 84, 154
Jeremiah, 65
John, 65, 77, 107, 180
John R., 77
Joseph S., 255
Judith, 91
Lydia, 65
Lydia S., 252
Mary, 83, 149, 154
Mary Anna, 77
Mary B., 225
Mary S., 180
Mary Thornton, 77
Moses, 52, 65, 171
Nancy, 84, 187
Nathaniel Howland, 77
Olive W., 214, 239
Samuel, 107
Sarah, 107, 210
Sarah Caroline, 235
Susan, 101
Thomas, 107
Walter, 77
William, 65, 79, 149, 154
William Henry, 77
Bruce, Harriet S., 244
Bryer, Abigail, 107
Elisha, 107
Margaret, 107
Mary, 107
Samuel, 107
Sarah, 107
Buckingham, Edgar, 104, 105, 257
Buckley, Daniel, 260
Ellen, 261
Jeremiah, 261
Margaret, 260
Buckminster, ——, 168
Joseph, 63
Bullard, Augustine, 129
Bunker, Abigail, 159, 174
Benjamin, 154
Daniel, 41
Deborah, 147
Dorcas, 41, 152
Elijah, 150, 161, 164, 165, 210

Bunker, Elizabeth, 35, 41, 149, 150
Esther, 79, 150
Hannah, 35, 150, 164.
James, 165
John, 11, 35, 41, 152
Judith, 78, 159, 175, 210
Martha, 159
Mary, 8, 164
Mary Jane, 238
Phillip, 152
Sarah, 41
Sarah B., 236
Silas, 35
Stephen, 152
Susan, 82, 161
Susanna, 161
Thomas Millet, 154
Tobias, 236
Zechariah, 41, 147, 152, 171
Burleigh, Charles E., 102
Burley, Grace F., 243
Hiram, 103
Martha, 231
Oliver P., 245
Parkman, 231
Paul, 179
Burnham, Abigail Stevens, 231
Deborah, 247
Elizabeth, 44
Hannah, 132
Jeremiah P., 251
Joseph, 190, 232
Josiah C., 234
Mary, 90
Mehitable, 178
Robert, 44, 106
Sophia, 182
Susanna, 44
Burns, Eliza, 262
Mark, 260
Thomas, 262
Burrows, Abigail, 228
Amos, 226, 228
Eliza, 226
Eunice, 183
Mary, 217
Thomas, 82
Burtell, Mary, 261
Burton, Ebenezer, 179
Buss, John, 3
Butler, George, 178
Hester Ann, 221
James, 171
Joseph, 94
Mary, 185, 243
Buzzell, Abigail, 158
Abraham, 144
Benjamin, 142
Ebenezer, 157, 215
Hannah, 142
Henry, 145, 151, 209
Ichabod, 147
Jane, 151
John, 142, 144, 146, 158
Lydia, 172
Mary, 147
Nathaniel, 145
Rhoda, 257
Samuel, 147
Sarah, 146
Susan, 183
Tabitha, 147
William, 107, 147, 150
Byrne, Mary, 260
Cady. Susanna, 94
Cahill, Mary, 260
Caldwell. Agnes, 171

Alexander, 159, 165, 189, 193
John, 220
Mary, 82, 165
Sarah, 159, 174
Calef, { James, 57, 67, 188, 190, 191, 192
Calf, } John. 67
John S., 251
Jonathan, 212
Mary, 67
Sarah, 67
Zeceariah Z., 67
Campbell, Archibald, 175
Duncan, 174
John, 26,
Margaret, 11
Canada, Abigail, 51, 52; 161
George, 52
John, 51, 161
Mary, 161
Nicholas, 51, 52, 161
Sarah, 51, 161
Canney, { Abigail, 25
Kenney, } Benjamin, 194
Caroline, 180
Daniel, 62
Deborah, 137
Elizabeth, 81
Hannah S., 89, 222
Izetta, 214
James, 92
Jane, 62, 109, 203
John, 36, 44, 101
Joseph, 25, 109, 130
Judith, 26
Leah, 25
Liberty E., 62
Love, 191
Lydia, 137
Martha, 119, 128
Mary, 36, 80, 109, 124, 128, 130, 172
Mary J., 251
Mary W., 187
Otis, 26
Rebecca, 26. 79, 199
Richard, 26, 81, 117, 128, 167, 180, 194, 195, 196
Rose, 81
Samuel, 44, 130, 135
Sarah, 36, 44, 203
Susanna, 44, 82
Thomas, 44, 109
Carberry, John, 262
Card, Abigail, 183
Archelaus, 177
Daniel, 222
Dorothy, 183
Eliza J., 244
Hannah, 245
Henry, 247
Phebe, 181
Sarah, 181
Susan T., 185
Thomas, 179
William, 245
Carle, Timothy, 131
Carleton, Benjamin, 181
Carlisle, Daniel, 181
Lydia, 182
Carpenter, Deborah, 174
Carr, Dudley, 89
Joanna, 108
John, 146
Mary, 208
Moses, 146, 208
Sarah A., 224
Susan, 226
Carter, Abigail, 39, 138, 139

Carter, Benjamin, 85, 205
Frances, 39
Hannah, 177
John, 39, 138, 139
Mary, 39
Oliver, 231
Sarah, 231
Carver, Sabrina, 95
Cash, Joseph, 109
Cass, Joseph, 109
Mary, 109, 122
Cassidy, Hannah, 260
Cassily, Phillip, 259
Caswell, Richard, 156
Timothy, 171
Cate, Elizabeth, 168
John, 146, 246
John, G., 89
Joseph, 168
Rebecca, 109, 125
Sarah, 144
Sarah Ann, 247
William, 141, 144, 146
Cater, John, 244
Mary, 245
Sarah A., 246
Caverley, Almira H., 252
Hannah, 171, 234
Susan, 223
Cawley, James, 262
Cearll, (See Searle.)
Chadbourne, Phebe, 170
Chadwick, Elizabeth B., 75
Jacob, 79
John, 76
John S., 100
Mary Woodman, 76
Nathaniel Gookin, 76
Chmaberlain, Albert, 258
Dorothy, 139
Ebenezer, 138
Jacob, 143
Joseph, 103
Mary, 17, 134. 206
Mary E., 248
Rebecca, 17, 135
Samuel, 141
William, 17, 134, 135, 138, 139, 141, 143, 206
Champion, John N., 102
Chandler, Abigail, 86, 225
Eliza, 63, 180, 242
Elizabeth, 63
Joseph Socrates, 86
Lydia Gray, 63, 184, 215
Mary, 232
Mary Ann, 63, 240
Philemon, 63, 86, 212, 215, 225, 242
William, 96
William Lovejoy, 63, 232
Chapin, Derrick W., 246
Elmer D., 244
Chaplin, Calvin, 92
Chapman, Elizabeth, 108, 131
Jeremiah Y., 182
Johh, 255
Mercy, 131
Phebe, 110
Robert, 108
Samuel, 110
Chase, Abigail G., 181
Calvin, 183
E., 204
Eliza, 84
Elizabeth, 103, 184
Elizabeth L., 253
Enoch, 170, 194

Chase, Harriet, 63
  Herman, 245
  James, 203
  Joanna, 85
  John G., 181
  Maria, 254
  Nancy, 184
  Nathan B., 254
  Nicholas, 92
  Patience, 58
  Sarah, 63
Cheney, Israel E., 231
  Sarah, 231
Chesley, —— 194
  Ann, 39
  Benjamin, 146
  Ebenezer, 158
  Elizabeth, 66, 108, 186
  George, 146
  Hannah, 145
  Hester, 131
  James, 27, 79, 131, 158, 167, 189, 190
  James G., 245
  Jonathan, 16
  Joseph, 141
  Louisa Ann, 100
  Lydia, 80
  Martha, 39
  Mary, 16, 130, 150, 163
  Mehitable, 167
  Miles, 250
  Moses, 158
  Nancy, 66
  Philip, 79
  Richard F., 66
  Samuel, 39, 142, 150
  Stephen P., 183
  Susanna, 39, 146
  Tamson, 27
  Thomas, 108, 145
  William J., 247
Chick, Hannah, 85
  Noah, 177
  Priscilla, 172
  Richard, 130
Child, ⎫ Enoch L., 217
Childs, ⎭ Lucinda, 217
  Mary, 217
  Sarah, 129
  Solomon, 217
Choate, Eliza, 223
  Elizabeth, 170
Christie, Daniel M., 183
  Ira, 257
Church, —— 194
  Abigail, 10, 43, 47, 109, 129
  Ann, 47
  Benjamin, 43, 81, 145
  Daniel, 140
  Deborah, 131
  Ebenezer, 43, 47, 109
  Elizabeth, 10, 138
  Eunice, 177
  Israel P., 252
  James, 47
  John, 10, 43, 47, 109, 130, 140, 143, 145
  Jonathan, 10, 43, 47, 109
  Mary, 10, 43, 140
  Mercy, 10
  Nathaniel, 47
  Tamson P., 252
Churchill, Sarah, 132
Cilley, Daniel P., 101
  James, 23
  Martha, 109
  Mary, 23
  Thomas, 129

Claggett, Wiseman, 57
Clapham, Charles, 195
Clarke, Abigail, 229
  Abraham, 33, 35, 100, 147
  Alfred Metcalf, 225, 229
  Ann, ⎫
  Anna, ⎬ 33, 35, 105, 147
  Anne, ⎭
  Elizabeth, 91
  Elizabeth McNeal, 239
  Emily W., 228
  Enoch, 181
  Esther, 81
  George, 176, 182
  Greenleaf, 187
  Hannah, 220
  Horace, 93
  Huldah T., 186
  Isaac, 145
  Jacob, 174, 232
  Jacob S., 96
  James. 8, 90
  James V., 101
  Jonathan, 109
  Levi, 251
  Love, 33, 145
  Mary, 7, 35, 147, 197, 226
  Nathan, 184
  Samuel, 145
  Samuel S., 104
  Sarah, 100
  Smith, 258
  Susan, 232
  Thomas, 78, 175
  William H., 203, 220, 225
Clary, Anna, 214
  Joseph W., 74, 75, 176, 213, 214
Clay, Richard, 187
  Sarah, 182
Clements, Abigail, 7, 156, 172
  Anna, 164
  Charlotte, 181
  Ebenezer, 170
  Elijah, 79
  Elizabeth, 158, 173, 202
  Enoch, 165
  Hannah, 21, 177, 207
  James, 7, 153
  Jeremiah, 160
  Joanna, 3
  Job, 7, 21, 109, 128, 134, 135, 153, 156, 158, 159, 160, 162, 164, 165, 166, 193, 202, 207
  John, 153, 199
  Mary, 80, 93, 109, 159
  Miriam, 153
  Moses, 166
  Robert, 108
  Samuel, 21, 134
  Thomas, 78, 175
  William, 85
Clifford, Ann, 109
  Harriet M., 99
  Israel, 109
  John, 109
  Julia, 259
  Mehitable, 109
  Sarah, 109
Clinton, John, 260
Cloggston, William H. S., 248
Cloudy, Michael, 171
Clough, John, 109
Cloutman, Edward, 130
  Eliphalet, 98
  John, 171
  Thomas, 172
Cluncart, Mary, 260

INDEX OF PERSONS.

Cocklin, John, 259
Cochrane, Lilly, 170
Cocking, Edward, 253
Cody, John, 261
Coe, Ebenezer, 176
Coffin, —— 114, 195
    Abigail, 11, 85, 108, 134
    Deborah, 144, 182
    Edmund, 243
    Edward, 108
    Eliphalet, 150, 173
    Elizabeth, 108
    Hannah, 141, 240
    James, 108
    Jane, 11, 14, 21, 134
    Jethro, 108
    John, 139
    Judith, 108
    Lydia, 183
    Mary, 108
    Parnell. 82, 152
    Peter, 108
    Rebecca, 183
    Stephen, 183
    Susan, 178
    Susanna. 140
    Tristram, 11, 14, 21, 108, 134, 135,
        139, 140, 141, 144, 150, 152, 206
    William, 84
Cogswell, Abigail, 180, 214, 242
    Amos, 83, 212, 242
    Elizabeth, 242
    Francis, 180, 225, 233, 242
    Lydia, 177, 212, 242
    Mary, 225
    Nathaniel P., 200
    Sophia, 242
Colbath, King, 258
    Susan P., 252
Colby, Benjamin, 237
    Benjamin L., 88
    Dorothy, 88
    Emily T., 243
    Hannah, 217
    John, 236
    Susan E., 237
Colcord, Elizabeth, 109
    Jonathan, 109
    Mary, 109
    Samuel, 109
Cole, —— 192
    Ann, 107
    Elizabeth, 85
    James, 102
    Jeremiah, 103
    John, 130, 183
    Tamson, 184
Coleman, Calvin, 181
    Enoch T., 247
    Joseph, 183
    Mark, 244
    Samuel S., 178
Collier, Ann, 257
Collins, Benjamin, 230
    Patrick, 261
    Philenia, 258
Colomy, Sarah, 101
Conant, Joshua, 182
Conner, —— 193
    John, 191, 192
    Joseph, 138, 189
    Mary, 99
    Mercy, 32
    Sarah, 82, 138, 170
Conners, Mary Ann, 261
Connerty, Patrick, 261
Connelly, Thomas, 262

Cook, Abigail, 24, 36
    Abraham, 36
    Daniel, 43
    Dorothy, 8, 222
    Ebenezer, 17, 43, 82
    Eli, 95
    Elizabeth, 245
    Hezekiah, 16
    Ichabod, 81
    Jedediah, 231
    John, 16, 17, 43, 110, 128, 185, 222, 223
    John Langdon, 224
    Joseph, 24
    Lydia, 16, 17, 43, 79, 167, 211
    Mary, 17, 232
    Mary A., 243
    Mercy, 16
    Nathaniel, 24, 82
    Peter, 24, 36
    Phebe, 43
    Rebecca, 8
    Reuben, 36
    Richard, 43
    Samuel, 80
    Sarah, 172
    Stephen S., 98
    Susanna, 175
    William, 232
Cooley, John, 171
Coomes, Abigail, 130
Cooper, —— 211
    Abigail, 59, 197
    Deborah, S., 194
    Deborah Shackford, 59, 167
    Elizabeth, 59, 167
    John, 129
    Martha, 59, 166
    Nathaniel, 59, 60, 83, 165, 166, 167
        168, 188, 198, 210, 212
    Venus, 165, 166
    Walter, 59, 60, 61, 166
    William Shackford, 59, 168
Copp, Abigaill, 39
    Adeline, 62
    Avery, 55
    Benjamin. 55
    Charlotte King Atkinson, 258
    David, 62
    Elizabeth, 55
    John Manning, 62
    Jonathan, 139, 140
    Mary, 62
    Mary W., 105
Corson, Ann, 181
Courson, Hannah, 137
    Hatevil, 23
    Ichabod, 137
    Irena, 182
    Joanna, 23, 137
    John, 185
    Josiah A., 101
    Mary, 23, 88, 137
    Michael E., 243
    Rachel, 214
    Samuel, 23, 137
    Zebulon, 23
Costelloe, John, 174
Cotton, George O., 237
Cowan, James Wellington, 233
Cox, John, 129
    Lucy, 89
    Moses, 109
Craffort, —— 109, 125
Cram, Benjamin, 110
    Eliza, 187
    Elizabeth, 110
    F., 252

INDEX OF PERSONS.

Cram, Hebzibah, 110
    John, 110
    Jonathan, 110
    Mary, 110
    Nehemiah, 84
    Sarah, 110
Crane, Frances Elizabeth, 236
    J. Henry, 248
    William Henry, 236
Crawford, Alexander, 72, 88
    Lucy, 72
Creeber, Alice, 123
Crockett, John, 147, 177
    Joshua, 131
    Martha D., 248
    Mary, 82
Cromwell, Ann, 4
    Dorothy, 35
    Eliphalet, 35
    Elizabeth, 4, 199
    John, 11, 110, 189
    Mercy, 131
    Philip, 4, 199
    Rachel, 35, 136
    Samuel, 32, 35, 136
    Sarah, 79, 112
Crook, Susan, 213
Crosby, Asa F., 249
    Cornelia, 63
    Daniel, 140
    Elizabeth, 140
    Hannah, 8
    Harriet, 63, 213
    Henrietta, 63
    John, 8
    Jonathan, 8, 135, 140
    Oliver, 63, 213
    Sarah, 8, 135
    William Chase, 63
Cross, Alexander, 262
    Belinda, 184
Crawley, Hannah, 262
Crown, Agnes, 109
    Alice, 109
    Elizabeth, 109
    Henry, 109
    John, 109
    Rebecca, 109
    William, 109
Cunningham, Ellen, 260
    Michael, 262
Currell, Margaret, 174
Currier, Ann, 100
    Elizabeth C., 184
    Jacob, 63
    Jacob M., 63, 64, 202
    John, 64
    John L., 100
    Samuel, 95
    Sarah, 64
    Sarah C., 257
    Thomas, 64
Curtis, Benjamin F., 101
    Caroline, 227
    Daniel, 256
    James M., 181
Cushing, ——110, 164
    Asenath, 229
    Caroline, 182
    Daniel, 83
    Deborah, 134
    Eliza, 226
    Elizabeth, 59, 137, 206
    Hannah, 78, 85, 138, 175, 225
    James, 207
    John, 59
Cushing, Jonathan, 6, 7, 11, 12, 40, 41, 42, 44, 48, 50, 51, 56, 59, 133, 134, 206, 225, 226
    Jonathan H., 215
    Lydia Abigail, 230
    Lydia W., 179
    Mary, 200
    Mary H., 216
    Nancy, 220
    Peter, 59, 82, 88, 133, 191, 214
    Robert H., 218
    Samuel W., 229
    Sarah A., 183
    Thomas, 79, 220
    William, 135, 220
Cushman, J. H., 226
Cutt, Eleanor, 110, 121
    Elizabeth, 108
    Hannah, 108
    John, 108, 110
    Margaret, 125
    Mary, 108, 121
    Samuel, 108, 110
Cutter, Charles W., 77
Cutting, Azro P., 243
Dalton, Samuel, 114
Dame, Abigail, 37, 110, 123, 128
    Abner, 161
    Alice, 110
    Ann, 90, 248
    Anna, 200
    Calvin, 246
    Charles, 219
    Elizabeth, 110
    Hannah S., 250
    John, 36, 110, 217, 224
    Jonathan, 161
    Joseph, 150, 232
    Judith, 110
    Leah, 2, 11
    Martha, 2, 130
    Mary, 110, 150
    Mehitable, 226
    Mehitable B., 232
    Phebe, 251
    Pomfret, 2, 131, 142
    Samuel, 2, 185
    Sarah, 2, 36, 37, 173
    Susanna, 110
    Theophilus, 202, 212
    Thomas, 80
    William, 2, 36, 37, 110, 131
Daniels, Abigail, 148
    Anna, 80, 172
    Bridget, 112
    David, 145, 150, 151, 153, 155
    Eliphalet, 145
    Eliza, 246
    Jacob, 173
    Jane, 43
    Joanna, 145
    John, 43, 153
    Joseph, 43, 135, 148, 155, 231
    Mehitable, 148
    Nathaniel, 145
    Obadiah, 148
    Pelatiah, 148
    Samuel, 148
    Solomon, 151, 155
Danielson, Arthur, 144, 151
    Hannah, 151
    Levi, 144
    Lydia, 144
    Mary, 144
    Sarah,
Danforth, —— 108
    Elizabeth, 187

INDEX OF PERSONS.

Danvers, James, 260
Darling, Harriet Elizabeth, 237
Davidson, ——210
Davis, Aaron, 78, 175
  Anna, 147
  Constant, 157
  Daniel, 46, 154, 156
  Ebenezer, 29
  Eleazer, 151, 153, 172, 237, 249
  Elijah, 155
  Elizabeth, 39, 46, 47, 157, 207
  Ephraim, 154
  Francis, 156
  Hannah, 110, 149, 154, 172
  Jabez, 204
  James, 7, 8, 32, 36, 39, 46, 47, 110,
    139, 151, 153, 154, 155, 158, 181,
    207, 227
  James H., 255
  Jane, 48, 110
  Joanna, 111
  Joanna M., 250
  John, 47, 80, 110, 111, 153, 158
  Jonathan, 81, 146
  Jonathan J., 104
  Joseph, 110
  Judith, 100
  Lavina Powers, 235
  Leonard, 256
  Lydia, 227
  Lydia Sherburne, 229
  Martha J. P., 252
  Mary, 46, 111, 153, 240
  Moses, 29, 110, 256
  Nancy, 227
  Nathaniel, 147, 149, 153, 155
  Newell C., 249
  Olive F., 99
  Reuannah, 29
  Ruth, 39, 46, 139, 207
  Samuel, 141, 146, 151, 153, 157, 240.
  Sarah, 153
  Stephen, 182, 227
  Thomas, 46, 141, 155
  Timothy, 111
  William H., 226
  Zervia, 156
Dawley, Huland, 185
Dealand, ⎰ Sarah, 104
Deland,   ⎱ Ursula, 102
  William, 104
Dealing, Maria, 94
Dean, Benjamin, 197
  Eliza Ann, 242
  Elizabeth, 212, 242
  Nathaniel Benjamin, 242
Dearborn, Hannah, 111
  Henry, 216
  Jonathan, 111
  Levi, 83
  Naomi, 244
  Thomas, 111
Deere, George, 100
DeJean, Eugene, 250
Delaney, Joseph, 235
  Sarah, 255
Demeritt, Abigail, 146
  Anna, 148
  Benjamin, 20
  Daniel, 161
  Deborah, 141
  Ebenezer, 80, 147, 155, 156, 157, 161,
    162, 164, 165, 166, 210
  Ebenezer T., 180
  Eleanor, 183
  Eli, 20, 143, 147
  Eliza, 166, 177

Demeritt, Eliza H., 186
  Elizabeth, 254
  Hannah, 162, 210
  Hannah T., 180
  Hopestill, 20
  Jacob J., 99
  Jeremy, 165
  Job, 20, 141, 143, 146
  John, 141, 143, 146
  Jonathan, 157
  Joseph, 146
  Lydia, 155, 173
  Mary J., 245
  Nathaniel, 248
  Oliver Cromwell, 225
  Paul, 143
  Samuel, 20
  Sarah, 147, 164
  Susan, 103
  Susanna, 80, 156
  Tabitha, 20
  William, 148, 209
Deming, R. H., 98
Denmark, Hannah, 111
  James, 111
  Patrick, 111
Dennett, Amy, 111
  Anna, 111
  Elizabeth, 111
  Ephraim, 111
  Hannah, 111
  John, 111
  Joseph, 111
  Lydia, 111
Dennis, James, 217
Derrigan, Michael, 262
Devitt, Mary, 261
Dexter, Eliza A. S., 258
Dilhanty, James, 261
Dimon, Maria, 94
Dinsmore, Cynthia Verrill, 220
  Solomon, 177
Dittey, Mary 141
  Sarah, 144
Dixon, Hannah, 130
  James, 183, 219, 223
  Lydia, 219,
Dockham, Catherine, 258
Doe, Caroline, 220
  Elizabeth, 111
  John, 111
  Joseph, 96
  Martha, 111
  Mary Ann, 222
  Nicholas, 111
  Ruth, 180
  Samson. 111
Doherty, Grace, 260
  Margaret, 262
  Richard, 260
Dolan, Michael, 262
Donahoe, Anthony, 260
  Bridget, 261
Donnelly, Ellen, 262
Donovan, Michael, 259
Doran, Patrick, 259
Dore,——,201
  Elizabeth. 101
  Frances, 181
  Henry, 92
  Jonathan, 173
  Margaret, 244
  Mary, 129
  Wentworth, 98
  William, 193
Dorr, Eliza, 249
Dorset, Mary, 81

INDEX OF PERSONS.

Douglass, John, 111, 128
Douse, Anna, 111
    Joanna, 111
    John, 111
    Ozem, 111
    Samuel, 111
    Solomon, 111
    Susanna, 111
Dow, Abigail, 111
    Hannah, 227
    Jabez, 227
    John, G., 95, 97
    Joseph, 111
    Mary, 111, 129
    Samuel, 111
    Sarah, 111
    Simon, 111
Downing, Ebenezer, 213
    Mary, 183
    Mary, H., 95
    Palfrey, 92
    Palfrey W., 219
Downs, Aaron, 175
    Abigail, 30
    Anne, 30, 246
    Catherine, 110
    Dorcas, 215
    Edmund, 87
    Elizabeth, 29, 110, 183
    Eunice, 173
    Gershom, 6, 131, 133, 134, 135, 138, 142, 256
    Hannah, P., 251
    James M., 250
    John, 134
    Joseph, 142
    Martha, 6, 134
    Mary, 29, 31, 110, 128, 187
    Mercy, 30
    Patience, 30,
    Paul, 142
    Phebe, 136
    Pomfret, 174
    Rebecca, 134
    Richard, 135
    Samuel, 31, 136, 182
    Sarah, 6, 29, 30, 138
    Thomas, 6, 29, 30, 110, 130, 134, 138
    William, 11, 31, 136, 138, 186
Drake, Abraham, 111
    Abram M., 251
    Guy, 183
    Sarah, 111
Draper, Caroline, R., 187, 216
    Hannah C., 216
    Hannah Rogers, 227
    Lemuel, 216
    William Cutter, 218
Drew, Abigail, 20, 107, 149
    Abigail B., 99, 222
    Ann, 6, 38, 133
    Anne Ellzabeth, 258
    Benajah, 151
    Clement, 8
    Daniel, 172
    Elijah, 146, 192
    Eliza, 254
    Elizabeth, 28, 91, 145, 247
    Elizabeth W., 244
    Elsa O., 97, 101
    Francis, 20, 28, 38, 145, 146, 151, 153, 179
    Hannah, 11, 20
    James, 230, 247
    Jeremiah, 187, 200
    Joanna, 204
    John, 8, 20, 28, 131, 146

Drew, Joseph, 38, 82, 133, 146, 152, 154
    Julia Ann, 247
    Lemuel, 20
    Lois, 80, 145
    Lydia, 81
    Maria, 180, 221
    Martha, 243
    Martha Abigail, 235
    Mary, 92, 98, 152
    Mary E. N., 96
    Mary L., 248
    Mary P., 257
    Meshech, 149
    Nancy M., 257
    Nathaniel, 257
    Nicholas, 202
    Patience, 39, 146, 149
    Rebecca, 20
    Sarah, 131, 148
    Sarah C., 246
    Sophia, 181
    Tamson, 84
    William, 256
    William P., 180, 182
    William Pickering, 186
    William Plaisted, 221
    Zebulon, 20
Drisco, Sarah, 131
Drown, Elizabeth, 142
    Maria J., 96, 222
    Samuel, 142
Dudley, Clarissa, 182, 215
    Orin, 104
Duncan, Abraham, 242
    Charlotte Margaret, 242
    Mary, 242
Dunn, Ann, 103
    Jane, 258
    John, 97
    Samuel, 256
Duplesis, Henry, 198
Durant, James, 84
Durell, Charles James Fox, 66
    Daniel Meserve, 66
    Elizabeth, 66
    Elizabeth Slater, 66
    Mary Jane, 66
    Nicholas St. John, 66
    Sarah A., 183
    Sarah Adeline, 66
Durgin, Louisa M., 99
    Walter, 94
Dwyer, Elizabeth, 79
Dyer, Hannah, 129
    James, 260
Earle, Frances, 178
    Relief, 85
Eastman, Miriam, 124
Eastwick, Nathaniel, 112
    Phesant, 112
    Sarah, 112
Eaton, Philip, 136, 153
Eddy, Abraham, 246
Edgecomb, James, 190
Edgerly, Daniel, 144
    Elizabeth, 34
    John, 141
    Sarah 94
    Thomas, 112
    Zechariah, 141, 144
Edson, Emily, 96
Ela, Benjamin, 73
    Caroline, 73
    Charles, 73
    Esther, 73, 88
    George, 73
    John Furnald, 73

INDEX OF PERSONS. 275

Nathaniel, 73
Nathaniel Whittier, 72, 73, 201, 204
Ruth, 73
Susanna, 73
Elkins, Hester, 117, 128
Ellingworth, Joseph, 260
Ellins, Margaret, 116
Elliot,——202
    Andrew, 54
    Deborah, 254
    Elizabeth, 84, 125
    Henry, 227
    Henry S., 183
    Moses, 85
    Russ H F., 94
    Ruth, 54
    Sarah, 211
    Sarah Ann, 227
Ellis,——, 193
    Simeon, 185
Ellison, James, 247
    Statira A., 89
    Susan, 244
Emerson, Abigail, 3, 57, 82, 140, 142, 161
    Ann, 181
    Benjamin, 155
    Daniel E., 249
    Deborah, 57, 81, 162, 186
    Dorothy, 56, 211
    Edward Winslow, 158
    Elizabeth, 142, 238
    Elizabeth M., 245
    Esther, 72, 73
    Hannah, 3, 56, 79, 138, 140, 157, 173
    Jeremiah, 251
    John, 151
    Jonathan, 155
    Joseph, 57, 144, 166
    Judith, 3
    Lydia J., 252
    Mary, 56, 78, 140, 159, 175
    Mary A., 249
    Micah, 3, 57, 82. 138, 140, 142, 160
    Moses, 158, 211
    Phillis, 174
    Samuel, 3, 56, 57, 141, 146, 155, 157, 159, 160, 161, 162, 164, 165, 166, 193, 200, 211
    Sarah, 56, 144, 155
    Solomon, 142, 144, 146, 151, 155, 174
    Susan, 180
    Timothy, 140, 141, 142, 144
    William, 57, 165
Emery, Eliza P., 101
    Elizabeth, 97, 119
    Frances, 11
    Job, 214
    John, 182
    Kezia, 93
    Olive J., 255
    Oliver, H., 93
    Rhoda, 285
    Sarah, 89
Estabrook, Joseph E., 227
Estes,——, 189, 192, 199
    Abigail K., 100
    Caleb, 195
    Caroline, 225
    Caroline Elizabeth, 230, 254
    Elijah, 195
    Elizabeth, 61, 176
    Israel, 61, 180, 225, 230
    Jane Mary, 254
    Mary, 61
    Olive, 61
    Robert, 61
    Samuel, 61, 82, 196

Estes, Sarah, 181
    William F., 193
Evans,——190, 203
    Abigail, 236
    Ann, 16, 134, 206
    Benjamin, 16, 17, 35, 56, 148, 162, 174, 189, 211
    Charles, 236
    Daniel, 23, 191
    Dorcas, 3
    Edward, 3, 112
    Eleanor, 3
    Elizabeth, 17, 112, 163, 166
    Ephraim, 155, 167, 173
    Eunice, 179, 222
    Frances, 94, 218
    George, 171
    Hannah, 16, 132, 238
    Hosea, 94
    Ichabod Chesley, 167
    John, 23, 236
    John L., 222
    John Leighton, 231
    Jonathan, 17, 112
    Joseph, 3, 16, 17, 23, 131, 148, 155, 158, 175, 200, 209
    Julia, 174
    Lois, 182
    Lydia, 166
    Martha, 167
    Mary, 17, 23, 35, 79, 115, 148, 156, 159
    Mary A., 248
    Mercy, 23, 149
    Miles, 177, 200
    Nathaniel, 82
    Patience, 16. 128, 173
    Phebe, 156
    Rachel, 3
    Robert, 16, 23, 112
    Sarah, 16, 164, 175
    Stephen, 35, 148, 155, 156, 158 159, 162, 163, 164, 166, 167, 174, 209
    Temperance, 166
    Thomas, 112
    William, 23
Everson,——200
    Hannah, 176
    Mary, 171
Ewers,——, 199
Eyres, see Ayers
Eystick, Richard, 190
Fabian, John, 130
Fagin, Henry, 262
Fall) Louisa Maria, 238
Falls) Lydia F., 100
    Thomas, 99
Farewell,——, 198
    Isaac, 171
Farnham,——, 235
    Abigail, 90
    Joseph, 11
    Martha, 239
    Samuel W., 238
Farniside, Hannah, 215
Farnsworth, Asa, 220, 231
    Elizabeth, 220
    Mary Ellen, 231
Fawley, James, 261
Faxon, Ebenezer, 97, 221, 229
    Olive, 229
Feeney, Catherine, 260
Fernald,) Clement, 170
Furnel,) John, 201
    Martha H., 99
    Mary, 120
    Nathaniel, 130
    Oliver, 248

INDEX OF PERSONS.

Furnel, Robert, C., 250
 Sarah, 117
Field, Abigail, 130, 152
 Benjamin, 79
 Daniel, 18
 Elizabeth, 116
 Hannah, 18
 John, 131, 188
 Joseph, 173
 Mary, 131
 Sarah, 172
 Zecharias, 18, 132
Fifield, Benjamin, 112
 Mary, 112, 114
 Mehitable, 112
Filierty, Mary, 260
 Patrick, 260
Finn, Thomas, 261
Fisher, Janvrin, 195, 201
 Jonathan, 241
 Priscilla, 177
 Sarah, 198, 241
 Silas, 184
Fiske, Charles A., 254
 Moses, 185, 260
 Sarah, 212
 William J, 212
Fitts, Nathaniel, 11
Fitzgerald, Daniel, 171
Flagg, Arlo, 223, 225
 Esther D., 223
 Harriet T., 228
 James M., 224
 Lucy, 222
 Rufus, 221, 222
Flanders, ——, 238
 John, 89
Flannigan, John, 262
 Timothy, 260
Flood, Martha, 84
Flynn, Edmund, 260
 Patrick, 261
 Peter, 259
 Thomas, 261
Fogg, John, 257
Fonett, Abigail, 129
 Deborah, 147
 Hannah, 3
 Ichabod, 147
 Nicholas, 3, 112
 Samuel, 112
Folsom, Abigail, 213
 Abigail Smith, 232
 Abraham, 232, 257
 Benjamin, 178
 Henry, 184
 Isaac L., 183
 Josiah, 78, 175, 189, 202
Foot, James L., 216, 219
 Margaret, 219
Footman, Hannah, 86
 John, 112
 Joseph, 100
 Rebecca S., 214
 Susanna, 200
 Thomas, 80, 193, 194
Ford, John, 131
 Mary Jane, 182
 Rachel, 183
 Susan D., 94
Foss,) Benjamin, 81, 136, 141, 207
Faus,) Catherine, 189
Faust,) Chadbourne, 40, 140
 D. W., 99
 Daniel, 140
 Eliza, 183
 Eliza A., 249

Faust, Elizabeth, 81
 Elizabeth L., 217
 Elizabeth R., 100
 George, 80, 84
 George L., 217
 Hannah J, 91
 Humphrey, 134
 Jeremiah, 80
 John, 40
 Joshua, 154
 Lois, 91
 Lucretia, S., 102
 Lydia, 5, 136, 143, 180
 Margaret, 136
 Mary, 40, 139, 141, 179
 Nathan, 157
 Samuel, 219
 Sarah, 5, 154
 Stephen, 157
 Sylvina H., 102
 William, 5, 40, 130, 136, 139, 140,
   143, 190, 191, 198, 209
Foster, Elijah, 94
 Herschel, 89
Fox, Samuel W., 185
Foye, Ann, 100
 John, 144
 Lydia, 244
Frederick, Aaron K., 93
Freeman, Aaron H., 250
 Abby A., 255
 Asa, 179, 214, 254
 Franklin, 250
 George, 246
 Sarah Huntington, 254
French, ——, 228
 Chase W., 178
 Eli, 223, 227
 Elizabeth, 97
 Increase, 222
 John A., 235
 Joseph Y., 258
 Mary Elizabeth, 235
 Sarah, 43
 Susan, 92
Friend, John, 194, 204
 Phebe, 171
Frost, ——, 112
 Hannah, 179
 Lucinda S., 249
 Margaret, 182
 Olive T., 243
Fry,) Adrian, 131
Frye,) Charles G., 246
 Elizabeth, 130
 Ivory, 89
 Statira Ann, 220
 William, 220, 256
Fuller, Lucinda, 104
Fullington, Jane, 165
 Mary, 165
Fulton, Robert, 187
Furber, Elizabeth, 110, 112
 Jethro, 244
 Mark L., 98
 Mary, 95
 Mary Jane, 244
 Samuel, 78, 175
 Susanna, 112
 William, 112, 129
Furbush, John, 183
 Sarah, 56
Gafney, Catherine, 261
Gage, Caesar, 201
 Dover, 199
 Eliza, 179
 Elizabeth, 55, 173

INDEX OF PERSONS.

Gage, Hannah, 55, 79, 169, 212
John, 57, 141, 143, 172, 188, 194, 200, 201, 202
Jonathan, 50, 55, 56, 141, 179, 180, 203
Joseph, 68, 204
Joseph Hanson, 55
Lois, 82
Lydia, 81
Margaret, 55
Martha, 95, 221
Mary, 68, 80, 178, 201
Moses, 141, 204, 237, 246
Rebecca, 55
Samuel, 221
Samuel F., 182
Sophia, 183
Susanna, 55, 80
Tamson, 204
William, 143, 203
Gahan, Joanna, 262
Gale, Daniel R., 185, 221
Galloway, Mary, 256
Garland, ——, 190
Abigail, 21, 37
Anna, 82, 175, 178
Dodavah, 37
Dorcas, 1, 2, 11
Ebenezer, 1, 11, 37
Eliza, 183
Elizabeth, 11, 112, 225
Hannah, 37
Jabez, 1, 2, 21
Jacob, 174, 183
Jeremiah, 79
John, 81
Lydia, 2
Mary, 176
Nathaniel, 2, 80, 148, 176, 225
Olive Furber, 228
Peter, 112
Rebecca, 1
Reuben, 21
Samuel, 185
Sarah, 81
Garmine, Elizabeth, 129
Garr, Mary, 259
Patrick, 259
Garvin, Elizabeth, 96
John, 182
Gear, Anna, 174
Gideon, 189
Isaac, 257
Rebecca, 79
Gellett, Susan W., 259
Gentleman, Martha Jane, 241
George, Alice, 248
Josiah, 79
Gerald, see Jerrill.
Gerrish, ——, 148, 142, 202
Abigail, 41, 134, 158
Andrew, 41, 50, 156, 157, 158, 160
Anna, 41, 133
Benjamin, 39, 41, 42, 140, 143
Dorothy, 153
Edward F., 256
Eleanor, 81, 157
Elizabeth, 38, 41, 50, 129, 154, 156, 171, 208
Eunice, 49, 155, 159
George, 42, 143
Hannah, 50, 81, 156, 170
James Tobey, 49, 160
Jane, 41
Joanna, 209
John, 7, 42, 43, 141, 143, 145, 148, 151, 153, 208
Jonathan, 38, 49, 136, 159, 160, 162

Gerrish, Joseph, 41, 50, 157, 177, 181
Lucy, 80, 160, 210
Lydia, 38, 139, 155, 171
Margaret, 42, 43, 148, 162, 208
Martha, 162
Mary, 38, 39, 42, 49, 54, 134, 151, 155, 156, 159, 173, 207
Mary A., 258
Nancy, 49, 159
Nathaniel, 135
Paul, 2, 38, 39, 42, 54, 81, 134, 135, 138, 139, 140, 143, 151, 155, 158, 193, 205, 207
Primus, 149
Robert Elliot, 7
S., 202
Samuel, 38, 134, 154, 155, 156, 157, 159, 160, 161, 189, 210, 230, 254
Sarah, 7, 8, 41, 42, 50, 145, 156, 158, 160, 161, 180
Sarah M., 254
Susanna, 135
Thomas, 155
Timothy, 7, 8, 41, 50, 133, 134, 135, 151, 152, 158
Venus, 148
William, 41, 134, 151, 152, 155, 158, 181, 256
Gerry, Samuel, 102
Gibbs, John T., 258
Giddes, William, 36
Gile,) Daniel C., 187
Guile,) John H., 182, 221
Mary Ann, 97
Susan L., 184
Giles, Abigail, 14
Ann, 14
Elizabeth, 55
Esther, 14
Hannah, 228
John, 10, 130
Joseph, 55
Lydia, 55
Mark, 14, 55, 130
Mary, 10
Paul, 14, 55
Sarah, 14
Gilligan, John, 260
Gilman, Abigail T., 223
Ann, 83
Bridget, 173
Clarissa, 91
E., 233
Ebenezer, 101
Eliza, 83, 190, 223
Elizabeth, 55, 221
Elizabeth S., 253
Esther, 239
George, 257
Hannah Phillips, 75, 189
Jesse, 182
Joanna, 83
John P., 75, 83, 221
Lorenzo, 238
Mary, 224, 234
Mary Ann, 83
Mary Jane, 218
Nathaniel, 224, 234
Sarah, 83, 172
Sarah Phillips, 85
Susan C., 218
Ward E., 249
Gilpatrick, John, 101
Gleason, Hiram, 104
Glidden, Deborah, 157
Elizabeth, 48
Mary, 93
William, 157

278　　　　　　　　　　INDEX OF PERSONS.

Glidden, William B., 249
Glines, Albon, 101
　　　　John, 38, 39
Glover, Richard, 147
Goodrich, Abigail, 256
　　　　　Lydia, 93
Goodwin, ——, 192
　　　　　Abigail, 30, 31
　　　　　Albion, 252
　　　　　Amy, 31
　　　　　Armenia, 217
　　　　　Daniel, 30, 31, 94
　　　　　Edward, 259
　　　　　Elizabeth, 134
　　　　　Fidelia Abbott, 238
　　　　　Hannah, 137
　　　　　James, 31
　　　　　Jeremiah, 180
　　　　　Lemuel, 246
　　　　　Lydia, 30
　　　　　Mary, 31
　　　　　Richard, 134, 135, 137, 221
　　　　　Sarah, 31
　　　　　Sarah P., 101
　　　　　Susan, 227
　　　　　Thomas, 98
　　　　　Uriah, 203
Gordon, Ebenezer, 184
　　　　James Munroe, 253
　　　　Mary, 224
Gorman, Bridget, 259
Goss, Robert, 129
Gotham, David, 91, 184
Goudy, Thomas, 204
Gould, ——, 198
　　　　Isaiah, 201
　　　　John, 215, 226
　　　　Joseph, 183
　　　　Mary, 215
Gove, Rebecca Jane, 248
Gowell, Sarah, 227
Gowen, Mary, 171
　　　　Thomas A., 183
Gratfort, Thomas, 112
Graham, Henry V., 91
Grant, Edwin, 240
　　　　Eli, 95
　　　　Elizabeth, 240
　　　　Joseph L., 239, 240
　　　　Rebecca, 94
　　　　Sarah Ann, 89
　　　　William, 129
Graves, Francis, 128
　　　　Philena, 96
Gray, Abby H., 247
　　　　Abigail, 199, 241
　　　　Dorothy, 244
　　　　Elizabeth, 242
　　　　Elizabeth W., 104
　　　　George, 185
　　　　George W., 246, 248
　　　　Jeremiah, 172, 245
　　　　Lydia, 199, 203, 241, 242
　　　　Martha, 182
　　　　Martha Tufts, 242
　　　　Oliver Crosley, 242
　　　　Peter, 241
　　　　Robert, 63, 84, 199, 241, 242
　　　　Sarah C., 180
　　　　Thomas, 99
　　　　William H., 249
Greeley, Jonathan, 85
Green, ——, 109, 117, 123, 191
　　　　Charles, 169
　　　　Deborah, 213
　　　　Deborah Shackford, 341
　　　　Esther, 118

Green, Eunice, 168, 213, 242
　　　　Ezra, 80, 168, 169, 195, 197, 198, 199, 211, 212, 213, 241, 242
　　　　Henry, 129
　　　　James D., 183
　　　　John, 112
　　　　Lucy Ann, 222
　　　　Martha, 242
　　　　Reuben Hayes, 168
　　　　Samuel, 242
　　　　Sarah, 213, 241
　　　　Silas, 244
　　　　Susanna, 212, 241, 242
　　　　Walter Cooper, 242
Greenough, Daniel, 138
　　　　Mary, 138
Greward, Lucy H., 248
Grieve, Margaret, 183
Griffin, Abner C., 228
　　　　George Graham, 75
　　　　Hannah, 122
　　　　Olive, 75
　　　　Olive Minnort, 75
　　　　William E., 184
　　　　William H., 75
Griffith, Caleb, 112
　　　　Edward, 112
　　　　Gershom, 112
　　　　Joshua, 112
Grimes, Peter, 261
　　　　Thomas, 259
Groudy, Nathaniel, 90
Guilford, Orlo, 91
Gullison, Elihu, 112
Guppey, ——, 193, 197
　　　　Abigail, 90
　　　　Emily, 258
　　　　George F., 102
　　　　Hannah, 175
　　　　J., 204
　　　　James, 166, 168
　　　　James B., 102
　　　　Jeremy, 168
　　　　John, 90
　　　　Mary, 168
　　　　Oliver, 244
　　　　Samuel, 166
　　　　Sarah Ann, 257
　　　　Sophia, 168
　　　　Thomas B., 247
Guptill, Moses, 96
　　　　Robert, 96
Guy, Anne, 254
Hackin, Bridget, 261
Hadley, Andrew Quincy, 73
　　　　David F., 72
　　　　Hannah, 72, 73
　　　　James N., 72, 73
　　　　Louisa, 257
Haggens, Elizabeth, 71
Haines, see Haynes
Hale, Aroet Lucius Little, 76
　　　　Elizabeth, 215, 256
　　　　Jonathan H., 76
　　　　Joseph W., 180
　　　　Martha, 256
　　　　Mary Ann, 179
　　　　Olive, 76
　　　　Samuel, 180, 208
　　　　Thomas Wright, 81
　　　　William, 201, 256
Haley, John B., 280
　　　　Rhoda M., 91
Hall, ——, 164
　　　　Abigail, 25, 56, 114, 130, 147, 152
　　　　Alfred, 245
　　　　Andrew, 56, 256

INDEX OF PERSONS.   279

Hall, Angelina, 235
       Anna, 70, 140
       Benjamin, 51, 147, 151
       Bethia, 139
       Daniel, 56, 149
       Diana, 92
       Dorothy, 56
       Ebenezer, 56, 81
       Elizabeth, 3, 7, 113, 121, 128, 131,
           148, 173, 179, 248
       Elizabeth M., 246
       Esther, 25
       Federal B., 251
       Frances, 51, 147, 148
       Grace, 113
       Hannah, 142, 155
       Hatevil, 56, 131
       Isaac, 147
       Jedediah, 56
       John, 6, 7, 36, 56, 113, 114, 131, 147
       John S., 102
       Joseph, 25, 36, 40, 131, 138, 140, 142,
           144, 147, 148, 149, 152, 154, 155,
           191, 193, 207
       Josiah, 99, 218, 253
       Lois, 148
       Mark, 181
       Mary, 36, 40, 113, 142, 245
       Mercy, 56
       Moses, 98
       Nicholas, 56
       Patience, 100
       Peniel, 174, 207
       Prudence, 185
       Ralph, 40, 113, 130, 148
       Rhoda A., 90
       Samuel, 51, 151, 154, 173, 181
       Sarah, 6, 7, 36, 56, 113, 131, 134
       Sarah Jane, 220
       Solomon, 148
       Stacy, 187
       Thomas, 36, 114
       William, 56
Halligan, William, 226
Hallowell, Rebecca, 112
Halpin, Ann, 260
Ham,   Aaron, 141, 162, 163
        Abigail, 15, 98, 138, 154, 182, 199
        Abigail Dame, 217
        Ann,   } 15, 141, 143, 151, 154
        Anna, }
        B., 197, 199
        Benjamin, 11, 15, 21, 79, 143, 144,
            155, 191, 200
        Caroline, 180
        Charles, 184, 217
        Clarissa M., 96, 217
        Clement, 15, 147, 152, 153, 172, 208
        Daniel, 15, 85, 145, 146, 150, 153, 154,
            155, 157, 160, 162, 2 8
        David, 175, 192
        Deborah, 200
        Dodavah, 9, 148, 168, 172, 212
        Dudley, 168
        Ebenezer, 142, 167, 172
        Eliza, 228, 245
        Eliza B., 183
        Elizabeth, 9, 15, 80, 114, 138, 154,
            155, 166, 172, 177, 179, 211
        Ephraim, 82, 141, 143, 144, 151, 153,
            154, 155, 178, 212, 227, 242
        G., 205
        George, 205
        George Jefferds, 166
        Hannah, 84, 183, 187, 211, 227
        Harriet, 180
        Ichabod, 144, 199

Ham,   Israel, 82, 143
        James, 203
        Jane, 15, 135, 152, 157
        Jeremy Wheelwright, 166
        Joanna, 9, 155, 162
        John, 9, 113, 114, 130, 138, 139, 140,
            142, 143, 145, 150, 154, 156, 168,
            189-193, 243
        John Coffin, 161
        John H., 244
        Jonathan, 15, 147, 152, 153, 154
        Joseph, 15, 103, 114, 135, 146, 161
        Joshua, 141, 183, 227, 235, 242
        Lucy, 250
        Lucy C., 249
        Lydia, 82, 144, 162, 163, 168, 184, 212,
            225, 242
        Margaret, 183
        Mary, 9, 15, 21, 81, 114, 139, 143, 160,
            181, 187
        Mary D., 250
        Mary Jane, 218
        Mehitable, 239
        Moses, 141, 239
        Nathaniel, 9, 166, 167, 168, 171, 172,
            211
        Olive, 235
        Patience, 9, 15, 21, 143, 144, 156
        Paul, 145, 160
        Ruth, 181, 187
        Samuel, 9, 98, 104, 144, 163, 165, 166,
            167, 168, 170, 176, 180, 191, 225
        Sarah, 81, 152, 155, 162, 163, 208, 248
        Sarah Baker, 235
        Sarah F., 187
        Sarah Jane, 239
        Sarah V., 257
        Seth W., 184
        Shadrach, 145
        Stephen, 144
        Susan, 183, 227
        Susanna, 80, 153
        Tamson, 15, 135, 139
        Thomas, 150, 154, 189
        Thomas T., 99
        Titus, 87
        Walter, 220
        William, 15, 148, 166, 193
        Zoah Hillard, 178
Hamick, Thomas, 174
Hamilton, David, 114
          Jonathan, 114
          Solomon, 114
Hammack, John, 48
Hammott, Elizabeth Pearl, 216
Hanniford, Olive, 257
Hanscom, Alpheus Augustus, 230
         Daniel, 231
         Lorenzo, 248
         Thomas, 183
Hanson, ——, 148, 188, 189, 204
        Abby J., 258
        Abigail, 17, 29, 64, 75, 81, 132, 156,
            159, 176
        Abijah, 62, 152
        Abraham, 50, 81
        Ahijah, 191
        Albee, 244
        Albert Franklin, 66
        Amos, 62
        Ann,   } 3, 28, 43, 49, 166, 214
        Anna, }
        Anthony, 156, 172, 192
        Bathsheba, 49, 50, 155, 171
        Benjamin, 28, 139, 157, 158, 160, 162,
            170, 180, 194, 209, 224
        Bridget, 49, 170

INDEX OF PERSONS.

Hanson, Caleb, 13
Charles, 180
Cato, 167
Clarissa Jane, 75, 180
Corydon, 165, 199
Daniel, 13, 59
David, 158
David S., 91
Dinah, 165
Dominicus, 55, 59, 63, 64, 65, 66, 67, 68, 69, 70, 85, 86
Ebenezer, 11, 13, 157, 159, 160, 162, 163, 165, 166, 191, 195
Eliza, 91, 92
Elizabeth, 13, 28, 39, 50, 53, 55, 59, 61, 83, 84, 137, 142, 156, 159, 173, 204, 207
Enoch, 162
Ephraim, 44, 50, 51, 52, 53, 82, 139, 157, 291
Esther, 28, 78, 175
Eunice, 199
Ezra, 62
Francis, 179
George, 28, 172, 194
Hannah, 10, 11, 13, 29, 45, 53, 59, 64, 79, 82, 157, 173, 176, 213
Horatio G., 182, 236
Humphrey, 44, 55, 59, 83, 144
Isaac, 13, 47, 115
Israel, 49, 151, 204
Israel T., 216
Ivory, 65
J., 214
Jacob, 59, 151, 172
James, 79, 142
Jeremiah, 247
Joanna, 50, 55, 83, 156
John, 13, 68, 80, 139, 192, 201
John Burnham, 44, 57, 59, 82, 83, 190, 195
John T., 176
Jonathan, 81, 147, 169, 192
Joseph, 3, 28, 43, 44, 18, 49, 50, 51, 55, 59, 75, 90, 139, 141, 149, 188, 201, 217
Josiah, 147
Kezia, 51, 174
Lois, 53
Lydia, 65, 66, 79, 139
Lydia Rotch, 65
M., 201
Margaret, 43, 50, 51
Martha, 17, 39, 191
Mary, 17, 28, 49, 69, 64, 66, 79, 82, 115, 118, 142, 156, 157, 168, 170, 177, 191, 211
Mary Ann, 65, 66, 181
Mary Ann H., 88
Mary Ellen, 70
Mary L., 255
Maul, 200
Mercy, 68, 130
Miriam, 53, 198
Moses, 83
Nahum, 178
Nancy, 203
Nathaniel, 17, 39
Pamelia, 65, 183
Patience, 53
Paul, 17, 39
Peter, 165, 166, 197, 196, 211
Phebe, 68, 186
Philip, 149
Phillis, 166, 197
Pierce, 189
Rebecca, 44, 59, 207

Hanson, Rhoda, 165
Richard, 233
Robert, 59, 81
Rose, 174
Ruth, 208
Samuel, 43, 68, 152, 184
Samuel H., 94
Sarah, 13, 44, 53, 54, 55, 59, 62, 79, 80, 82, 169, 202, 203, 212, 241
Sarah Ann, 89, 217
Sarah Jane, 228
Shadrach, 165
Silas, 39, 188
Solomon, 10, 43, 191
Sophia, 179, 180
Stephen, 62, 65, 66, 70, 97
Susan, 59
Susanna, 44, 59, 60, 62
Thomas, 10, 11, 29, 43, 53, 64, 142, 165, 166, 188, 191, 199, 211
Thomas R., 182, 215
Timothy, 54, 139
Tobias, 3, 43, 48, 130
William, 28, 49, 59, 101, 149, 151, 154, 155, 156, 157, 159, 171, 189, 191, 208, 212, 241, 248
William Hodgdon, 236
William Rotch, 65
Venus, 138, 165, 166
Zaccheus, 43, 62, 189
Harby, Fidellah, 134
Hardy, Mary A., 103
Sarah F. E., 255
Harold, John, 262
Harper, Richard P., 253
Harriden, Henry, 90
Harrigan, Ellen, 261
Margaret, 261
Harriman, Elizabeth, 244
Harrington, Dennis, 260
Patrick, 260
Harris, Lydia B., 184
Hart, Jane, 115
John, 115
Joseph, 115
Mary, 115
Matilda, 182
Robert, 115
Samuel, 115
Sarah, 115
Thomas, 115
Hartford, Ann, 9, 12, 143
Benjamin, 9
Charity, 8
Deborah, 158
Elizabeth, 8, 9, 42, 143, 171
J., 158
Joanna, 81
John, 9
Joseph, 8
Joshua, 203
Lydia, 45, 158
Mary, 79, 104
Nicholas, 8, 9, 173
Patience, 8, 11
Paul, 9, 45, 158, 171
Rebecca, 224
Samuel, 202
Sarah, 80, 171, 219
Sarah H., 181
Silas, 158
Simeon, 91, 224
Solomon, 9
Stephen, 9
William, 9
Hartwell, Mercy, 100
Harty, Pailip, 91

INDEX OF PERSONS. 281

Harty, Rebecca, 180
Harvey, Catherine, 103
    Daniel, 142, 144
    Deborah, 142
    Elizabeth, 128
    John, 177
    Jonathan, 144
    Mary, 129
Haselton, Benjamin, 229
    Ira, 181
    Mary, 229
Haskell, Emily, 232
    Ezra, 232, 238
    Henry Mills, 238
    Mary, 256
    Moody, 215
Hasty, Paulina, 218
Latch, Olive, 248
Lathaway, Lydia, 94
Haughey, Ann, 259
    Bridget, 260, 261
    Catherine, 259
Hauck, Leonard M., 261
Haven, ——, 167
    Joseph, 66
    Samuel, 62
Hawkins, Abigail, 51
    Ann, 51
    Benjamin, 51
    Elizabeth, 51, 173
    Patience, 148
    George, 51
    Hannah, 51
    John, 34, 51
    Mary, 51
    Rachel, 34, 51
    Sarah, 51
    Stephen, 6, 34, 51
    Thomas, 51
    William, 51
Hayden, Abigail, 232
    Isaac, 232
Hayes, Aaron, 39, 52, 137, 156, 168, 169, 173, 175, 212, 213
    Abigail, 8, 11, 18, 36, 39, 40, 41, 46, 52, 59, 79, 133, 138, 139, 141, 149, 155, 156, 161, 206, 208, 210
    Abra, 27, 52, 80, 135, 150, 156, 159, 203, 209
    Andrew, 159
    Ann, 29, 134
    Benjamin, 21, 29, 135, 137, 138, 139, 140, 141, 150, 155, 158, 159, 195, 207, 208
    Brackett, 94
    Daniel, 18, 52, 150, 154, 155, 156, 157, 158, 160, 161, 162, 163, 164, 165, 166, 208, 244
    Deborah, 168, 212
    Diana, 220
    Dodavah, 141
    Dorothy, 156
    Ebenezer, 155
    Elihu, 27, 44, 45, 133, 147, 150, 152, 153, 154, 155
    Elijah, 146
    Elijah Hussey, 233
    Elizabeth, 27, 52, 67, 135, 140, 152, 155, 160, 161, 185, 198, 209
    Elizabeth R., 258
    Eunice A., 248
    Ezekiel, 18, 46, 52, 66, 67, 84, 134, 153, 164, 171, 180, 203, 215
    George, 139
    Hannah, 12, 21, 41, 46, 67, 140, 141, 148, 159, 190, 208
    Hanson, 179
    Hercules M., 67

Hayes, Hezekiah, 27, 134, 150, 152, 154, 157, 208
    Ichabod, 7, 8, 18, 36, 39, 40, 41, 52, 134, 135, 136, 137, 139, 143, 149, 151, 153, 154, 155, 156, 158, 159, 160, 161, 162, 165, 171, 198, 209
    James, 80
    James Chesley, 52, 160
    Joanna, 140
    John, 7, 12, 21, 27, 30, 40, 41, 44, 52, 82, 114, 133, 134, 135, 136, 137, 138, 139, 140, 147, 150, 162, 180, 207
    John W., 231
    John Wingate, 168, 213
    Jonathan, 41, 140, 168, 176, 194
    Joseph, 29, 135, 171, 209
    Joseph M., 67
    Leah, 16, 39
    Lucy, 215
    Lydia, 140, 141, 169, 213
    Martha, 16, 44, 45, 147
    Mary, 7, 12, 21, 30, 39, 67, 102, 114
    Mary Ann, 90, 234
    Mehitable, 33, 82, 136, 150, 163, 208
    Moses, 36, 52, 136, 155
    Nathaniel, 81, 158, 166
    Oliver K., 228, 245
    Oliver P., 231
    Oliver Peabody, 233
    Patience, 148
    Paul, 27, 168
    Peter, 29, 33, 134, 135, 136, 138, 140, 141, 143, 146, 207
    Reuben, 29, 134, 150, 160, 209
    Richard, 157
    Robert, 40, 136, 150, 156
    Samuel, 11, 16, 30, 39, 41, 139, 171
    Samuel W., 67
    Sarah, 8, 29, 33, 155, 162, 187, 207
    Sarah Jane, 238
    Susan, 46, 179
    Susanna, 80, 160
    Tamson, 27, 40, 41, 44, 45, 52, 82, 83, 138, 152, 153, 157, 158, 162, 171, 207
    Thomas, 27, 46, 133, 155, 156, 158, 159, 162, 188, 208, 210
    Wentworth, 41, 137
    William, 12, 21, 44, 45, 147, 148, 154
    William B., 92, 220
Haynes, Daniel, 171
    Eleanor, 114
    Elizabeth Wiggin, 238
    Hannah, 225, 239
    Jane, 114
    Joshua, 114
    Julian, 247
    M. M., 239
    Mary, 114, 115
    Mathias, 114
    Samuel, 114, 115
    Sarah, 114
    William, 114
Hayte, John, 129
    William, 130
Hazeltine, Charles, 218
Heard, } ——, 192, 202
Hurd, }
    Abigail, 28, 29, 113, 128
    Anna, 155
    Benjamin, 12, 113, 133, 154, 155, 156, 160
    Caroline, 224
    Charity, 209
    Daniel, 141, 170, 188, 193, 194
    Deborah, 12, 21, 37, 133, 207
    Ebenezer, 141
    Eliza, 96

Heard, } Elizabeth, 6, 21, 29, 113, 132, 134,
Hurd, }   157, 161, 209
    Experience, 6, 134
    Ezekiel, 89, 95, 100, 102, 202
    Frederick B., 257
    Hannah, 7, 11, 113, 119, 139
    Jacob, 157
    James, 11, 12, 21, 37, 133, 134, 135, 136, 139, 155, 207, 248
    Jane, 11, 20, 207
    Jethro, 157, 171
    John, 20, 21, 28, 113, 129, 135, 141, 142, 144, 146, 155, 157, 175, 198, 202
    Joseph, 28, 113, 136, 138, 139, 156
    Josiah, 146
    Joshua, 155
    Judith, 136, 150
    Kezia, 29, 157
    Lydia, 12, 134
    Maria Augusta, 250
    Martha, 83, 143
    Mary, 12, 29, 87, 113, 133, 160
    Mercy, 157
    Nathaniel, 29, 113, 161
    Paul, 141
    Phebe, 21, 135
    Rebecca, 136, 139
    Reuben, 20, 134, 161
    Samuel, 6, 21, 29, 113, 134, 135, 136, 140, 141, 143, 151, 157, 170, 195, 209, 210
    Sarah, 83, 130, 140
    Silas, 160
    Stephen, 141
    Susan F., 185
    Thomas, 155, 162
    Tristram, 20, 28, 29, 113, 134, 135, 161, 207
    William, 141, 144
    William Wentworth, 162
Heath, Caroline E., 251
Heddle, William, 237
Henderson, Abigail, 234, 258
    Benjamin, 160, 179
    Daniel, 163
    Elizabeth, 82, 164, 181
    Howard, 131, 160, 161, 162, 163, 164, 172, 197
    Love, 80, 160
    Lydia, 177
    Mary, 239
    P., 80
    Samuel H., 90, 257
    Sarah, 200
    Sarah Elizabeth, 235
    Stephen, 161, 193
    Stephen S., 251
    Thomas, 161, 258
    William, 94, 162
    Zoath, 82, 193
Henry, Patrick, 262
Hern, George, 151, 152, 154, 208, 209
    Mary, 151
    Morris, 79
    Ruth, 154
    Sarah, 152
    Susanna, 154
Hersom, } Bathsheba, 82, 157
Horsom, } Bridget, 46, 159, 173, 209
    Elizabeth, 150
    Eunice, 162
    Hannah, 156
    Jacob, 46, 146, 150, 156, 157, 159, 162
    John H., 246
    Mary, 146
    Sarah, 146

Hicks, } David, 182
Hix,   } Elizabeth, 145
    John, 36
    Joseph, 36, 145, 153
    Mary, 36
    Sarah, 36
Higgs, Mary, 254
Hildrup, Elizabeth, 102
Hill, Abigail, 115, 145, 147, 149
    Benjamin, 113, 115, 145
    Eliphalet, 147, 149, 183
    Elizabeth, 113, 115, 119, 147
    Hannah, 115, 129, 147
    Jerusha, 148
    Joanna, 172
    John, 113, 115, 193
    John M., 254
    Johnson, 223
    Joseph, 115
    Lucretia, 147
    Lydia, 145
    Mahala C., 244
    Mary, 2, 115, 179, 257
    Nathaniel, 2
    Nathaniel R., 88
    Patience, 144
    Robert, 145
    Ruth, 162
    Samuel, 115
    Sarah, 115
    Sarah C., 229
    Sobriety, 150
    Valentine, 2
    William, 39, 144, 145, 150
    William H., 252
Hills, Joseph G., 250
    Mary Ann, 239
    Nathaniel, 239
Hilliard, ——, 71
    Aphia, 115
    Timothy, 115
Hilton, Edward, 108
    Nathaniel, 85
Hines, Richard, 259
Hoag, Enoch, 189
    Mary, 198
    Silas, 80
Hobart, Elizabeth, 150
Hobbs, Abigail, 22, 34
    Deborah, 22
    Elizabeth, 180, 245
    Hannah, 27
    Henry, 27
    James, 22, 34, 39, 136, 138
    Joanna, 22
    Lurana, 103
    Mary, 27, 115
    Mercy, 22, 180
    Morris, 22, 115
    Nathaniel, 99, 214
    Phebe, 22
    Rebecca, 22, 34, 39
    Sarah, 22, 39, 115, 129, 138
Hoddey, Arthur, 114
    John, 114
    Mary, 114, 117
    Samuel, 114
Hodgdon, Abigail, 46, 58, 152
    Abner, 173
    Ann, 14, 142
    Benjamin F., 187
    Caleb, 45, 188, 203
    Caroline, 183
    Chase, 58
    Daniel, 155
    Dorcas, 203, 211
    Edmond, 45

INDEX OF PERSONS.

Hodgdon, Eleazer, 194, 211
    Elijah, 198
    Eliza, 214
    Elizabeth, 80, 130, 177, 213
    Hannah, 45
    Hanson, 82
    Henry, 179
    Hester, 125
    Israel, 14, 45, 46, 47, 142, 149, 158, 201
    J., 198
    Joanna, 162
    Job, 84
    John, 46, 58
    John J., 227, 238
    John Perkins, 158
    Jonathan, 58
    Joseph, 143, 162, 163, 164
    Louisa, 99, 100
    Lucy, 84
    Mary, 45, 46, 47, 58, 142, 145, 164
    Moses, 47, 174, 201
    Patience, 58
    Peter, 46, 58
    Rebecca G., 178
    Russell, 237
    Sarah, 45, 58, 97, 103, 221
    Shadrach, 142, 143, 145, 148, 152, 154, 155, 189, 195, 199, 208
    Stephen, 58, 163, 221
    Susan Hanson, 234
    Susan Margaret, 180, 214
    Susanna, 154
    Timothy, 45
    William, 178
Hodge, Ann, 150
    Elizabeth, 143
    Mary, 211
    Samuel, 143, 145, 150, 166, 170, 194, 210
    William, 166, 198
Hoffy, Ann, 261
Hogg, Mary, 173
Holden, Elizabeth, 172
    Fabian, 81
    Robert, 92
Holland, Alice, 84
Holmes, Jeremiah, 128
    John, 177
Homan, Joanna, 129
Hook, Mary, 92
Hooper, George P., 90
    John, 182
    Sarah, 257
Hopkins, James, 89
Hopley, Elizabeth, 131
    Mary, 131
Horan, Thomas, 261
Horn, ——, 190, 200, 204
Horne, Abigail, 33, 40, 141, 151, 168, 172, 182, 183, 214
    Abraham, 153
    Benjamin, 33, 85, 137, 220
    Caleb, 79
    Daniel, 10, 30, 33, 40, 133, 134, 135, 137, 139, 141, 151, 152, 154, 156, 158, 159, 184, 190, 193, 207, 211
    Deborah, 79, 159
    Drusilla, 33, 141
    Drusilla Ellen, 228, 248
    Ebenezer, 159, 160, 165, 172
    Eleanor, 32, 98, 149, 169
    Elizabeth, 48, 81, 113, 138, 141, 143, 145, 156, 159, 177, 208, 215
    Ephraim, 168
    Esther, 33, 43, 141, 208
    George, 143, 145, 146, 150, 151, 152, 153, 154, 157, 171, 173, 192, 209

Horn, Gershom, 98
Horne, Hannah, 48, 152, 177
    Hannah S., 220
    Harriet, 181
    Heard, 203
    Henrietta, 98
    Ichabod, 6, 10, 134, 152, 190, 201, 213
    Ira, 184
    Isaac, 138, 153, 191, 192, 195, 199
    Isaac Libbey, 168
    Isaiah, 160
    James, 41, 157, 168, 176, 194, 195, 201
    James Madison, 233
    Jane, 215
    Jeremiah, 165
    Joanna, 233
    John, 113, 114, 132, 138, 141, 149, 151, 153, 168, 189, 190, 193, 208
    Jonathan, 81, 153, 257
    Joseph S., 184
    Judith, 6, 33, 41, 151, 209
    Judith A., 249
    Leonard, 233
    Lydia, 79, 84, 178, 185, 211, 214
    Lydia H., 218
    Margaret, 32, 33, 41, 113, 141, 157, 178, 209
    Mary, 10, 30, 33, 40, 82, 114, 130, 133, 135, 138, 141, 143, 149, 158, 159, 168, 171, 174, 178, 207, 209, 233, 246
    Mary Elizabeth, 235
    Mary Jane, 184
    Mercy, 131, 174, 178, 211
    Moses P., 247
    Nathan, 141, 177
    Nathaniel, 48, 142, 143, 146, 152, 154, 168, 169, 192, 195, 211, 215
    Nicholas P., 103
    Oliver S., 181, 233
    Patience, 151, 171, 174, 184
    Paul, 40, 43, 139, 144, 154, 174, 193
    Rachel, 146
    Samuel, 33, 141, 179, 182, 218, 233, 235
    Samuel Heard, 81
    Samuel M., 221
    Sarah, 6, 48, 95, 136, 141, 146, 150, 168, 201, 213, 233
    Sophia, 215
    Stephen Greely, 230
    Stephen Wentworth, 159
    Susan, 247
    Susan Y., 183
    Susanna, 153
    Thomas, 6, 33, 43, 113, 130, 141, 144, 154, 171, 235
    Tristram, 183
    William, 6, 32, 41, 48, 113, 159, 172, 174, 189
Horton, Jotham, 88
    William, 253
Hough, Henry, 254
    John, 103
    Leonard, 257
    Ralph, 255
    Thomas, 77
Houson, Levi W., 89
Houston, James, 129
Hovey, Charles, 254
Howard, Amasa, 182
    Amos, 194, 201
    Anna, 176
    Charity, 82
    Edward, 128
    Elisha, 104
    Esther, 171
    Judith, 172
    Kezia, 172

INDEX OF PERSONS.

Howard, Mary Ann, 262
    Samuel, 79, 88, 226
    William T., 93
Howcroft, David, 254
    William L., 253
Howe, Comfort Boody, 226
    Elijah, 163
    Josiah Farewell, 160
    Mary, 164
    Moses, 160, 161, 162, 163, 164, 189
    Relief, 162
    Sarah, 161
Hoy, James, 261
Hoyt, Benjamin R., 91, 92, 93
Hubbard, Elizabeth, 209
    John, 102, 246
    Joseph T., 182
    Mary, 117
Huckins, Abigail, 141
    Hannah, 147
    James, 114
    John, 140, 141, 143, 146
    Mary Ann D., 224
    Rebecca, 146
    Robert, 147
    Sarah, 114
    Welthean, 140
Hudson, John, 128
Hughes, Edward, 261
    Ellen, 261
    Felix, 260
    Henry, 259
    James, 260
    Jane, 260
    John, 260
    Michael, 261
    Owen, 261
    Phebe, 259
    William, 256
Hull, Alfred, 185
    Dodavah, 115
    Elizabeth, 115
    Hannah, 115
    Joseph, 115
    Mary, 112, 115
    Reuben, 115
    Sarah, 115
Humphrey, Milo A., 248
Hunking, Agnes, 113
    Hercules, 113
    John, 113
    Mark, 113, 129, 174
    Peter, 113
    Richard, 174
    William, 113, 129
Hunt, Elizabeth, 169
    Mark, 183
    Nathan, 169
    Thomas, 169
    William, 169
Huntress, George, 130
    James L., 246
    Martha, 183
    Mary, 129
    Sarah, 260
Hurn, see Hern
Hussey, Abigail, 33, 222
    Ann, 186
    Benjamin, 34
    Daniel, 221, 222, 234
    Eleanor, 33
    Elizabeth, 11, 33, 225, 246
    Elizabeth A., 100
    Ezekiel, 178, 215
    Hannah, 18
    Jane, 33, 34, 226
    Job, 33

Hussey, John, 178
    Joseph, 33, 225
    Lydia, 177
    Lydia H,, 91
    Margaret, 33
    Mary, 18, 33, 83, 123, 172
    Mary E., 186
    Mercy, 90, 215, 249
    Moses, 96, 217
    Oliver Perry, 233
    Paul, 199
    Priscilla, 176
    Rachel, 82
    Richard, 18, 33, 34
    Robert, 33
    Samuel, 247
    Sarah, 179
    Sarah H., 220
    Sophia Parker, 234
    Susan J., 185
    Timothy, 187
    William, 33, 190, 198
Hutchins, Enoch, 113
    Joseph, 180
    Samuel, 56
Hutchinson, Hammon, 99, 216, 223
    Samuel S., 90
Hynes, James, 260
Ingalls, John C., 243
Ingersoll, Elisha, 3
    Mary, 3
Ingraham, John H., 88
Jacklin, Rosamond, 130
Jackman, Jacob W., 184
Jackson, Charles D., 105
    Clara Augusta, 258
    Daniel, 183
    Dexter, 104
    Ebenezer, 146, 173, 225, 228
    Enoch, 173
    George W., 236
    Hannah, 145
    James, 142, 153
    James M., 245
    John, 116
    Joseph, 146, 147
    Joshua, 116
    Judith, 145
    Lydia Margaret, 230
    Margaret, 116
    Mary, 129, 153, 225
    Meribah, 146
    Nathaniel, 116
    Patience, 153
    Robert, 142
    Samuel, 129, 145, 153
    William, 146, 200
Jacobs, Abigail, 148
    Daniel, 130, 148, 152, 156
    Elijah, 156
    Elizabeth, 152
    Lydia, 152
    Mary, 148, 152
    Patience, 152
    Samuel, 152
    Sarah, 231
    Seth, 80, 152
Jambrin, John, 131
James, Catherine, 261
    Eleanor, 170
    John, 94
Jaquis, Henry, 131
Jefferds, ——, 202
    Samuel, 80
Jenkins, Ebenezer, 83
    Elijah, 99, 204, 222
    Hannah Jane, 247

INDEX OF PERSONS.

Jenkins, John, 85
    Mary, 112
    Mary S., 95
    Rowland, 130
    Tabitha, 189
Jenks, Anna, 198
    Elizabeth, 182
Jenness, Esther, 251
    George, 185
    Mary Ann, 246
    Prudence, 95
    Stephen, 102
    Susan Hall, 236
Jennings, Anne, 116
    Hezekiah, 116
Jepson, Elizabeth, 98
Jerrill, Edward, 84
Jewett, Clarissa, 60
    David, 60
    David H., 60
    Thomas, 178
Joce, } Christopher, 116
Jose, } Hannah, 79, 116
    Jane, 116
    Joanna, 116
    John, 116
    Margaret, 116
    Martyn, 116
    Mary, 116, 122
    Richard, 116
    Samuel, 116
    Sarah, 116
    Thomas, 116
Johnson, Daniel, 186
    David, 145
    Ebenezer, 116
    Edmund, 180
    Eleanor, 116
    Hannah, 116
    James, 116
    Joanna, 129
    John, 116
    Joseph, 145
    Mary, 45
    Nancy W., 251
    Nelson Swift, 218
    Oliver W., 185
    Rosamond, 116
    Sarah W., 219
    Thomas, 145
Jones, Abigail, 133
    Ann, 143
    Charles, 104
    Deborah, 157
    Dorcas, 137
    Dorothy, 155
    Ebenezer, 137
    Eleanor, 25, 135
    Eliza, 185
    Eliza J., 258
    Elizabeth, 130, 137, 143, 221
    Ephraim M., 251
    Esther, 133, 137
    Hannah, 25, 36, 134, 137
    Ivory, 245
    John, 133
    Joseph, 131
    Joshua, 153, 221
    Lydia, 100, 185
    Mary, 133, 137
    Richard, 145, 146, 153, 155, 157, 209
    Samuel, 133, 137, 145, 261
    Sarah, 93, 145, 256
    Sophia W., 185
    Stephen, 116, 145
    Tobias, 173
    Ursula, 209

Jones, Vaughn, 183
    William, 11, 25, 36, 134, 135, 136, 137
Jordan, Barbara, 201
    James K., 181
    Jeremiah, 84
Joy, Eliza H., 182
    Emmeline L., 247
    Mary Ann, 89
    Tabitha, 130
Joyce, Margaret, 262
Kane, Mary, 261, 262
Kase, John, 129
Kauffer, Francis, 184
Kay, James, 261
    Mary Ann, 99
Keais, Samuel, 117
    William, 117
Keating, Margaret, 262
    Susanna, 173
Keay, William, 178
    William G., 255
Kelley, } Aaron, 49, 151
Kielle, } Abigail, 54, 69, 212
    B., 198
    Benjamin, 48, 54, 69, 200
    Deborah, 48, 49, 146, 210
    Ebenezer, 49, 153
    Eleanor, 261
    Eliza Jane, 221
    Hannah, 54, 82
    Ivory, 69
    James, 48, 49, 69, 85, 98, 151, 153, 159, 189, 195, 210, 261, 262
    John, 18, 54, 69, 151, 200, 212, 260
    John F., 184, 226
    Kezia, 69
    Lydia, 226
    Mary, 82, 159, 221, 260
    Moses, 49, 151
    Philip, 172
    Samuel, 49, 151, 249
    William, 48, 69, 100, 151, 256
Kennedy, Thomas, 262
Kendall, Rebecca, 237
Kennicom, Elizabeth, 170
Kenniston, Jane, 89
    Jerusha S., 223
    John, 97
    Mary F., 94
Kenney, see Canney
Kernan, Bridget, 261
Kettle, John, 117
    Sarah, 117
Kilmington, Hannah, 261
Kim, Elizabeth, 130
Kimball, Abigail, 84, 141, 158
    Abigail Gray, 61, 242
    Anna, 212
    Charles, 185, 222
    Clara A., 250
    Cynthia, 178
    Daniel, 143
    Daniel W., 95
    Eliza, 222
    Elizabeth, 139, 142, 168
    Elizabeth W. H., 240
    Ephraim, 156, 173, 197, 211, 241
    Ezra, 61, 139, 140, 141, 142, 144, 162, 201, 203, 212, 242
    George, 183
    Hannah, 241
    Isaac Hasey, 242
    James, 238
    John, 80, 101, 190, 204
    John H., 228
    John Horne, 236
    John M., 249

Kimball, Luther C., 258
　　　Lydia, 112, 231
　　　Lydia Jane, 238
　　　Mahala, 226
　　　Maria, 61, 177, 213, 242
　　　Mary, 61, 82, 139, 141, 160, 192, 211, 212, 213, 242
　　　Moses, 161
　　　Nathaniel, 165
　　　Nehemiah, 141, 142, 143, 149, 152, 191, 193, 211
　　　Olive, 238
　　　Paul, 152, 171
　　　Richard, 140, 158, 159, 160, 161, 162, 164, 165, 168, 189, 191, 197, 212, 240, 257
　　　Samuel, 87, 88, 168
　　　Sarah, 159, 211
　　　Solomon, 241
　　　Susan G., 187
　　　Tamson, 233
　　　William, 85, 161, 231, 233, 240
Kimmin, Sarah, 131
King, Daniel, 117
　　　Daniel S., 254
　　　Mary, 117
　　　William, 117
Kingman, Charles H., 255
　　　Jeremiah, 185
Kingsbury, Benjamin, 257
　　　Elisha, 171
Kinsman, Mary, 81
Kirke, Eleanor, 129
Kittredge, Abigail, 68, 69
　　　George Washington, 68
　　　Hannah, 68, 254
　　　Jacob, 68, 69, 254
　　　John, 68
　　　Thomas Wallingford, 68, 257
　　　William Wight, 69
Kivel, Patrick, 261
Knapp, John N., 89
Knight, Alpha, 234
　　　Elizabeth, 130, 131
　　　Joseph, 139
　　　Leah, 2
　　　Mary, 2
　　　Robert, 138, 139
　　　William, 138
Knott, Richard, 261
Knowles, James, 162, 163
　　　Sarah, 162, 163
Knox, Henry, 99
Ladd, Eliphalet, 62, 204
　　　Eliza, 62
　　　Elizabeth, 62, 200
　　　James, 84, 227
　　　Samuel, 62
　　　Sarah Ann, 235
　　　William, 62
Laird, Ann, 227
　　　George, 256
Lambert, Edmond, 172
　　　James, 179
　　　Thomas R., 253
Lambeth, Philip, 130
Lamm, William H., 235
Lamos, Abigail, 37
　　　Elizabeth, 37
　　　James, 37
　　　Jonathan, 202
　　　Nathaniel, 37
　　　Phebe T., 184
　　　Samuel, 37
　　　Susanna, 200
Lamprell, Henry, 117
Lamson, Elizabeth P., 229

Lane, ⎰ Bridget, 262
Layn, ⎱ Ebenezer, 89
　　　Edmund, 52, 148
　　　Edmund James, 223, 229
　　　Elizabeth Barker, 229
　　　George W., 258
　　　Jane, 52, 148
　　　John Hussey, 52, 148
　　　Joseph, 259
　　　Samuel, 148
　　　Styles, 148
Langdon, ——, 166
　　　Elizabeth, 117
　　　John, 58, 117
　　　Joseph, 117
　　　Mark, 117
　　　Martha, 117
　　　Mary, 117
　　　Richard, 117
　　　Samuel, 117
　　　Tobias, 117
　　　William, 117
Langley, Sarah, H., 246
Lapish, Mehitable, 85
Larry, Mary, 80
　　　Mercy, 160
　　　Samuel, 160
　　　Sarah, 160
　　　William, 80
Laskey, Anna, 147
　　　John, 147
Lawler, Catherine, 260
　　　Patrick, 261
Lawrence, Samuel, 96
Lear, Susanna, 130
Leathers, Thomas, 79
Leavitt, George W., 100
　　　Harriet M., 243
　　　J., 203
　　　Joseph, 80
　　　Lucinda Pease, 237
　　　Mercy, 122
Lee, Abraham, 117, 128
　　　Benjamin F., 182, 222
　　　Lois, 222
　　　Mary Ann, 234
　　　Stephen, 81
Legg, Abigail, 213
　　　Jane, 220
　　　Jeremiah, 220
　　　Lucien B., 187, 244
　　　Otis, 213
Leighton, Aaron, 146
　　　Abigail, 53, 99
　　　Deborah, 53
　　　Dorothy, 18, 47, 173
　　　Eliza, 217
　　　Elizabeth, 47, 244
　　　Ephraim, 81
　　　George, 47, 152
　　　Gideon, 47
　　　Hannah, 172, 209
　　　Hannah C., 181
　　　Hannah E., 258
　　　Hatevil, 53, 79, 152, 153, 156, 160
　　　Isaac, 144
　　　James, 53, 144, 146, 160
　　　Joanna, 109
　　　Joanna H., 178
　　　John, 4, 18, 47, 53, 150, 152, 153, 160, 193
　　　John W., 250
　　　Jonathan, 53, 150
　　　Joseph, 47, 102
　　　Kezia, 156
　　　Leonora F., 257
　　　Lydia, 4

INDEX OF PERSONS.   287

Leighton, Mary, 2, 53, 97, 153, 160, 202, 221, 244
    Mary Ann, 181
    Olive, 53, 152
    Paul, 53
    Ruth, 181
    Samuel, 47
    Sarah, 4, 8, 18, 47, 153, 184, 216
    Sarah C., 243
    Susanna, 18, 47
    Theodore, 47
    Thomas, 18, 47, 117, 174
    Tobias, 53
    William, 53
Lew, Peter, 247
Lewis, Caroline B., 244
    Hannah, 124
    James R., 91
    William H., 252
Libbey, Abigail, 85
    Anna, 81, 142
    Benjamin, 54, 195, 210
    Bennett, 183
    Daniel, 137, 200, 201, 203
    Eliza, 249
    Elizabeth, 54, 155, 195, 210, 236
    Enoch, 180
    Isaac, 142
    James, 54, 118, 170, 194, 196
    John, 85, 129
    Joseph, 137
    Lydia, 203
    Mary, 86, 118
    Mehitable, 217
    Oliver, 181, 236
    Phebe, 179
    Rebecca, 203
    Sarah, 81, 118
    William Pickering, 258
Light, Dorothy, 117
    John, 117
    Mary, 117
    Robert, 117
Lindsay, Henry M., 178
    John, 198
Linton, John, 182
Litchfield, Elizabeth P,, 246
Little, Moses, 201
Littlefield, David F., 250
    James, 97
    John, 219, 237
    Joseph, 226
    Joseph Horne, 238
    Phebe, 129
    Theodore, 89, 180
Locke, ——, 235
    Abner, 183
    Ann, 178
    Daniel, 179
    Harriet S., 257
    Jeremiah, 91
    Sabina, 129
    Sarah, 73, 85
Long, Hannah, 67
    John F., 258
    Nathaniel R., 257
Loo, Sarah, 12
Lord, Ann, 130
    Benjamin, 100
    Dorothy, 129
    Elizabeth, 178
    Eunice, 250
    Frances, 103
    Gershom, 78, 175, 195
    Jefferson, 252
    John, 248
    Lydia, 174

Lord, Mark, 174
    Margaret, 50
    Martha, 130
    Mary, 139
    Sarah, 129, 217
    Simon, 173
    Temple, 249
    Theodore, 244
Lothrop, Samuel K., 256
Loud, } Solomon, 83, 193
Lowd, }
Lougee, Charlotte, 93
    Dearborn, 184
    Nicholas, 96
Lovering, Mary, 124
Lovitt, Aretas, 117
    John, 129
    Ruth, 117
    Thomas, 117
Low, } Joanna, 117
Lowe, } John, 117
    Mary, 117
    Mary Ann, 227
    Mary Sheafe, 254
    Nathaniel, 179, 227
    Sarah, 117
Lowden, Anthony, 129
Loyde, } Allen, 117, 118
Lyde, } Eleanor, 118
    Francis, 118
    Sarah, 117
Loyns, Susanna, 79
Lucas, Andrew, 173
    Ann Maria, 104
    James, 165
    Jane, 165
    Sirena M., 183
Ludecas, David, 117
    Elizabeth, 117
Lufkin, Hannah, 104
Lyman, William B., 100
Lynn, Andrew, 101
Lyons, Patrick, 259
Mace, Eliphalet, 80
    Hannah, 177
Macey, James E., 216
Macfield, Elizabeth, 7
Mack, John, 240
Mackaugh, Neal, 11
Maffit, John N., 89, 90
Magoon, ——, 219
    Benjamin, 96
    Mary, 109
Mahan, Michael, 261
Maine, ——, 160
    Esther, 225
Malcolm, Anne, 161
    Patrick, 161
Malone, James, 260
Maloon, Henry, 181
Maltby, ——, 218
Mann, George Gains, 62
    Gustavus Hodgdon, 238
    John, 177, 213, 238
    Lucy, 85
    Patience, 199
    Peter, 200
    Statira, 62
    Susanna, 61, 62
    William, 60, 61, 62
Manning, Patrick, 209
Mannyard, Ruth, 122
Mansfield, Jesse, 104
Marble, Newton Epaphroditus, 254
March, Anna T., 258
    Joseph W., 86
Marcy, Samuel, 183
Marden, Ann, 153

INDEX OF PERSONS.

Marden, Elizabeth, 144
 Hinkson, 157
 James, 119, 157
 John, 119, 142, 143, 144, 153
 Mary, 143
 Rachel, 119
 Sarah, 143
 Stephen, 119
Marion, Margaret, 118
Marlow, Bridget, 259
Marrifield, William, 132
Marshall, Andrew, 151, 152, 153, 155
 Elizabeth, 153
 George, 119
 John, 152
 Lydia, 119, 152, 197
 Martha Ann, 182
 Thomas, 118
 William, 152
Marston, Winthrop A., 257
Martin, Hannah, 93
Martyn, Elias, 118
 Elizabeth, 118
 Hannah, 116, 118
 John, 118
 Mary, 118
 Michael, 118
 Richard, 118
 Sarah, 118
Mason, Benjamin, 12, 34, 165
 Elijah, 246
 Elizabeth, 12, 34, 131, 172, 211
 Erksine, 227
 Isaac, 165, 211
 Jeremiah, 227
 Mary L., 229
 Nathaniel, 99
 Peter, 34
 Shubael, 172
Mathes, Elizabeth, 240
 Love S., 250
 Samuel H., 228
 Samuel Hanson, 233
Matthews, Elizabeth, 150
 Francis, 118
 John, 150
 Sophia H., 101
May, Phebe Ann, 185
McBennett, Alice, 259
 Thomas, 260
McCabe, Mary, 259
McCarty, Charles, 261
 Dennis, 262
 Honora, 261
 Julia, 260
 Mary, 261
 Margaret, 262
McClintock, ——, 166
McCloskey, Ellen, 260
 Margaret, 260
McCollister, William S., 100, 221
McCrellis, Philip, 98
McCullock, Esther, 157
 William, 157
McDaniel, John, 100, 172
McDanielson, Arthur, 153
 Charles, 153
McDavitt, Ann, 76
 Eminty, 76
 William, 76
 William Francis, 76
McDuffee, Caroline, 234
 James, 140
 John, 138, 140
 Mary, 234
 Sarah Ann, 244
 William, 138

McElroy, Martha, 151
McEvoy, Bridget, 259
McGregor, ——, 211
McGuinness, Andrew, 259
 Catherine, 261
McIntire, Hugh, 261
 Johathan, 178
 Silas, 257
McIntosh, Lydia, 100
 Robert, 176
McKenley, Catherine Elizabeth, 75
McKinley, Robert, 75, 93
 Sarah, 75
McKenney, Hannah, 222
 Robert, 129
McKone, Alice, 261
 Arthur, 261
 Elizabeth, 260
McLaughlin, James, 255
McLucas, Mary G., 251
McManus, Patrick, 261
McMillan, John, 240
McMullen, Catherine, 260
 James, 260
McNally, Agnes, 260
 Rose, 260
McNeal, Joseph D., 96
 William, 79
McNorton, Jane, 232
McNulty, Bridget, 261
McScovy, Jane, 138
 John, 138, 139
 Matthew, 139
McShane, Mary, 262
Meader, Abigail, 118
 Anna, 80
 Daniel, 6, 18
 David, 172
 Eleanor, 18
 Elizabeth, 18, 79, 118
 Harriet N., 103
 Isaac, 257
 John, 6, 118
 Kezia, 5
 Lydia, 5, 6, 18
 Moses, 79
 Nathaniel, 18, 118
 Nicholas, 5, 6, 84
 Ruth, 174
 Samuel, 6
 Sarah, 98, 118, 126
 Timothy E., 245
Meed, Elizabeth, 111
Meicher, Almira, 221
 Ellen M., 257
 Mary, 129
 William, 101
 William N., 103
Mellen, ——, 198
 Eliza Hovey, 69
 George Washington Frost, 69
 Henry, 62, 63, 69, 212, 242
 Henry Orlando, 62
 John Prentice, 63, 242
 Martha, 62, 63, 69, 242
 Martha Wentworth, 63, 242
 William Pepperill, 69
Meroney, Joseph, 181
Merriam, ——, 165
Merrill, Emily W., 246
 John, 262
 Phineas, 252
Merrow, Abigail, 51
 Dorcas, 170
 Elisha, 257
 Elizabeth, 51
 Jonathan, 51, 189

INDEX OF PERSONS.   289

Merrow, Maria, 257
    Samuel, 172
    Thomas, 195
Meserve, ——, 204
    Abigail, 49, 139, 159
    Clement, 49, 130, 145, 202, 203
    Daniel, 49, 139, 145, 159
    Deborah, 49, 149
    Ebenezer, 257
    Elizabeth, 82, 129
    George, 256
    John, 149, 150, 151, 258
    John S., 218, 229
    Jonathan, 49
    Joseph, 49, 139
    Lois G., 182
Middleton, Mary J., 100
Miles, Abraham, 182
Miller, James, 93
    Martha, 131
    Rebecca, 226
    Robert C., 89, 226
    Thomas, 138, 139
Millet, Abigail, 143, 153
    Benjamin, 143
    Elizabeth, 143
    Hannah, 143
    John, 143
    Love, 143
    Lydia, 143
    Susanna, 144
    Thomas, 143, 144
Mills, Elizabeth, 150, 209
    John, 148, 149, 151, 209
    Mary, 151
Minnehan, Mary, 262
Mitchell, Elizabeth, 117
    George W., 250
    Isabella, 262
    Mary Jane, 90
    Thomas E., 182
Monroe, Cyrus, 102
Monsey, William, 130
Montgomery, John, 157, 209
    Jonathan, 157
Moody, ——, 223
    Charles C. P., 94, 218
    Edwin, 184
    Elizabeth, 251
    Esther, 118, 119
    Joseph G., 184
    Joshua, 118
    Mary, 119
    Samuel, 118, 119
Moon, Abby, 260
    Alice, 260
Mooney, Archelaus, 155
    Elizabeth, 148, 155
    Hannah, 66, 67, 171
    Patrick, 262
Moore, Mary, 184
    Thomas, 261
    William, 173
Moran, Thomas, 261
Morey, Harvey, 87
Morgan, Deborah, 102
    Elizabeth, 262
    Thomas, 262
Morrill, ——, 63
    Ada, 130
    Edward, 250
    John, 130
    Jonathan, 220, 232
    Joseph, 182
    Mary, 80
    Nancy, 220
    Peaslee, 170

Morrill, Sarah, 98, 130
Morrison, Jonathan, 80
    Mary, 259
Morse, } Edward M., 239
Moss, } Eliza Jane, 77, 225
    John Boardman, 77
    Martha, 220
    Mary, 129
    Sarah, 170, 173
    Thomas G., 77, 225
Moses, ——, 50
    Benjamin, 179
    Kezia, 154
    Martha, 40
    Mary, 40, 153 157
    Timothy, 40, 150, 153, 154, 157
Moulton, Adelia A. P., 251
    Benjamin, 118
    Daniel, 119, 247
    Dorothy S., 185
    Edward, 182
    Hannah, 118
    James, 118
    Jeremiah, 101
    John, 119
    Josiah, 118
    Lydia, 245
    Lucy, 118
    Mary, 119
    Samuel A. M., 92
    Sarah J., 250
Mullen, Charles, 262
    James, 259, 261
    Patrick, 260
Mulligan, Edward, 259
Munden, Elizabeth, 121, 128
Murdock, Elisha, 90
    Mary, 96
Murphy, Catherine, 261
    Ellen, 260, 261
    Jeremiah, 262
    Peter, 260
Murray, Daniel, 244
    John, 81
    Mary, 261
Nailor, James, 160
    Martha, 160
Nason, ——, 181
    Benjamin, 119, 128
    Eliza, 226
    Elizabeth, 104
    Elizabeth Wingate, 234
    John, 80, 119
    Jonathan, 130
    Joseph, 226
    Lois, 185
    Mary Elizabeth, 234
    Sarah, 99
    Shuah, 111, 128
    Stephen, 83
    Susan Amanda, 234
    Temple, 180
Nathersell, Elizabeth, 159, 210
Neal, Content, 88
    Elizabeth, 251
    Joseph L., 88
    Lydia J., 253
    Mary, 119
    Samuel, 119
    Sophia, 179
    Walter, 119
Nealley, John B., 96, 221, 222
Nell, William, 203
Nelson, Elizabeth, 130
    Hannah, 124, 128
    Louise, 249
Nesmith, John, 128, 230, 255

INDEX OF PERSONS.

Newall, Daniel, 91
    Thompson L., 96
Newbegin, Maria, 248
Newcomb, Elizabeth, 222
Newman, ——, 229
Nichols, Lucy, 88
    Mary, 173
    Samuel B., 257
Noble, Martha, 153
Nock, Abigail, 22, 79
    Benjamin, 26, 137
    Dorothy, 172
    Drisco, 30
    Ebenezer, 30
    Elizabeth, 119
    Esther, 30
    Hannah, 22, 135
    Henry, 30, 119
    James, 22, 135
    Jonathan, 40
    Joseph, 26, 137
    Joshua, 26, 137
    Love, 137
    Mary, 22, 27, 135
    Mercy, 22, 30, 135
    Nathaniel, 22, 135
    Olive, 40
    Rebecca, 107, 119
    Samuel, 130
    Sarah, 26, 27, 30, 40, 119, 137
    Silvanus, 30, 119, 131
    Temperance, 40, 137
    Thomas, 22, 40, 119, 135, 137, 207
    Zecharias, 26, 27, 40, 137
Noonan, Margaret, 261
Nooney, Catherine, 261
Norraway, Dorothy, 4
    Elizabeth, 4
    James, 4
    William, 4
Norris, Arthur F. L., 234
    Daniel L., 224
    Martha, 102
    Sophia Ann, 224
Norton, George, 257, 258
Noyes, Abigail, 163
    Ebenezer, 163
Nudd, Thomas L., 103
Nute, ——, 199
    Abigail, 86
    Abraham, 3, 131
    Ann, 32
    Clarissa, 187, 237
    Clarissa Matilda, 230
    Daniel, 175
    Elizabeth, 32, 101, 129
    Elizabeth P., 210
    Francis, 89
    Hannah, 204
    Isaac, 199
    James, 32, 189
    Joanna, 3
    Jonathan, 202
    Joseph, 247
    Joseph P., 240
    Joshua, 85
    Joshua B., 249
    Jotham, 204
    Mary, 88, 90, 218
    Moses, 237
    Paul, 32, 199
    Priscilla, 82
    Prudence, 32
    Samuel, 7, 171
    Sarah P., 256
    Thomas, 233, 235
Nutter, Anthony, 119

Nutter, Hannah C., 104
    Henry, 131
    John, 119, 183, 213
    Mary, 95
    Sarah, 119
Oates, Nancy, 248
Occleston, Maria, 257
O'Brien, Margaret, 261
    Robert, 260
O'Connell, Timothy, 261
Odell, Ebenezer F., 99
Odiorne, Ann H., 184
    Benjamin, 170, 185, 227
    John B. H., 181
    Martha, 227
    Susanna, 81
O'Donald, John, 260
O'Donnell, Joanna, 262
    Mary, 260
Oliver, Ira, 221
Osborne, Charles, 252
    Irena, 97
    Marble, 192, 193
    Mary Little, 228
    Sarah, 129
Osgood, Bradley, 216
    Eliza, 252
    John, 229
    Mehitable, 216
    Sabra, 244
Otheman, Bartholomew, 93
Otis, Elijah, 53
    Experience, 120
    Freeman, 245
    Jane, 52, 53, 79
    John, 95
    Joshua, 52, 53
    Joyce, 130
    Mary Ann, 245
    Micajah, 52
    Nicholas, 52
    Richard, 120
    Rose, 120
    Sarah, 53, 178
    Solomon, 120
    Stephen, 8, 41, 98, 120
    Susanna, 78, 175
Owen, Benjamin, 99
Packard, Priscilla F., 248
Packer, Thomas, 121, 128
Page, Eunice W., 184
    Francis, 121
    James, 95
    Joseph, 121
    Mary, 129
    Meribah, 121
    Rebecca W., 251
Paine, Elizabeth, 46
Palmer, Aaron, 176
    Abigail, 181
    Abizag, 118
    Ann, 121
    Barnabas, 166
    Barnabas H., 71, 218
    Charlotte M., 231
    Christopher, 121, 219
    Deborah, 121, 215
    Dudley, 166
    Edmund Haggens, 71
    Elihu H., 257
    Elizabeth, 71, 218
    Growth, 178
    Hannah P., 231
    John G., 236
    Joseph, 121
    Lydia, 181
    Mary Elizabeth, 71

INDEX OF PERSONS. 291

Palmer, Merrill D., 251
    Rebecca, 231
    Ruth, 121
    Samuel, 121
    Sarah, 231
    Stephen, 183
    Susan Haggens, 71
    Susan Hamilton, 71
    William, 177, 213, 231
Parcher, Elias, 131
Parker, ——, 86
    Catherine, 122
    Elizabeth, 121
    Elizabeth B., 224
    John, 122
    Noah, 121
    William, 122
Parkman, John, 258
Parks, ——, 189
    Asa, 186
    Mary, 183
    Thomas, 162
Parmalee, Horace, 67, 68
    Horace Gerrish, 68
    Jesse Sherman, 68
    Mary, 67, 68
Parmenter, George Franklin, 233
Parshley,) Elizabeth Jackson, 234
Parsley,) Elizabeth R., 258
    John G., 258
    Martha, 180
    Mary, 247
    Tamson, 247
Parsons, Harriet, 245
    Obadiah, 171
Parol, Thomas, 92
Partridge, Abigail, 120, 122
    Elizabeth, 120
    Hannah, 120
    Joanna, 117
    John, 120
    Mary, 120, 121
    Nehemiah, 121
    Patience, 120
    Rachel, 120
    Sarah, 120, 121, 129
    William, 121, 122
Patten, Harriet, 216
    Joshua, 216
    Nancy, 85
    Rebecca, 85
    Sarah, 177
    Stephen, 213
    William, 250
Paul, Abigail, 71, 90
    Abigail C., 179
    Almira, 99, 223
    Ambrose, 71
    Ambrose B., 180
    Charlotte, 202
    Charles, 91, 232
    Clarke, 185, 235
    Delia, 90, 214
    Edmund, 214
    Eliza, 179,
    Eunice, 179, 180
    Ivory, 91, 236
    Jane, 224
    John H., 254
    Judith Smith, 236
    Lois, 232
    Maria, 102
    Mary, 235
    Mary Ann, 71, 254
    Moses, 180, 214, 215
    Rebecca, 257
    Rosella, 181

Paul, Samuel, 185
    Sidney, 100
Payson, Orin M., 219
Pearl, Abraham, 19
    Benjamin, 19, 157, 158, 208
    Eleanor, 157
    Elizabeth, 19
    John, 19
    Joseph, 19
    Mary, 19
    Pamellar, 258
    William, 158
Pearson, Mary Jane, 184
Pease, Dorcas T., 222
    Elizabeth, 124
Peaslee, Abigail, 79
    Amos, 70, 82, 94, 194
    Ann, 70
    Benjamin Titcomb, 70
    Elizabeth, 81
    Elizabeth A., 258
    Elizabeth Austin, 70
    Hannah, 70
    John Noble, 70
    Joseph, 191
    Joseph Tibbets, 70
    Mary Noble, 70
    Nicholas, 70, 84
Peavey, Edward, 135, 207
    Esther, 137
    Joseph, 137
    Mary, 207
    Oliver, 87
    Pamelia, 245
Pecker, James, 158
    Sarah, 158
Peirce, Abigail, 71
    Abigail Smith, 71, 217, 257
    Andrew, 70, 71, 87, 88, 169, 217
    Ann, 245
    Benjamin, 3, 27, 58, 133, 167, 168, 169, 197, 211
    Clarissa Wheeler, 71
    Daniel, 167, 216
    David, 182
    Ebenezer, 27
    Elizabeth, 27, 133, 167, 218
    Hannah, 27, 122, 184
    Israel, 27
    James, 244
    Joanna, 180
    John, 27, 133, 168, 188
    John Osborne, 229
    Joseph, 27, 167, 201
    Joseph Andrew, 71, 258
    Lydia, 71, 168, 203
    Lydia A., 231
    Martha, 27
    Mary, 122, 167, 182, 211, 215
    Mary Ann, 71, 217
    Mary L., 252
    Mehitable, 122, 167
    Nancy, 87
    Rachel, 99, 218
    Rebecca, 91, 96
    Rebecca Elizabeth Wheeler, 71
    Sarah, 122, 167, 214
    Tamson, 167
    Thomas, 27, 79, 122, 175, 208
Pendexter, Drusilla B., 219
    George, 84
    Hannah C., 183
    Joseph, 221
    Lydia, 221
    Margaret J., 257
Pendleton, Ann, 120
    Brian, 120

INDEX OF PERSONS.

Caleb, 120
Edmund, 120
Hannah, 120
James, 120
Joseph, 120
Penhallow, Samuel, 121
Percival, Laura, 104
Perkins, Abigail, 16, 31, 37, 121, 134, 179
  Adam, 81
  Anne, 31, 145
  Ann Augusta, 257
  Asa, 181
  Daniel, 138, 154, 164
  Dorothy, 37, 142, 208
  Eleanor, 147, 150
  Elijah, 194
  Elijah Bunker, 163
  Eliza, 214
  Elizabeth, 147
  Ellen, 250
  Ephraim, 37, 80, 136, 159
  Ezekiel, 174
  Frances, 16, 130
  Hannah, 15, 25, 134, 208
  James, 121, 142, 159
  Jared, 102, 104, 243
  Jeremiah, 202
  John, 25, 195
  Jonathan, 121
  Joseph, 16, 147
  Joseph A., 235
  Joshua, 37, 136, 138, 142, 143, 145, 148, 152, 154, 163, 164, 165, 202, 208
  Leah, 121
  Lemuel, 31
  Louisa, 219
  Margaret, 159
  Mary, 15, 16, 121, 131, 213
  Mary Thompson, 228
  Mary, W., 179
  Mercy Plumer, 228
  Morris, 179
  Moses, 213
  Nathaniel, 25, 31, 134, 138
  Olive, 81, 163
  Paul, 147
  Penniah, 31
  Rebecca, 80
  Robert, 85, 97, 257
  Samuel, 15, 16
  Sarah, 121, 159
  Sarah Ann, 93
  Solomon, 194, 217
  Susanna, 152, 173
  Thomas, 176
  William, 165, 179, 182
Perry, Mary, 23
  Matthew, 23
  William, 23
Philbrick, Elizabeth, 121, 122, 129
  Joseph, 121, 122
  Mary, 121
  Mehitable, 121
  Thomas, 121
  Tryphena, 122
  Walter, 121
  William, 121
Philpot, John, 80
  Lydia, 238
  Moses, 179
  Olive G., 258
  Richard, 80
  Sarah, 179
  Sarah Rollins, 228
Phipps, Eleanor, 121
  Mary, 121

Philpot, Solomon, 121
  Thomas, 121
Pickering, Abbie P., 253
  Charlotte, 101
  John, 120, 121, 128
  Joseph, 225
  Mary, 120, 130, 186
  Rebecca, 131
  Sarah, 121
  Thomas, 120
  William, 104
Pigeon, Mary B., 185
Pike, ——, 108, 110, 146, 164
  A. W., 255
  Benjamin, 180
  Daniel, 178
  Elizabeth, 122
  James, 48
  John, 8, 122, 128, 131
  Robert, 122
  Sarah D., 247
  Theodore, 122
  William, 245
Pillsbury, Caroline M., 250
Pinkham, Abigail, 37, 81, 146, 152
  Achsa, 178
  Amos, 25
  Ann, 36, 37, 81
  Clement, 171
  Daniel, 181, 236
  Deborah, 154, 162
  Edward J., 234
  Elizabeth, 7, 25, 28, 32, 45, 149, 154, 158, 184, 226
  Emeline, 247
  Enoch, 181, 226
  Eri, 258
  Hannah, 25, 28, 92, 136, 150, 158, 181
  Hepzibah, 146
  Isaac, 152
  James, 28, 134, 135, 136, 137, 139, 151, 152, 154, 155, 156, 158, 182
  Joanna, 25
  John, 45
  Jonathan, 139, 158, 159, 160, 162, 163, 184
  Joseph, 152
  Lois, 28, 135, 159
  Lydia, 81, 223
  Lydia Neal, 234
  Mary, 28, 134, 146, 152, 158
  Nathaniel, 163
  Otis, 37
  Patience, 146
  Paul, 190, 199
  Phebe, 171
  Phebe Tuttle, 237
  Rebecca, 172
  Richard, 45, 154
  Rose, 37
  Samuel, 37, 151, 223
  Sarah, 137, 147, 148, 152, 156
  Sarah A., 244
  Sarah E., 251
  Solomon, 131
  Sophia, 236
  Stephen, 146, 149, 152, 154
  Thomas, 130, 152, 158
  Ursula, 28, 155
  William, 253
Piper, Ellen Clarke, 74
  Emily, 245
  George, 74, 181
  Martha W., 99
  Mary Smith, 74
  Samuel, 129
  Sarah Bell, 74

INDEX OF PERSONS. 293

Piper, Sarah Fisher, 74
       Susan S., 96
Pishon, Charles, 181
Pitman, Abigail, 137
        Derry, 208
        Dorothy, 208
        Mary, 11, 120
        William, 120
        Zechariah, 32
Place, ——, 198
       Ebenezer, 161
       Eliza, 78
       Harrel, 78
       Harrel F., 104
       John Wesley, 78
       Jonathan, 178
       Rachel, 161
       Richard, 184
       Samuel, 202
Plaisted, Elisha, 128
          Ichabod, 122
          John, 121
          Joshua, 121
          Mary, 121, 122
          Olive, 122
          Samuel, 122
Plumer, Abigail, 161
        Ann, 88
        Benjamin, 138
        Bidfield, 137
        Daniel, 12, 26, 136, 138, 139, 193
        Dodavah, 162
        Ebenezer, 139
        Elizabeth, 135, 178
        Ephraim, 12, 136, 165, 199
        Hannah, 26, 135, 136
        James, 90
        James P., 221
        Jeremiah, 180
        John, 135, 178, 256
        Jonathan, 199
        Joseph, 93
        Lucinda, 182
        Lydia, 172
        Mary, 181
        Mary Ann, 221
        Mercy, 159
        Richard, 135, 137
        Robert, 257
        Samuel, 162
        Sarah, 26, 136
        Susan G., 257
Pollard, Rebecca, 89
Polley, David, 148
Pomeroy, Rebecca, 128
         Richard, 130
Pomfret, William, 121
Porter, Arthur L., 225, 226
        Catherine Evans, 230
        Charlotte, 222
        Elizabeth Crocker, 226
        George, 103
        Hannah, 96
        Isaac A., 217, 230, 237
        Lucy Kent, 237
        Mary Ann, 227
        Mary K., 217
Potter, William, 90
Pott,) Joanna, 3, 4
Potts, j Joyus, 4
        Lavina, 246
        Mary, 3
        Thomas, 3, 4, 129
Powell, Abigail, 11
Power, Judith, 137
Powers, ——, 191

Pratt, Abigail, 133
       Alice, 78, 175
       Peirce, 80
       Hannah, 215
       John, 215
Pray, Benjamin, 100
      Dorcas, 100
      Dorothy, 180
      Isaac C., 224
      Janette, 218
      John, 251
      Mary A., 244
      Mehitable, 217
      Thomas J. W., 240
Preble, Abraham, 197
Prentice, Lydia, 214
Prescott, Dorothy M., 257
          Mary, 251
          Rebecca, 129
          Samuel, 215
          Woodbury T., 256
Preston, Henry P., 248
         Mary, 259
         Priscilla B., 251
         Samuel R., 247
         Sarah, 176
Prestwitch, Anastasia, 254
Priest, Mary Adaline, 183
Prime, Aphia, 187
       Deborah R., 89
       Emmela, 92
       Joseph, 92
       Mary, 96
       Oliver, 184
Prince, Caleb, 156
        Isaac, 157
        Joseph, 156, 157
Printy, Catherine, 259
Proudman, Sarah A., 258
Pugsley, John, 131
Pumpkin,) Margaret, 199
Punkin, j Mercy, 189
Purinton, ——, 201
          Amy, 128
          Anna, 202
          Daniel, 95
          Peace, 290
          Thomas, 128
          Zaccheus, 201
Putnam, ——, 228
        John W., 248
        Osgood, 90
Quimby, Elizabeth, 235
        Henry, 100, 182
        Israel P., 248
        Joseph C., 248
        Lucy Ann, 252
        Mary Elizabeth, 235
        Moses, 90
        Nancy A., 182
Quinn, William, 262
Quint, Alonzo Hall, 240
       George, 240
Rabbin, Samuel, 95
Rackley, William, 129
Rand, Margaret, 261
Randall, Benjamin, 159
         Daniel, 82, 190
         Deborah, 171
         Eliphalet, 137
         Elizabeth, 131, 137, 138, 161
         Ephraim, 159
         John, 161, 171
         Jonathan, 139
         Joseph, 129
         Mary, 79, 137

Randell, Mary M., 103
　　Moses, 194
　　Nathaniel, 136, 139
　　Richard, 131
　　Samuel, 7, 137, 138
　　Sarah, 171, 184
　　Simon, 136
　　Tobias, 159, 161
　　William, 203
Rankin, Martha, 226
　　Sarah, 130
Ransom, Ebenezer, 172
　　Lydia, 201
　　Thomas, 190
Rawson, J., 198
　　Jonathan, 212
　　Jonathan A., 178
Raymond, Lydia, 183
Reade, Lydia, 179
　　Mary, 222
　　Michael, 79, 198, 226
　　Nancy, 179
　　Sarah, 226
Reading, Abigail, 121
Reddon, Mary, 114
Redford, Elizabeth, 126
Reed, Henry R., 257
　　Moses F., 185
　　Sarah, 124
Regan, Julia, 251
Remick, Ai, 257
　　James, 81, 195
　　John, 173
　　Mary, 179
Reynolds, Daniel, 183
　　Hannah, 84
　　Joseph, 93
　　Olive, 99
　　Oliver L., 95
　　Susan, 261
Richards, Abigail, 207
　　Benjamin, 130
　　John, 161
　　Joseph, 129, 138, 207
　　Tristram, 161
　　William, 129
Richardson, Augustus, 72
　　Charlotte King Atkinson, 72, 228
　　Elizabeth, 98
　　Eunice F., 247
　　Hannah, 177
　　J[ames], 70, 71, 72, 73, 74, 75, 76, 77, 84, 87, 88, 89, 90, 91, 92, 93, 94, 95, 97, 98, 99, 100, 101, 225
　　John Tebbets, 72
　　Joseph, 82
　　Lewis, 89
　　Lydia Ann, 72, 230, 255
　　Mark S., 246
　　Mary A., 90
　　Susan, 85
　　Tamson, 226
Ricker, ——, 177
　　Abigail, 22, 179, 182, 242
　　Asa, 173
　　Belley, 42
　　Bridget, 23
　　Charles L., 221
　　Daniel, 177, 181
　　Dorcas, 23, 137, 183
　　Eleanor, 46
　　Eliphalet, 46
　　Elisha, 46
　　Eliza, 98
　　Elizabeth, 7, 22, 135, 177, 207, 220,

Ricker, Ephraim, 11
　　Ezekiel, 163
　　G., 205
　　George, 22, 81, 192, 214
　　Gershom, 175
　　Hannah, 7, 11, 22, 23, 30, 42, 134, 138, 222
　　Isaac, 165, 242
　　Israel, 95
　　Jeremiah, 205, 242
　　John, 7, 22, 46, 135, 164, 245
　　Joseph, 11, 22, 46, 79, 135, 136, 138, 207
　　Judith, 130
　　Lydia, 242
　　Lydia Ann, 250
　　Lemuel, 172
　　Mark, 82
　　Mary, 22, 42, 159, 172, 174, 212, 242
　　Mary A., 90
　　Maturin, 22, 23, 30, 42, 134, 136, 137, 138, 139, 206
　　Mercy, 42, 159
　　Nancy, 181
　　Nicholas, 162, 163, 164, 165, 204
　　Noah, 136
　　Olive, 7
　　Oliver, 181
　　Reuben, 30, 136, 212, 242
　　Richard, 22
　　Samuel, 23, 42, 139, 159, 192, 202, 203
　　Sarah, 22, 136, 228, 242
　　Sophia, 181
　　Susanna, 159, 174
　　Tamson, 100
　　Timothy, 91, 176, 242
　　William, 82, 95, 162, 198, 246
Ridley, Mary, 11
Riley, ——, 202, 254
　　Abbie Waldron, 239
　　Anna, 60, 238
　　Ann Boardman, 238, 254
　　Catherine, 60
　　Eliza, 60
　　Hazen K., 230, 237
　　John, 60, 79, 176, 238
　　Mary, 60, 238
　　Sarah, 60
　　Sarah B, 76, 176
　　Susan, 179
　　Susanna, 60
Rines, Christina, 147
　　Elizabeth, 147
　　Hannah, 155
　　John, 147, 148
　　Joseph, 147, 149, 155
　　Thomas, 148
Roades,) Jacob, 131
Roads,) Mary, 130
Robbins, Sarah, 180
Roberts, ——, 191, 199, 203
　　Aaron, 24, 170, 193, 200
　　Abigail, 14, 30, 42, 114, 149, 160, 183
　　Alexander, 35
　　Alice, 81
　　Benjamin, 14, 32, 83, 192
　　Clarissa, 178
　　Deborah, 25, 35
　　Ebenezer, 14, 25, 137
　　Elizabeth, 14, 24, 25, 29, 42, 142, 149, 163, 172, 211
　　Elizabeth H., 246
　　Elizabeth R., 249
　　Ephraim, 42, 154, 159
　　Frances, 25, 35

INDEX OF PERSONS. 295

George, 81
George W., 186
Hannah, 29
Hanson, 177
Hatevil, 30
Heard, 174
Hiram R., 187
Huldah, 176
Isaac, 174, 191
Isabella G., 250
James, 165
Joanna, 25, 98, 129
John, 11, 14, 25, 35, 131, 137, 142, 144, 145, 150, 179, 208
Joseph, 14, 42, 142, 149, 159, 160, 162, 163, 165, 201, 204, 211
Joshua, 30
Love, 29
Lydia, 14, 30, 32, 42, 149, 181
Lydia G., 96
Margaret, 172
Martha Ann, 245
Mary, 11, 14, 25, 30, 42, 79, 145, 149, 165
Mary Ann, 90, 223
Mary Jane, 181
Mercy Ann, 243
Miriam, 24
Moses, 25, 193
Nathaniel, 24, 25, 131
Paul, 24, 144
Phebe, 25
Rebecca, 96, 182
Ruth, 96
Samuel, 14, 30, 32, 142, 174, 198
Sarah, 25, 32, 80, 131, 144, 177, 208
Stephen, 14, 80, 204
Susan, 185, 222
Tamson, 175
Thomas, 24
Thomas J., 215
Tobias W., 258
Robey, Ichabod, 122
Robinson, Ann, 223
Anna, 213
George P., 97
John, 216
Jonathan, 84
Paul, 202
Samuel, 100
Thomas C., 258
Timothy, 192
William, 192, 245
Roby, Tappan, 249
Rodgers, ⎰ ——, 224
Rogers, ⎱ Abigail, 71, 219
Abigail Ann, 71
Alice, 109
Amasa S., 248
Ann, 259
Artemas, 71, 219, 244
Catherine, 187
Daniel, 143, 173
Elizabeth, 59, 181
Elsie, 204
George W. T., 104
John Davis, 143
John F., 253
John P., 96
John T., 230
Lucretia, 257
Margaret, 260
Mary, 173
Owen, 261
Robert, 85, 174, 175, 236
Samuel, 177
Rogers, Susan, 103
William Harris, 71
Rollins, Abigail, 129, 171, 173, 219
Andrew, 179
Calvin, 247
Daniel, 181, 226
Deborah, 21, 137
Elizabeth, 21, 27, 137
Hannah, 27, 100, 179
Ichabod, 21, 27, 131, 137
James, 91, 179
Jeremiah, 21, 137
Joanna W., 182
John A., 181
Lorenzo, 184, 226
Lydia, 21, 137
Mary, 21, 137, 224, 226
Mary C., 226
Sarah, 137
Timothy E., 248
Root, David, 97, 101, 224
Elizabeth L., 230
Mary Elizabeth, 224
Ross, James, 93
Phebe, 233
Richard Nutter, 233, 234
Simon, 233
Rossiter, Mary, 259
Rounds, Gerry, 178
Joseph, 97, 101
Rouse, Thomas, 128
Rowe, James, 151
John, 146, 151, 153
Martha, 128
Tamson, 203
William Gray, 153
Rowell, Samuel, 253
Royse, Vere, 172
Ruggles, Gardner, 100, 223
Rumerill, Clement, 128
Rebecca, 128
Rumney, Ezra, 93
Rundlett, Nancy, 186
Satchel, 122
Runnells, Hannah, 175
Joseph, 81
Lydia, 98, 170
Mary, 174
Russell, ——, 194
Eliezer, 11
John, 174
Lydia, 193
Rosamond, 98
Thaxter, 89
Ryan, James M., 250
John, 262
Sales, see Sayles.
Salter, Thomas G., 254
Saltmarsh, E., 89
Sampson, James, 98
Luther, 97
Sanborn, Charlotte, 179
Clara, 252
Daniel, 179
Hannah, 12
James, 93
John, 123, 144
Jonathan, 129
Judith, 123
Lydia, 123
Mary, 123
Nathaniel, 129
William, 123
Sanders, ⎰ Abigail, 173
Saunders, ⎱ Abraham Burnham, 234, 244
Mary J., 244

INDEX OF PERSONS.

Sands,   Martha W., 236
  Richard, 129
  Sarah, 130
Sands, Mary, 98
Sankey, Sarah R., 257
Sargent, Abigail, 232
  Amos, 232, 239
  Clarissa Jane, 238
  David, 179, 215, 216, 238
  Edward, 129
  Walter, 249
  Ezekiel Hussey, 237
  George Washington, 237
  Harriet, 100
  John B., 90, 215, 235, 237, 239
  John P., 216, 232, 235
  Julia A., 239
  Lucy, 216
  Lucy Ann, 235
  Lucy W., 216
  Mary Bagley, 228
  Sarah, 226
  Susan B., 232
Sawyer, Benajah, 60
  Edward, 60
  Elizabeth, 60
  George, 50
  Hannah, 50
  Hosea, 60, 225
  Huldah, 50, 54
  J., 204
  Jacob, 54, 55, 204
  Justin, 60
  Kezia, 54
  Levi, 60
  Lois, 57
  Lydia, 54, 60
  Mary, 50, 60
  Mary V., 223
  Micajah, 54
  Moses, 50, 54, 57, 194
  Nahum, 60, 202
  Patience, 54
  Rebecca, 57
  Ruth, 60
  Samuel, 50
  Sarah, 54, 55, 57, 204
  Stephen, 54, 60, 83
  Susanna, 54
  Thomas E., 95, 251
  Timothy, 54
  Walter, 60
  Zaccheus, 54
Sayles, Alfred, 251
  John, 89
Sayward, Nancy Elizabeth, 228
  Richard P., 228
Scagel, Abigail, 80
Scammon, Elizabeth, 123
  Hope, 191
  Jane, 123
  Mary, 123
  Prudence, 123
  Richard, 123
  Sarah, 44
  William, 123
Scanlan, Ann, 72, 74, 75
  Francis Peter, 72
  Mary, 74
  Phillip, 72, 74, 75
  Teresa, 75
Sceggell, Jerusha A., 237
Scolly, Thomas, 182
Scott, Elihu, 245
Scovy, see McScovy.
Scribner, John, 174

Scriggins, Dorothy, 179
Scruton, Jonathan, 181
  Joseph H., 94
  L., 244
Scully, Maria, 262
Searle, Ann, 35
  Benjamin, 35
  Nathaniel, 35
  Patience, 35
  Robert, 35
  Samuel, 35
  Sarah, 35
  Timothy, 35
Seaverne, Mary, 108
Seavey, Henry, 214
  James, 247
  John, 123
  Mehitable, 79
  Nathan F., 97
  Thomas, 123
  True, 256
Sellars, ——, 84
Severance, Sarah, 93
Sewall, Gilbert T., 239
  James C., 184
Sewer, Henry, 129
Shackford, Anna, 212, 242
  Deborah, 160
  John, 159
  Joshua, 131
  Mary, 131
  Nancy Walker, 242
  Richard, 158
  Samuel, 212, 242
  William, 158, 159, 160
Shannon, Cutt, 45, 154
  Mary, 45
  Thomas, 172, 190, 191, 193
  William, 45, 81, 154
Shapleigh, Alpheus, 184
  Content, 245
  Elisha, 171
  Oliver, 184
Shaw, Ichabod, 183
  John, 254
  Levi, 100
  Smith M., 94
  Sophronia, 184
Shay, Joanna, 269
Shearman, Caleb H., 72, 84, 85, 86
Sheavallier, ——, 131
Shepard, Leonard, 231
  Rebecca, 43
  Verona, 234
Shepway, Ann, 122
  John, 122
Sherburne, Elizabeth, 129
Shorey, Francis A., 250
  Samuel, 130
Shortridge, Ann, 126
  Richard, 123
Shumway, James, 101
Shute, Andrew W., 245
Silley, see Cilley.
Simpson, Abigail, 124
  Caroline, 257
  Hannah, 124
  John, 124
  Joseph, 124
  Woodbury M., 98
Sinclair, John, 165
  Samuel Conner, 165
Sise, Ann, 238
  Edward, 61, 198
  John, 61
  John Hodgdon, 61

INDEX OF PERSONS.

Sise, Maria, 61
　　 Nancy, 61
　　 Shadrach Hodgdon, 61
Skinner, John, 245
Slattery, William, 261
Sleeper, Aaron, 123
　　 Elizabeth, 123
　　 Moses, 123
　　 Sherburne, 184
　　 Thomas, 123
Small, Elizabeth, 131
　　 Samuel, 80
Smallcorn, J., 202
Smart, Burleigh, 180
Smiley, Ellen Maria, 76
　　 Ephraim Haley, 76
　　 John, 76, 91
　　 John Samuel, 76
　　 Josiah Haley, 76
　　 Rhodia M., 76
　　 Susan Gilchrist, 76
Smith, ——, 75, 166, 194
　　 Aaron B., 243
　　 Abel C., 219
　　 Abigail, 123
　　 Abram, 244
　　 Archibald, 142
　　 Benjamin, 10, 142
　　 Caroline, 70, 257
　　 Catherine, 72, 254
　　 Charles, 248
　　 Charles N., 251
　　 Charlotte, 182
　　 Cheney, 146, 151, 153, 155, 157, 158
　　 Dryden, 254
　　 Ebenezer, 10, 57, 177
　　 Eleazer, 243
　　 Elizabeth, 10, 61, 85, 123
　　 Eunice, 81, 151, 209
　　 George, 73
　　 Hampden Sidney, 73
　　 Hannah, 10, 157, 174
　　 Henry, 185
　　 Henry W., 258
　　 Horace C., 234
　　 Huldah, 123
　　 Isaac, 185, 248
　　 Jabez, 171
　　 Jacob Jewett, 234
　　 James, 82, 197, 218
　　 Jeremiah, 215, 256
　　 John, 10, 73, 85, 123, 157, 166, 182, 231
　　 John D., 99
　　 John M., 246, 251
　　 John Q. A., 238
　　 Joseph, 10, 61, 62, 70, 72, 123, 142, 200, 202, 212, 217, 253, 254
　　 Joseph Belknap 70
　　 Josiah, 166
　　 Judith, 61, 62, 212
　　 Leonard, 72
　　 Lucy, 155
　　 Lydia G., 93
　　 Mary, 70, 72, 217
　　 Mary Ann, 260
　　 Mary E., 257
　　 Mary Emerson, 70
　　 Mary F., 258
　　 Mary G., 225
　　 Mary Jane, 73
　　 Mary T., 222
　　 Mehitable, 176
　　 Mercy, 146, 199
　　 Nathaniel Emerson, 72
　　 Richard P., 88

Smith, Samuel, 10, 124, 132, 157, 171
　　 Sarah, 72, 73, 85, 153, 181, 219
　　 Sarah A., 250
　　 Sarah Ann, 73
　　 Sarah Fisher, 74
　　 Sarah K., 93
　　 Sarah Locke, 73
　　 Sophia, 72, 230, 253
　　 Susan Hodgdon, 73
　　 Susan Watkins, 73
　　 Susanna, 10, 72
　　 Thomas Elliot, 70
　　 Thomas Leonard, 72
　　 Uriah S., 92
　　 William B., 103
　　 William Jarvis, 62
　　 Winthrop, 10
Snell, Abigail, 81
　　 Hannah H., 92
　　 Mary, 226
　　 Mary Ann, 95
　　 Samuel, 180
　　 Sarah, 230
　　 Thomas, 186
Souther, Mary M., 255
Spalding, Mary E., 98
　　 Parker, 187
Sparkes, Rebecca, 129
Spear, Thomas S., 253
Spelan, Ellen, 259
Spencer, Abigail B., 246
　　 Harriet, 185
　　 James T., 187
　　 Louisa, 179
　　 Lydia, 181
　　 Mary, 131
　　 Mary F., 94
Spinney, Oliver P., 244
　　 William, 248
Spooner, Jane, 102
Spurling, Jonathan, 93
　　 Robert, 84, 89
　　 Sabrina, 257
　　 Susan, 218
Stackpole, ——, 197
　　 Abigail, 101
　　 Augustus, 88, 98
　　 Dorcas, 183
　　 Douglass, 201
　　 Elisha, 139
　　 Joseph, 200
　　 Lydia, 139
　　 Martha, 179
　　 Mary, 245
　　 Mary B., 236
　　 Mary J., 255
　　 Otis, 225, 236, 238
　　 Philip, 139
　　 Sabina, 182
　　 Sarah, 139
　　 Tobias, 252
　　 William, 139
　　 William W., 89
Stacy, Dorcas, 217
　　 Ebenezer, 168, 169, 192
　　 Eleanor, 168
　　 Joanna, 169
　　 Mary, 168
　　 Rebecca, 168
　　 Ruth, 168
Stanley, Surviah, 122
Stanian, } Ann, 129
Stanyan, } Mary, 120
Stanton, Benjamin, 34
　　 Eleanor, 34
　　 Elizabeth, 161

298   INDEX OF PERSONS.

Stanton, Ezekiel, 251
        Joanna, 131
        John M., 246
        Tamson, 161
        William, 161, 162
Stanwood, Ann S., 185
        Mary, 216
Staples, Abigail, 187
Star,   Hannah, 108
Starbird, Abigail, 31, 149, 150
        Agnes, 31
        Elizabeth, 31, 37
        Hannah, 26, 150
        Jethro, 26, 31
        John, 26, 31, 146, 150
        Margaret, 26
        Nathaniel, 26
        Rebecca, 37, 148
        Samuel, 26, 31, 37, 148
        Sarah, 146, 150, 172
        Thomas, 26, 31, 123, 128, 135, 207
Stark, Lewis, 186
Stearns, Mary Ann, 95
Stebbins, Mary G., 252
Steele, Andrew, 181
Stevens, ——, 166
        Alpha, 75
        David R., 182
        Deborah, 36
        Elijah, 25
        Elizabeth, 25, 178
        George W., 249
        Hobart, 140, 158
        Hubbard, 210
        Jacob, 74, 247
        James, 9, 29, 36
        James Alpha, 75
        Jemima, 227
        John, 90, 177
        Jonathan, 174
        Joshua, 158
        Lover, 253
        Martha, 25, 28, 35
        Mary, 35, 123, 140
        Nathaniel, 123
        Olive, 25, 74
        Samuel James, 9
        Sarah, 75, 83
        Sarah A., 219
        Sarah Ann, 220
        Susanna, 36
        Thomas, 25, 28, 35
        Willard, 74
        William H., 97
Stevenson, Abraham, 7
        Bartholomew, 7, 12
        Deborah, 12
        Elizabeth, 7
        Joseph, 7
        Margaret, 122
        Mary, 7, 113
        Sarah, 7
        Thomas, 7, 122
        William S., 252
Stewart, James, 231
        James R., 232
        Jane, 232
Stickney, J., 204
        Joseph, 100
Stileman, Elias, 122, 124
        Elizabeth, 123
        Mary, 123
        Richard, 123
        Ruth, 107
        Sarah, 123
Stiles, Abigail, 24

Stiles, Deborah, 24, 93
        Elizabeth, 24, 181
        Mary, 24
        Samuel, 24, 180
        William, 24
Stillings, Daniel, 98
Stimpson, ——, 203
Stimson, Joseph, 82
Stocker, John, 179
Stokes, Benjamin, 183
        Deborah, 117, 128
Stone,   Sophia W., 216
        Stephen, 216
        Stephen S., 185
Storer, Sarah, 124
Storrs, Lois, 80
Stratton, Elias, 250
Straw,   Abigail, 251
        Clarissa, 89
        Moses W., 182
Street, Ellen, 74
        Isaac Dollive, 74
        John F., 74
Streeter, Ethan, 247
Stuart, Ann, 74
        Margaret, 74
        William, 74
Sullivan, ——, 57, 58, 78
        John, 261
        Owen, 259
Sumner, Eliza H., 98
Swain,   Ebenezer P., 244
        Nancy, 247
Swan,   Elizabeth, 256
        Joseph, 213
Swanton, Sarah, 223
Swasey, Ambrose, 64
        Asa, 64, 178
        Charles, 64, 180
        Henry S., 64
        Joanna, 64
        Nathaniel, 64, 177
        Sarah, 64
        Sarah K., 64
        Sarah T., 84
        Sophia, 64, 176
Swinerton, Amos, 244
Swett,   Moses, 123
        Samuel B., 254
Synnot, Thomas. 259
Tapley, John, 179, 218, 223
        Lydia, 223
        Mary Elizabeth, 237
Tarleton, Elias, 124
        Richard, 124
        Ruth, 124
Tarr,   see Torr.
Tasker, Abigail, 158
        Curtis, 247
        Deborah, 80
        Ebenezer, 142
        Elizabeth, 157
        Hannah H., 88
        Henry, 237, 239
        Horatio G., 100
        John, 142, 158
        Joseph, 158
        Lydia, 90
        Lydia Leonard, 231
        Mary, 157, 256
        Rebecca, 142
        Samuel, 80, 142, 157
Taylor, Ann, 178
        Christina, 184
        Daniel R., 185
        Deborah, 124

INDEX OF PERSONS.

Elizabeth F., 182
John, 124
Mary, 124
Simeon W., 94
William, 85
Tebbets, } ——, 233
Tibbits, } Aaron, 13
Abigail, 1, 13, 14, 15, 38, 81, 137, 138, 181, 213, 217, 241
Alonzo F., 238
Ann, 13, 149
Benjamin, 25
Bridget, 21
Caroline, 242
Catherine, 12
Charles, 169
Daniel, 151
Deborah, 171
Dorothy, 2, 148, 158, 173
Ebenezer, 168, 169, 195, 241, 242
Edward, 25, 141
Elijah, 13
Elisha, 13
Elizabeth, 1, 2, 3, 4, 13, 21, 91, 129, 180, 184
Ephraim, 1, 12, 13, 15, 16, 148, 153
Esther, 12, 15, 16, 78, 175
Hannah, 12, 15, 124, 137, 151, 226
Henry, 13, 25, 130, 148
Ichabod, 14, 33, 38, 136, 138, 143, 146, 148, 149, 191, 193, 196
Irena, 104
James, 143
Jeremiah, 34, 43, 124, 148
John, 1, 12, 13, 15, 16, 34, 84, 137, 147, 151, 153, 158, 174, 179, 190, 191, 193, 203
John G., 85
Jonathan, 184
Joseph, 2, 3, 4, 12, 13, 124
Joshua, 137
Joyce, 25
Judith, 1, 2, 14, 32, 33, 38, 136, 138, 148
Judith E., 253
Kezia, 34
Lydia, 3, 176
Margaret, 2, 148
Martha, 43
Mary, 12, 13, 15, 16, 32, 34, 124, 130, 136, 137, 145, 151, 184, 208
Moses, 1, 16, 34, 137
Nathaniel, 21, 34, 38, 138, 151
Olive J., 251
Paul, 25
Philip P., 183
Rebecca, 146, 241, 242
Rose, 13
Ruth, 179
Samuel, 1, 12, 15, 32, 33, 124, 128, 136, 148, 171
Samuel H., 184
Sarah, 12, 15, 34, 43, 104, 131, 136, 151
Sophia, 96
Susanna, 25, 81, 84, 141, 168
Temson, 34, 71, 72, 84, 85, 151, 191
Thomas, 1, 11, 13, 15, 38, 78, 124, 131, 136
Timothy, 15, 137, 192
William, 16, 137
Tenney, ——, 167
Tetherley, Andrew, 88
Thing, Sarah, 236
Thomas, Abigail, 171
David, 131
Elisha, 195

Thomas, Elizabeth, 108, 110
William R., 257
Thompson, ——, 258
Benjamin, 158
Charles, 237
Charles E., 246
Edmund, 82
Gustavus, 250
James, 130
John, 156, 160
Jonathan, 156, 210
Joseph, 179
Martha W., 185
Mary J., 240
Olive, 97
Rebecca, 247
Robert, 158
Sarah, 210
Thomas, 173
Thomson, Abigail, 144
Benjamin, 142
Calvin, 93
James, 148
Jonathan, 144
Joseph, 144
Robert, 142
William, 124
Thurston, ——, 66
Nathaniel, 98
Tierney, William, 261
Tilden, William P., 258
Tilton, John, 216
John G., 181, 217
Mary Ann, 216
Titcomb, ——, 194, 198
Abigail, 84, 141
Ann, 38, 40, 133, 134
Benjamin, 150, 173, 201
Daniel, 6, 38, 40, 134, 135, 136, 138, 140, 141, 143, 150, 207
David, 40, 141
Elizabeth, 40, 138, 155
Enoch, 143
Hannah, 70, 84
Jeremiah H., 182
John, 38, 57, 81, 136, 155, 157, 158, 160, 161, 162, 193, 197, 199, 213
Lydia H., 183
Martha, 160, 184
Mary, 38, 155, 179, 209
Samuel Waterhouse, 158
Sarah, 38, 57, 83, 135, 157, 162, 166, 174, 213
William, 38. 86, 135, 166
Tobey, Stephen, 124, 128
Todd, ——, 195, 198
Joanna, 157
Lois, 190
Mehitable, 159
Samuel, 157, 159
Sarah, 157
Tolman, Gaward, 179
Toppan, ——, 194
Stephen, 184
Torr, Andrew, 152, 193, 198
Benedictus, 2, 149
Elizabeth, 63
Eunice, 154
Harriet A., 104
Lois, 209
Mary, 146
Mary A., 251
Phebe, 149
Sarah A., 103
Vincent, 146, 149, 152, 154, 188, 209
Towle, Joshua, 142

INDEX OF PERSONS.

Tracy, Daniel, 176
Traffton, Theodosia, 182
Trainor, Alice, 262
Trask, Martha, 179
    Mary, 178
Treadway, Lavina, 224
Tredick, Adeline, 257
    Ann, 256
    Catherine N., 103
    Charles, 228
    John, 105
    Mary, 101
Trefethen, Charles, 251
    Daniel, 181, 245
    Henry, 200
    Lucretia, 162
Trickey, Ann, 185
    Elizabeth, 8, 131
    Jonathan, 81, 213
    Lydia, 213
    Martha, 112, 222
    Miriam H., 245
    William, 102
Tripe, Lucy, 177
    Mary, 227
    Nancy, 82, 85
    Nicholas, 181
    Richard, 194
    Sylvanus, 80
Trufant, Gilbert, 180
Trussell, Sarah Ann F., 256
Tubbs, Benjamin, 180
Tuck, Bethia, 124
    John, 124
    John, 124
    Jonathan, 184
Tucker, Abigail, 186
    Dorcas, 170
    Eliza, 237
    Lucy Maria, 240
Tufts, Ann L., 178
    Asa, 75, 201
    Asa Alford, 75, 180, 215
    Caroline Gilman, 75
    Charles Augustus, 75, 230
    David K., 182
    Ellen Foster, 75
    Hannah Phillips, 75, 215
    John Wheeler, 75
    Martha, 75
Tuttle, ——, 190
    Abigail, 197
    Andrew, 103
    Angeline, 228
    Anna, 79
    Benjamin, 172
    Dorothy, 5, 124, 128
    Ebenezer, 194, 200
    Elijah, 5, 182, 194
    Esther, 84
    Eunice, 173
    Fanny P., 256
    Hannah C., 247
    James, 4, 5, 195, 249
    John, 3, 4, 5, 6, 89, 199
    Judith, 3, 5
    Judith T., 89
    Lucy, 175
    Martha, 85
    Mary, 4, 5, 97, 126, 128, 148, 151, 153, 186, 214
    Mary Ann, 249
    Nancy B., 256
    Nicholas, 5
    Otis, 86
    Phebe, 5, 80

Tuttle, Rose, 5, 174, 256
    Samuel, 79, 176
    Sarah, 80, 130, 181
    Silas, 200
    Susan, 178
    Thomas, 4, 5, 188, 228, 245
    Tobias, 200
    William, 81, 151
Twombly, Abigail, 104, 171, 182
    Abra, 138
    Andrew, 157, 172
    Ann, 37
    Anne, 79
    Benjamin, 22, 135, 136, 137, 138, 149
    Christina, 62, 178
    Daniel, 20, 82, 154, 157
    David, 81, 82, 183, 204
    Ebenezer, 151
    Eleanor, 149
    Elizabeth, 18, 134, 145, 147, 206, 208, 253
    Ephraim, 81
    Esther, 131
    Eunice, 80, 140
    Hannah, 22, 135
    Hannah S., 249
    Hepzibah, 152
    Hope, 245
    Huldah, 220
    Isaac, 17, 178
    Israel, 213, 214
    James, 84, 85, 183
    James C., 62
    John, 20, 36, 37, 124, 128, 129, 135, 140, 148, 161, 178, 219
    Jonathan, 38
    Joseph, 152, 157, 206
    Joshua, 150, 157
    Judith, 37, 38
    Lemuel, 152
    Lydia, 148, 157, 215, 216
    Martha, 20
    Mary, 17, 18, 36, 141, 145, 192, 213, 219
    Mehitable, 62
    Moses, 147, 154
    Nancy, 66
    Nathaniel, 152, 232, 235
    Paul, 152
    Rachel, 37, 137
    Ralph, 17
    Reuben, 79, 177, 251
    Samuel, 37, 38, 160
    Sarah, 20, 214, 257
    Solomon, 152
    Susan, 158, 249
    Tamson, 136, 161, 172
    Thomas B., 186, 220
    William, 17, 18, 36, 62, 84, 140, 141, 145, 147, 149, 150, 151, 152, 153, 154, 157, 178, 190, 195, 215, 216
Tydie, Hannah, 131
Underwood, Abigail, 80
    Olive, 174
Upham, Alfred, 223
    Joseph B., 257
    Sophia, 223
Varney, ——, 192
    Abigail, 74, 125, 176, 180
    Abigail Ann, 76, 228
    Benjamin, 190
    Charles Green, 74
    Charlotte Augusta, 77
    Clarissa, 184
    Daniel, 204
    Dorothy, 60

Varney, Ebenezer, 189
    Elias, 249
    Elijah, 89
    Elizabeth, 141, 173
    Eveline L., 251
    Ezekiel, 59, 60
    Franklin, 234
    Hannah, 67
    Hope, 83
    Humphrey, 124, 125
    Ichabod, 195
    Isaiah, 87
    James, 76, 83, 188, 205
    James B., 76, 77, 176
    Jedediah, 200, 201
    Jesse, 74, 84
    John, 84, 124
    John H., 184
    John Riley, 76, 229
    Joseph, 124, 178, 191
    Joshua, 195
    Judith, 83, 198
    Lafayette, 233
    Martha, 141, 182
    Mary, 60, 84, 198
    Mary Ann, 180, 218
    Mary Ann Boardman, 74
    Mary Riley, 76, 230
    Mercy Matilda, 77
    Moses Lafayette, 77
    Nathan, 191, 197
    Paul, 191
    Peter, 124
    Rhoda Ann B., 87
    Robert, 80, 179
    Samuel, 67, 83
    Samuel Bragg, 74
    Sarah, 83, 85, 95, 101, 124, 125, 202
    Sarah Ann, 67
    Sarah B., 76
    Shubael, 257
    Stephen, 177, 194
    Susanna, 60
    Theodore, 74
    Thomas, 67, 175
Vasey, John, 177, 180
Vaughn, Abigail, 125
    Bridget, 125
    Cutt, 125
    Eleanor, 125, 127
    Elizabeth, 125
    George, 125
    Margaret, 125
    Mary, 125
    Sarah, 125
    William, 125
Velden, Mary, 262
Vicker, Hannah, 81
Vickery, Daniel, 244
    John S., 243
    Josiah P., 247
    Mahala, 92
Victor, Elizabeth S., 257
Vincent, Abigail, 216
Vrin, John, 109, 125
Waburton, John, 99
Wade, John, 129
    Patrick, 260
Wadleigh, ——, 109
    Elisha, 258
    Hannah, 90, 231
Wakeham, Edward, 126
Walbridge, Mary, 85
Waldron, ——, 110, 112, 114, 116, 119, 120, 188, 201
    Abby, 254

Waldron, Abigail, 61, 127, 153, 163, 165, 175
    Alexander, 126
    Ann, 125, 126, 127
    Ann P., 249
    Benjamin, Q., 181
    Bridget, 159
    Charles, 164, 196
    Clementine, 93
    Dinah, 193
    Daniel, 167
    Ebenezer, 159
    Eleanor, 82, 127, 163
    Eliezer, 125
    Eliza, 184
    Elizabeth, 126, 130, 163, 164, 171, 173, 175
    Elizabeth A., 104
    Ephraim, 161
    Hannah, 81, 164
    Jeremiah, 165
    Joanna, 166, 210
    John, 57, 58, 130, 136, 159, 160, 161, 162, 163, 164, 165, 166, 167, 168, 181, 188, 190, 198, 209, 210
    Joseph, 172, 190, 192, 193
    Lucy, 222
    Lydia, 176
    Marah, 126
    Margaret, 11, 127
    Mary, 79, 80, 159, 178, 209
    Mary Bowers, 167
    Mary C., 184, 257
    Mehitable, 182
    Nancy, 191
    Patience, 81
    Plato, 85
    Richard, 7, 83, 125, 126, 127, 163, 166, 173, 187, 191
    Richard Canney, 153
    Samuel, 79
    Sarah, 162
    Sarah Ann, 237
    Solomon, 179
    Susan, 168
    Thomas, 160
    Thomas Westbrooke, 56, 57, 58, 78, 79, 163, 164, 165, 167, 192, 193
    Timothy Winn, 167
    Wells, 222, 223, 237
    William, 89, 127, 159, 163, 191, 192, 198, 199, 206
Walker, George, 129
    Gideon, 169, 174
    Hannah, 123
    John, 79
    Joseph, 102
    Judith, 169
    Mary, 80
    Robert, 244
    Sarah, 128, 204
    Seth S., 85
    Sophia C., 249
Wallace,) Emma, 228
Wallis, } George, 126
    George Burns, 233, 235
    John, 229
    Judith P., 232
    Nancy, 229
    Olive Willard, 234
    Salome Reed, 235
    Sophronia, 230
Wallingford, Abigail, 37
    Ebenezer, 37
    Hannah, 23
    John, 126, 128
    Judith, 23

Wallingford, Lavina, 178
  Lydia, 83
  Margaret, 23, 34, 37, 138
  Nicholas, 34
  Rachel, 6, 34
  Samuel, 74
  Thomas, 23, 37, 138
Walsh, Ann, 259
  Bridget, 262
  Elizabeth Ham, 229
  Jane, 222
  Lucy, 261
  Maria, 262
Ward, Catharine, 259
  Mary, 259, 261
Warner, Margaret, 177
  Tobias, 171
Warren Angeline, 91
  Eliza, 181
  Eliza W., 219
  George K., 234
  Hannah, 226, 244
  Jane, 129
  Joseph H., 229
  Susan, 90
  Thomas, 226
Washburne, Abigail P., 187
  Oliver, 219
Wastefall, William, 235
Waterhouse, Richard, 126
  Samuel, 126
  Sarah, 126
Waters, James, 260
Watson, Aaron, 177, 223
  Abigail, 176, 238, 256
  Alice, 173
  Benjamin, 50, 192
  Caroline S., 248
  Christina, 180, 208
  Daniel, 85, 158, 214
  Daniel H., 183
  David, 16, 146
  Dudley, 112, 144, 146, 151, 152, 155, 156, 157, 159, 160, 208
  Elizabeth, 54, 95, 150, 158, 168, 184, 212, 219, 221, 230, 241, 242
  Elizabeth G., 220
  Elizabeth Hamilton, 167
  George, 57, 158, 168, 169, 171, 191, 194, 195, 202, 212, 241, 242
  Hannah, 85, 87, 92, 156, 168, 172
  Harriet, 89
  Isaac, 50, 54, 149, 150, 158, 167, 168, 169, 173, 190, 192
  James, 54, 175, 195
  Jane, 235
  Joanna, 149, 192, 210
  John, 169, 202
  John N., 221
  John S., 250
  Jonathan, 147
  Joseph, 54
  Joshua, 238
  Julia A., 246
  Lillias, 50, 172
  Lucy, 144, 235
  Lucy Cutts, 242
  Lydia, 169, 168
  Mary, 16, 62, 155, 168, 174
  Mercy, 118, 209
  Nancy, 167
  Nancy H., 182
  Nathaniel, 194, 200
  Olive, 214
  Otis, 195
  Otis Baker, 157
Watson, Priscilla, 218
  Robert, 169
  Samuel, 152, 168, 218, 219, 220
  Sarah, 54, 143, 159, 183, 184, 185
  Sarah H., 95
  Seth, 249, 250
  Susan R., 257
  Thomas, 151, 172, 204
  William, 191, 202
  Winthrop, 16, 174, 176, 230, 238
  Zervin, 158
Weare, Abigail, 31
  Meshech, 57, 90
  Peter, 129
  Sarah, 246
Webster, Abigail, 119
  Andrew, 249
  Cynthia, 98
  Daniel K., 187
  Elizabeth, 220
  Emily, 254
  John, 99
  Mary, 97
  Reuben, 84
  Robert S., 234
  Susan, 229
  William G., 91
Wedgwood, Dearborn, 102
  Lot, 178
Weeks, Ann, 180
  John, 126
  Joseph, 126
  Joshua, 126
  Leonard, 126
  Margaret, 126
  Mary, 126
  Samuel, 126
Welch, Joseph W., 237, 239
Wells, Dependence, 179
  Hannah, 85
  Hanson H., 183
  William, 192
Wendell, George, 95
  Mary Ann, 103
  Sophia L., 99
Wentworth, ——, 195
  Aaron, 150
  Abigail, 21, 48, 135, 155
  Abra, 26, 226
  Adaline F., 185
  Anna, 152, 170
  Benjamin, 4, 21, 26, 35, 37, 135, 138
  Benning, 126, 178
  Caroline, 239
  Damaris, 133
  Daniel, 126, 170, 246
  Deborah, 37
  Disco, 81
  Dorothy, 26, 126, 245
  Dorothy Frost, 167, 177
  Ebenezer, 4, 126
  Edwin, 248
  Elihu, 150
  Elizabeth, 21, 26, 35, 66, 91, 135, 166, 180, 207, 209, 218
  Ephraim, 145, 150, 152, 163, 164, 189, 208
  Eunice, 97
  Ezekiel, 3, 133, 140, 141, 146, 150, 209
  George, 91
  Gershom, 3, 134, 138, 206, 207
  Grant, 145
  Hall, 178
  Hannah, 3, 138, 178
  Ichabod, 160

INDEX OF PERSONS. 303

Wentworth, Jacob, 83, 92
  James, 179, 249
  Jedediah, 84
  John, 21, 57, 58, 126, 127, 131, 135, 165, 166, 167, 168, 190, 194, 211, 240
  John Frost, 167
  John H., 255
  Jonathan, 155, 156, 164, 195, 244
  Joseph, 4, 259
  Judith S., 91
  Kezia, 79, 80, 175. 208
  Lewis, 92, 176
  Lucretia, 173
  Lydia, 156
  Margaret, 166, 208, 211
  Mark, 26
  Martha, 26, 133, 145, 206, 208
  Mary, 35, 126, 139, 145, 159, 163, 207, 209
  Mercy, 92
  Meshech, 201
  Meshech Weare, 167
  Moses, 141, 146
  Nahum, 228
  Nancy, 178
  Niobe, 140
  Paul, 168, 177, 206
  Phebe, 155
  Phineas, 212
  Reuben, 170
  Richard, 133, 165
  Rosilla, 234
  Samuel, 126, 222
  Sarah, 4, 26, 37, 17, 207, 217
  Spencer, 143, 145, 188, 208
  Susanna, 4
  Tamson, 4, 131, 136
  Thomas, 133
  William, 4, 136, 138, 139, 145, 159, 190, 207
  Zebulon Y., 98
West, Thomas, 181
Wetmore, Nathaniel D., 100
Weymouth, ——, 209
  Benjamin, 29, 138
  Edward, 125
  Lucinda, 181
  Mary, 29, 208
  Sarah, 138
Wheedon, see Whidden.
Wheeler, Clarissa, 214
  Dorothy D., 180, 212
  Elizabeth, 214
  Elizabeth C., 105
  Henrietta, 184
  James, 186
  John, 61, 212, 214, 225, 242
  John H., 182, 218
  John Hancock, 215
  Lydia A., 249
  Lydia M. 182
  Mary B., 218
  Rebecca, 61, 212, 242
  Rebecca Elizabeth, 61, 178, 242
Whelan, Mary, 260
Whidden, Eliza, 232
  Eliza H., 237, 247
  Hannah, 216
  Jane, 112
  Josiah P., 237
  Lavina, 92
  Lydia, 56
  Mary Ann, 103
  Michael, 129, 232
Whipple, Ruth, 89

Whitan, Nathaniel, 98
White, ——, 227
  Amos, 162, 213
  Asa, 89
  Charles, 106
  Eunice R., 102
  Japheth D., 184
  Lydia, 161, 211
  Sarah, 213
  Timothy, 161, 162, 211
  Warren, 182
  William, Q., 251
Whitehouse, Benjamin, 168
  Caroline, 247
  Caroline T., 104
  Charles, 175
  Charles Carroll, 77
  Daniel, 81, 241
  David, 241
  Edward, 19
  Edwin, 104
  Elizabeth, 19, 34, 137, 162, 168, 175, 182
  Ephraim, 165
  Eunice, 86
  George, 229
  George L., 77
  George Washington, 77
  Jacob Kittredge, 241
  James, 258
  John, 20, 48, 139, 162, 165, 174
  Jonathan, 79, 168
  Joseph, 103, 168, 201, 212, 241
  Judith, 19, 81
  Laura Ann, 77
  Liberty N., 77
  Lucy, 140
  Lydia, 168
  Mary, 143, 185
  Mary Jane, 94
  Moses, 20, 147, 154, 173
  Nancy Ann, 244
  Nathaniel, 152
  Paul, 165
  Pomfret, 19, 20, 162
  Rachel, 34, 48
  Rebecca, 19, 20
  Reuben, 241
  Rose, 19
  Samuel, 20, 144
  Sarah, 144, 145
  Silas, 65
  Susan, 103
  Susanna, 212, 241
  Thomas, 19, 34
  Turner, 150
  Walter Scott, 77
  William, 19, 137, 139, 140, 141, 143, 145, 150, 152, 154
Whittle, Mary Ann, 100
Whitton, Abel, 233, 238, 254
Whittier, Adaline Mendum, 72
  Ann, 72
  Joseph, 72
  Joseph Albert, 72
  Lydia Ann, 72
  Moses, 247
  Nathan, 90
  Phebe, 180
  Samuel Hall Locke, 72
Wiberd, Elizabeth, 127
  John, 127
  Richard, 126, 127
  Thomas, 127
Wiggin, Andrew, 129, 165
  Asa, 228

INDEX OF PERSONS.

Wiggin, Benjamin, 73, 74
    Benjamin Horace, 73
    Ellen Frances, 74
    Martha Jane, 74
    Mary, 73
    Mary H., 73
    Moses, 165
    Nancy D., 73, 258
    Norris Dow, 73
    Samuel L., 244
    Stephen, 181
    William B., 96
    Zelia, 73
Wiggins, John S., 258
Wigglesworth, Elizabeth, 171
    Samuel, 80
    Wright H., 93
Wilbur, Ann T., 230
Wilkinson, John Henry, 233
Willand, ——, 189
    Elizabeth, 16, 57
    Hannah, 8, 16, 36
    Lydia, 57, 203
    Mary, 202
    Nathaniel, 57
    Nathaniel Heard, 8
    Paul, 57
    Sarah, 36, 174
    William, 7, 8, 11. 16, 36, 199
Willard, Samuel, 44
Willey, Anna, 147
    Caroline A., 256
    Caroline G., 224
    Elizabeth, 9, 101, 142, 151
    Enoch T., 103
    Ezekiel, 147, 156
    Frances, 146
    Hannah, 146
    Isaiah, 156
    Josiah, 165
    Margaret, 175
    Mary, 9, 142, 146, 156, 171
    Robert, 147
    Samuel, 9, 139, 131, 136, 142, 165, 221
    Stephen, 146, 151, 219, 224
    William, 142
    William H., 243
Williams, Charlotte A., 228
    Elizabeth, 115, 125
    Frances, 240
    George W., 93
    Gibbon, 99
    John, 125, 220
    Margaret, 125
    Martha Fitch, 228
    Mary S., 218
    Rachel, 128
    Sophia M., 220
    Washington, 228
    William, 125
Wilmet, Sarah, 48
Wilson, David, 184
    Eliza Ann, 218
    Elizabeth, 129
    Joseph, 131
    Nancy, 185
Wingate, ——, 202
    Aaron, 143, 151, 184, 256
    Aaron P., 237
    Abigail, 19, 57, 81, 91, 139, 222
    Ann, } 17, 18, 19, 38, 126, 142, 148,
    Anna, } 154, 156
    Benjamin, 145
    Daniel, 17, 135
    Deborah, 139, 175, 202

Wingate, Dorothy, 17, 35, 140
    Ebenezer, 140, 149
    Edmond, 19
    Edmund, 57, 139, 156, 157
    Eliza C., 237
    Elizabeth, 19, 57, 139, 178
    Hannah, 185
    Jeremy, 179
    Joanna, 19
    John, 2, 17, 18, 19, 35, 82, 126, 133, 134, 135, 136, 137, 139, 140, 141, 143, 144, 148, 151, 153, 157, 208
    Jonathan, 137
    Joshua, 35, 57, 136, 198, 199
    Mary, 18, 57, 80, 96, 126
    Mary Frances, 240
    Mehitable, 19, 153, 171
    Moses, 19, 139, 140, 142, 144, 145, 149, 151, 191
    Noah, 141
    Samuel, 17, 18, 134, 154
    Sarah, 19, 144, 179, 211, 256
    Sarah Elizabeth, 230
    Shadrach, 177
    Simon, 19
    Stephen, 57
    Susan C., 244
    William P., 180, 184, 215, 225, 237, 240
Winkley, Asa, 185
    Francis, 81, 257
    John H., 238
    Joseph, 245
    Samuel, 244
    William, 179
Winn, Dorcas, 234
    Hannah, 231
    Josiah, 217
    Priscilla, 223
Winslow, H., 219
    Hubbard, 186
    Martha, 219
    Susan Ward, 219
Wise, Jeremiah, 32
Witham, } Moses, 178
Wittum, } Ruth, 130
Wood, ——, 192, 230
    Aaron, 156
    C., 224
    Daniel Gerrish, 154
    Elizabeth, 42, 43, 146, 210
    Harriet Eliza, 224
    James, 186
    John, 42, 43, 143, 145, 146, 150, 152, 154, 155, 156, 188, 208
    John B., 258
    Lydia, 42, 150
    Mary, 42, 143
    Moses, 155
    Susanna, 42, 145, 210
Woodbury, Robert, 88
Wooden, Catharine, 171
Woodes, Clara D., 249
    John F., 245
Woodhouse, Sarah, 186
Woodman, Charles, 180
    Charles W., 100
    Dorothy D., 183
    Ebenezer, 155, 162, 204
    Edward, 156, 162, 209
    George S., 254
    Hannah, 94
    John, 2, 145, 155, 210
    Mary Esther, 228
    Rebecca Elizabeth, 221
    Samuel, 156

Woodman, William, 178, 216, 221
Wooward, Elkanah S., 185
Worcester, Nancy, 100
Wormwell, William, 178
Wright, Amos, 103
    Thomas, 90
Wyatt, Charlotte L., 100
    Samuel, 216
    Sophia, 216
Wyman, Zebadiah, 217
Yeaton, ——, 189
    George S., 182
    James, 158
    John, 97
    Mary, 157, 178
    Phebe, 137, 181
    Philip, 137
    Samuel, 157, 158
    William, 137
York, Abigail F., 102
    Comfort, 246
    James, 260
    James M., 258
    John, 195
    Susanna, 84
Young, ——, 189, 192, 204
    Abigail, 23, 24, 36, 101, 148, 159, 226
    Alice, 149
    Ann, 142
    Caroline, 253
    Catharine, 236
    Charles, 74, 77, 78, 102, 103, 104, 105
    Daniel, 10, 160
    Deborah, 175
    Dorothy, 235
    Ebenezer, 209
    Effalina Emmela, 71
    Eleazer, 24, 149
    Eliza, 227, 242
    Elizabeth, 71, 80, 142, 148, 161, 212, 241, 242, 256
    Elizabeth Jane, 71
    Elizabeth S., 92
    Ephraim, 161
    Ezra, 70, 80, 103, 156, 199, 200, 212, 236, 241, 242
    Fordyce R., 71
    Frances Ellen, 70
    George, 204, 234, 235
    Hannah, 70, 146
    Hannah Smith, 227
    Harriet Boardman, 224
    Harriet F., 232
    Isaac, 24, 148, 190
    Irena, 240
    Jacob K., 248
    James, 24, 79, 82, 148, 152, 159, 160, 161, 188, 193, 194, 242
    Jeremiah S., 232, 236
    Jeremy, 70
    John, 142, 146, 158, 226
    John C., 184
    John K., 71
    Jonathan 23, 24, 36, 85, 132, 148, 152, 216, 226, 241
    Joseph, 201
    Lucy, 149, 172
    Lurana, 99
    Lydia D., 70
    Margaret, 248
    Martha Ann, 250
    Mary, 8, 36, 52, 92, 142, 146, 148, 171, 183, 184, 185, 211, 218, 220, 241
    Mary R., 70
    Mercy, 10, 148
    Moses C., 95

Young, Nathaniel, 10, 24, 71, 146, 155, 156, 158, 159, 161
    Roxary Augusta, 71
    Ruth, 226
    Sarah, 89, 174, 235
    Sobriety, 148
    Solomon, 149
    Stephen, 174, 198
    Susan, 88, 182
    Susan Ela, 234
    Susanna, 80, 146
    Thomas, 24, 82, 142, 146, 198, 204
    Thomas J., 71
    Timothy, 155, 173
    Timothy R., 70
    William, 194
    William Augustus, 70

www.ingramcontent.com/pod-product-compliance
Lightning Source LLC
Chambersburg PA
CBHW070722160426
43192CB00009B/1285